HYPNOSIS 1979

HYPNOSIS 1979

Proceedings of the 8th International Congress of
Hypnosis and Psychosomatic Medicine, Melbourne,
Australia, 19-24 August, 1979

Editors
GRAHAM D. BURROWS
DAVID R. COLLISON
and

LORRAINE DENNERSTEIN

1979

ELSEVIER/NORTH-HOLLAND BIOMEDICAL PRESS
AMSTERDAM · NEW YORK · OXFORD

ISBN: 0-444-80142-1

Published by:
Elsevier/North-Holland Biomedical Press
335 Jan van Galenstraat, PO Box 211
Amsterdam, The Netherlands

Sole distributors for the USA and Canada:
Elsevier North-Holland Inc.
52 Vanderbilt Avenue
New York, N.Y. 10017

Library of Congress Cataloging in Publication Data
International Congress of Hypnosis and Psychosomatic
    Medicine, 8th, Melbourne, 1979.
    Hypnosis 1979.

    Bibliography: p.
    Includes index.
    1. Hypnotism--Congresses. I. Burrows, Graham D.
II. Collison, David R. III. Dennerstein, Lorraine.
IV. Title.
BF1119.I57 1979   615'.8512   79-16095
ISBN 0-444-80142-1

Printed in The Netherlands

PREFACE

The Australian Society for Clinical and Experimental Hypnosis (ASCEH) was given the task of organizing the 8th International Congress of Hypnosis and Psychosomatic Medicine on behalf of the International Society of Hypnosis. The Congress was sponsored by University of Melbourne, Departments of Psychiatry, Psychology, and Dental Medicine and Surgery.

The Australian Society was founded in 1971 and has been involved in training more than one thousand members. The Congress has stimulated the growth and interest of hypnosis and encouraged training programmes, co-ordination and co-operation, increased standards, research, and clinical applications of hypnosis. The ASCEH is extremely grateful to the International Society for their support and encouragement.

This volume continues the tradition of publishing the proceedings of triennial major world congresses of hypnosis. The contributors to the scientific programme were invited to submit their papers prior to the congress in order that this volume should be available and provide a permanent record of what we trust will be a most successful meeting.

Graham D. Burrows
David Collison
Lorraine Dennerstein

CONTENTS

Preface   V

The use of hypnosis in the treatment of psychogenic impotency
    H.B. Crasilneck   1

Isolation, EEG alpha and hypnotizability in Antarctica
    A. Barabasz   9

High and moderate hypnotizables: A study of brain function
    differences in a plateaued sample exposed to cold pressor pain
    R. Karlin, D. Morgan and L. Goldstein   17

Expectancy reactions in hypnosis
    P.W. Sheehan   25

Hypnotizability and the treatment of dental phobic illness
    J. Gerschman, G.D. Burrows, P. Reade and G. Foenander   33

The case against relaxation
    K.F. Thompson   41

Hot amethysts, eleven fingers and the Orient Express
    F.J. Evans   47

Imagery differences between anxious and depressed patients
    D.J. De L. Horne and J. Baillie   55

Adjunctive trance and family therapy for terminal cancer
    G.A. Pettitt   63

Guided self-hypnosis
    H.K. Goba   71

An approach to hypnotherapy : My method
    D.R. Collison   79

Beyond hypnosis
    A.E. Bernstien   87

Experimental exacerbation and relief of asthma under hypnosis
    P.S. Clarke   95

Autogenic training, basic and advanced level: Its technique,
    application and indications, especially for children
    K. Thomas   97

Audio-video-polygraphy during hypnosis: A contribution to the
    verification of hypnotic states
    U.J. Jovanović   105

Hypnosis in the management of chronic pain
    D. Elton, G.D. Burrows and G.V. Stanley   113

Hypno-analytic therapy of hysteric hemiplegia by means of secondary
  personalities
  R. Kampman, R. Hirvenoja and O. Ihalainen   121

Group meditation therapy
  S. Inglis   127

Hypnosis - A diagnostic tool in epilepsy
  M. Gross   133

Hypnosis in the treatment of prolonged grievance over a death
  G.S. Jennings   139

Hypnotherapy for Raynaud's disease
  B.G. Braun   141

L'Abbe de Faria : His life and contribution
  S. Sharma   149

Tension headache treated with hypnosis
  A.M. Damsbo   157

Mutually-induced trance as a therapeutic mode
  J.C. Hancock and E. Hackett   165

Insomnia and hypnotherapy
  M.A. Basker   173

Hypnotic susceptibility, EEG theta and alpha waves and hemispheric
  specificity
  C.MacL. Morgan   181

Pain control through hypnosis
  A. Rappaport   189

Hypnotic strategies in the daily practice of anesthesia
  J.C. Erickson III   195

Hypnotherapy of a psychogenic seizure disorder in an adolescent
  T.J. Glenn and J.F. Simonds   201

Hypnosis in the treatment of long term sequelae of sexual assault
  on children
  N. Malcolm   209

The hypnotherapeutic placebo
  H.E. Stanton   215

The use of hypnology as an adjunct in curbing smoking, obesity
  and hypertension
  C.A.D. Ringrose   223

Clinical medical hypnotic treatment of physiological
  disease - A holistic approach
  J.A. Jensen   231

Neuropsychology, bioethics and hypnosis
    M. Senk   239

A case of hysterical blindness with symptom removal in one session
    M.D. Zannoni   247

Pain sensitivity biological timidity and psychosomatic disorders
    Z. Pleszewski   253

Hypnotic regression into past lives : A case of resistance to
    hypnosis
    E. Fiore   261

Hypnosis in burn therapy
    D.M. Ewin   269

Contractual aspects of hypnosis in psychotherapy
    N. Phillips   277

The cognitive prerequisites of posthypnotic amnesia in chronic
    schizophrenia
    L. Girard-Robin and G. Lavoie   285

The effects of post hypnotic suggestion on maximum endurance performance
    and related metabolic variables
    J.A. Jackson and G.C. Gass   293

Hypnotic preparation of athletes
    L.-E. Uneståhl   301

Conflict in hypnosis : Reality versus suggestion
    K.M. McConkey   311

Bilateral EEG alpha activity in hypnosis
    G. Foenander and G.D. Burrows   319

Biofeedback and hypnotizability
    J. Holroyd, K. Nuechterlein, D. Shapiro and F. Ward   335

Relaxation and biofeedback : Clinical problems in research with
    essential hypertensive patients
    M. Goebel, G.W. Viol, G. Lorenz and T.S. Ing   345

Author index   353

© 1979 Elsevier/North-Holland Biomedical Press
Hypnosis 1979
G.D. Burrows, D.R. Collison and L. Dennerstein

THE USE OF HYPNOSIS IN THE TREATMENT OF PSYCHOGENIC IMPOTENCY

HAROLD B. CRASILNECK, PH.D.

The University of Texas Southwestern Medical School Health Science Center

Barnett Tower-Suite 901; 3600 Gaston Avenue; Dallas, Texas 75246 - U.S.A.

Hypnosis is an altered state of consciousness in which we are transacting treatment with the patient's unconscious mind. In reviewing the literature in the use of hypnosis with various urological problems Allen[2] (1972) Brown[4] (1959) Cheek[5] et al (1948) Choinottas[6] (1961) Collison[7] (1970) Crasilneck[8] et al (1959) Crasilneck[11] et al (1975) Kroger[17] et al (1956) Schneck[18] (1963) Wolberg[19] (1948) the results are generally excellent. Similar reports may be found in the literature describing the successful use of hypnosis in the treatment of sexual dysfunction, Alexander[1] (1974) August[3] (1959) Cheek[5] et al (1948) Crasilneck[9] et al (1959) Crasilneck[11] et al (1975) Deabler[13] (1975) Erickson[14] et al (1964) Fabbri[15] (1975) Jacks[16] (1975) Kroger[17] et al (1956) Schneck[18] (1963) Wolberg[19] (1948).

This paper is concerned with the use of hypnosis in the investigation and treatment of psychogenic impotency which is a condition manifesting an inability to obtain full erection, partial erection, or no erection at all often accompanied by premature ejaculation. Some patients report an incapacity to ejaculate usually followed by loss of erection, anxiety and complete exhaustion. Quite often the patient becomes extremely depressed because this condition is so frustrating.

Most men have experienced occasional difficulty with erection at some time in their lives for one reason or another. Should this condition become constant however, anxiety and apprehensive reactions toward the situation may develop. As the condition worsens the anxiety may manifest itself in psychological trauma resulting in moderate to severe depression, and in some cases the patient may attempt suicide.

> In most life activities a man in modern culture can rely on any num-
> ber of props for his sense of adequacy--his clothing, his income,
> his identification with a business, social, or sports group. Well
> wishing and social approval from peers can compensate for many fears
> of inadequacy.
>
> In the sexual act though, a man functions entirely alone in the most
> intimate contact with a woman who may approve or disapprove of his
> adequacy in the situation. It is not surprising then, that fail-
> ure in the sexual act may cause severe anxiety in a man who is
> functioning well in his other roles. Crasilneck and Hall (1959).

The writer has used this therapeutic modality for the past 25 years and

feels that the results obtained are sufficiently worthwhile; that hypnotherapy

should be considered as one of the principle methods employed by urologists,

psychiatrists and psychologists in the treatment of psychogenic impotency.

Before a patient is referred for hypnotherapy a complete genito-urinary

work-up is necessary. Most often a trial of medication has been administered

by the referring physician which failed to accomplish the task. Psychological

screening of the patient by the hypnotherapist is definitely required prior to

the first session of hypnosis.

Successful application of hypnosis in any type of problem requires both con-

scious and unconscious motivation by the patient. Crasilneck[8] (1958) Crasilneck[9]

et al (1959) Crasilneck[10] et al (1968) Crasilneck[11] et al (1975) Crasilneck[12] et al

(1956) Kroger[17] et al (1956) Wolberg[19] (1958). The patient should be psychological-

ly cooperative in the opinion of the referring physician, and must be willing

to accept this method of treatment in order for hypnotherapy to be successful.

During the psychological screening session the hypnotherapist may discover

one or more contraindications to hypnosis in the psychogenic impotency case, re-

vealing that the patient has a long-standing history of conversion neurosis, a

history of psychotic behavior, obvious masochistic tendencies, and/or extreme

severe depression. Also, patients with a history of diabetes who are on medi-

cation for hypertension such as Inderol, should not be treated with hypnosis

because a possible side effect of this medication is impotency.

If however, there are no contraindications good rapport should be established during the first session. Any and all questions should be answered concerning all aspects of hypnotherapy in an honest and forthright manner. Since most men with the chief complaint of psychogenic impotency manifest some type of psychological involvement, these psychogenic components should be investigated before and during the treatment program. This may be done in the form of hypno-analysis, hypnotherapy or in a waking state using psychotherapy. It is a well accepted theory that removing a psychologic symptom which has meaning to the patient by hypnosis, may cause a substitution of neurotic symptoms. Crasilneck[8] (1958) Crasilneck et al (1975)[11] Schneck (1963)[18] Wolberg (1948)[19]. Therefore, discussing the basic etiology of the problem with the patient and giving him good intellectual and emotional insight into his problem is of utmost importance during the combined treatment course of psychotherapy and hypnotherapy, thereby avoiding neurotic symptom substitution. This judicious measure is necessary to successful treatment of psychogenic impotency.

The most common causes for impotency reported by our patients include: loss of penile erection, fear of premature ejaculation, fear of castigation by the partner for failure during coitus, self-condemnation for failure, anger toward the partner for whatever reasons, guilt for extra-marital relations, failure in extra-marital relations, and failure in homosexual relationships. Also, some patients refer to anxiety over children disturbing the act, fear of impregnating the partner, and anxiety concerning exposure to venereal disease. Some patients relate to having been taught by their parents that sex is dirty and sinful while others admit unresolved oedipal conflicts. Many patients indicate their impotency exists at home but not with their paramour or vice versa.

A number of patients report that they were able to masturbate successfully but became impotent during sexual intercourse while other patients were capable of practicing homosexuality with erection but became impotent in the hetero-sexual act.

Weekly 30 minute hypnotic sessions on an individual basis is sufficient time to treat the psychogenic impotency problem. Prior to hypnotic induction the patient is advised that hypnotherapeutic treatment for impotency may either be completely successful, partially successful or totally unsuccessful. If appropriate, statistical results may be cited to the patient concerning the success factor of hypnosis in the treatment of impotency.

The patient is hypnotized into the deepest level of trance possible. Most of the time he is given the suggestion of catalepsy in one arm and hand with the following suggestion: "Make a fist with your right (or left) hand. Your arm and hand will become hard as steel, stiff as a board which has been soaked in water for days." When the arm becomes rigid the patient is told to touch his arm and hand with the non-cataleptic hand and feel the hardness. "If your unconscious mind can create this rigidity in your arm and hand then your penis can become as rigid and you can sustain an erection. You will have good blood supply to your penis. You will not ejaculate prematurely. You can and will enjoy this pleasurable and natural act with success." Following the repetition of these words a suggestion is given for the cataleptic arm to return to normal, and for the patient to relax.

Also, patients are instructed that, "because of the omnipotency of your unconscious mind over your body you can sustain erection for a normal period of time. There will be no loss of erection; no premature ejaculation. You will want to continue this natural act that feels good to you." These suggestions are given repeatedly during the remainder of the hypnotherapy session followed by constructive therapeutic and appropriate questioning later during the waking state, thereby strengthening the patient's insight as treatment proceeds.

The present series of 100 consecutively referred male patients manifested a chief complaint of psychogenic impotency. All these patients had a complete genito-urinary evaluation, and had been placed on a recommended therapeutic pharmacological regimen (of testosterone) for an appropriate period of time with negative results. While on medication the impotency had either continued or followed a partial or total remission. However, since there was no relief of the psychological component the symptom exacerbated.

The average age of the patients was 45 years. Eighty-five percent of them were married and 90% were hypnotizable. The chief complaint had existed for an average of four months per patient prior to consultation with their physician. Return of good erection occurred on the average during the week of the fifth hypnotic session. A ten month follow-up indicated that 80% of the patients in this series were relatively free of impotency with only an occasional loss of erection when they were "too tired" or "had too much to drink."

The average total number of therapeutic sessions required by the patient was twelve. It was not uncommon however, for patients to elect to remain in treatment for additional problems which could easily contribute to further states of impotency. None of the patients reported side effects due to the use of hypnosis nor symptom substitution.

All the patients were instructed in the use of self-hypnosis as an aid in reinforcing the post-hypnotic suggestion. Most responded positively to learning self-hypnosis which could be used at will.

All individuals who were not able to be hypnotized were omitted from this study. Among these were the patients who were unable to respond to hypnosis in terms of trance depth necessary for post-hypnotic suggestions to be effective. After the third session, if negative response persisted these patients were advised that hypnotherapy would probably be useless, and that there were other forms of psychotherapy in which to treat the problem.

CASE HISTORY I

A 40 year old male construction worker was referred to hypnotherapy with a chief complaint of psychogenic impotency. The problem, although spasmodic, had existed for about one year. The urological examination was essentially negative, and a course of testosterone had been administered with results completely unsuccessful.

The patient stated that his impotency started about three months following a flirtation. He experienced some guilt, and when he endeavored to tell his wife about it. His fear concerning her reaction prevented his doing so for he felt he had "let down the best person in the world".

The patient was agreeable to hypnosis and responded very well achieving a deep level of trance during the first session. It was suggested that he could achieve catalepsy in his right arm and hand, and he responded positively. He was given the suggestion that he could have good penile erection just as he had achieved the "rigid, hard response in his right arm." He was instructed in the use of self-hypnosis as a means of reinforcing the suggestions.

During the second to tenth hypnotic sessions suggestions were given for permanent return of erections. Simultaneously I began probing the basic conflict which gave him good insight into his problem. He revealed that his flirting was merely a means of testing his masculinity. He discontinued this activity once he realized the implication factors. This was indicative of his fidelity and his love for his wife. He realized that his guilt and self-condemnation were manifested by impotency. By the sixth session he reported his erections had returned with maximum development, and ejaculation was normal. Therapy was discontinued after 14 sessions and there has been no recurrence of symptomatology for the past year.

CASE HISTORY II

A 35 year old male who worked in a grocery store was seen by his urologist for psychogenic impotency. His complaint had existed for almost four months. During the past year he had divorced his third wife, had numerous affairs, and had "either been drunk or on pot" virtually every night. He was a negative and hostile person with a low frustration tolerance, and had been arrested numerous times for assault and battery, and disturbing the peace.

He stated "I want a miracle cure so that I can have a permanent erection." It was explained that this was not the purpose of hypnotherapy, that I would attempt to understand and treat the basic cause of his impotency and that he must be cooperative. The patient was noticeably anxious and apprehensive during the initial induction in spite of my attempts to establish good rapport. He stated at one point that "I am afraid to let go - to lose control" and was incapable of entering a depth of trance below the hypnoidal level.

On the second session he appeared hostile stating that he had been demoted in his position at work. He feared that hypnosis would be used to question him about secret facts in his life despite my assurance that this was not the purpose of treatment. He responded negatively to hypnotic induction. The attitude of this patient was slightly better during the third session but he cancelled his fourth session terminating all future meetings. His inadequate motivation negated any response to hypnotherapy and the case was considered a failure.

These studies reveal some important factors: a) with motivation and cooperation most patients presenting a problem of psychogenic impotency can respond favorably to hypnosis b) hypnosis can and does control the symptom c) hypnosis can bring into consciousness repressed material which precipitated the onset of the problem d) there is no indiscriminate removal of symptoms without adequate discussion of the basic etiology and e) a major advantage to hypnosis is that only a minimum amount of treatment time is required. Patients are instructed in the use of self-hypnosis some time during each visit which yields positive results and decreases the need for an excessive amount of heterohypnotherapy. As treatment proceeds the time between appointment sessions may be lengthened.

The basic conclusions of this study substantiate the findings of Crasilneck and Hall who reported the use of hypnosis in a series of more than 400 patients presenting functional impotency with improvement in approximately 80% of the cases. There were no severe side effects to this form of treatment nor were there any indications of symptom substitution.

ACKNOWLEDGEMENTS

The writer sincerely thanks Ms. Sherry Knopf for her research assistance in the collection of data, and also in the preparation of this article.

REFERENCES

1. Alexander, L. Treatment of impotency and anorgasmia by psychotherapy aided by hypnosis. Amer J of Clin Hypn (1974) 17, 33-43.

2. Allen, T.A. Psychogenic urinary retention. Swst Med J (1972) 65130-304.

3. August, R.V. Libido altered with the aid of hypnosis: A case report. Amer Soc of Clin Hypn (1959) 2,88.

4. Brown, T.D. Hypnosis in genito-urinary disease. Amer Soc of Clin Hypn (1959) 1, 165-168.

5. Cheek, D.B. Clinical Hypnotherapy N.Y. Grune & Stratton (1948).

6. Choinottas: Acute urinary retention successfully treated with hypnosis. Amer J of Clin Hypn (1961) 3, 201.

7. Collison, D.R. Hypnotherapy in the management of nocturnal enuresis. Med J of Anes (1970) 1, 52-54.

8. Crasilneck, H.B. The control of pain and symptom management. Bowers M.K. (ed.); Introductory lectures in medical hypnosis (1958) N.Y., Inst for Research in Hypn.

9. Crasilneck, H.B. Physiological changes associated with hypnosis: A review of the literature since 1948. Inst of Clin Hypn (1959) 7, 9-50.

10. Crasilneck, H.B. The use of hypnosis in controlling cigarette smoking. J of Swst Med Assoc (1968) 61, 99-1002.

11. Crasilneck, H.B. Clinical Hypnosis: Principles and Applications. N.Y., Grune & Stratton (1975).

12. Crasilneck, H.B. Special Indications for hypnosis as a method of anesthesia. J of Amer Med Assoc (1956) 162, 1608.

13. Deabler, H. Hypnotherapy of impotence. Amer Soc of Clin Hypn 18th annual meeting, Seattle, WA (1975).

14. Erickson, M. et al. The practical application of medical and dental hypnosis. The Julian Press, Inc. N.Y., Hall. (1964).

15. Fabbri, R. Hypnosis and the treatment of sexual disorders. Amer Soc of Clin Hypn 18 annual meeting. Seattle, WA (1975).

16. Jacks, F. Hypnosis and the treatment of sexual dysfunction. Amer Soc of Clin Hypn 18th annual meeting, Seattle, WA (1975).

17. Kroger, W.S. Psychosomatic gynecology. N.Y. Free Press (1956)

18. Schneck, P.M. (ed): Hypnosis in modern medicine (ed 3). Springfield, Ill., Thomas (1963).

19. Wolberg, L.R. Medical Hypnosis. Volume 1, N.Y., Grune & Stratton (1948).

© 1979 Elsevier/North-Holland Biomedical Press
Hypnosis 1979
G.D. Burrows, D.R. Collison and L. Dennerstein

ISOLATION, EEG ALPHA AND HYPNOTIZABILITY IN ANTARCTICA

Arreed Barabasz

Director of Clinical Psychology Training, University of Canterbury,

Christchurch, New Zealand.

The motivation for this study arose from the discrepancy between self report studies (Mullin, 1960) (Rivolier, 1976) about impairment of memory and difficulty in concentrating following Antarctic wintering-over isolation and objective measures (Gregson 1978a, 1978b) of actual pre-post winter performance showing, slight improvements rather than decrements. An investigation of EEG responses to veridical and suggested olfactory stimuli was conducted on an Antarctic wintering-over party (Barabasz & Gregson, 1978). Suppression of EEG amplitude, consequent upon stimulation, decreased for veridical odorants following wintering-over, but suppression consequent upon suggested odorants increased. This finding was viewed as supportive of a shift in suggestibility following winter isolation. Such a suggestibility shift might account for self reports of performance decrements, considering the recurrent iconography of base decor and literature featuring Antarctic explorers suffering and dying under stress.

Antarctic wintering-over isolation involves a considerable degree of sensory restriction, including total lack of diurnal variation for 4 months of the period. Olfactory stimulation is severely limited by the anosmic sub zero working environment. During the winter period there are no flights or ships and intermittent radio contact constitutes the only communication with the outside world.

Engstrom (1976) suggested that restriction of sensory experience may be a variable basic to hypnosis and skills involved in becoming hypnotised may include a subject's predisposition to restrict sensory input because of lower levels of cortical arousal. In Zubek's (1973) review of the effects of prolonged sensory and perceptual deprivation the slowing of EEG activity was reported in several investigations. The extent of alpha frequency slowing has been reliably shown to be dependent upon deprivation conditions.

Several studies have shown a significant positive relationship between waking eyes closed alpha density and hypnotizability while others have failed to support such a correlation (Barabasz, 1979). Dumas (1977) suggested that in experiments where the sample consisted of non-naive volunteers there was a significant correlation, while investigations using invited subjects or subjects unaware of the experimental focus found no correlation. A correlation results when subjects volunteer for a "brainwave and hypnosis" study but no such relationship is evidenced when subjects are drafted. It was hypothesized that subject self-selection, rather than environmental factors, is primarily responsible for alpha-hypnotizability correlations.

It seemed that further study of potential suggestibility shifts in Antarctica might eventually help to explain discrepancies in self report versus objective test performance. The environment was also considered to be an ideal laboratory for testing the Dumas hypothesis. The purpose of this study was to investigate the stability of EEG alpha and hypnotizability employing invited subjects, unaware of the experimental focus, who experienced a prolonged, but limited restriction of sensory and perceptual stimulation.

An additional purpose of the investigation was to determine whether or not alpha-hypnotizability correlations could be enhanced for invited subjects by omitting portions of EEG records coincident with skin conductance indices of arousal. Psychophysiological arousal, vigilance or even relatively simple cognitive tasks have been shown by numerous studies to be incompatible with alpha production (Beatty, 1975). Electrodermal response indices have been found to be negatively correlated with alpha production (Pelletier and Peper, 1977). It was hypothesized that Dumas' (1977) consistent findings of no correlation between alpha and hypnotizability might be accounted for by the suppression of Ss typical eyes closed alpha due to arousal. Crosson et al (1977) suggested that arousal responses in a novel environment, soon after having electrodes attached, could block alpha activity. It could be expected that naive or invited subjects might demonstrate greater psychophysiological arousal during experimentation than informed volunteers.

METHOD

Subjects - Invited Ss, naive with respect to the focus of the investigation consisted of nine men wintering-over at Scott Base, Antarctica. This New Zealand station is located near McMurdo Sound, 1300 km from the South Pole. Ss were told only that they were participating in a study of stability of various psychophysiological and psychometric responses. The sample was considered to be technologically oriented. Pre winter hypnotizability scores, on the instrument described later, were significantly lower (p <.05) on a Wilcoxon contrast than a group of 34 upper level university students.

Apparatus - Eight channels of EEG activity were simultaneously recorded on a San-Ei 1A61 electroencephalograph[1] at a sensitivity of 5 mm/50 μ volts and chart speed of 3 cm/second. Recordings were monopolar employing the left and right earlobes for reference sites. Electrodes were placed in compliance with the International 10-20 system at left and right frontal (F3 and F4), left and right temporal (T3 and T4), left and right parietal (P3 and P4) and left and right occipital (01 and 02).

Beckman silver/silver chloride electrodes were used for frontal, earlobe and earthing sites. Wire scalp electrodes were placed with bentonite paste for temporal, parietal and occipital sites. Electrode to skin contact conditions were monitored for all sites on the San-Ei LED display board. Maximum scalp to reference electrode resistance was 15 k ohms.

Skin conductance (SC) was also monitored during EEG recording sessions. Beckman silver/silver chloride electrodes were attached to the medial phalanx on the volar surface of each S's second and third digits following standardized procedure. SC measures were recorded on a Lafayette 76100-30 Barabasz Desensitization Quantifier. SC sensitivity was set at 0.1 μmho per centimeter.

Hypnotizability Instrument - To help preserve the naivete of the Ss for the pre and post test measure the Barber Suggestibility Scale (BSS) Barber and Glass, 1962) was selected as the measure of hypnotizability.

In contrast to other scales, the BSS can be administered without induction of hypnosis. On the basis of a pilot study (Barabasz, 1976) employing a Solomon four group design, it was determined that even the use of the BSS resulted in significant alteration of the Ss' awareness of the hypnotic focus of the study. Since it was the aim of the present study to maintain naivete of Ss and to minimize potential habituation effects   the BSS was not in its entirety. Item (1) Arm Lowering, (2) Arm Levitation and (4) Thirst Hallucination were found to correlate significantly with full scale suggestibility scores while showing no significant influence on Ss' naivete regarding focus of the measures. Items (1) and (2) were scored on the basis of inches of arm movement (Barabasz, 1976).

1 Special thanks are expressed to the San-Ei Instrument Corporation, Tokyo, Japan for the 1A61 Electroencephalographic equipment grant.

The present study employed items (1) and (2) of the BSS as above. Item (4) was limited to the scoring of the swallowing response upon imagination of the drinking of a refreshing glass of water.

The modified BSS and the Stanford Hypnotic Clinical Scale (SHCS) Hilgard & Hilgard, 1975) was administered to 34 upper level students enrolled at the University of Canterbury, New Zealand. A rank order correlation (.37) between the measures was significant (p < .05). Broad (1979) independently found a significant (p < .05) correlation (.42) between the modified BSS and the SHCS with an N of 20.

Procedure - All tests were conducted at Scott Base, Antarctica. Hypnotizability, EEG and SC data were collected eight weeks after Ss arrived at Scott Base and ten months later immediately following winter isolation.

Following attachment of electrodes S's maximum skin conductance level was established following standardized procedure, (Lykken and Venables, 1971). Ss closed their eyes while EEG and SC data were recorded.

A 25 minute recording period, was chosen to control for novelty effects on alpha production. Frontal records were used to help correct for onset of sleep. After the recording period, hypnotizability measures, announced only as tests of imagination, were administered without induction of hypnosis.

Scoring - EEG alpha (8-13 Hz > 20 µvolts) data for all eight channels was hand scored by two independent scorers using a San-Ei precision frequency templet. Records were scored for total percent-alpha and for total percent-alpha less the portion of each record during which Ss demonstrated SC arousal responses.

All channels, except frontals, were averaged in determining total percent-alpha. Frontal data was omitted because of between scorer inconsistency relating to artifact interpretation. An SC arousal response was operationally defined as a pen deflection amounting to 50% or greater of the S's SCR max (Lykken & Venables, 1971).

The three hypnotizability tests were scored on a 0 - 3 point basis for each item. Arm lowering and arm levitation were scored 1 pt. for 4" - 8" response, 2 pts for 8+" - 12", 3 pts for 12+" and over. The swallowing response/drinking of water item was scored 1 pt for a single swallow or mouth movements, 2 pts for more than one swallow or one swallow combined with mouth movements. An additional point was given if the S reported, "actually felt like I was drinking a glass of water" during post test questioning.

RESULTS

S's pre-wintering over and post-wintering over hypnotizability scores were analysed using a Wilcoxon Matched-Pairs Signed-Ranks test. A significant ($p < .05$) increase in hypnotizability was found (Wilcoxon T = 3 (NS - R = 8).

Rank order correlations were performed for hypnotizability scores and percent-alpha and for hypnotizability and percent-alpha omitting portions of the EEG record coincident with SC arousal indices.

TABLE 1

PERCENT-ALPHA & HYPNOTIZABILITY CORRELATIONS FOR ANTARCTIC WINTERING-OVER PARTY

Period	Total Percent-Alpha	Percent-Alpha Corrected for SC arousal periods
Pre-Winter Isolation	.21	.61
Post-Winter Isolation	.58 *	.86 **

   * $.05 < p < .1$

  ** $p < .01$

The results appearing in Table 1 show a significant ($p < .01$) correlation between percent-alpha per record, less periods of SC arousal, and hypnotizability for Ss exposed to Antarctic wintering-over isolation. Correlations for pre-winter SC corrected alpha and post-winter uncorrected alpha showed a tendency toward significance ($.5 < p < .1$). No significant correlation was demonstrated for the pre-winter total percent-alpha data.

Pre versus post wintering-over percent-alpha scores and SC corrected percent alpha scores were compared by a t-test for matched samples.

14

TABLE 2

ALPHA DENSITY t TEST RESULTS FOR WINTERING-OVER PARTY

Contrast	N	Mean % Alpha	S.D.	t-Value
Pre-winter Total Alpha	9	32.00	15.44	
VS				4.78*
Post-Winter Total Alpha	9	44.22	18.81	
Pre-Winter SC-corrected Alpha	9	38.33	17.17	
VS				3.53*
Post-Winter SC-corrected Alpha	9	49.44	21.54	

* $p < .01$

The results appearing in Table 2 demonstrate significant ($p < .01$) increases in alpha density for total percent-alpha and SC corrected percent-alpha following wintering-over isolation.

DISCUSSION

This study supports the hypothesis that a significant relationship exists between hypnotizability and EEG alpha density. A significant increase in hypnotizability and alpha density was found following the restriction of sensory and perceptual input while wintering-over at Scott Base, Antarctica.

The study fails to support the Dumas (1977) conclusion that the personality factor of subject self-selection is primarily responsible for alpha-hypnotizability correlations. The results appear to support the view that environmental factors or their interaction with another personality factor, choosing to winter over in Antarctica, can significantly influence hypnotizability and waking eyes closed alpha density.

Ss were drafted for both pre and post testing sessions. Informal interviews conducted with all Ss following all data collection failed to reveal any awareness of attitudinal change but preservation of naivety seemed to be confirmed.

It is of interest to note that had this study been limited to a simple total alpha density and hypnotizability measure for invited Ss, prior to wintering-over isolation the results would have appeared to further support Dumas' findings.

The long EEG/SC recording period control for novelty was apparently unnecessary. No significant differences were found between SC corrected alpha density for the first versus last five minutes of recording in pre or post winter comparisons.

The Crosson et al (1977) suggestion that arousal responses could block alpha activity was supported. While the total percent-alpha and hypnotizability correlation approached significance in the post wintering-over testing period, the omission of portions of EEG record coincident with SC arousal indices appeared to greatly enhance this correlation. The SC correction procedure also enhanced the pre wintering-over correlation. Further enhancement of EEG alpha and hypnotizability correlations might be obtained by additional refinement of SC criteria of arousability.

The Scott Base, Antarctica situation provided an ideal environment for restriction of sensory and perceptual input over time while maintaining naivete of Ss with respect to the focus of the experiment. Further investigations aimed at identifying specific environmental factors relevant to the enhancement of hypnotizability are planned focusing on summer Antarctic field parties where deprivation is more acute but for only one or two months duration.

REFERENCES

1. Barabasz, A.F. Treatment effects and subject awareness in the administration of the Barber Suggestibility Scale. Departmental Report, University of Canterbury, Christchurch, New Zealand, 1976.

2. Barabasz, A.F. New techniques in behavior therapy and hypnosis. So. Orange, N.J. Power, 1977.

3. Barabasz, A.F. EEG alpha, skin conductance and hypnotizability in Antarctica. International Journal of Clinical and Experimental Hypnosis, 1979, July, In press.

4. Barabasz, A.F. & Gregson, R.A.M. Effects of wintering-over on the perception of odorants at Scott Base. New Zealand Antarctic Record, 1978, 1, 2, 23-44.

5. Barber, T.X. & Glass, L.B. Significant factors in hypnotic behavior. Journal of Abnormal and Social Psychology, 1962, 64, 222-228.

6. Beatty, J. Self-regulation as an aid to human effectiveness and bio-cybernetics technology and behavior. Annual Report to the Defense Advanced Research Projects Agency, Arlington, Virginia, 1975. ARPA order Nos. 1595 and 3065.

7. Broad, G.S. Hypnotic suggestibility and the hand warming response. Unpublished MA Thesis, University of Canterbury, New Zealand, 1979.

8. Crosson, B. et al. EEG alpha training, hypnotic susceptibility and baseline techniques. International Journal of Clinical and Experimental Hypnosis,1977, 25, 4, 348-360.

9. Dumas, R.A. EEG Alpha-hypnotizability correlations: A review. Psychophysiology, 1977, 14, 5, 431-438.

10. Engstrom, D.R. Hypnotic susceptibility, EEG alpha, and self-regulation. In G.E. Schwartz and D. Shapiro (Eds.). Consciousness and Self-Regulation, New York, Plenum, 1976.

11. Gregson, R.A.M. An application of gustatory psychophysics in Antarctica. Chemical Senses and Flavour, 1978a, 3, 141-147.

12. Gregson, R.A.M. Monitoring cognitive performance in Antarctica. New Zealand Antarctic Record, 1978b, 1, 24-32.

13. Lykken, D.T. & Venables, P. Direct measurement of skin conductance: A proposal for standardization. Psychophysiology, 1971, 5, 92-96.

14. Mullin, C.S. Some psychological aspects of isolated Antarctic living. American Journal of Psychiatry, 1960, 117, 323-325.

15. Pelletier, K.R. & Peper, E. Developing a biofeedback model: Alpha EEG feedback as a means for pain control. International Journal of Clinical and Experimental Hypnosis,1977, 4, 361-371.

16. Rivolier, J. Selection et adaptation psychologiques due sujets vivant en groups isoles en hivernage dans l'Antarctique, Paris; Comite National Francais des Recherches Antarctiques, 1975, Report No. 34.

17. Zubek, J.P. Behavioral and physiological effects of prolonged sensory and perceptual deprivation: A review. In J. Rasmussen (Ed.), Man in Isolation and Confinement, Chicago, Aldine, 1973.

© 1979 Elsevier/North-Holland Biomedical Press
Hypnosis 1979
G.D. Burrows, D.R. Collison and L. Dennerstein

HIGH AND MODERATE HYPNOTIZABLES: A STUDY OF BRAIN FUNCTION DIFFERENCES IN A
PLATEAUED SAMPLE EXPOSED TO COLD PRESSOR PAIN

ROBERT KARLIN and DONALD MORGAN
Rutgers – The State University of New Jersey, New Brunswick, New Jersey, U.S.A.
LEONIDE GOLDSTEIN
CMDNJ-Rutgers Medical School, Piscataway, New Jersey, U.S.A.

INTRODUCTION

For the most part, studies devoted to hypnotic analgesia have failed to
find robust physiological correlates of the phenomenon.[1] However, recent work
by Saletu and his colleagues[2] has revealed some differences in gross EEG activity during hypnotic pain control. In another line of research, a number of
investigators have examined the relationship of laterality effects to hypnotic
phenomena. Studies of conjugate lateral eye movements have demonstrated that
stressed high hypnotizables show more tendency to activate the nondominant
hemisphere than do their less hypnotizable counterparts.[3]

Hypnotic analgesia is one of the most robust and clinically useful hypnotic
phenomena; and although one study[4] has failed to reveal hemisphere-related EEG
correlates of hypnotizability, it seems possible that true hypnotic pain control might well have cortical correlates that would emerge if EEG activity
were measured bilaterally. The present research attempts to explore that possibility.

OVERVIEW OF THE EXPERIMENT

Two hundred right-handed male volunteers were exposed to a modified 14-item
version of the group form of the Stanford Scale of Hypnotic Susceptibility:
Form C.[5] Thirty members of this original group were chosen for individual
testing: 15 potential high hypnotizables (HHs) and 15 potential moderate hypnotizables (MHs). These subjects were then tested in individual sessions
during which hypnotizability and response to cold pressor pain were assessed.
During the second of these sessions, subjects were given hypnotic analgesia
instructions and asked to immerse their hands in ice water for one minute.
Extremely cold water ($0-1^{\circ}C$) was used for the HH subjects in order to ensure
that they were able to control pain. This same temperature was used for all
subjects during the subsequent actual testing sessions. During the preliminary
screening, however, slightly warmer water was used for the MH group in order

to foster the belief among these less hypnotizable subjects that cold water stimulation during hypnosis was only minimally painful.

On the basis of these preliminary screening sessions, 12 of the 30 subjects were excluded, having failed to consistently fulfill the criteria for their respective groups. The remaining nine MH and nine HH subjects were exposed to EEG measurement and hypnosis during an acclimation session. During a separate session, tasks used by Graham and Evans[6] and Wallace et al.[7] as well as a paper and pencil measure were employed to determine whether differences in attentional abilities were related to the ability to control pain. (Recent research has indicated that HH subjects demonstrate superior ability in certain attentional tasks.[6,8]) Data analyses on these attentional measures have not been completed, and this report must therefore be seen as preliminary in nature.

The acclimation and attentional testing sessions took place during a one-month interlude between preliminary exposure to cold pressor pain and the final testing session. During the final session, EEG responses were recorded and pain reports obtained during five separate administrations of cold pressor pain.

METHOD
Subjects

The original sample consisted of 200 right-handed male volunteers ranging in age from 18 to 22. All were undergraduate students at Rutgers University who had responded to an advertisement in the student newspaper. They were paid $4 an hour for participating in the experiment, and all signed a detailed informed consent statement.

Group screening session

A revised version of the group form of the Stanford Scale of Hypnotic Susceptibility: Form C was administered. This scale, a self-scored inventory of hypnotic behavior, included four motor items, four challenge items, and six hallucinatory items. Fifteen subjects who reported passing the majority of all three types of items were selected for further testing as potential HH subjects. Fifteen subjects who had passed the majority of the motor and challenge items but had consistently failed the hallucinatory ones were selected for further testing as potential MH subjects.

Individual screening sessions

The 30 subjects selected from the original group were then tested at least twice to ensure that they satisfied the criteria for the groups to which they had tentatively been assigned. The SSHS:C was employed in the first of these sessions. During the second, a number of motor and challenge items from the Stanford Scale of Hypnotic Susceptibility: Form A[9] and several items from the Revised Stanford Profile Scale[10] were used. Negative hallucinations were emphasized.

At the end of the second session, HH subjects engaged in a cold pressor task during hypnotic analgesia. Circulating ice water at $0-1^{\circ}C$ was used. Both hands were placed in the water and standard analgesia instructions were administered. MH subjects were exposed to the same procedure except that the water was $4-5^{\circ}C$. For the HH subjects, the purpose of this procedure was to exclude those who could not demonstrate hypnotic analgesia. For the MHs, the purpose was to induce the belief that cold water stimulation during hypnosis was only minimally painful. In all cases, this procedure took place at least one month prior to the final testing session in order to ensure that the subjects' memory of the temperature during the screening session would be obscured.

Six MH and six HH subjects were excluded during the screening session for either of two reasons: (1) they did not consistently satisfy the requirements for high or moderate hypnotizability, but appeared to fall between the two categories; or (2) they had been classified on the basis of their other responses as highly hypnotizable, but did not show major analgesic effects during cold pressor stimulation and analgesia instructions. The remaining sample comprised nine HHs and nine MHs.

Preliminary EEG exposure

In order to stabilize response to EEG testing, all subjects were exposed to an initial recording session in which EEG was measured with and without hypnosis. A resting baseline was obtained. Then, following Morgan et al.,[4] subjects were asked to engage in verbal and nonverbal tasks. Finally, the SSHS:A was administered.

Attentional testing session

In this session, subjects were asked to complete attentional items from the Test of Attentional and Interpersonal Style,[11] a paper and pencil task that assesses attentional style. In addition, they engaged in a random number generation task developed by Graham and Evans[6] and a dual-tape task developed by the author[8] and reported the number of illusory shifts they observed during ten one-minute exposures to the Necker Cube and Schroeder Staircase illusions.[7] As analysis of data from this session has not yet been completed, no further mention of the attentional measures will be made in this report.

Final testing session: EEG response to cold pressor stimulation

Baseline measurement and stimulation pre-hypnosis. At the beginning of the final testing session, subjects were asked to relax for 10 minutes; a resting baseline, consisting of the last five minutes of that period, was obtained. Subjects were then exposed to the first of five hand immersions. The first immersion occurred prior to the induction of hypnosis. During this immersion, subjects did not receive any analgesia instructions. As in all hand immersions, subjects gave oral pain reports every 10 seconds. Pain was reported on a 0-10 scale, with 0 indicating no pain and 10 indicating pain so severe that the subject experienced a very strong desire to remove his hand(s) from the water. In the first immersion, both hands were immersed in 0-1°C ice water.*

Stimulation during hypnosis and post-hypnosis. Hypnosis was then induced using an eye closure induction. Induction was followed by three hand immersions. These occurred in one of two orders—either both hands were immersed first and then the left hand and finally the right hand alone were immersed or the reverse order was used. Order was counterbalanced within the hypnotic susceptibility groups. During these three administrations, standard analgesia instructions were administered. Next, two filler items were used to give subjects time to recover. Finally, hypnosis was terminated and both hands were again immersed in ice water without hypnosis or analgesia instructions.

EEG recording procedure. EEG was recorded using conventional gold-plated cup electrodes located at O1, O2, T3, and T4, with Cz as a common reference, and a mid-forehead ground. Unfiltered EEG (1.3-30 Hz) was digitized on line over successive five-second recording epochs. Thus, during each five-second period, integrated amplitude was separately recorded on a the right occipital, the right temporal, the left occipital, and the left temporal regions. Periods during which artifact was present were eliminated through examination of a hard-copy record that was simultaneously recorded on a Beckman type RM eight-channel dynograph. As alpha constitutes the majority of variance in the integrated amplitude of waking records and there are wide individual differences

---

*It should be noted that because of 60 Hz artifact created by the pump motors, water did not circulate during the final testing session, and local hand warming of the water could not be prevented.

in baseline alpha production, it was necessary to examine each record in light of individual patterns of activity. A global mean ratio of right to left integrated amplitudes was computed for the entire session. Ratios for the occipital and temporal records were computed separately. Each recording epoch was then designated as a period during which either the right or the left hemisphere was more active. During this final testing session, EEG recording was faulty for the first seven subjects. These subjects were excluded from further analyses. The final sample included six MH and five HH subjects, upon whose responses data analyses were performed.

RESULTS

Pain reports

Pain report data were analyzed in two ways. First, we performed a 2x2x5x6 ANOVA in which the factors were level of hypnotizability, order of hand immersion during hypnosis, type of hand immersion (both hands pre-hypnosis, right hand during hypnosis, left hand during hypnosis, both hands during hypnosis, both hands post-hypnosis), and time during each one-minute exposure at which the pain report occurred (10, 20, 30, 40, 50, or 60 seconds). Pain increased linearly over duration of exposure ($F=22.04$, $df=4.28$, $p<.001$). Hand immersions during hypnosis were reported to be less painful than without hypnosis ($F=15.09$, $df=5.35$, $p<.001$). HHs displayed greater pain control during hypnosis than did the MHs ($F=4.53$, $df=4.28$, $p<.001$). This last effect emerged most clearly as time went on during each hand immersion ($F=2.67$, $df=5.35$, $p<.05$).

A second analysis was performed using a 2x2x3x6 ANOVA with the same factors but in which only immersions of both hands were considered. This analysis allowed us to exclude variation based on single vs. dual hand immersion. Again in this analysis, pain increased linearly over time ($F=12.16$, $df=5.35$, $p<.001$). Reported pain was lower during hypnosis than during either of the two nonhypnotic immersions ($F=21.26$, $df=2.14$, $p<.001$). Finally, a condition x time interaction emerged ($F=2.76$, $df=5.35$, $p<.05$), which was qualified by a three-way interaction of condition x type of hand immersion x time ($F=2.75$, $df=10.70$, $p<.01$). This interaction revealed that while pain increased linearly over time, it did so far less for the HHs during hypnosis and post-hypnosis than it did for them pre-hypnosis or for the moderates on any occasion. While the finding during hypnosis for the highs was expected, the finding post-hypnosis for the highs was not. It results from a major increase in reported pain during the first pain report by highs post-hypnosis and is discussed below.

EEG responses

EEG responses were examined separately for dual hand and single hand administration. The percentage of five-second epochs in which the left hemisphere was more active was the dependent variable. Responses when a single hand was in the water were examined by means of a 2x2x2x2 ANOVA in which the factors were level of hypnotizability, order of hand immersion, recording site (temporal or occipital), and type of hand immersion (right or left). During single hand immersion, there was a significant difference in EEG activity during left vs. right hand immersion ($F=6.37$, $df=1.7$, $p<.05$), qualified by a hand x hypnotizability interaction ($F=6.73$, $df=1.7$, $p<.05$). Contralateral activation was seen among the MHs when either hand was immersed alone. The left hemisphere was relatively more active during 59.4% of the time during right hand stimulation, while during left hand immersion it was relatively more active only 30.4% of the time. The HHs did not show this pattern of contralateral activation. The left hemisphere was relatively more active 43.7% of the time during right hand immersion and relatively more active 44.1% of the time during left hand immersion. No significant main effects or interactions were found for either recording site or order of hand immersion.

Dual hand immersion was examined by means of a similar 2x2x2x3 ANOVA in which the final factor was whether hand immersion occurred pre-, during, or post-hypnosis. The condition x order x site interaction was significant ($F=9.60$, $df=1.6$, $p<.05$) as was the condition x order x time interaction ($F=3.81$, $df=2.12$, $p=.05$). (One subject was excluded due to muscle artifact during the first immersion.) Neither effect is readily interpretable as both are largely dependent on differences between the moderate hypnotizables run in different orders during the first hand immersion. This hand immersion occurred prior to the part of the experiment during which order was manipulated. These effects will therefore not be discussed further in this report.

DISCUSSION

Measurement of EEG response was based on several assumptions. First, we assumed that the cold water was a painful stimulus and that reported pain would verify this. Verification would consist of increasing reports of pain as hands were immersed in water. Second, we assumed that subjects in both groups would experience less pain during hypnosis and analgesia instructions than without hypnosis and analgesia instructions. It was expected that the placebo effects of hypnotic instructions and the changes in demand characteristics of the situation when analgesia instructions were administered would cause a lowering of reported pain during hypnosis. Finally, we assumed that HH subjects would be able to negatively hallucinate the absence of pain while the MHs would not. Thus, the highs should report less pain during hypnotic analgesia than the moderates.

The pain report data, for the most part, suggested that these assumptions were valid. The one data point that did not conform to our expectations was obtained from the first report post-hypnosis. Prior to hypnosis, the initial pain reports of highs and moderates during dual hand administration are relatively similar. However, during the post-hypnotic dual hand administration, the pain report after 10 seconds of hand immersion was considerably higher for the highs than moderates ($p<.01$, Tukey HSD). One, admittedly speculative, interpretation is that the MHs had become accustomed to the temperature of the water by the fifth hand immersion. On the other hand, the HHs had just experienced true hypnotic analgesia. Their first response to the water post-hypnosis may reflect their surprise at the quality of the sensation without hypnosis. Other interpretations are, of course, possible.

As for the EEG data, under ordinary circumstances we would expect to see clear contralateral activation when a single hand is immersed in $0-1^{o}C$ ice water. The moderates showed this effect. The reduction in pain that they reported during hypnosis was most probably related to expectancy and relaxation effects. MH subjects are clearly hypnotizable to some degree, and these subjects had been specifically prepared to expect that hypnotic analgesia instructions would provide an analgesic effect. Indeed, they report less pain during hypnosis than when they are not hypnotized. However, their EEG responses remained what we would expect in normal waking subjects. For the HHs, on the other hand, the results were quite different. The effects of hypnotic analgesia instructions on reported pain were clearer and more profound. Their EEG responses to single hand cold pressor pain showed practically no change in hemispheric activation. It would seem that, to some degree, the HHs were able to prevent the pattern of cortical activation that otherwise occurs with single hand stimulation.

It might be argued that, despite homogeneity of variance, the effect reflects either only statistical artifact or the insensitivity of our dependent variable. In order to examine the relationship between lack of contralateral activation and reduced pain perception, we examined the within group correlations between pain report and change in cortical activation during single hand stimulation. Although the numbers of subjects in both groups were small, the relationship for MHs was significant ($r=.82$, $n=6$, $p<.05$). However, the correlation within the group of HH subjects was not significant. Thus, while there is some indication that our data are not artifactual, the results remain suggestive rather than definitive.

In sum, these data add further support to the notion that hypnotic analgesia among HH subjects represents a true negative hallucination. In addition, they suggest that differences in gross cortical activation related to hypnotizability may be found during hypnotic analgesia under some conditions. It should be noted that we are familiar with the long history of findings of physiological correlates of hypnotic analgesia that have failed to withstand careful controls and/or replication. At present, we are planning a replication of the present experiment with a larger group of subjects.

ACKNOWLEDGEMENTS

This research was supported by a Behavioral Science Research Grant from Rutgers University. The authors are grateful to Julia Ward for her assistance. Requests for reprints should be sent to Robert A. Karlin, Department of Psychology, University College, Rutgers University, 39 Easton Avenue, New Brunswick, New Jersey, 08903.

REFERENCES

1. Hilgard, E. and Hilgard, J. (1975) Hypnosis in the Relief of Pain, William Kaufmann Inc., Los Altos, Cal.
2. Saletu, B. et al. (1975) Neuropsychobiology, 1, 218-242.
3. Gur, R. and Gur, R. E. (1974) J. Abn. Psych., 83, 635-643.
4. Morgan, A. et al. (1974) Psychophysiology, 11, 275-282.
5. Weitzenhoffer, A. and Hilgard, E. (1962) Stanford Hypnotic Susceptibility Scale: Form C, Consulting Psychologists Press, Palo Alto, Cal.
6. Graham, C. and Evans, F. (1977) J. Abn. Psych., 86, 631-638.
7. Wallace, W. et al. (1976) J. Abn. Psych., 85, 558-563.
8. Karlin, R. (1979) J. Abn. Psych., 88, 92-95.
9. Weitzenhoffer, A. and Hilgard, E. (1959) Stanford Hypnotic Susceptibility Scale: Forms A and B, Consulting Psychologists Press, Palo Alto, Cal.
10. Weitzenhoffer, A. and Hilgard, E. (1967) Revised Stanford Profile Scales of Hypnotic Susceptibility, Consulting Psychologists Press, Palo Alto, Cal.
11. Nideffer, R. (1977) Test of Attentional and Interpersonal Style: Interpreter's Manual, Behavioral Research Applications Group, Rochester, N.Y.

Hypnosis 1979
G.D. Burrows, D.R. Collison and L. Dennerstein

EXPECTANCY REACTIONS IN HYPNOSIS

PETER W. SHEEHAN

Department of Psychology, University of Queensland (Australia)

INTRODUCTION

Theorizing about hypnosis has clearly converged upon internal processes of
the organism and substantial data have accumulated to implicate processes such
as imaginative involvement, dissociation, and delusion. Such data aside, the
nature of the hypnotic situation itself clearly implicates these processes of
internal functioning. Hypnosis guarantees a situation where the investigator
typically requests that the subject engage in fantasy and imagery and presents
a variety of specific tasks in which subjects are motivated to experience as
cooperatively as they can. The hypnotist also actively urges the subject to
accept the truth of the communications that are given while at the same time
assumes that the subject has a grasp on reality that will permit the hypnotist
to change, alter or remove suggestions without any untoward effects. Active
imagination is permitted by the hypnotist who attempts to create the most
favourable situation possible for the display of the subject's capacities and
cognitive skills, reality and fantasy coexisting to potentially influence the
subject in how he or she chooses to behave.

One internal process that has faded into the background of contemporary
theorizing about hypnosis is the process of motivation, yet, conceptually
speaking, much would seem to highlight its potential relevance. The literature[1]
has, for example, long argued the importance of motivation to understanding the
processes of imagination and fantasy. In assessing recent data regarding
internal processes and their operation in hypnosis it seems necessary to
distinguish between the imaginative involvement of hypnotic subjects in the
events of trance and subjects' "motivated commitment"[2] to what the hypnotist
intends. Subjects may accept the suggestions given to them and translate them
into imaginative terms, but some hypnotized subjects appear to work cognitively
to construct the response that they consider is attuned to what the hypnotist
wants. The structuring of information is in accord with subjects' expectancy
about appropriate response. The notion of expectancy response specifically
describes the situation in which the expectancies or cognitive anticipations
of hypnotic subjects influence or structure distinctively their behaviour
through motivated involvement in what the hypnotist wants. The term needs to

be differentiated from general conformity reactions to standard hypnotic suggestions where there is no clear-cut objective indications of motivated commitment on the part of the hypnotized person. The commitment in question is a motivated and positive one, and depicts the hypnotic person as an active rather than passive recipient of the communications that the hypnotist sends.

For the most part, theorizing in hypnosis has taken the concept of "expectancy" and stripped it of its potential motivational significance. It has been formulated largely as a functional variable affecting outcomes in hypnosis. Subjects, for example, are said to typically bring expectancies about appropriate response (viz. that hypnotic response is easy or difficult) with them to the hypnotic setting and considerable evidence exists to illustrate their influence. Preconceptions about hypnosis that subjects have acquired can also readily influence the forms of behaviour that hypnotic subjects will show; hypnotic subjects, for example, who believe they will show catalepsy of the dominant arm will show that response when there is no real reason other than the induction of the preconception for their doing so. The notion of expectancy response advocated in this paper argues something different. It refers to the anticipation of the hypnotic subject stemming from the commitment of the hypnotized person to pursue cognitively what the hypnotist wishes or intends. Viewed in this way it stresses processes other than social attitudes or other sources of influence that occur outside the hypnotic setting and are brought with the subject to the trance context. And it indexes, directly, internal processes of psychological functioning.

The present paper attempts to review three major sources of evidence which illustrates the relevance of expectancy reactions in hypnosis. The first two studies reported have been published; the third extends data on the issue and reports unpublished work.

REVIEW OF THE EVIDENCE

The first programme of work[3], completed in 1971, employed susceptible hypnotizable subjects who volunteered to take part in a study on the correlates of trance. All subjects who participated were given a lecture demonstration in which crucial attributes of hypnosis (e.g., compulsive response) were illustrated by a model subject who took the part of a hypnotized person in front of a large audience. Months later, subjects were recruited from this same audience and asked to participate in an actual hypnosis study. Two groups of subjects (real and simulating) were tested. In the hypnosis session the hypnotist pitted his intent against the social influence of the lecture

demonstration in order to examine any special impact of the subject's willingness to please. In the session, the hypnotist prepared subjects for coming
out of hypnosis by telling them that soon he would count them into the waking
state. In doing so, he deliberately implied that he was going to remove all
suggestions and make sure everything was normal. Implicitly, his intent was
that subjects need no longer respond compulsively. In this way, subjects were
put into a subtle conflict. They had learnt outside the hypnotic setting
through the lecture demonstration that they should respond compulsively every-
time until they are actually out of hypnosis - they had seen a subject in a
demonstration respond in just that way - but now the hypnotist was implying
they needn't do that, even though he actually didn't say so.

The results of this experiment are illustrated in Table 1. Hypnotic
subjects responded according to the implicit intent of the hypnotist and
countered what they had learned was appropriate from the demonstration given
outside the trance setting; simulating subjects, on the other hand, opted for
the response dictated by the lecture demonstration. The results illustrate
the concept of expectancy reaction. The anticipation or expectancy of the
hypnotic subject about what was wanted was influential enough that it overcame
the influence of social factors operating in the setting to determine how
other subjects behaved.

TABLE 1

FREQUENCY OF EXPECTANCY REACTIONS (COMPULSIVE RESPONSE) IN STUDY 1

Subject Group	Expectancy Reaction	
	Present (Response in Favour of Hypnotist)	Absent (Response in Favour of Demonstration)
Hypnotic	6	10
Simulating	13	2

Note. Adapted from a monograph by the author, published in the Journal of
Abnormal Psychology, 1971, 78, 299-322. Copyrighted by the American
Psychological Association, Inc., 1971.

Evidence of another kind - using different procedures and methods of
control comparison - bear down on the same hypothesis. Epstein and Rock in an
important study of perception[4], suggested that expectations may play less of a
critical role in influencing our perceptions than we at first believe. They

isolated particular conditions of testing which guaranteed that events immediately preceding, and not our expectations of what is to be seen, influence later perception. Their procedures were simple. Subjects were shown three of the same slide and led to expect that the fourth one would be different. They used (among other stimuli) Boring's Wife/Mother-in-Law figure and presented either the old or the young woman in series for the first three of four trials. On the fourth (test) trial, the slide presented was the ambiguous figure which could be resolved perceptually by subjects as either young or old. Under very tightly controlled conditions of stimulus presentation, the data showed that subjects resolved the ambiguity of the test slide and reported the figure that had most recently preceded and not the figure that they expected would be seen.

Epstein and Rock's situation lends itself well to the pursuit of subjects' motivated cognitive commitment in the trance setting. If hypnotized subjects have a particular motivated involvement in what the hypnotist says then the hypothesis suggests itself that some hypnotic subjects at least may follow their expectancy when hypnotised and overrule the influence of most recent perceptual events. It was predicted in this second study, then, that Epstein and Rock's recency phenomenon would revert to expectancy behaviour when subjects move from the waking to the trance setting.

As a demanding test of subject's willingness to respond according to expectancy, this programme of work[5] tested subjects in one condition where the expected resolution of the ambiguous figure was "old" and tested the same subjects in a different series where the expected resolution was "young" - an entirely opposite response to what subjects had given before. The question was asked whether hypnotic subjects would "switch" from one expected response to an altogether different one when the hypnotist required it.

Table 2 sets out the results. The table lists results for imagination and hypnotic subjects who switched from reporting they saw the old woman on the first occasion of testing (Task 1) to reporting they saw the young woman in the same slide on the second occasion of testing (Task 2). Seven subjects did so and data showed that the only subjects to respond consistently in this manner were those in the hypnotic group. Mismatching (of the figure actually seen to the one reported) was associated distinctively with the performance of the seven subjects who switched from one expectancy response to another. Six of the seven subjects who switched from one expected response to another also showed long delays (M=2708 m secs.) suggesting in these cases that there was substantial cognitive effort involved in subjects' structuring the figure in the anticipated way.

TABLE 2

FREQUENCIES OF EXPECTANCY REACTION AND MISMATCHING IN STUDY 2

Response	Instruction Group		
	Hypnotic	Task Motivational	Control (Imagination)
Expectancy Reaction Present	7	0	0
(Old on Task 1; Young on Task 2)	2 mismatchings to old on Task 1		
	3 mismatchings to young on Task 2		
Expectancy Reaction Absent	13	20	20

Note. Adapted from an article by R. M. Dolby and the author, published in the Journal of Abnormal Psychology, 1977, 86, 334-345. Copyrighted by the American Psychological Association, Inc., 1977.

EXPECTANCY REACTIONS AND APTITUDE FOR HYPNOSIS

In arguing for the utility of categorizing subjects' expectancy responses, it is important to establish that expectancy behaviour may not simply be explained in terms of the level of subjects' aptitude or ability for trance response, their performance reflecting the specific skills that susceptible persons may easily display on request from the hypnotist in the hypnotic setting.

A third programme of work relevant to this issue followed on from the first study. The phenomenon evidenced in Study 1 can be labelled "countering" - the tendency for real hypnotic subjects to counter the message of the lecture demonstration in favour of the hypnotist. The prediction was made that relationship factors ought to affect this countering index. Specifically, countering ought to diminish in a context which inhibits a positive, warm relationship between subject and hypnotist and increase in a context of rapport that encourages such a relationship. The research involved ten experiments, each of which established an incidence of countering response for the group of hypnotic subjects who were tested. Each experiment involved independent samples of highly susceptible subjects and in each study, the susceptibility of counterers and those who did not counter in favour of the hypnotist

was examined. Table 3 sets out the mean susceptibility scores in the studies
that were conducted and contrasts the susceptibility level of counterers and
noncounterers for each experiment.

TABLE 3

MEAN SUSCEPTIBILITY SCORES ASSOCIATED WITH COUNTERING (EXPECTANCY REACTION)
AND NON-COUNTERING IN TEN INDEPENDENT STUDIES

Reaction	Study				
	Phase 1 Study 1	Phase 2 Study 1	Phase 3 Study 1	Phase 4 Study 1	Phase 5 Study 1
Countering	8.61	8.70	9.42	8.11	6.65
Non-Countering	8.83	9.20	10.08	8.06	7.26

Reaction	Study				
	Phase 1 Study 2 (-ve rapport)	Phase 2 Study 2 (-ve rapport)	Phase 3 Study 2 (+ve rapport)	Phase 4 Study 2 (-ve rapport)	Phase 5 Study 2 (-ve rapport)
Countering	7.29	10.42	6.57	7.00	6.00
Non-Countering	7.48	11.32	6.79	7.69	7.09

Note. The term Study 1 and Study 2 refer to control (no manipulation of
rapport) and experimental studies, respectively, in analysis of negative
(Phases 1, 2, 4 & 5) and positive (Phase 3) rapport factors as they affect
countering in the hypnotic setting. Different samples of hypnotic test items
were used in the separate experiments that are reported.

Results show that in nine of the ten studies, that were carried out,
counterers passed fewer SHSS:C items, on the average, than did noncountering
subjects. Only in one experiment was there a trend for this pattern in the
data to be reversed. The stability of the data in this respect suggests it is
quite inaccurate to associate expectancy behaviour with greater behavioural
compliance with suggestion, or overall conformity to respond. The same persons
who detected and responded to the hypnotist's intent were not those subjects
who necessarily responded best to the hypnotist's overt, direct communications
about appropriate standard response. The argument here is not that subjects'

aptitude for hypnosis is unimportant to the occurrence of hypnotic phenomena;
aptitude for trance is critically important in the laboratory setting.
Rather, the data point to inter-individual differences in behaviour among
highly susceptible subjects which cannot be explained simply in terms of
variation in subjects' overall ability to perform well in the hypnotic context.

CONCLUSION

Clinical data would support the notion that it is inappropriate to compart-
mentalize subjects' behaviour in a way that emphasizes simply one aspect of
internal process functioning. Cognitions relate importantly to motivational
states, and the concept of expectancy response serves to highlight the relevance of this interaction and so bring the scientific analysis of interpersonal rapport into methodological reach. The major advantage of the concept
lies in the kinds of differences between hypnotic and nonhypnotic subjects
that the term implicates and the concept is useful in the sense that it
orientates us to look for distinctive alterations in cognitive functioning and
changes in consciousness that may reflect subtle and possible dynamic[6]
cognitive effects.

Contemporary theorizing has focussed on the relevance, in particular, of
imaginative involvement, dissociation, and delusion. Susceptible persons, for
example, accept the hypnotist's communications and translate them easily into
imaginative events. The significance of the present concept is that it
argues further that some hypnotized subjects, because of the special per-
suasiveness of the hypnotist's intent, will work in a committed fashion to
cognitively construct the behaviour that they consider is appropriate to what
the hypnotist wants. The cognitive aspects of that translation clearly relate
to current theorizing on the multiple levels of consciousness of hypnotic
subjects[7] and to the importance of isolating the "cohesive cognitive organisa-
tions"[8] that characterize hypnotic as distinct from waking consciousness.

Two major empirical findings index the utility of expectancy reactions, in
particular, and they jointly draw needed attention to the internal processing
features of subjects' motivational states. First, such reactions are
characterized by the hypnotic subject distinctively overiding good reasons to
respond in other ways (reasons that waking subjects follow), and, second,
expectancy responses do not simply parallel differences in level of susceptibility as one would expect if such reactions were merely tied to the
hypnotist's overt communications to subjects. If subjects who respond in a
fashion that is particularly attuned to the intent of the hypnotist are not

necessarily those who respond most overtly to the demands of test suggestions, then the correlates of subjects' differing levels of involvement in hypnosis require close examination. It seems plausible to argue that such individual differences as exist in the extent to which subjects will resolve conflict situations in which they are placed - when strong reasons are present to respond otherwise in the way we have examined - are meaningfully associated with differences that have been observed in hypnotic subjects' styles, or modes of cognition[9]. Data from the third programme of work did, in fact, suggest that subjects altered their cognitive orientation as shifts occurred in their positive commitment following the manipulation of rapport. The results point firmly to the need to study individual difference variables and their cognitive correlates among susceptible subjects themselves, not in isolation, but in reciprocal interaction with process (e.g., rapport) and situational variables (e.g., hypnotist characteristics) that influence behaviour in the hypnotic setting.

ACKNOWLEDGEMENTS

Part of the research reported in this paper was funded by the Australian Research Grants Committee. The author wishes to thank the Committee for its support.

REFERENCES

1. Holt, R.R. (1972) On the nature and generality of mental imagery. In P.W. Sheehan (Ed.), The Function and Nature of Imagery, Academic Press, New York, pp. 3-33.

2. Sheehan, P.W. (in press) In R.H. Woody (Ed.), Encyclopedia of Clinical Assessment. Jossey-Bass, New York.

3. Sheehan, P.W. (1971) J. Abn. Psychol., 78, 299-322.

4. Epstein, W., and Rock, I. (1960). Amer. J. Psychol., 73, 214-228.

5. Dolby, R.M., and Sheehan, P.W. (1977) J. Abn. Psychol., 86, 334-345.

6. Sheehan, P.W., and Dolby, R.M. (in press) J. Abn. Psychol.

7. Hilgard, E.R. (1977) Divided Consciousness, Wiley, New York, pp. 1-300.

8. Rapaport, D. (1951) Organisation and pathology of thought. Columbia University Press, New York, p. 184.

9. Sheehan, P.W., McConkey, K.M., and Cross, D. (1978) J. Abn. Psychol., 87, 570-573.

Hypnosis 1979
G.D. Burrows, D.R. Collison and L. Dennerstein

HYPNOTIZABILITY AND THE TREATMENT OF DENTAL PHOBIC ILLNESS

JACK GERSCHMAN, GRAHAM D. BURROWS, PETER READE, GEORGE FOENANDER

Depts. of Dental Medicine & Surgery, & Psychiatry, Univ. of Melbourne, Australia

INTRODUCTION

A continuing multi-disciplinary study at the Oro-Facial Pain Clinic, The Royal Dental Hospital of Melbourne has demonstrated that hypnotherapy is useful in the management of previously resistant, chronic facial pain disorders, discomfort conditions and dental phobic illness[1].

Little systematic attention has been given by the dental profession to the problems of the management of patients' fears and phobias. Effective studies evaluating treatment methods are scant.

Methods of reducing dental fears have included hypnosis, relaxation, modelling, systematic desensitization, cognitive rehearsal, implosion, flooding, operant conditioning, psychotherapy, psychotropic agents, conscious sedation techniques and leucotomy. Behavioural psychotherapy techniques, relaxation and hypnotherapy have in recent years assumed increasing prominence as effective treatment regimes.

Dentists have used a number of methods in the management of dental phobic illness through hypnosis. They have treated the anxiety directly and symptomatically, relying largely on relaxation. Behavioural techniques have also been found to be effectively combined within the hypnotic framework. Hypnosis has also been found to be useful in more sophisticated uncovering techniques of age-regression and hypno-analysis as part of more analytical insight-oriented psychotherapies.

The relationship between hypnotizability and phobic behaviour is not well understood. From a study of the case histories of phobic patients Frankel[2] observed that the dissociative experiences reported by these patients were similar to those described by persons in the hypnotic state. He therefore hypothesised a relationship between phobic behaviour and hypnotizability. He suggested that these findings lend strong empirical support to the view that phobic patients show a tendency to the same kind of mental functioning that is involved in responding to hypnotic induction. He also suggested that individuals who develop phobic symptoms must have the capability of manifesting the kind of cognitive functioning that characterises the hypnotized individual. Foenander et al.,[3] in a continuing study, tested Frankel's hypothesis of this relationship.

Thirty-three subjects were assessed for phobic behaviour and hypnotisability using standardized rating scales.

The main findings of the study were as follows: (1) The hypnotizability scores of a group of phobic subjects were significantly higher than those of the normal population. This partially supported Frankel's results that the dissociative experiences of phobic patients resembled those of high hypnotizable subjects; (2) High hypnotizable subjects showed a significantly higher mean response to treatment than medium and low hypnotizable subjects.

The aim of the present study was to further investigate the relationship between hypnotizability and the treatment of phobic behaviour in patients presenting with dental phobic illness.

SUBJECTS

During the past five years more than 500 patients have been intensively investigated and treated at the Oro-Facial Pain Clinic. Of this group, 100 patients (20%) presented with dental phobic illness. The first forty consecutive cases receiving hypnotherapy for their illness, were included in the study. There were fourteen males and twenty-six females. Their age ranged from four to seventy-nine years (mean=30 years) and when first attending the Clinic had been experiencing phobic symptoms for three to thirty years (mean=10.6 years).

DESIGN OF STUDY

Initial patient assessment included a detailed medical and dental history and examination, psychiatric assessment and the completion of a series of objective and subjective rating scales and questionnaires.

Hypnotizability was measured by the Diagnostic Ratings scale of Hypnotizability[4]. Patients were classified as a low, medium or highly hypnotizable according to their scores on this scale. A

chi-square analysis was carried out in order to compare the distribution of these scores from that expected in the normal population.   The expected frequencies were calculated on the basis
that in the normal population 20 percent are low in hypnotizability, 60 percent are medium in hypnotizability and 20 percent are
highly hypnotizable.

Patients were grouped according to the type of phobia (single
or multiple).   This was decided on the basis of the main predom-
inating symptom present.

Patients were also grouped according to the severity of their
phobic behaviour, which was measured by means of a four point
clinical rating scale (0=none, 1=mild, 2=moderate, and 3=severe).

The severity of the specific dental phobic behaviour was
measured by the Dental Anxiety Scale[5] and a visual Analogue
Rating Scale[6], and also scored by means of a four point clinical
rating scale (0=none, 1=mild, 2=moderate, and 3=severe).

Comparisons were made of the patients' degree of hypnotizability with the response to treatment.   Response to treatment,
which consisted of a combination of behaviourally oriented hypnotherapeutic techniques and psychotherapy was rated as follows:
none=0, slight=1, moderate=2, and very much=3.

RESULTS

TABLE 1

DISTRIBUTION OF HYPNOTIZABILITY SCORES ON THE DIAGNOSTIC RATINGS
SCALE OF HYPNOTIZABILITY

| Frequencies | Hypnotizability | | | |
	Low	Medium	High	
Observed	7	14	19	40
Expected	8	24	8	40

χ^2=19.43, 2 d.f.
p < 0.001

Table 1 shows the distribution of the patients' hypnotizability
scores as measured on the Diagnostic Ratings Scale.   A chi-square
analysis showed that the distribution of the scores were significantly different from that expected in the normal population

(χ^2=19.43, 2 d.f., p < 0.001). The observed frequencies were comparable to those found in Frankel's data and in our previous study.

TABLE 2

FREQUENCY DISTRIBUTION OF THE TYPE AND SEVERITY OF PHOBIAS

Severity of Phobia	Type of Phobia		
	Single	Multiple	
Mild	0	0	0
Moderate	5	5	10
Severe	6	24	30
	11	29	40

Table 2 shows the frequency distribution of the type and severity of phobias. There were more people with multiple phobias than single phobias and more severe multiple phobias than severe single phobias.

TABLE 3

THE RELATIONSHIP OF HYPNOTIZABILITY WITH THE SEVERITY OF PHOBIC BEHAVIOUR

Clinical Rating of Phobic Behaviour	Hypnotizability			
	Low	Medium	High	
Mild	0	1	2	3
Moderate	1	8	7	16
Severe	6	5	10	21
	7	14	19	40

Table 3 shows the relationship of hypnotizability with phobic behaviour as measured on a clinical rating scale. The results suggested a trend towards a positive correlation of hypnotizability with phobic behaviour. The cell frequencies were too small for a test of significance to be carried out.

TABLE 4

THE RELATIONSHIP OF HYPNOTIZABILITY WITH THE SEVERITY OF DENTAL
PHOBIC BEHAVIOUR

Rating of Dental Phobic Behaviour	Hypnotizability			
	Low	Medium	High	
Mild	0	1	0	1
Moderate	2	5	3	10
Severe	5	8	16	29
	7	14	19	40

Table 4 shows the relationship of hypnotizability with dental
phobic behaviour as measured by the Dental Anxiety Scale and an
Analogue Rating Scale. The results suggested a trend towards a
positive correlation of hypnotizability with dental phobic behaviour. Because of the small cell frequencies it was not possible
to test the significance of this relationship.

TABLE 5

THE RELATIONSHIP OF HYPNOTIZABILITY WITH THE RESPONSE TO TREATMENT

Hypnotizability	Response to Treatment			
	Slight	Moderate	Very Much	
Low	4	2	0	6
Medium	3	8	6	17
High	0	1	16	17
	7	11	22	40

$\chi^2=25.42$, 4 d.f.
$p < 0.001$

Table 5 shows the relationship of hypnotizability with the response
to treatment. A chi-square analysis showed a positive correlation
of hypnotizability with a favourable response to treatment
($\chi^2=25.42$, 4 d.f., $p < 0.001$).

DISCUSSION

   The main findings of this study were that:- The hypnotizability
scores of a group of patients with dental phobic illness were
significantly higher than those of the normal population. This
supports the findings of our previous study and partially supports
Frankel's hypothesis that the dissociative experiences of phobic
patients resembled those of highly hypnotizable subjects.

   The finding that there were more people with multiple phobias
than single phobias and that there were more severe multiple
phobias than severe single phobias is of significance to dental
treatment. The dentist who is not adequately trained in psychological medicine may not be fully aware of the extent of his
patient's psychological problems and may not provide adequate
treatment for his patient. Dental phobic illness is still too
often managed by purely physical means,such as nitrous oxide
conscious sedation or intravenous sedation techniques without
the evaluation of the psychological status of the patient.

   There was a suggested trend towards a positive correlation
of hypnotizability with total phobic behaviour and with specific
dental phobic behaviour. Severe phobias seemed more hypnotizable
than mild to moderate phobias.

   Frankel did not report any correlation of hypnotizability with
phobic behaviour as he did not use a phobic scale to measure the
severity or type of phobia present.

   The finding that highly hypnotizable patients showed a significantly more favourable response to treatment than medium or low
hypnotizable subjects supports both Frankel's results and the
findings of our previous study.

   The finding of marked alleviation of symptoms and fears in
the majority of the patients (83%) was a significant result, as
these patients had experienced little or no success with previous
treatment, having attended multiple dental practitioners or
having totally avoided treatment. The majority of dental patients
can be managed readily by orthodox techniques. Hypnotherapy
seems to be most useful with problem patients who are resistant to
standard techniques. The use of suggestion or relaxation techniques in dentistry without the formal induction of a hypnotic
state may however assist for a wide range of dental procedures.

More detailed statistical analyses and further research are in progress using a larger sample size and including other ratings of phobic behaviour.

REFERENCES

1. Gerschman, J. A., Burrows, G. D. and Reade, P. C. (1978) Aust. Dent. J., 23, 6, 492-496.

2. Frankel, F. H. (1976) Hypnosis: trance as a coping mechanism. Plenum Medical Book Company, New York.

3. Foenander, G., Burrows, G. D., Gerschman, J. A., Horne, J. de L. Phobic behaviour and hypnotic susceptibility. In press.

4. Orne, M. T. and O'Connel, D. N. (1957) J. Clin. and Exp. Hypnosis, 14, 125-133.

5. Corah, N. L. (1969) J. Dent. Res., 48, 596-598.

6. Aitken, R. C. B. (1969) Proc. Royal Soc. Med., 62, 989.

© 1979 Elsevier/North-Holland Biomedical Press
Hypnosis 1979
G.D. Burrows, D.R. Collison and L. Dennerstein

THE CASE AGAINST RELAXATION

KAY F. THOMPSON, D.D.S.
University of Pittsburgh, School of Dental Medicine, Pittsburgh, PA 15261, USA

Ancient and modern teachings in the literature concerning hypnosis present
one or another model of relaxation as the primary means of teaching hypnosis
to individuals. Relaxation is a practical, useful tool for many people like
the apprehensive medical or dental patient, or the patient in therapy who can
use relaxation to stimulate recall and reduce anxiety. Relaxation provides
enough adjunctive benefit to the patient to enable the doctor to treat him.
What it is critically important to recognize is that, for many people, hypnosis is not synonymous with relaxation and that complete dependence on relaxation will often retard the individual who is learning the technique.

Relaxation techniques teach the patient to expect the doctor to "do" the
hypnosis, since the patient is required to participate only by sitting and
listening and relaxing physically and mentally. Further, relaxation techniques demand that the patient "go into a recognizable trance," which means that
he should look relaxed, with his eyes closed, his body loose and semi-slumped
in a chair, and relatively unresponsive to stimuli. The nature of relaxation
encourages the doctor to use the "I want you to ..." approach to the patient;
to expect compliance at least, and possibly complete subservience. Before a
patient can progress beyond relaxation, he must learn that this stereotypic
response is not a necessary component of trance, nor a true indicator of hypnosis. Perhaps one reason so many people find it difficult to acknowledge the
spontaneous trance is that it does not require relaxation. It is easy to demonstrate that closed eyes do not imply relaxation: think of the many regular
dental patients who keep their eyes closed, but who most definitely are not relaxed. Many a patient who wishes to use hypnosis during surgery, childbirth
or some other traumatic procedure is apprehensive because the doctor continues
telling him to "relax..relax...". The patient knows he is not what he per-
ceives as relaxed, at least on the physiological and emotional levels; though
he may be quite capable of undergoing surgery and controlling pain and bleeding, the process requires such hard work and concentration on his part that
relaxation is the last thing on his mind. The patient does not need to relax;
he needs confidence in his ability to control his autonomic nervous system.

For 25 years I have taught individuals hypnosis. I have increasingly turned
away from the relaxation/sleep model and have demanded more from the patient
than that he sit there and listen to me drone on and on, until he becomes so

lulled that relaxation is the natural consequence of boredom. In the more
active physiological approach, the patient is taught and expected to rely on
his own unconscious and to learn that his unconscious can initiate behavior
which his conscious mind is not controlling, nor even expecting. When he understands this type of trance, he is more willing to accept active responsibility
in the cooperative venture of getting him well. He recognizes that at no time
is he "under the control" of the doctor teaching him hypnosis (although he may
be restricted in what he can learn if the doctor's teaching is inhibited). The
patient learns that he can - and must - talk, walk, react, think, and, in general, interact and participate in the procedure. One of the most important
aspects of the non-relaxed trance is that the patient is more immediately
aware of his own control. When he is encouraged to move around, talk, and do
whatever he needs to do spontaneously, he realizes it is his own trance. He
also learns to take responsibility for himself.

The confusion which surrounds doctor-patient relationship in a situation
involving hypnosis may be partly explained using the terms "to", "for" and
"with". The earliest concept of hypnosis required an authoritarian doctor/
hypnotist who did something "to" the subject/patient. This evolved into a relationship in which the doctor/hypnotist did something "for" the subject/
patient. The modern approach is one in which the doctor/facilitator does something "with" the patient in a cooperative teaching/learning situation. Patients with whom I work understand that once they have learned to achieve trance,
"You have your job and I have mine." I assume that the patient will do his
part, which may or may not include relaxation.

There are real semantic difficulties in interpreting the word "relaxation."
What does the doctor mean, and what does the patient understand, when the doctor continually emphasizes "relax, relax, your whole body is getting heavy,
loose, limp and relaxed?" To the doctor it may imply being comfortable and it
may certainly include the ideas of dissociation, cognitive control or the letting go of anxiety; sometimes it means safety. For the patient these same
words must imply a change from anticipating the worst and dreading the unknown,
to feeling secure in the knowledge that everything is under control. Relaxation is convenience and the freedom to concentrate on the task at hand, and the
realization that the patient is in control of himself. How difficult it is for
the doctor and the patient to understand one another if all that is communicated in words is the need to relax.... which may well be interpreted by the
patient as mere muscle looseness, lethargy and a disinclination to function or

think. What are we really communicating to our patients? Are we saying what we think we are saying? Do we permit the patient to transcend our words or do we restrict him to a narrow, literal view of trance and its associated behaviors? A doctor asks a patient in trance to "control" his bleeding; does the doctor mean "control", or does he really mean "stop"? Do we pay enough attention to the meaning our words have for the patient? One way to improve communication which I have been encouraging for years, involves tape recording our sessions with our patients, and later studying the recording to determine all possible meanings of what we have said. This may oversimplify the problems, but at least it is a start toward understanding our own interpretation of "relaxing", and patients' understanding as well. This exercise can help us to clarify the meaning of our words.

One wonders why facilitators* continue to talk about and insist on relaxation as a precondition for hypnosis. Do we need to see this relaxation to believe our patients are truly in a hypnotic state? Would it shake our confidence in ourselves if the patient did not "look" as if he were in trance? Surely if we can learn confidence in our ability to work with a patient under any circumstances, we need not demand that he "prove" to us he is in trance. Erickson says, "My learning over the years was that I tried to direct the patient too much. It took me a long time to let things develop and make use of things as they developed."[1] (Perhaps the cultural and professional educations we have received make us unable to trust the patient to control himself. Possibly our own experience of trance, or our lack of experience, inhibits our willingness to trust the patient's unconscious.)

Attitudes toward clinical hypnosis seem to divide facilitators reliably into two categories: those who have experienced hypnosis for themselves, and those who have not. It is difficult for me to accept anyone's interpretation of trance in anyone else, if he has not experienced usable trance in himself. Clinical trance is so often indicted as a non-measurable, subjective, interpersonal response that we must recognize how greatly our understanding and interpretation of the experience is influenced by what we have undergone. For too long practitioners have assumed that an external, "objective" view of the state of clinical trance is more valuable in helping patients than an internal, "subjective" view. I do not accept this. Valid descriptors can be obtained using, for instance, the Gracely et al[2] verbalization technique - and this should be done.

*Facilitator: Alternative word for operator as used by the faculty of the hypnosis course at the University of Pittsburgh.

We should ask those most directly concerned - the patients and the doctors who have experienced trance themselves - how <u>they</u> define relaxation, and whether or not it is a necessary condition of trance. (We might also ask these doctors who have worked with hypnosis before and after having themselves experienced clinical trance, whether that experience changed their understanding of hypnosis or their approach to their patients.) In my own very small sample, both patients and doctors who work without relaxation maintain that the trance is the patient's own; that relaxation is not necessarily a part of it, and may in fact detract from it; but that until a state of close communication has been established, the patient will necessarily rely on a literal interpretation of the doctor's instructions.

It is understandable that the manipulative, practitioner-centered approach to hypnosis has prevailed in the practice of medicine in the United States: until recently, most of the doctors who used hypnosis had been taught it by stage hypnotists. The stage hypnotist could not discard the concept that he was indeed doing something "to" his subjects. In fact, the same authoritarianism extended to most aspects of the practitioner-patient relationship. Recently, however, the humanizing of the health professions in general has resulted in the widespread notion that the patient has both the right and the obligation to involve himself in his treatment - particularly when that treatment includes hypnosis. Too few clinical patients and too many experimental subjects have been involved in the study of relaxation. In the laboratory situation, in which the urgent motive of pain-control does not really obtain, experimenters may well view the hypnosis as a surrendering of self-control by the subject. Even in the clinic, some doctors rely on tests to determine whether a patient will be a good "subject"; if the patient "fails" the test, the doctor relieves himself of the responsibility for working with him and the patient accepts the judgement that he will fail at hypnosis. (The role of the healer is exchanged for the impersonal demands of the instructor, and the self-fulfilling prophecy is completed.)[3] Those patients who remain are taught to "relax", and in general they will do well; the rest are not counted, and the score for "relaxation" remains high. It is important to remember, also, that even when the doctor provides the patient with a legitimate opportunity to learn hypnosis, the patient may - for a variety of reasons which are not immediately apparent - either refuse to go into trance, or prove unwilling to use trance in working with his particular problem. Erickson, as far back as 1954, emphasized that the induction of trance is not the same as the utilization of trance.[4]

In my opinion, when the patient is learning to induce hypnosis, the doctor should explain to him that hypnosis is a normal, natural, human capacity, that learning it is a process that is curious and interesting, and can even be fun, so that while an individual is in trance he can do all the things he normally does, but that he <u>gains</u> certain controls over himself. The patient's active participation must be acknowledged, and he and the doctor must recognize that his conscious and his unconscious minds may have different expectations of appropriate procedures. The patient's physical appearance has little to do with the situation; he will achieve a trance profound enough to accomplish whatever it is that his unconscious recognizes as necessary whether or not he <u>looks</u> as though he is relaxed. He will certainly concentrate fixedly on the demanding task at hand and, as a result, will appear to ignore outside interference, but that does not mean he is relaxed. Indeed, it may mean just the opposite: he is relaxed only when he is <u>not</u> required to call upon <u>profound</u> trance, or to control his autonomic nervous system.

The advantages of eliminating relaxation as a precondition for trance include the elimination of the need to re-learn the non-relaxed state, the admission of more natural responses to the therapeutic situation, the recognition of spontaneous trance, and a freer communication between the doctor and patient which should result in a more comfortable use of hypnosis and its more widespread acceptance in medicine.

REFERENCES

1. Erickson, M. H., Ernest L. Rossi, Sheila I. Rossi (1976): Hypnotic Realities, New York, Irvington Publishers, Inc., pp. 266-67.

2. Gracely, R. H., Patricia McGrath and Ronald Dubner (1978): New Methods of Pain Measurement and Their Control, International Dental Journal, Vol. 28, pp. 52-65.

3. Rosenthal, Robert (1966): Experimenter Effects in Behavioral Research, New York, Appleton-Century-Crofts.

4. Erickson, M. H. (1954): Deep Hypnosis and Its Induction, in Experimental Hypnosis, Lecron, Leslie, Editor, New York, MacMillan Company, pp. 78, 83.

© 1979 Elsevier/North-Holland Biomedical Press
Hypnosis 1979
G.D. Burrows, D.R. Collison and L. Dennerstein

HOT AMETHYSTS, ELEVEN FINGERS, AND
THE ORIENT EXPRESS

FREDERICK J. EVANS

The Institute of Pennsylvania Hospital and University of Pennsylvania

111 North 49th Street, Philadelphia, Pa. 19139

While the mystery implied in the title may be more appropriate to an Agatha Christie novel, the mystery that we have been trying to solve is that of post-hypnotic amnesia. The dramatic ease with which some subjects become unable to recall any of their hypnotic experiences following a simple verbal suggestion of the hypnotist is a powerful demonstration of the dissociative effects of hypnosis, but has also provided grist for the mill of those who inherently reject verbal report as unreliable and subsume the phenomena of hypnosis under the cloak of compliance, role playing, and other motivational influences. Our on-going interest in posthypnotic amnesia has been partly based on our desire to understand the nature of dissociative processes occurring during hypnosis. In so doing we hope to shed light on similar functional amnesias and the psycho-pathology of temporary memory quirks and lapses of everyday life. Phenomeno-logically at least, posthypnotic amnesia provides an heuristic paradigm to in-vestigate a variety of phenomena including functional amnesias and fugues, as well as simple everyday problems such as misplacing the car keys, tip-of-the-tongue effects, or momentarily blocking an acquaintance's name at a cocktail party[1].

POSTHYPNOTIC SOURCE AMNESIA

Our search for clues about the nature of posthypnotic amnesia really began with an observation at the University of Sydney by Wendy Thorn[2] who first systematically described the phenomenon of *source amnesia*. Under hypnosis subjects are taught esoteric information not commonly known to college students such as: "An amethyst is a blue or purple gem stone: what color does it become when it is exposed to heat?" After satisfying the subject's curiosity by provid-ing him with the answer, the hypnosis session proceeds, and suggestions for amnesia for the total hypnotic session are given. After the termination of hypnosis, and after the deeply hypnotizable subject has asserted that he remem-bers none of the events under hypnosis, he is casually asked: "An amethyst is a purple gem stone: what color does it turn when it is heated?" Subjects with source amnesia spontaneously answer "Yellow": When asked how they know the answer, they appear to have no awareness that they learned this information a few minutes before during hypnosis. Instead, they may rationalize: ("I guess I learned it in a geology course;" "My girlfriend knows all about jewelry;" "I just saw a yellow flash of light.").

While source amnesia occurs in some deeply hypnotizable subjects, we have never observed this phenomenon in subjects who are simulating hypnosis[3] with a blind experimenter.[4, 5] Indeed, a moment's reflection suggests that acknowledging the correct answer would be a "dumb" response from a subject who is protesting complete amnesia. It is precisely the casual, paradoxical nature of the reaction of the hypnotizable subject in giving the correct answer, while maintaining that he knows nothing of what has happened to him, that perhaps provides compelling evidence that is most inconsistent with motivational compliance accounts of hypnotic amnesia.

In source amnesia there is an apparent dissociation between the recall of the content of hypnosis and the failure to be able to locate the context in which the information was acquired. Similarly, in cases of clinical amnesia and in fugue states, the patient typically does not know who he is, where he is, or what has happened over a period of time. Nevertheless, a wide range of other verbal, cognitive, motor, and sensory skills remains quite intact. Clinically, memories may remain functionally intact except for the context in which certain events occurred. Nonpathological examples have been cited in which a novelist has been inspired by a personal insight into the perfect plot, or a scientist has designed a brilliant experiment, only to discover later that, for example, the budding novel was recently on the bestseller list, or, even worse, that the potential Nobel Prize-winning experiment has already been carried out. Unconscious plagiarism seems to involve amnesia for the original context in which the insight occurred. Most of us probably do not remember the process of learning to walk or first writing our name, or even which shoe we first put on this morning. More commonly, we have all had the experience of meeting somebody whose name or face is hauntingly familiar, but we cannot remember where we have met this particular person before, sometimes with disastrous social consequences.

In the foregoing examples the skill or information has become dissociated from the context in which it occurred. The *content* is recalled, but the *context* is forgotten.

GENERIC, VAGUE RECALL

The apparent dissociation of the content from the contextual aspects of the memory process is quite typical during posthypnotic amnesia. Amnesic subjects often recall some material but have considerable difficulty in elaborating upon the details of what they did[6].

For example, a subject with some recall of the hypnosis events may seem confused about whether it was the right or left arm that became stiff and rigid, or whether that happened before or after he chased the buzzing mosquito--or was it a fly? The phenomenological vagueness of the accessible information and the ease with which the memories are described in precise detail when a cue to lift the amnesia is given places the phenomena of posthypnotic amnesia squarely within the province of recent cognitive studies of the selective processes and strategies involved in the process of recalling one-of-a-kind autobiographical events.

In an analysis of two samples totaling 725 subjects, generic recall was found to occur significantly more often in the memory reports of the high hypnotizable subjects than in those of the low hypnotizable subjects (23% vs. 6%, respectively). Within the group of hypnotizable subjects, generic recall was most often found in those who were most completely amnesic. Moreover, there was a marked shift from generic to particular (or detailed) recall following cancellation of the amnesia suggestion. The relative poverty of the memory reports of hypnotizable subjects, including their vague, fragmentary, and generic qualities, appears to mark the partial influence of suggestions for posthypnotic amnesia as the subject struggles to recall material that he cannot readily access in his efforts at remembering.

DISRUPTION OF RETRIEVAL PROCESSES DURING POSTHYPNOTIC AMNESIA

The observations summarized suggest that in most instances amnesic subjects are actively trying to recall, but are limited in their success because of some inefficiency, inaccessibility, or disruption of those mechanisms that would otherwise produce easy and efficient retrieval of target experiences.

Typically, if you are asked to remember what you have been doing today, you might start in the morning and trace your activities sequentially through the day; alternatively, you may focus upon some specifically salient event that was meaningful to you. Such organizational schema are necessary both to determine that which will be recalled and the ease with which it is recalled[7]. It is for such reasons that some events will be forgotten temporarily, only to be recalled later when more appropriate organizational cues are available, as any mnemonic system of memory will attest.

We have shown in several studies that it is precisely these kinds of retrieval mechanisms that seem to be temporarily unavailable to the subject who is experiencing posthypnotic amnesia. For example, Evans and Kihlstrom[8] have documented that even when hypnotizable subjects recall some of the events of hypnosis, they are unable to recall them in the same temporal order in which they were experienced. For each subject we calculated the rank order correlation between the order in which the subject recalled those hypnotic suggestions he could remember during posthypnotic amnesia, and the chronological order in which they were administered. Hypnotizable subjects recall in significantly more random sequence than unhypnotizable subjects who are not experiencing amnesia. This disrupted use of sequential organization occurs even when the subject is exhorted "Try hard to recall" and even if he is asked to try to recall in correct temporal sequence, but it does not occur posthypnotically if the amnesia suggestion is omitted from the hypnotic procedure. The original documentation of the reduced temporal sequencing in hypnotic amnesic subjects has been documented by several investigators, some of whom have used more traditional verbal memory paradigms[9]. This research is reviewed in more detail by Kihlstrom and Evans[1].

More recently, we have been able to demonstrate that other cognitive schemata often used to facilitate the recall of autobiographical material may also be disrupted during posthypnotic amnesia. For example, highly hypnotizable subjects who show reversible amnesia (thereby distinguishing the amnesia from normal forgetting) do not selectively favor either the successful or failed hypnotic suggestions in their recall of the amnesic period, even though non-hypnotizable subjects are much more inclined to recall successful rather than failed hypnotic experiences[10].

SIXES ON THE TIP-OF-THE-TONGUE

It appears that the experiences during hypnosis are not successfully integrated into the normal stream of consciousness in the manner in which we automatically process similar events in our waking experience. The intriguing implication that information may be processed differently in hypnosis is supported by such notions as Orne's concept of trance logic[3] and Sheehan's[11] work on the tolerance of ambiguity. This suggested that our understanding of memory processes during hypnosis might be facilitated by tracing the effects of a highly specific induced amnesia.

In work begun in Sydney, and continued since, we have been studying the effects of the suggestion "in a moment you are going to find that you are not going to be able to use the number 6 in your counting system; when you count, it will be 1, 2, 3, 4, 5, 7, 8, 9, 10, and that's just the way it's going to be for you." Not surprisingly, most of the hypnotic subjects easily avoid using the number 6 in simple counting tasks. Simulating subjects are also adept at this relatively easy task.

The task becomes more challenging if the subject is asked to count his fingers. A simulator will typically avoid the obvious problem and cleverly maintain the reality of 10 fingers by the time he is finished counting: he may count, "1, 2, 3, 4, 5, and 5 on this hand makes 10;" or "1, 2, 3, 4, mumble, mumble, 8, 9, 10." However the hypnotized subject studiously counts "1, 2, 3, 4, 5, 7, 8, 9, 10, --11?" perhaps grinning slightly, but hardly with the same affective involvement that you might have if you suddenly discovered that you had an extra digit.

We made the task progressively harder by asking the subject to complete simple problems of addition. On the first page it was impossible to obtain a 6 in any answer, or in a subtotal, barring any errors over which we had no control. However, the second page was loaded with 6s. To our surprise, neither hypnotized nor simulating subjects differed in the length of time taken to do these problems, nor the number of wrong answers obtained.

It was particularly instructive to examine the nature of the wrong answers that the subjects came up with. It was possible to divide most of the wrong answers into two types of solution strategies. In the strategy we called arbitrarily *logical* a 6 was systematically transformed into a 0 or a 7; or a variety of compromise solutions were used that appeared to make use of the next best mathematical operation in solving the problem. Thus, if a column summed to less than 10 if a 6 were omitted, the existence of the 6 was implicitly acknowledged by carrying the "1" into the tens column. The second strategy we labeled a *blocking* strategy in which the wrong answers implied the 6 was not seen or processed, or else was perceived as, for example, "a strange foreign symbol" that was not to be included in the mathematical operations used. The 6 was, simply, ignored, in much the same way that the hypnotized subject ignores the incongruity in the double hallucination trance logic described by Orne[3]. Briefly, hypnotizable subjects tended to use blocking strategies in solving problems while simulating subjects and other unhypnotizable subjects resorted to logical strategies in making erroneous answers. The hypnotized subjects simply did not process the 6 as a number. This was true in simple tasks like counting on fingers and in more complex mathematical tasks of the kind described, and also in maintaining randomness when asked to generate a series of 100 random numbers, using the digits 1 through 10 inclusive, at a rate of one a second. Whether this finding is best thought of as a trance logic phenomena, or as a return to a more primitive level of functioning, or as an example of the dissociation of a specific content from the normal context in which it is experienced, remains a mystery which I will leave you to ponder.

POSTHYPNOTIC AMNESIA AND NORMAL MEMORY

While the evidence seems compelling that posthypnotic amnesia involves a temporary disruption of normal cognitive strategies that aid efficient recall, an alternative hypothesis that good hypnotic subjects simply have poor and disorganized memories even in their normal wake state could also account for much of the data so far summarized. However, our trip on the Orient Express suggests that this is not so.

In a classroom lecture having nothing to do with hypnosis, a description of the infamous train itinerary was given to the students, associating each city visited with a specific event (for example, a trip to the Tower of London or to the diamond cutters of Amsterdam). At a later point the subjects were asked incidentally, to list the cities they visited on their imaginary train trip. Many of these subjects were subsequently assessed for hypnotic responsivity. No significant differences between high and low hypnotizable subjects in either number of events recalled nor the sequence of recall were found. If anything, hypnotizable subjects were able to remember many of the cities in slightly better temporal sequence than their insusceptible classmates. This, and other evidence[12], suggests that the memory disruption that occurs is not a function of typical memory styles, but is a product of hypnosis in which the content of the experience and the context in which the experience occurs becomes dissociated, or at best, only partially integrated.

SUMMARY

These studies seem to provide clues about the mechanisms used by amnesic subjects as they go about the task of trying to remember. Posthypnotic amnesia seems to involve a blurring of the context resulting in cognitions that are, for a time, only tenuously linked with waking experience and memory. Phenomenologically, the hypnotized subject knows, but does not know how, why, or even what he knows.

ACKNOWLEDGMENTS

These studies were supported in part by Grant #MH 19156-09 from The National Institute of Mental Health, United States Public Health Service, and in part from the Institute of Experimental Psychiatry. I wish to thank David F. Dinges, R. Lynn Horne, John F. Kihlstrom, Emily Carota Orne, Martin T. Orne, Helen M. Pettinati, Stuart K. Wilson, and William M. Waid for their valuable suggestions and comments during the preparation of this paper. Author's current address: Director, Research Division, Carrier Foundation, Belle Mead, N.J. 08502.

REFERENCES

1. Kihlstrom, J.F. and Evans, F.J. (1979) Functional Disorders of Memory, Lawrence Erlbaum Associates, Hillsdale, New Jersey, pp. 179-215.
2. Thorn, W.A. (1960) Unpublished Bachelors (Hons.) Thesis, University of Sydney, Australia.
3. Orne, M.T. (1959) J. abnorm. soc. Psychol., 58, 277-299.
4. Evans, F.J. and Thorn, W.A. (1966) Int. J. clin. exp. Hypnosis, 14, 162-179.
5. Evans, F.J. (1979) J. abnorm. Psychol., 88, in press.
6. Kihlstrom, J.F. and Evans, F.J. (1978) Bull. Psychonom. Soc., 12, 57-60.
7. Tulving, E. and Donaldson, W. (1972) Organization of Memory, Academic Press, New York.
8. Evans, F.J. and Kihlstrom, J.F. (1973) J. abnorm. Psychol., 82, 317-323.
9. Spanos, N.P. and Bodorik, H.L. (1977) J. abnorm. Psychol., 86, 295-305.
10. Pettinati, H.M. and Evans, F.J. (1978) Int. J. clin. exp. Hypnosis, 26, 317-329.
11. Sheehan, P.W. and Dolby, R.M. (1975) J. abnorm. Psychol., 84, 331-345.
12. Evans, F.J. (1979) In G.D. Burrows and L. Dennerstein, Handbook of Hypnosis and Psychosomatic Medicine, Elsevier Biomedical, Amsterdam, in press.

Hypnosis 1979
G.D. Burrows, D.R. Collison and L. Dennerstein

IMAGERY DIFFERENCES BETWEEN ANXIOUS AND DEPRESSED PATIENTS

DAVID J. DE L. HORNE AND JENNIFER BAILLIE

Department of Psychiatry, University of Melbourne, Parkville, Victoria,

3052, Australia

INTRODUCTION

Current literature reports very little experimental information on the
ability of both anxious and depressed people to image. There is also little
reliable information about the hypnotic susceptibility of depressed people.
In accordance with the relationship between hypnosis and imagery, and the
evidence of effects of expectations and motivations on hypnosis, hypnotic
susceptibility in depressives may be expected to be different from that of
other people.

Furthermore, recent clinical observation has suggested that depressed
people may not be able to image vividly and with emotional arousal. It could
be postulated that the depressed person's inertia, lethargy and loss of
interest, plus his negative outlook on life, make it difficult to voluntarily
image particular events. Alternatively, or additionally, the agitation and
impaired concentration often observed in depression may also affect the ability
to image.

It may be that for depressives, the use of imagery in therapy is too like
the "pull-yourself-together" doctrine, which would tie in with Barber et al's[1]
theory that negative expectations and low motivation reduce the effectiveness
of therapy. A further possible explanation is that both very low and very high
levels of arousal may lead to the poorest imagery[2].

The aim of the present experiment was to specifically test the difference
between anxious and depressed people, in imagery and hypnotic susceptibility,
using non-depressed, non-anxious subjects as a control group. The facets of
imagery investigated were vividness and quality. The former was measured by
Sheehan's shortened form of Bett's Questionnaire Upon Mental Imagery or the
Q.M.I.[3,4]. Quality of imagery, in a modified replication of the experiments
of Schwartz et al.[5,6], was measured by Electromyograph recordings from the
zygomatic muscle of the face, and Izard's Differential Emotion Scale (D.E.S.)[7].
These measures were taken while subjects were asked to "think" about a happy
scene, and to "feel or re-experience" the same happy scene. Hypnotic susceptibility was assessed by Wilson and Barber's Creative Imagination Scale or

W.B.Q.I.[8].

Hypotheses.

1. Depressed people would have less vivid imagery or, operationally
   defined, higher Q.M.I. scores than anxious or control subjects.
2. Depressed people would be less hypnotically susceptible, as shown
   by lower W.B.Q.I. scores than anxious or control subjects.
3. Depressed subjects would have less happy imagery than the anxious
   and control groups, as shown by lower E.M.G. recordings, and lower
   scores on the D.E.S. Enjoyment-Joy factor and higher scores on the
   D.E.S. Distress-Anguish factor when asked to "think" or "feel" a
   happy scene.

METHOD

Subjects. There were three groups of subjects:

Experimental 1 - Depressed Group. There were 10 subjects (five men and
five women), all of whom were receiving medication for primary depression.
None was having E.C.T. Mean age was 42.9 years (range 21 to 54).

Experimental 2 - Anxious Group. There were 11 subjects (six men and five
women), all of whom were diagnosed as suffering from anxiety neuroses, and
were receiving behaviour therapy treatment. In some cases adjuvant chemotherapy
was also being taken. Mean age was 31.7 years (range 19 to 46).

Control Group. There were 12 subjects (six men and six women), nine of whom
were university students. Mean age was 30.5 years (range 20 to 63).

Unfortunately, the classification of anxiety posed a problem, since the
control group were nearly as anxious as the anxious group. This was thought
to be because they were mostly students, who in Australia are known to come
from an anxious population. However, none of the control subjects was having
any form of treatment for psychological problems. The depressed group, in fact,
had the highest ratings on the anxiety scales, but this was in accordance with
the norms. Scores on the Carroll Rating Scale for depression (C.R.S.)[9] showed
the depressed group to be more depressed than the other two groups.

Procedure. All subjects were tested individually in a quiet room while
seated in a comfortable armchair. At the beginning of the testing session,
subjects were given the Spielberger[10] state-trait anxiety inventory, and the
C.R.S.[9], in alternating order within each group. Following this the three
other measures: the Q.M.I., the W.B.Q.I. and the E.M.G. combined with the
D.E.S. were given in a balanced order within each group. The instructions for
the W.B.Q.I. were read on to an audio tape by the experimenter. This tape was
then used for administering the scale.

For the E.M.G., a baseline was established after two minutes, during which subjects were required to relax as completely as possible. After this, the "think" and feel" instructions were presented by the experimenter in alternating orders between subjects, and the E.M.G. changes were recorded over three minutes. After each presentation subjects completed the D.E.S. questionnaire.

RESULTS

Hypothesis 1. Less vivid imagery in depressed patients.

The results for the three groups on the Q.M.T. are presented in Table 1. Inspection of the data suggests that far from having the least vivid imagery the depressed group showed the greatest vividness. However, a univariate analysis of variance (F = 0.957) and t-test results between all three groups, showed there were no statistically significant differences between the groups.

Hypothesis 2. Less hypnotic susceptibility in depressed patients.

The results for this, as measured by scores on the W.B.Q.I., are also displayed in Table 1. By inspection, it does appear that the depressed group were less hypnotically susceptible than either of the other two groups. A univariate analysis of variance (F = 0.456) failed to reveal any statistical significance in the results, as did t-test calculations between the individual groups.

TABLE 1

IMAGERY AND HYPNOTIZABILITY

Scores for the Questionnaire Upon Mental Imagery (Q.M.I.) and the Creative Imagination Scale (W.B.Q.I.)

Group		Q.M.I. Score[1]	W.B.Q.I. Score[2]
Depressed	$\bar{x}$	84.5	14.6
(n = 10)	S.D.	23.4	9.8
Anxious	$\bar{x}$	94.5	18.0
(n = 11)	S.D.	32.8	6.9
Control	$\bar{x}$	102.5	17.8
(n = 12)	S.D.	34.8	10.1

1. The lower the score, the greater the vividness of imagery

2. The higher the score, the greater the hypnotic susceptibility.

58

Hypothesis 3. Less happy imagery in depressed patients.

The results for the E.M.G. recordings, the D.E.S. Enjoyment-Joy factor, and the D.E.S. Distress-Anguish factor during the "think" and "feel" conditions are shown in Figures 1, 2 and 3 respectively.

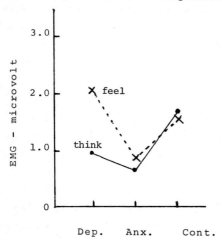

Fig. 1 Mean EMG Scores

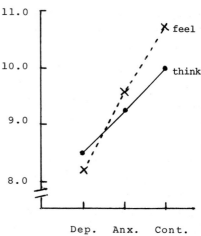

Fig. 2 Mean D.E.S. Enjoyment-Joy Scores

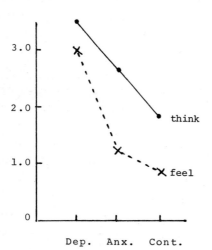

Fig. 3 Mean D.E.S. Distress-Anguish Scores

The trends in Figure 1 indicate that in the "think" condition the control group had the highest E.M.G. recordings, followed by the depressed group, with the anxious subjects having the lowest recordings. In the "feel" condition the depressed group had the highest recordings, while the anxious group again had the lowest recordings. Thus, the prediction that depressed people would have significantly lower E.M.G. recordings than anxious and control subjects in the "think" condition, was definitely not supported. The only result nearing statistical significance was the t-test for the "feel" condition (t = 1.94; $p < 0.067$), such that depressed people had higher E.M.G. recordings than anxious subjects. Again, this trend was in a direction opposite to that expected.

An examination of Figures 2 and 3 indicates that under both conditions the control subjects scored the most highly on the D.E.S. Enjoyment-Joy factor, while the depressed subjects had the lowest scores. In both conditions the depressed group scored most highly on the Distress-Anguish factor, with the control group having the lowest scores. It can be seen from the graphs that anxious subjects, on average, were scoring midway between the other two groups. These findings are in the predicted direction.

Although the overall between group comparisons for "think" and "feel" conditions on these two D.E.S. scales were not significant, the difference between the depressed and control subjects for the Distress-Anguish factor with the "feel" condition (Figure 3) approached significance (t = 1.78; $p < 0.09$).

DISCUSSION

Vividness of imagery. One major limitation of the present study was the small number of subjects, so that, the findings are probably best considered as preliminary data that could suggest areas of investigation worth further exploration.

The prediction that depressed people would not image as vividly as anxious and normals was not supported. In fact, there were non-statistically significant findings that the depressed group had the most vivid imagery, followed by the anxious group and then the normal controls.

Because it is known that even within primary, or endogenous depression, the symptomatology may vary, a further analysis was carried out within the ten depressed subjects to investigate the effects of psychomotor retardation and agitation on imagery vividness and hypnotic susceptibility. This was done by separately extracting the "retardation", "agitation" and "depression" factor scores from the C.R.S., and correlating them with scores on the Q.M.I. and

W.B.Q.I. The results are presented in Table 2, along with the Pearson Product
Moment correlations for the total score on the C.R.S.

TABLE 2

IMAGERY, HYPNOTIC SUSCEPTIBILITY AND DEPRESSION CORRELATES

Pearson Product Moment correlation coefficients between C.R.S. factors and
scores on the Q.M.I. and W.B.Q.I. for the 10 depressed subjects

	RETARDATION	AGITATION	DEPRESSION	TOTAL SCORE C.R.S.
Q.M.I.	r = 0.834	r = 0.685	r = 0.487	r = 0.720
	P = 0.003	P = 0.029	P = 0.153	P = 0.019
W.B.Q.I.	r = 0.175	r = 0.122	r = 0.471	r = .247
	P = 0.629	P = 0.736	P = 0.170	P = 0.492

It can be seen that the Q.M.I. correlated significantly with all but one of
the measures of depression. This showed vividness of imagery *decreased* with
increases in levels of retardation, agitation and total score on the C.R.S.
Although all the other correlation coefficients in the table were positive,
none of those for the W.B.Q.I. were significant, revealing no directly significant correlation between the different indices of depression on the C.R.S. and
hypnotizability.

Such findings could have important implications for behavioural and cognitive
therapies, aiming to treat depression with imagery techniques. There have been
studies requiring depressed people to imagine positively reinforcing, or
rationally acted situations[11,12,13,14]. But, if the depressed person is too
agitated, too retarded, or too severely depressed, his ability to do this may
well be impaired. Thus, it would seem that very low levels of arousal, inertia
and loss of interest, or too high levels of arousal, agitation, restlessness
and anxiety, may reduce the ability to vividly image particular events.

Hypnotizability. Since it was not found that depressed people had significantly poorer hypnotic responsiveness than other subjects, a possibility is
that hypnosis can be used with depressed subjects, before requiring them to
imagine positive events. Lazarus[14], in fact, did use hypnosis for some subjects in the method of time projection. Thus, the viability of this method is
not questioned by the findings of the present experiment.

<u>Quality of imagery</u>. The third hypothesis, that when asked to imagine a
scene which has made them very happy in the past, depressed people would have
significantly less happy imagery than anxious and non-depressed, non-anxious
people, was supported to some extent. While the E.M.G. recordings did not
indicate this (Figure 1), some factors of the D.E.S. did. Depressed subjects
did have more complicated self reports than either other group. The depressed
subjects scored lowest on the D.E.S. Enjoyment-Joy factor, and highest on the
Distress-Anguish factor (Figures 2 and 3).

Other factors on the D.E.S., about which no particular predictions had been
made, also discriminated between the groups. The depressed subjects scored
highly on the Anger-Disgust-Contempt, Guilt, and Anxiety-Fear factors; while
anxious subjects scored particularly highly on the Shyness factor. The anxious
subjects, on the whole, did not group closely with the control subjects, but
lay in between the other two groups on such variables as guilt, anger and
distress.

It would seem that asking a depressed person to imagine a past happy event
is not a clear cut procedure. Very generally, the results of this study indicated that depressed people are likely to experience a variety of emotions
connected with their depressed state, when imagining a supposedly happy scene.
It would also seem that behavioural and cognitive therapies which use positive
imagery as part of their treatment, may have to take such a possibility into
account.

In conclusion, the topic of this study is as yet a very new area of research.
No other studies were found which specifically tested the difference between
anxious and depressed people in imagery and hypnotic susceptibility. There were
a number of limitations to the present study, which further studies could avoid.
Larger samples could be used, and such variables as age, educational level and
anxiety should be more carefully controlled. The type of depression, whether
agitated or retarded, should be assessed, and level of arousal to the imagined
scene measured more accurately, with for example, other physiological measures
than the E.M.G. It would be preferable to test depressed people while they are
not on medication. Though the effects of antidepressant drugs on imagery were
not actually documented, it would seem very likely that significant effects
could exist on the ability to image; these obviously warrant investigation.

REFERENCES

1. Barber, T.H., Spanos, N.D. and Chaves, J.F. (1974) Hypnosis, Imagination and Human Potentialities. Pergamon Press Inc., New York.

2. Lang, P.J. (1977) Behav. Therapy, 8, 862-887.

3. Betts, G.H. (1909) The Distribution and Function of Mental Imagery. Teachers' College, Columbia University, New York.

4. Sheehan, P.W. (1967) J. Clin. Psychol., 23, 386-389.

5. Schwartz, G.E., et al. (1976a) Science, 192, 489-491.

6. Schwartz, G.E., et al. (1976b) Psychosom. Med., 38, 337-347.

7. Izard, C.E. (1972) Patterns of Emotions: A New Analysis of Anxiety and Depression. Academic Press, New York.

8. Wilson, G.C. and Barber, T.X. (1976) The Creative Imagination Scale: Applications to Clinical and Experimental Hypnosis. Medfield Foundation, Medfield, Massachussetts.

9. Carroll, B.J. and Shaw, J. (1978) Manual for the Carroll Rating Scale for Depression. Department of Psychiatry, University of Melbourne.

10. Spielberger, C.D., et al. (1970) STAI Manual for the State-Trait Anxiety Inventory. Consulting Psychologists Press Inc., California.

11. Shelton, J.L. and Ackerman, J.M. (1974) Homework in Counselling and Psycho-therapy. Charles C. Thomas, Illinois.

12. Beck, A.T. (1974) The Development of Depression: A Cognitive Model. In: Friedman, R.J. and Katz, M.M. (eds.) The Psychology of Depression: Contemporary Theory and Research. V.H. Winston, Washington D.C.

13. Ellis, A. and Harper, R.A. (1977) A New Guide to Rational Living. Wilshire Book Co., California.

14. Lazarus, A.A. (1968) Behav. Res. Therapy, 6, 83-89.

Hypnosis 1979
G.D. Burrows, D.R. Collison and L. Dennerstein   63

ADJUNCTIVE TRANCE AND FAMILY THERAPY FOR TERMINAL CANCER

G.A. PETTITT, MRCP DObst RCOG, General Practitioner, Motueka, N.Z.

INTRODUCTION

   Patients can spontaneously use trance when desperate; I have seen this in a
woman dying of breast cancer. Kubler-Ross[1] who did so much to make us aware
of the needs of the dying and their families, described the same phenomenon.
Family therapy first made advances in psychiatry, now also in rehabilitation.
Except for Horowitz[2] it has rarely been reported for terminal illness. Common
to both trance and family therapy is the growing awareness of the neuropsychology of the non-dominant hemisphere, and the communication of ideas by
symbols and indirect suggestion, that can evoke new use of past experiential
learnings to achieve therapeutic goals[3].

THE PATIENT'S HISTORY AND AIMS

   The family consisted of Joan, the patient, 53; her husband, Robert, an
insurance salesman, a little older; four children, Tom 22, an artist, Andrea
19, a student nurse, Harold 17, and Dick 14, both at school. In late 1976 Joan
found she had disseminated ovarian adenocarcinoma. Oophorectomy and radio-
therapy were followed by cytotoxic treatment. By Sept. 1977 her main symptoms
were vomiting, and intermittent fevers once or twice a week, during which her
body pains in back and abdomen became severe. As chemotherapy was not holding
her disease, it was stopped. She was using occasional methadone 5 mg or
Panadeine tablets. She asked for hypnotherapy and her family agreed to all
sessions being tape recorded.
   First visit (8.11.77.): she walked only with difficulty, had pain in her
back and abdomen, and breathlessness. Her aims were (1) to control pain and
fear. (2) To keep her mind clear and analgesics down. (3) To see her husband
in better health before she died. For 3 years he had suffered repeated hospi-
talisation for catatonic schizophrenia. (4) To feel secure about her family's
future. From 8.11.77. to 14.2.78. 15 visits were made to the house - 20 hours
in all. There were 3 conjoint family sessions before Joan died, and 1 after.
There were 11 hypnotherapy sessions with Joan, with peripheral involvement of
the family.

INITIAL LEARNING

The first 2 sessions Joan was introduced to trance by recall of an early learning process[4], learned relaxation, hallucination of a garden, and analgesia of her hand. Early on she was given ideas of: (1) Protection against negative attitudes in others. (2) Exploring past experiences to be used in new ways. (3) Improved appetite and sleep. (4) Learning to use her forgetting ability to diminish pain. She expressed anger and frustration at her emaciated condition, and anticipatory grief. She learned to let that ebb as trance occurred. She learned sensorimotor hypnoplasty[5] in which symbolic moulding of pottery was associated with progressive adaptations to her condition. She learned body analgesia by hallucinating herself in an icy lake, and was taught time dissociation and time distortion to shorten experience of unpleasant symptoms and restore healthy body sensations predating her illness[6]. She was taught to reinterpret pain as a heavy, weak sensation. She was offered the idea that present pain might be worsened by guilt feelings from the past, and it was suggested that she could now shed all such parts of it and that this could occur without it being shared with her conscious mind, or by myself. She learned to induce trance herself, and was offered, in an experimental way, the idea that unconscious processes might influence her central temperature control mechanism and diminish her fevers.

FIRST FAMILY SESSION

Members were encouraged to express needs honestly. Family strengths were emphasised. We explored: (1) The hurt each felt watching Joan die so slowly. (2) Feelings that they were a "family with cancer" and felt its brooding presence everywhere. (3) Joan's feeling that her cancer was punishment for not coping with her husband's psychosis. (4) That everyone's frayed nerves had found outlet in disputes over household duties. We discussed grief:- denial, isolation, anger, bargaining, depression, guilt, hope, acceptance. aimed to let each find their place in that sequence and at their own pace express resentments, and complete unfinished business, to prevent storing hurtful feelings. I asked them to teach me how improvements could be made in our handling of their situation. Once, the parents were retelling the development of the family and the atmosphere changed to laughter and hope, the family's movements recreating the ideomotor language of those memories. The younger generation was fascinated by their background, and realised how strengths that had seen them through previous hard times were still available to them. The myth was disposed of that Joan might pass her disease to her children. Next day, Joan said, they had begun to sleep and communicate better.

Joan emphasised how she had guessed her fatal prognosis from the non-verbal body language of the hospital staff. She described her mixed feelings for the oncologist, whom she felt had "brushed her off" when she asked if she would get well again - but she also admitted she had not been ready then for full state- ment of her prognosis. She had felt rejected and angry ("cut off", "dropped") when chemotherapy had ceased and she had lost contact with the cancer clinic.

FURTHER HYPNOTIC LEARNING

By 18.11.77. she was using trance on her own, and had changed the image of the icy lake to one of a cold local river she preferred. There had been no more fevers, and she was using only 2 Panadeine tablets a day. The flowers of her trance garden were all purple, the colour of melancholy. So she was induced to hallucinate the germination of seeds planted "at the time of the first family session", and she watched as nasturtiums, marigolds, lillies and daffodils developed in her garden. Interspersed was the idea that symbolised progress her family was starting to make and intermingling with depression of something new, fresh, fragrant, calm and peaceful.[7] She learned body dissociation, and reported delightedly that she had spontaneously experienced something similar 3 weeks before. This emphasises that this is an inate capacity not alien to ordinary life. She said: "We must learn to trust our bodies. We don't use our intuition, which comes naturally if we let it."

By 25.11.77. Joan was much stronger and had made 3 trips away from home. Her trance garden was full of colours. She looked less ill and was using only occasional Panadeine tablets for pain. She was offered the idea that certain gestures by family members could act as cues to deepen her trance. We all know how soothing gestures from nurses or relatives (holding the hand, stroking the forehead) can be. When these cues were linked to her trance capability, they acquired added significance and enabled the family to feel they were contributing even more to her comfort. Over the next few days, her diary records, she could use trance to alleviate dyspnoeic attacks, and the cues from her husband and daughter enabled her to control pain adequately. As things were going well, it was agreed that Andrea take a much needed holiday, and I should call less frequently. Sadly, two parts of her support system gone at the same time, she deteriorated. There was a period of fever and pain, though less long than previous ones. She began using a morphine (10 mg) cocaine (10 mg) mixture for her dyspnoeic attacks, lost her appetite, and her

ability to maintain trance on her own adequately.   The visit on 9.12.77. was
therefore devoted to rebuilding her confidence.

2ND FAMILY SESSION, HUSBAND'S ILLNESS & IMPROVED FAMILY FUNCTION.

   On 13.12.77. Joan commented on improved family rapport, but Robert was
showing signs of withdrawal.   Their anger of grief was still expressed in
feuds over domestic chores, despite home help and district nursing service.
Two structural interventions were made.   (1) To notice Dick's clarity on the
domestic issue, because he was not directly involved in the power struggle
among the elder sibs.   Gradually they moved towards his solution and let him
work out a duty roster.   This was a lengthy task for they had to do it without
mother, as if she was already dead.   (2) To ask Andrea to allow Tom to move
physically into her place next to mother.   In a thoughtful silence, the family
experienced that changed responses were possible.   Tom's current identity
crisis was touched on, but inadequately.   First he became more helpful, but
withdrew a little from the family later.

   By 16.12.77. Robert had been rehospitalised for catatonia, on the
anniversary of Joan's laparotomy that discovered her cancer.   He stated: "I
want to suffer too, because you (Joan) are suffering".   This affected Joan,
who more tired and unhappy, began using 2 doses of morphine (10 mg) and
cocaine (10 mg) mixture, 2 Panadeine, and Amytal (200 mg) per day.   She was not
suffering much physical pain, she said, mostly the pain of missing her husband.
On 20.12.77. she and Andrea were to express their resentful sadness over
Robert's illness, with its serious emotional and financial impact.   Joan
described how her trance garden had become a pleasing formal Elizabethan garden,
full of colourful flowers.   She was able to use the affective imagery it provided to realise how she had been working to achieve a firm structure for her
departure.   She was guided to planting a tree in her garden, and to being aware
that, because of her careful preparation, this tree would grow strongly, and
beautify her garden.   It would represent the next generation of her family,
helped by her contributions made in her lifetime, especially the last weeks.

   Then, for Christmas, for a woman who couldn't tolerate actual food in any
quantity, she was able to enjoy a hallucinatory picnic in her garden, of her
favourite dishes - crayfish salad, tomatoes, fresh and fragrant from the plant,
crisp crunchy lettuce, cool cucumbers, small tender radishes, brown bread and
butter, and a sprinkling of chives.   Her pleasure at this was a joy to behold.

   By 27.12.77. Robert now improved by ECT had returned home, and they had
enjoyed Christmas together.   Joan was now so weak she couldn't turn in bed

without help, but despite her emaciation, she looked radiant on the feast of
family co-operation current at this time. She reviewed previous trance learning, was asked to discover other areas she wished to work in, and given a
series of multiple level permissive communications to continue inner growth
processes, within the protection of the trance state. By 6.1.78. Robert had
begun work again, the 2 youngest sons had holiday jobs, the 2 oldest sibs were
evolving realistic plans for after Joan's death, and she approved. Father was
less withdrawn, even to the point of making arrangements with the undertakers.

THE POWER OF NEGATIVE EXPECTATION, DOCTOR'S OWN ANTICIPATORY GRIEF REACTION,
& JOAN'S DEATH.

Joan began attacks of nocturnal dyspnoea and panic, fearing how she would
die. She said she was "surprised at the lack of pain", and that it had been
worth "holding on" to see what she and her family had achieved in the last
months. Her mind was lucid and she listened to concerts. Despite her lack of
pain she had been using her morphine (15 mg) and cocaine (10 mg) mixture 4
times daily, on the advice of the visiting nurse, as a calming influence.
There had been no fevers but she was intensely weak. She was trained therefore to trigger a relaxation response and trance, not only by methods she had
learned, but also conditioned to the onset of breathlessness and panic.

One most important task with this family was countering the great weight of
negative expectations for themselves, that they had from their history, and
from the verbal and non-verbal actions of key figures around them. The
subtelties of non-verbal and extra-verbal communications are influences that
have to be "controlled out" of drug trials because they are enough to distort
the results - for good as well as bad. They can be strong enough to adversely
affect our patients if we dislike them, or have poor expectations, and there
is no tonic more effective than the indirectly implied expectation that our
patients will fulfil their potential.

Joan was coping now, and we made no further appointments for me to call.
She lived, after all, 32 miles away. I was unprepared for my own depression
that came a few days later. Even though I had tried to build Joan's confidence,
I had not prepared myself for her gracious statement of her independence,
which I had felt as a "dismissal". I contacted the family again. I
discovered that Joan had immediately felt from non-verbal cues that her dismissal of me had been taken badly by me (before I knew myself in fact). She
said: "you must have felt as I did when the doctor gave me the brush off from
the cancer clinic. But I hadn't meant it like that, to be honest its for

financial reasons – our outgoings exceed our incomings. I felt it would be easier if the suggestion to disengage came from me." This cleared the air. We discussed the doctor's own needs in terminal caring and our unpreparedness. I thanked her for her lesson. She then described successful use of trance to ease, shorten, and terminate dyspnoeic attacks.

The last occasion I guided her, 13.1.78. was profoundly meaningful for both of us. As I re-read the transcript I saw how much I was in debt to Dr Erickson for the style of indirect communication that had been so effective for Joan. She was very weak and her speech very soft. She was using only 1 dose of morphine (15 mg) and cocaine (10 mg) mixture and 1 Nitrazepam tablet per 24 hours. She expressed with modest realism, her awareness of her achievements. She had freed herself from unnecessary past, present, and future parts of the pain and dyspnoea experience. She was helping her family through this tragic time and beyond. We said our goodbyes without knowing if it would be for the last time. I wonder how often other doctors have been able to say "goodbye" to a dying patient? I think this was the first time for me. I thanked her for what she had taught me and I hope through this she will teach others.

At the 3rd family session on 17.1.78. Joan chose to be absent, so it would be as after her death. They were first reminded of their achievement, Joan's continued dignity at home. Then – the remaining difficulties in accepting Joan's imminent death, their own needs, and the restructuring they would do afterwards. There were practical difficulties: Andrea needed to feel free to leave home to continue her interrupted education. Tom too would need to leave home to find work. This meant that the 2 youngest sons and father would be left to run the home. How could school age boys be left with the responsibility of hospitalising their father if his mental state deteriorated? He was usually unaware of his need for treatment when it did so. Negative expectations for father's mental health dominated the issue of family leadership, but Harold was able to confront father with his need to be included in family and financial decisions. They made plans for extending hobbies when released from present chores, rehearsing constructively for the future. They accepted the idea of staying with Joan's body when she died, to complete inner unfinished business, and avoid haste in calling the undertaker. Afterwards Joan could be reassured that her family was working constructively together. On 21.1.78. Joan had a haematemesis, was visited by her priest, and the weekend doctor gave her an injection, and then died peacefully. The family spent time with her in various ways until next day.

THE AFTERMATH

The 4th family session was on 14.2.78. Asked to teach what they felt doctors should know to help care of similar families, they said trance therapy had helped Joan to cope with her pain and breathlessness, to come to terms with her illness, and had helped her to "hold on" until she recognised her family would continue to cope. By having something she could do for herself, she had felt less passive and helpless. Conjoint family sessions had improved communication, the younger ones appreciating not being excluded. All re-expressed feelings of rejection at the time when "active" treatment shifted to "terminal" care, and contact from the cancer clinic was lost.

One lesson stood out clearly:- for hospital base specialists and family doctors, we need to study more carefully non-verbal body language, extra-verbal intonation and timing, as well as our verbal communications. Some cause tranquility, even euphoria, others are as unpleasant in pharmacology as bad drugs. The foundations of terminal care are laid early in the illness, and Sacerdote[5] has written of the value of the adjunctive therapist working early with the usual medical attendants. Emotional involvement is considerable, but worthwhile, as shown by Andrea's own words: "I thought she had a really lovely death. It was just something she really deserved."

Nothing I say here should be taken to imply I think all terminal care is inadequate. There are many families who have good deaths, cared for at home by dedicated family doctors. Not all deaths in hospitals are dehumanised by technology. Adding Trance and Family Therapy approaches can help, and seem worth exploring further.

ACKNOWLEDGEMENTS.

To this family for permission to publish their story, and Dr Milton Erickson for his teaching. Recording and secretarial work has been supported by the Medical Research Council of New Zealand.

REFERENCES

1. Kubler-Ross E. (1969). On Death and Dying. New York, Macmillan.

2. Horowitz L. (1975). Treatment of the Family with a Dying Member. Family Process. 14:95

3. Rossi E. (1977). The Cerebral Hemisphere in Analytical Psychology. J.Anal. Psychol. 22: 32-51.

4. Erickson M.H., Rossi E.S. (1976). Hypnotic Realities. New York, Irvington.

5. Sacerdote P. (1970). Theory & Practice of Pain control in Malignancy and other protracted or recurring painful illnesses. Int. J. Clin. Hyp. 18: 160-180.

6. Erickson M.H. (1968). Further Consideration of Time Distortion: Subjective time condensation as distinct from time expansion. Am. J. Clin. Hyp. 1: 2: 83-88

7. Erickson M.H. (1966). The Interspersal Hypnotic Technique for Symptom Correction and Pain Control. Am. J. Clin. Hyp. 8: 198-209.

© 1979 Elsevier/North-Holland Biomedical Press
Hypnosis 1979
G.D. Burrows, D.R. Collison and L. Dennerstein

GUIDED SELF-HYPNOSIS

HERBERTS K. GOBA
Calgary, Alberta, Canada

The term guided self-hypnosis is not new. John C. Ruch[1] in his attempt to
establish the relationship between self-hypnosis and hetero-hypnosis and the primary or secondary role of each, suggests that all hetero-hypnosis is in effect,
guided self-hypnosis. In my technique of guided self-hypnosis, the emphasis is
placed on teaching the patient a specific way of thinking--the *how to think*--to
elicit the patient's voluntary, conscious cooperation while in hypnosis. Ruch
observes that the hypnotist is as capable of being inhibitory as helpful. In my
technique, the possibility of the hypnotist as an inhibitor is eliminated. The
patient may revise any suggestions that are unacceptable in the form given, and
is further encouraged to express objections to either the form or content.

R.E. Shor's[2] criterion for self-hypnosis is the total lack of interference by
the hypnotist throughout the hypnotic behaviour of the subject. He accepts that
guidance for the hypnotic behaviour is given prior to self-induction. In my
technique of guided self-hypnosis there is continuous input by the therapist.
At the same time, the active participation of the patient is expected to the
same degree that would be necessary in self-hypnosis.

Research into self-hypnosis has been largely directed towards establishing
the difference between self- and hetero-hypnosis, and comparing their relative
effectiveness. L.S. Johnson and D.C. Weight[3] concluded that procedures labelled
self-hypnosis and hetero-hypnosis are similar in most phenomenological and behavioural effects. They noted one specific difference, that there was more awareness, activity and control by the subject in self-hypnosis than in hetero-hypnosis. In my observations, the control and activity exercised by the subject in
self-hypnosis is possible only when there is a minimum conscious effort applied.

Induction techniques for self-hypnosis vary from the subject's response to a
cue learned in hetero-hypnosis, to response to specific instructions received in
the waking state which the subject is then expected to follow without further
guidance. In all induction techniques, the subject is instructed what to do and
what to think, but nowhere is it reported that the subject is instructed *how to
think*. The suggestions given following induction--usually in the form of "you
are, you will, you can, you may"--are prefacing instructions what to do and what

to think, but again not *how to think*. My observation that there is a specific way of thinking that is typical for hypnosis is supported by some of Erica Fromm's[4] observations in her research into self-hypnosis. In the same publication, some of Fromm's subjects reported that they felt their passivity increased the depth of trance and the slightest effort lightened it. In my opinion these subjective observations are significant and are similar to the subjective experiences of most of my patients. Increased passivity is synonomous with decreased consciously applied effort. If this is accepted as a principle it would explain another experience shared by many of Fromm's subjects, who reported that as time went on they found it progressively easier to concentrate. My interpretation is that the deepening of trance automatically reduces the effort needed to concentrate. An apparent contradiction of this principle is Fromm's conclusion that intense concentration is not incompatible with receptive spontaneity in self-hypnosis. This is based on reports from some of her subjects who concentrated on their imagery with no apparent effect on their hypnotic behaviour. Fromm states that this intense concentration is different than the active effortful kind of attention which is employed in the waking state. In my opinion the total involvement in their imagination and the intensity of the experience, may have been expressed by the subjects in terms of intensity of concentration. A spontaneous thought, memory or image can appear in the awareness with varying degrees of intensity, but this intensity is vastly different than the intensity which results from conscious effort. The intensity of a spontaneous image or thought or memory, does not interfere with the depth of hypnosis, whereas a consciously applied effort does interfere. A voluntary and consciously employed effortless way of thinking is the basis of my technique in guided self-hypnosis. This almost effortless way of thinking is used to induce hypnosis, to deepen trance, and to make self-suggestions more efficient.

There are few reports on the use of self-hypnosis in a clinical setting. Milton H. Erickson[5] in discussing his personal experiences with E.L. Rossi in the use of self-hypnosis to control pain, states that while inducing self-hypnosis he focuses on a thought that subsequently acts as a self-suggestion. Erickson also focuses on a thought or memory during hypnosis. It is not mentioned if this focussing involved any effort. J. Scagnelli[6] advised one of her patients to use self-hypnosis to change disturbing dreams and images. Again the suggestions are what to do but not *how to do*.

T.S. Barber[7] used "Think-With Instructions" for subjects who were not formally induced in hypnosis and proved that this group scored higher on a creative imagination test than either the group in a formal hypnosis or the control group.

Barber did not use his "Think-With Instructions" for the group in hypnosis, nor is it reported that instructions were given how to "Think-With."

The acceptance of two basic principles about thinking can explain different hypnotic phenomena. The less conscious effort that is applied to one's thinking or attention, the deeper the hypnotic trance, is the first principle. Second is that an effortless, or almost effortless thought has the potential to become an accepted suggestion in hypnosis. All induction methods are designed to suddenly, or gradually, reduce this conscious effort. A complete involvement in a perception, or one's own imagination, thought or physical activity automatically induces hypnosis. Initial involvement requires a certain effort to concentrate, to focus, to narrow one's attention. During the course of the involvement all responses become increasingly effortless, thereby inducing hypnosis. The involvement, and the fatigue of forceful concentration are the components of most induction techniques. The induction method of advising the subject to apply an extreme concentration is successful because resulting fatigue leads to a reduction of the effort or to giving it up entirely. Only then is the subject able to achieve the state of hypnosis. As long as the subject is able to maintain the effort to concentrate, hypnosis is impossible.

Another component of induction techniques is to gain the subject's acceptance that body responses are elicited by the suggestions given, and any effort by the subject to control these responses will be useless. With acceptance of these suggestions, the individual's effort to control is abandoned. The induction method of eye fixation requires an initial extreme effort by the subject-- resulting in fatigue, with a consequent sudden, or gradual release of the effort involved in keeping the eyes open and focused.

Any induction method utilizing visual imagery automatically leads to giving up of all conscious effort. While there is an initial, minimal effort necessary to stimulate the imagination and to manipulate the images, any forceful effort used in this direction will terminate the imagery. In confusion techniques the confused mind of the subject uses effort in attempting to achieve clarity. When this effort becomes tiresome or impossible, the effort to think is given up and hypnosis is induced.

Hand levitation is a deepening technique rather than an induction method. By narrowing the subject's field of attention to the arm and hand, a light hypnosis is induced. It is then that a thought, or image, of the arm lifting becomes an accepted hypnotic suggestion. Lack of voluntary effort used in raising the arm enhances the subject's belief in the power of the hypnotist. The subject then assumes the role of observer and withdraws all efforts to participate.

If the subject accepts the hypnotist's challenge to counteract levitation of the limb by a voluntary, forceful effort, and this is unsuccessful, the belief in the power of the hypnotist is reinforced. The inability of the subject to control the skeletal muscles is real, even though an honest attempt has been made to apply every possible voluntary effort. In reality, the arm remains under the subject's voluntary control but access to that control has not been employed. If conscious effort to regain control is replaced with a soft and gentle whispering way of thinking that the arm will go down, this thought becomes a self-suggestion in hypnosis which counteracts suggestions given by the hypnotist. This does not necessarily mean that the subject has terminated hypnosis but has simply terminated the control of the hypnotist in a specific area.

An analysis of the hand levitation technique can clarify certain aspects of response to post-hypnotic suggestions. This analysis demonstrates that skeletal muscle movement can be initiated and continued by two independent means of achieving the same control. One is the voluntary effort applied,and the other is the automatic response to accepted hetero- or self-suggestions in hypnosis. In hypnosis, the conscious and voluntarily applied effort has no control over automatic responses. In the waking state, a response may be automatic or it may be controlled by a conscious, voluntary effort. If a post-hypnotic suggestion is accepted that an arm will assume a particular position after the hypnosis is terminated, then the arm will automatically assume that position. A voluntary effort to change the position may be successful, but as soon as the voluntary effort is discontinued, the automatic control takes over and the arm returns to the specified position.

A post-hypnotic response to a suggestion can be explained as a computerized, set way of behaviour that is activated by a cue: a word, phrase, signal, set time, place or situation. If, at the beginning or during the response to the post-hypnotic suggestion, the subject experiences a spontaneous thought that is counter to the suggestion, the post-hypnotic suggestion is cancelled, and the response to it is halted. If initially, or during the response to this post-hypnotic suggestion, the subject tries to use force or effort to counteract the automatically set response, this effort will not be successful. If instead of using force, a positive self-suggestion is repeated in an almost effortless way, the subject will regain control.

Some post-hypnotic suggestions are constructed to produce a response so sudden as to exclude the fractional amount of time required for even a spontaneous thought to cancel the suggestion. However, if after the initial response to the suggestion, a spontaneous thought occurs which is contrary to the suggestion, this thought will be sufficient to cancel future responses to the previously accepted suggestion. The lack of any consciously applied effort to these spontaneous thoughts invests them with the potential power to affect the acceptance or rejection of suggestions. Hope, expectation and belief are established ways of thinking and feeling which cannot be forced. They are present without effort, although we may mistakenly use effort in attempting to achieve them. One simply does, or does not, believe, hope or expect. This effortlessness gives them the power to facilitate or inhibit the suggestions given in hypnosis. The art of effective treatment in hypnosis is to create in the mind of the patient, a positive expectation, hope and/or belief.

The technique of guided self-hypnosis was initiated by the author's personal experiences in self-hypnosis. It was further developed during sixteen years of the clinical application of it. The author's first description of this technique was contained in a printed booklet[8] available to participants of the ASCH Annual Scientific Meeting in Toronto in 1973. The author had utilized self-hypnosis for goal-directed, post-hypnotic suggestions. As an efficient technique was developed it was incorporated in the treatment of patients. The ensuing successful results validated the technique. It became apparent that if a goal-directed decision was made prior to self-induction, the goal was frequently achieved. Refinements of the methods of giving self suggestions led to condensing the pre-induction suggestions into a cue word or phrase which was then repeated during self-hypnosis. The author found that any force or effort applied to concentration on the cue had the effect of lessening the depth of hypnosis. More significantly, when the effort to concentrate was reduced, the depth of hypnosis was increased. The logical conclusion was to avoid any intensity in concentration or attention, and to adopt the almost effortless, soft, whispering way of thinking while in hypnosis. The author reasoned that if a patient's own thoughts while in hypnosis act as post-hypnotic suggestions, the effect of the patient's own thinking while in hetero-hypnosis is equally valid. Therefore the cooperation of the patient was sought by introducing guided self-hypnosis as a routine technique. Initially the technique was used with various traditional methods of induction, but subsequently it became the author's preferred method of both induction and deepening technique.

In the clinical application of guided self-hypnosis, the patient is first given an explanation of what hypnosis is, how it can be used, and how the patient's own thoughts can affect both induction and continuation of the hypnotic trance. The patient is assured that the first experience in hetero-hypnosis will be used only for induction and not for therapeutic suggestions. This approach takes into account the possibility of unexpressed misconceptions, reservations or concerns the patient may have about hypnosis. It also minimizes the patient's need to be "on guard" and reduces the attendant effort to maintain this defence. By reducing or eliminating this effort by the patient, the induction of hypnosis is facilitated. The initial hypnosis experience is terminated in about ten minutes, and the patient's subjective experience is discussed. Further explanations are given if necessary. The direction of the treatment is always discussed before induction to establish the patient's conscious acceptance of it. For all inductions, excepting the first, suggestions are given to "Close your eyes, relax, start following my voice, repeating in your own mind, word by word, what I say...thinking in the softest, gentlest way possible, with the least effort... as though you are softly, gently, whispering to yourself in your mind. You may revise my suggestions if you so desire, but try to maintain a positive attitude towards the given suggestions. If a sound--or a thought of your own--disturbs you, dismiss it as something that is not important for you at this moment. If you have any objections to something that I say, I would like to know it immediately." The patient's repetition of the given suggestions while in hypnosis and the voluntary reduction of any effort applied to thinking, automatically deepens the trance. In the author's experience, whatever depth of trance is reached by the patient is sufficient for the effectiveness of the treatment.

The highly significant role of the patient's negative thoughts and their consequent effect on the outcome of the treatment is stressed. The patient's own ability to enhance treatment by a positive way of thinking, logically leads to the acceptance that negative thoughts can adversely affect treatment by counteracting or negating the given suggestions. Some resistance to treatment can be the result of the patient's spontaneous, negative thoughts while in hypnosis. The author recognized that a patient may at any time be in a spontaneous, not recognized self-hypnosis.[9] Any negative thought occurring during that time acts as a self-suggestion, with the power to counteract any previously accepted suggestions in hypnosis. The accidental discovery that an hour of treatment in hypnosis had been cancelled by the patient's spontaneous thought, expressed as "Now I am going home and I will be sick, or depressed, again," made it abundantly clear that these spontaneous thoughts have a potential power at any time. All patients are consistently advised to become aware of negative thoughts at all times, and to immediately replace them with positive thoughts. To achieve this awareness without becoming compulsively absorbed in one's own thought processes, the suggestion is given in hetero-hypnosis that "You will become immediately aware of any negative thought and correct it by replacement with a positive one, without consciously paying attention to what you think." Patients are routinely taught self-hypnosis on their third or fourth visit. Ruch's[1] observation that hetero-hypnosis prior to self-induction interferes in learning self-hypnosis does not apply to my technique. Most patients learn in one session, not only self-induction, but how to use self-hypnosis for giving self-suggestions to enhance treatment and how to utilize it in other areas for personal benefit.

Patients are advised to give positive self-suggestions in any emergency. Many have learned to prevent the formation of blisters that normally result from minor burns and to inhibit subcutaneous haemorrhage in moderate bruising simply by having a positive thought at the critical moment. These self-suggestions have the same powerful effect as suggestions given in a formal self-hypnosis.

The fact that one's thoughts have this potentially powerful effect supports Barber's Cognitive-BehavioralTheory[7], in which he postulates that to have a positive response to suggestions, a formal hypnosis is unnecessary. This is partially correct. The positive response to suggestions in the waking state depends on the almost effortless way of thinking about the given suggestions-- a quality that is typical of hypnotic thinking.

Just as the decrease in any conscious effort will deepen the hypnotic trance, the less effort applied to a thought the more powerful it will become as a post-hypnotic suggestion. If two conflicting thoughts are concurrent or alternating, that one which involves the least effort will act as the more powerful post-hypnotic suggestion. Therefore any spontaneous, negative thought is more potent than a consciously chosen thought to counteract it. The correction technique in this instance, is the repetition of the positive thought until it becomes automatic, therefore effortless and extremely effective. The intensity of a negative thought is not decreased by a consciously applied effort of equal intensity. In the waking state, any attempt to force an unpleasant or disturbing thought from one's awareness gives this thought the tendency to spontaneously reappear[10]. The return of this thought will continue as long as force is used to exclude it. The effective counteraction is to use the almost effortless way of thinking about the replacement positive thought or attitude, and to continue with this until the negative thought disappears from awareness. It seems that when a balance of power is achieved between a positive and a negative thought, it is the final thought which effectively tips the balance. To decrease the intensity of any extremely forceful, spontaneous negative thoughts which may appear, this suggestion is given in hypnosis: "Any thought, any negative feeling, any desire when it comes to your awareness, will be tuned so low that you will be able to ignore it without any effort. Your common sense will tell you how to react."

Suggestions for controlling the intensity of thoughts are given to all patients.

To change behaviour patterns using the guided self-hypnosis technique, is similar to erasing old material on a tape by recording new material over it. The suggestions are repeated in the patient's mind, using the specific way of almost effortless thinking. Strongly established patterns of behaviour or feelings however, are resistant to change and will seldom respond to a single attempt to record the new material over the old. Continuous re-recording or repetition may be required to effectively erase the old patterns.

The limits of this paper do not permit the inclusion of case reports detailing specific applications of the technique of guided self-hypnosis. The basic principles have been explained in detail and an attempt has been made to integrate guided self-hypnosis with other techniques traditionally used by clinicians. The writer believes that an understanding of these basic principles will increase the efficiency of any other technique used. The author hopes that the almost effortless way of thinking described that is the key to this technique, can--and will--be included as another variable in hypnosis research.

REFERENCES

1. RUCH, J.C. (1975) Self-Hypnosis: The Result of Heterohypnosis or Vice Versa? International J. of Clin. and Exp. Hypnosis, 4,282-304.

2. SHOR, R.E. & EASTON, R.D. (1973) Preliminary Report on Research Comparing Self- and Hetero-Hypnosis, American J. of Clin. Hypnosis, 1, 37-44.

3. JOHNSON, L.S. & WEIGHT, D.G. (1976) Self-Hypnosis Versus Heterohypnosis: Experiential and Behavioral Comparisons, J.of Abn. Psychology, 5, 523-526.

4. FROMM, E. (1975) Selfhypnosis: A New Area of Research, Psychotherapy: Theory Research and Practice, 3, 295-300.

5. ERICKSON, M.H. & ROSSI, E.L. (1977) Auto Hypnotic Experiences of Milton H. Erickson, American J. of Clin. Hypnosis, 1, 37-44.

6. SCAGNELLI, J. (1977) Hypnotic Dream Therapy With a Borderline Schizophrenic, A Case Study, American J. of Clin. Hypnosis, 2, 136-145.

7. BARBER, T.X. & WILSON, S.C. (1977) Hypnosis, Suggestions, and Altered States of Consciousness: Experimental Evaluation of the New Cognitive-Behavioral Theory and the Traditional Trance State Theory of "Hypnosis", Ann. of the New York Academy of Sciences, 296, 34-44.

8. GOBA, H.K. (1973) Significance of Recently Repressed Thoughts, Unpublished Manuscript, ASCH Ann. Scientific Meeting, Toronto, Ont.

9. GOBA, H.K. (1974) Effects of Spontaneous and Not Recognized Hypnosis, Unpublished Manuscript, ASCH Ann. Scientific Meeting, New Orleans, La.

10.GOBA, H.K. (1977) Hypnotherapy for a Schizoid Personality, Unpublished Manuscript, ASCH Ann. Scientific Meeting, Atlanta, Ga.

© 1979 Elsevier/North-Holland Biomedical Press
Hypnosis 1979
G.D. Burrows, D.R. Collison and L. Dennerstein

AN APPROACH TO HYPNOTHERAPY : MY METHOD

DAVID R. COLLISON MB.BS.,FRACP.
Consultant Physician-Psychiatrist, P.O. Box 586, Chatswood, N.S.W., 2067,
(Australia).

INTRODUCTION

Since the time of Mesmer, hypnosis has had a colourful history.. There
have been many attempts to define hypnosis and in such defining to
characterise the essential components and characteristics of this state.
Three of these concepts will be briefly mentioned.

The first is the definition arrived at by the sub-committee of the
British Medical Association which was set up specifically to look at
hypnosis and hypnotism. This sub-committee[1] defined hypnosis as:

> "A temporary condition of altered attention in the subject
> which may be induced by another person and in which a variety of
> phenomena may appear spontaneously or in response to verbal or other
> stimuli. These phenomena include alterations in consciousness and
> memory, increased susceptibility to suggestions, and the production
> in the subject of responses and ideas unfamiliar to him in his usual
> state of mind. Further phenomena such as anaesthesia, paralysis and
> rigidity of muscles, and vaso-motor changes can be produced and removed
> in the hypnotic state."

From a practical point of view, hypnosis may be defined, secondly, as an
increased susceptibility to suggestion, as a result of which sensory and
motor capacities are altered in order to initiate appropriate behaviour. A
suggestion, for these purposes, is an idea that one accepts uncritically and
favourably, resulting in the initiation of appropriate behaviour. Thus,
a suggestion is a special kind of stimulus leading to simple or elaborate
responses.

Spiegel, H. and Spiegel, D[2] offer another conceptualization of
hypnosis, and they describe it as an experience which is characterised by
an ability to sustain in response to a signal a state of attentive, receptive,
intense focal concentration with diminished peripheral awareness. It is a
function of the alert individual who utilises his capacity for maximal
involvement with one point in space and time and thereby minimises his

involvement with other points in space and time. The hypnotised person is
not asleep, but awake and alert. The crux of the trance state is the
dialectic between focal and peripheral awareness. Any intensification of focal
attention necessitates the elimination of distracting or irrelevant stimuli.
Likewise, a position of diffuse and scanning awareness requires a relinquishing
of focal attentiveness. The trance state is a form of intense focal
concentration which maximises involvement with one sensory concept at a time.

Hypnotherapy may be defined, briefly, as the application of the state of
hypnosis with associated relaxation and its attendant phenomena to the
clinical situation and/or state.

The way in which the hypnotic state is used for therapeutic ends is, of
course, determined by the individual therapist. It has always been the
author's strong contention that hypnosis should be used within the overall
training and expertise of the individual therapist or researcher, be he doctor,
dentist or psychologist. This contrasts with the approach of so many "lay
therapists" who look upon hypnosis as the "be-all and the end-all", the total
therapeutic program. When used correctly, hypnosis may range from a small
part of a therapeutic program to the total program.

All too often, hypnotherapy is regarded as a very complex and detailed art
which has to be learned to the full before such can be contemplated and used
in therapy. Emile Coue published his book "My Method" in 1923 and the book
itself is beautifully simple; in it Coue describes the use of a simple
formulary "every day, in every way, I am getting better and better" and
demonstrates how this, as a total therapeutic program, can give outstanding
results.[3] A simple approach can lose its true worth and efficacy when it is
allowed to become complex.

I have explored all aspects of the application of hypnosis and hypnotic
techniques to therapy in a medical practice which has a bias towards
psychotherapeutic interests and psychosomatic problems. I have found that
virtually everyone can benefit from the inclusion of hypnosis in their program.

My method involves a four stage progression, depending upon both indication
and results of treatment. Such a method allows universal application. The
first stage would benefit everyone and the subsequent steps can be suitably

structured to individual needs as necessary.

RELAXATION

In this day and age in the western world, everyone can benefit from
learning the art of relaxation and practising relaxation as an ongoing means
to neutralise the tension and stress which is part of our competitive life.
Although this problem of anxiety, tension and stress and the various expressions
appears to be worse and apparently maximally developed in the present decade
of the twentieth century, if the benzodiazapenes had been available, the
Roman Gladiators would have been taking them. One cannot be anxious and
relaxed at the same time. Relaxation is the antidote to anxiety and tension.
If a state of physical and mental calm, tranquility, peacefulness and
relaxation can be achieved, anxiety and tension and the complications therefrom
will present no problem to the individual; there would be marked reduction in
the usage of tranquillizing drugs such as the benzodiazapenes, and the need for
non prescription drugs like alcohol would also be reduced.

The induction of the hypnotic trance is one of the best ways of achieving
and teaching relaxation. My method is to take a detailed history and give
appropriate explanation about the symptoms, the role of tension in the genesis
of the symptoms and the benefit to be gained by relaxation. It is the aim
to enable the individual to agree that, if relaxation can be learnt and
practised, benefit would result. Such an agreement based upon an intellectual
approach, is a type of contractual requirement, since the formal hypnosis in
the rooms is but a small part of the treatment program. If the patient
cannot see the logic and the purpose of relaxing and aiming for a relaxed
state throughout life, then the program will not be carried out and benefit
will be minimised. If the link between anxiety and tension and the symptoms
and hence the benefit of relaxation cannot be accepted, I believe there is no
purpose in pursuing relaxation therapy. However, almost everyone acknowledges
that benfit would result from being more relaxed.

Once this agreement has been reached, the patient is then directed to make
himself (herself) comfortable in a reclining chair with footstool. Induction
is by progressive relaxation technique. At times this may be part of the
first consultation. Generally, it is at the second consultation, the first

being devoted to history taking and psychometric assessment where indicated, and appropriate explanation. When the individual has become as comfortable as practicable, the induction involves the eyeroll technique of Spiegel (1978)[2] and he is asked to roll the eyes upwards and look upwards and backwards, past the eyebrows into the head and while looking up, to allow the eyes to close. Once the eyes have closed, he is instructed to allow the eyes to remain closed, to let the eyes relax, and to relax the forehead muscles. If the head has been tilted backwards during the upward gaze, he is asked to lower the chin and the head to a more relaxed position. He is asked to leave the eyes closed, to let the eyes relax and to forget about the eyes while he progressively relaxes each part of the body. I then request that the focus of attention is directed to the left leg, and, at that point touch contact is deliberately made with the leg to increase sensation awareness. The explanation is given that relaxation involves three elements: 1). To become aware of the feelings and sensations that are arising from and part of the area of the body to be relaxed. 2). Deliberate cooperation by relaxing that part of the body as completely as possible. 3). The use of the imagination to gain a mental picture, a visual image to "see in the mind's eye", the particular part of the body in the way it is to become, namely, relaxed. With that explanation, the patient is then asked to consider the left leg in those three ways and full details about this is given. For example, if there is a shoe on the foot, he is told to notice the feeling that is arising from the shoe on the foot, the feeling of the material against the skin, the sensations that are coming from inside the foot and leg. While this is going on he is asked to let the leg relax and to use the imagination as indicated. Watching the leg, it is apparent when it is relaxed and then feedback is given by rocking the leg from the foot and to point out just how relaxed it has become, thus giving reinforcement. The same procedure is then followed for the right leg and then the body itself, with specific reference to the abdominal musculature and the back muscles. I have found that a visual imagery of lying back and settling down into a soft heap of eiderdown and "letting go", heightens the relaxation of the back. When we consider the upper part of the chest, he is asked to note how the breathing is already relaxed (which happens in virtually every instance) giving further feedback: he is then asked to become aware of all the movements that are part of breathing and especially to consider the movements of the chest wall with each breath in and out, and also to note the feeling of the air as it passes in and out through the nostrils and across the back of the throat. The parallelism of relaxation and the breathing process, is then given: "every time you breathe out you will find yourself becoming increasingly more and more completely relaxed. With every breath that you breathe out, you are breathing away tension from your body....". I have found that the association between doing something and something else happening, is very beneficial. The left arm, right arm, area between the shoulders, neck muscles, muscles about the scalp, forehead muscles, facial muscles and in particular, the jaw muscles, are then briefly made the focus of attention along the lines as already mentioned.

Having considered the physical body, each patient is asked then to use his imagination to gain a mental image or picture of himself in a situation where there is no tension, anxiety, apprehension, fear, no worries and where there is complete freedom from any problems, difficulties, and in which he could expect himself to be completely at ease, tranquil, calm and peaceful. The selection of the scene that typifies this description is always left to the individual, and each is encouraged, not only to see just a scene, but indeed, to experience it through all the senses of his body. For example, if the scene is an outdoor one, the warmth of the sun on the body is to be experienced and the appropriate sounds are to be heard. In other words, all five senses are to be utilized since this heightens the experience and allows a carryover effect to occur, achieving not only an increasing physical relaxation, but also mental relaxation.

Achieving the combination of physical and mental relaxation is the first part of stage one of treatment and the second step involves getting the individual to agree to practise such relaxation at least once a day, for a period of approximately fifteen minutes. He is to replicate what has been done in the therapeutic session, at home or wherever a suitable time and place free from interruption, can be found. After taking up a comfortable position, (lying or sitting) the eyes are closed in the same manner and progression is made in the same order from the left leg to the right leg, finishing with a mental picture of the "shrangri-la" and experiencing total physical and mental calm and tranquility. This homework is a learning procedure aimed at behaviour modification and geared towards achieving an overall state of relaxation. At the next therapeutic encounter, a time for reporting success or otherwise is given and then the patient demonstrates his technique. The pattern of relaxation is then reinforced. In many instances such simple

relaxation is sufficient to gain worthwhile benefits. It has been shown that
once patients learn to relax completely, and then stay relaxed during their
daily affairs, psychoneurotic symptoms and disorders disappear spontaneously.[4]

EGO STRENGHTENING SUGGESTIONS AND SYMPTOM REMOVAL

   Once relaxed and in trance, ego strengthening-type suggestions can be
utilised to help the individual cope better, to improve his self image, and to
achieve greater motivation. Such suggestions are formulated appropriate to the
individual's needs and problems. Hartland has described fully the concept of
ego strengthening suggestions and sets out details of wording in his book
"Medical and Dental Hypnosis"[5]. The individual is asked to see himself, to
use his imagination to picture himself in the appropriate situation or set of
circumstances and to experience the full assimilation of the suggestions so
as to feel the imagined state as one of reality, doing or being or saying or
performing in accord with the specific needs and the suggestions given.
The addition of this visual imagery, especially if such imagery includes as
many of the senses as possible, greatly reinforces and heightens the benefit
from such ego strengthening suggestions.

   Suggestions specific to the symptomatology can also be given and, where
indicated, symptom removal can be attempted. Details of this are beyond the
scope of this paper, but it is important to recognise the individual problems
can be structured into this second stage of hypnotherapy. For example, an
individual with an organic pain can be directed that he will be less
concerned by the pain, the pain will appear to be separate from him, the
pain will not interfere with his thought and concentration, or that the pain
will lose its painful quality and be a sensation that he can tolerate.
Special care needs to be taken when dealing with symptoms that may be
important; for example, the asthmatic patient who is suffering from an attack
of asthma should never be told that he has no trouble breathing. Rather,
suggestions for calm, not fighting against the breathing difficulty, being
more at ease, allowing the bronchial muscles to relax, letting the air move
in and out more freely, are more correct[6].

HYPNOTHERAPY

This is psychotherapy carried out in the hypnotic state and the use of the various attendant phenomena of hypnosis to assist in such psychotherapy. The psychotherapeutic technique depends upon the individual therapist and I am interested in dealing with current problems, assessing reasons for the symptom, determination of goals and delineating successful approaches towards these goals. The uncovering of repressed psychic material is an important part of psychotherapy; the use of age regression in which the individual is asked to go back to an age which is relevant to and important in the development of his present problem, is a standard procedure in this stage of hypnotherapy and illustrates the use of specific hypnotic phenomena for therapeutic purposes. A variety of techniques are used to achieve regression. For example: the lift technique is where the patient sees himself in a lift and the number of floor buttons represents the number of years of age. A hand is observed reaching out automatically and pressing one of the buttons. After descending to that level, the doors open and the individual passes through the doors to that age and stage of their life which is then described. The red balloon technique is another useful method of therapy. The individual is asked to place into an appropriate container, the problems, worries, guilts, fears and the various burdens of life; then to seal the container and attach it to a helium filled red balloon and allow the balloon to carry the problems away and deposit them in a far distant mountain (able to be seen and be retrieved if need be in the future rather than be completely lost). Needless to say there are many variations and varieties of the actual application of hypnotic phenomena to hypnotherapy and these are set out in the various text books dealing with hypnotherapeutic mechanisms.

HYPNOANALYSIS

Finally, a progression from hypnotherapy to hypnoanalysis, in which deeper uncovering techniques are utilised, can take place. Hypnoplasty can be cited to illustrate this. "Play Dough" or modelling clay is used by the individual while in deep trance, to create, by modelling, objects which are linked into and part of subconscious conflicts. These can then be interpreted in later sessions, either in hypnosis or in ordinary therapy. Meares has detailed this in his book on hypnoplasty.[7] The subsequent use of objects created in hypnoplasty can be very interesting. One asthmatic who had enormous psychosexual problems that were part of her conscious conflict, subsequently took the dried clay objects (breasts and phallax symbols) and destroyed them utterly until they were just powder.

CONCLUSIONS

The progression from simple relaxation to complex hypnoanalysis can be tailored to fit the individual. Relaxation and ego boosting suggestions may be adequate in one individual whereas another, with what appears to be identical presenting signs and symptoms, may need a full hypnoanalysis.

My method is to start with relaxation, to assess the results and benefit and as necessary to progress right through to full hypnoanalysis if this is indicated. I do not believe that one should launch straight into hypnoanalytic techniques at the first or second session, but rather there should be a progression from relaxation to hypnoanalysis. My method is the result of my own personality, my knowledge and experience with hypnosis and is presented as an encouragement to those who are using hypnosis and wanting to develop their own method to achieve maximum therapeutic benefit and gain for their individual patients.

REFERENCES

1. NEEDHAM, F. and OUTTERSON-WOOD, T. (1955) Medical Use of Hypnotism, Brit. Med. J., Supplement, Appendix X, 1, 190-193.

2. SPIEGEL, H. and SPIEGEL, D. (1978) Trance and Treatment - Clinical Uses of Hypnosis, Basic Books Inc., New York, pp.22-23, 52-55.

3. COUÉ, E. (1923) My Method, William Heinemann, Ltd., London.

4. GRIM, P.F. (1972) Relaxation Therapies and Neurosis: A Central Fatigue Interpretation, Psychosomatics, 13, 353-370.

5. HARTLAND, J. (1971) Medical and Dental Hypnosis and its Clinical Applications, 2nd Ed., Balliere Tindall, London.

6. COLLISON, D.R. (1975) Which Asthmatic Patients Should be Treated by Hypnotherapy?, Med.J. Aust., 1, 776-781.

7. MEARES, A. (1960) Shapes of Sanity. Springfield, Ill., Charles C. Thomas.

© 1979 Elsevier/North-Holland Biomedical Press
Hypnosis 1979
G.D. Burrows, D.R. Collison and L. Dennerstein

BEYOND   HYPNOSIS.

A..E. BERNSTIEN
1039 Beaufort Street, Bedford Park, Perth, Western Australia 6052.

OVERVIEW

This short paper is the preliminary report upon results of the
investigation of one hundred pre-hypnotised subjects.   During the
apparent normal waking state of consciousness many of these
subjects displayed phenomena which are usually attributable to
hypnotic or post-hypnotic suggestion.   The question is why did
they do so and can the results be put to practical medical use?

INTRODUCTION

In 1886 Bernheim in his momentous book "De La Suggestion"
described the work which he and his associate Liebault had
carried out for some years preceding that date.   It concerned the
hypnosis of thousands of patients.   Numerous cures of illness
were described and it became quite obvious to the medical
profession that these two workers considered that the state of
hypnosis was a trance brought about by suggestion.

This closely followed upon the work carried out a few years
earlier by James Braid of Manchester, England.   Braid had
completely discounted the mesmeric theories of "animal magnetism"
and coined the term hypnotism from the Greek Hypnos meaning sleep.

Charcot, however, working at the Salpetriere hospital in Paris
was at this time teaching that hypnosis was only demonstrated in
patients suffering from pathological hysteria and therefore it was
an abnormal condition.   For some years a bitter war of argument
was kept up between the Nancy school of Bernheim and Liebeault
and the Paris school of Charcot and his co-workers.   Eventually,
however, the medical profession denigrated Charcot's theories
because he had carried out all his investigations with mentally
ill patients many of whom suffered from severe hysteria.   The
medical profession then accepted Bernheim's theory of suggestion.

From the mid eighteen hundreds, until early into the twentieth
century many workers offered theories in the field of hypnosis.
Jacuer, Sidis and Moreton Prince all considered that hypnosis was
a type of somnamulism and to some extent agreed with Charcot that

it was similar in certain ways to hysteria.   They claimed that in some fugue states in the hysterical personality, the stream of consciousness can split off so that groups of ideas and memories dissociate themselves from the main stream of cognition.   Today we accept the phenomena acting in such fugue states, for it is well known that some people in actual hypnosis can perform quite complicated feats of mental activity without the apparent interruption of normal conscious intellect.

Furthermore both Prince in 1906 and Riggale in 1931 brilliantly described the dissociation of personality in two hysterical patients.

Sigmund Freud proferred the theory that the hypnotic state comes about because the subject develops a libidinous attraction for the hypnotist and his associate Ferenczi went a stage further and believed that hypnosis was the direct result of a type of child-parent relationship of the subject to the hypnotist.

But in 1957 and 1960 Wyke in lectures to the British Society of Medical and Dental Hypnosis, discussed the "Neurological aspects of Hypnosis" and "Neurological Mechanisms of Hypnosis". He described that there exists a close relationship between hypnosis and certain other states of consciousness as verified by the E.E.G. and the studies he had persued.   He claimed that contrary to earlier belief, the reticular brain stem system is involved in hypnosis.

To quote Doctor Wyke, "Hypnosis does not involve some kind of peculiar psychological state imposed on the subject by the hypnotist.   Instead it is a physiological state inadvertently experienced by everyone in certain situations of normal life and into which the individuals can enter of their own choice or with the guidance of a hypnotist, who merely provides an appropriate environmental situation to facilitate such an excursion."

Ainslie Meares in his theory of "Atavistic Regression" offers the interesting concept that in hypnosis there is a regression from the normal adult mind at a logical level, to an archaic level of mental functioning in which suggestion determines how ideas will be accepted.   This theory assumes that primitive man dealt with ideas by a primitive process of suggestion, before he developed the ability to logically criticise at a conscious level.

Many authorities today, although not accepting Pavlov's
conditioned reflex theory as the underlying factor in hypnosis,
are prepared to consider that the conditioned reflex may be
involved when a person has been hypnotised on more than one
occasion'

To sum up this introduction, it would appear that none of the
theories thus far advanced are in themselves completely
acceptable in the consideration of the actual process of
hypnotic induction and indeed, Barber and his associates would
offer the opinion that hypnosis is not a trance state at all but
a peculiar state of controlled imagination.

Auther's Report.

For some years it has been found that individuals suffering
from conversion hysteria will very often respond in a positive
manner to suggestion put to them by a prestige figure, e.g. a
medical practitioner. The author conducted a series of
experiments with four patients suffering from conversion hysteria
and all the patients responded in a positive manner to
suggestions of:
1. Arm Rigidity.
2. Analgesia in the arm and hand.
3. Deafness.
4. Blindness.
5. Anosmia.
6. Loss of taste.
7. Mouth Dryness.
8. Salivation.
9. Arm levitation.
10. Positive visual hallucination.

It was decided to conduct a similar series of experiments on
apparently normal subjects who had been previously hypnotised,
some to somnambulistic depth. One hundred subjects were
involved and care was taken to ascertain as far as possible that
nobody in the group was suffering from hysteria.

Half the group had been hypnotised at some earlier time by the
author himself, whereas the other half had experienced hypnosis

induced by professional colleagues and had never before met the author himself, whereas the other half had experienced hypnosis induced by professional colleagues and had never before met the author, although they all knew him by reputation.

Of the hundred persons, sixty three were deep trance subjects or somnambules and thirty seven had never entered hypnosis deeper than the medium trance level or cataleptic stage.

All subjects during the course of the experiments were apparently fully awake and in possession of their normal conscious faculties.

Not one of the second group of thirty seven persons responded to any of the ten suggestions.

In the first group of sixty three persons, thirty one responded positively to all of the ten suggestions; eleven subjects responded to nine suggestions; Six subjects responded to eight suggestions; eight subjects responded to four suggestions; three subjects responded to two suggestions; four subjects responded to one suggestion.

DISCUSSION.

Why did thirty one people out of a group of one hundred pre-hypnotised subjects respond in some significant measure to suggestions given to them? If this proves to be a cross section of the population, what practical use can be made of it?

In attempting an answer to these questions, it first becomes necessary to consider the flow of conscious as against unconscious mental activity.

The principle function of the conscious mind is its analytical process. So long as the conscious mind is available to criticise incoming suggestions, the subject will react only in so much as his critical faculties will allow him. The unconscious is the repository of memory and basic emotions. It appears to have no power of analysis or criticism, yet under certain conditions it can take over many of the functions usually attributed to conscious activity.

Let us take a simple example to clarify our understanding of the mental finctions.

If you are offered a glass of water and told that it is brandy, you will look at it and see that it is colourless; you may smell it and note that it is odourless. You will bring up from your unconscious the memoty of what brandy tastes like and you will remember that it has a particular odour and has an amber colour. Thus you criticise the suggestion that it is brandy and you accept the true fact that the liquid is water.

If, however, by some means, your conscious processes are inactive, there is no criticism of what is suggested because unconscious thought processes are at an atavistic level. Therefore, the liquid now looks, smells and actually tastes like brandy.

Returning to the report, it becomes quite obvious that people who had on an earlier occasion been hypnotised no deeper than to a medium trance, retained full critical faculties because they did not respond to any of the suggestions, even though in the actual trance state they would have responded to a fair number of suggestions.

Those who were classed as somnambules retained only varying degrees of critical faculty and thirty one per cent of the whole group retained no obvious analytical process and yet apart from the experiment appeared perfectly normal in every way and quite able to persue their normal activities, some of which were of a highly intellectual nature such as medical practice or law practice.

CONSIDERATION.

That certain individuals who have been earlier hypnotised to a deep "trance" will be completely unable to resist a number of suggestions in their apparent "waking" state has now been proved to the satisfaction of the author.

The question now arises. Are these subjects truly awake and if not, what state of consciousness are they exhibiting? White described hypnosis as meaningful goal directed striving as defined by the operator and understood by the subject. The subjects in the report were apparently awake when they responded to suggestion and as such may have measured up to White's hypothesis.

With regard to the motivation of the group involved in this report it is somewhat difficult to reach agreement. Psycho-analytically orientated authorities consider that the motivation in hypnosis is derived from dependency and masochistic requirement. If this is true and the author feels doubtful about it, such motivation may be a spill-over from the hypnotic to a post hypnotic state which would suggest that the subjects in the report were in hypnosis.

It is also possible that hypnotic activity as persued by the subject is derived from an atavistic regression which allows of an easy transference. Thus, those of the subjects who displayed positive results may have entered spontaneous hypnosis in order to do so.

Most authorities today, whether state or non-state theorists, agree that in hypnosis the subject responds in the manner whereby he believes and understands he should respond and that the results depend upon the subjects willingness to accept the set of conditions laid down in a specific situation. As these subjects had earlier been in the hypnotic state, it is very possible that their suggestibility resulted from such a set of conditions.

It is also suggested by many authorities that subjects who take a positive attitude towards the hypnotic state perform better than those who remain negative in their attitudes. The reader will note that the best results obtained in this experiment were with those subjects who had earlier attained deep hypnosis.

It is suggested by the non-state theorists, hypnotic performance requires a peculiar set of imaginative abilities or skills so that the imagination is utilized for a specific purpose, the positive results in this experiment may have resulted because the subjects were in fact hypnotised and that a hypnotised subject does not require to look different from the normal.

Both state and non-state theorists are coming to the conclusion that hypnosis involves a shift from the pragmatic situation of our everyday existance to a set of purely controlled imaginings so that anything outside of the suggestion offered is ignored or translated as part of the suggestion. If this is so and if the subjects giving positive results to suggestion in this experiment were actually in hypnosis at the time, they must be strongly compared to those conversion hysterics who were described earlier.   Therefore the causative factors may be similar iin both cases.

Suggestion and suggestibility must play a powerful role here. The "positive" group of subjects were already proved to be susceptible to suggestion and in this experiment the author would have been regarded as a prestige figure.   Suggestion can work "miracles" among motivated subjects and it is the stock-in-trade at religious shrines such as Lourdes and in faith healing groups.

That spontaneous hypnosis may be involved in this experiment, cannot be overlooked.   For some considerable time many workers have believed that to carry out a post hypnotic suggestion, the subject unknowingly enters spontaneous hypnosis.   He may therefore enter spontaneous hypnosis here.   This would also explain the negative results found among the subjects who had never entered deep hypnosis but had only remained "light."

Against this, remains the fact that the subjects did not appear to be in a so called "trance state."

But Erickson and Hartland both consider that most patients have entered hypnosis long before an orthodox "trance" is established and much of Erickson's behavioural therapy appears to be based upon this assumption.

CONCLUSION.

It is far too early to reach any ultimate conclusions.   Many more experiments of this nature will be necessary before we can adapt pure scientific knowledge to medical treatment and it will become necessary to establish the causative factors behind hypnosis itself, for at present we find ourselves in a morass of theory and counter theory..

However, one important fact stands out.   Those people who have been taken to deep hypnosis will react positively to many suggestions without again being induced into hypnosis by standard induction techniques.

In other words, they are more susceptible to suggestion than would normally be expected.   The fact that a trance-like state does not appear to come about in such persons, speaks strongly on behalf of those who believe hypnosis to be a "non-state" phenomenon.

If hypnosis proves to be a condition of controlled imagination, so then might this phenomena be. In that case we can call this a state of controlled imagination and therefore hypnosis. What then of the response to suggestion by conversion hysterics? Are they in hypnosis during such experiments?

Here we begin to tread on very dangerous ground indeed, because for many years, hysteria has been dissociated from hypnosis and can such a high percentage of the population be hysterical?   (90% of the population are hypnotisable.)

Looking at this another way, it is theoretically possible that we are all born with a genetic predisposition to hysteria and that the pathological hysteria of Charcot is the clinical hysteria as we see it today, only found in a small number of the population who develop what we call psycho-neurosis as a result of psychogenic trauma.

As for the practical applications of the phenomena described in this early report, it is quite obvious to any hypnotist that all the responses obtained could quite easily be obtained by the normal means of post-hypnotic suggestion. Therefore at this time, the author feels that although much may be learned about states of consciousness from similar experiments and that they may hold the key as to what hypnosis is or is not, there would remain only a few occasions in which the phenomena can have practical application in medicine. This preliminary report was made to demonstrate that such a phenomena does exist.

© 1979 Elsevier/North-Holland Biomedical Press
Hypnosis 1979
G.D. Burrows, D.R. Collison and L. Dennerstein

EXPERIMENTAL EXACERBATION AND RELIEF OF ASTHMA UNDER HYPNOSIS

PAUL STEPHEN CLARKE

Allergist, Royal Hobart Hospital Hobart Tasmania Australia

INTRODUCTION

There has been considerable literature on the connection between emotion and asthma but little experimental confirmation. It has been demonstrated that hypnosis can be useful in the treatment of asthma. The experiments to be described show that airways resistance in asthmatic subjects can be increased under hypnosis by the suggestions of anger, fear, and asthma itself. Even more important is the demonstration that the increases in broncho obstruction thus induced can be reversed by the suggestion of relaxation. One can in fact under hypnosis talk directly to the bronchial muscles and have it obey one's commands.

The increases in broncho obstruction observed were abolished by the previous administration of atropine showing that they were mediated through the vagus nerve. Examples are given below.

TABLE 1.

CHANGES IN PULMONARY RESISTANCE DURING HYPNOSIS IN AN ASTHMATIC SUBJECT

Suggested State First Patient	Pulmonary Resistance (cm H_2O litre/sec (Normal 2.5.)
Before Hypnosis	6.8
During Hypnosis	
Control	8.3
Coughing	11.4
Asthma	12.4
Relaxed	7.5
Fear and Anger	16.1
Fear Anger and Asthma	11.9
Relaxed	6.4
After Hypnosis	7.6

Suggested State Second Patient	Pulmonary Resistance (cm H_2O Litre/sec (Normal 2.5.)
Before Hypnosis	5.2
During Hypnosis	
Control	5.3
Coughing	6.5
Relaxed	4.6
Anger and Fear	9.2
Relaxed	5.2
Anger Asthma and Cough	8.2
Relaxed	4.9

REFERENCE

Smith M.M. Colebatch H.J.H. Clarke P.S. 1970 Increase and Decrease in Pulmonary Resistance with Hypnotic Suggestion in Asthma. Am.Rev. Resp. Dis. 102: 236 - 242.

© 1979 Elsevier/North-Holland Biomedical Press
Hypnosis 1979
G.D. Burrows, D.R. Collison and L. Dennerstein

AUTOGENIC TRAINING, basic and advanced level, its technique, application
and indications, especially for children

KLAUS THOMAS, M.D., Ph.D., D.D.
Director of the I.H. SCHULTZ-Institute for medical hypnosis and Autogenic
Training, Glockenstr. 17, 1000 Berlin-West, Germany

1. Historical Remarks

One of the most effective methods in modern medical hypnosis had been
discovered before world war I by Prof. Johannes H. Schultz (1884-1970). Inter-
viewing patients in hypnosis he almost regulary found six groups of physical
experiences: heaviness and warmth in the limbs, calmness in heartbeat and
breathing, a warm abdomen and a cool forehead. Schultz did not only use these
reports, when he introduced hypnoses by suggesting these experiences, but he
also taught people to realize these feelings in order to introduce autohypnosis.
He called this "Autogenic Training", a method which meanwhile was introduced world-wide in modern medicine and found 3000 scientific publications.

During more than 65 years of research and experience J.H. Schultz and myself
evaluated more than 50 000 questionnaires thus constantly improving the
techniques, learning about hopeful indications in both levels, the basic and the
advanced Autogenic Training.

2. Technique of the Autogenic Training

The Training has been taught usually in groups, which is even more effective than instructing single patients. Small groups of five to 30 patients provide
time for individual counselling, large groups of 50 to 100 people are bound to
healthy people who need individual care only in case of difficulties, which may
rise during the training. Such difficulties may be serious and so relatively
frequent that according to Schultz exclusively physicians ought to spread the
Autogenic Training. All further details of the technique of the Autogenic
Training cannot be discussed here.

3. Effects of the Autogenic Training

Ten main effects for healthy people as a consequence of a deep hypnotic
relaxation have been carefully observed:

98

Physical consequences:

a) Overcoming of sleep-disturbances (exception: those of depressive origine which respond to antidepressive drugs)
b) Independence from climatic influences (temperature) and from food (to keep and preserve diet)
c) Childbirth considerable easier and shorter
d) Pain-relief
e) Strengthened resistence against many illnesses, even some infective diseases.

Psychic consequences:

f) Short and deep recreation at any time and place
g) Lasting calmness and relaxation including the inability of anger ("damping of the affects")
h) Concentration (by eliminating all disturbances and making thoughts stay at the topic by using posthypnotic suggestions)
i) Additional help for studying and passing examinations by removing anxiety, and enlarging capacities of the memory
k) Working at one's own character (especially in the advanced level of the Autogenic Training)

4. Indications for the Autogenic Training for sick persons

There is no need here to emphasize that all kinds of "psychosomatic" illnesses respond very well to the Autogenic Training.

In inner medicine many kinds of heart-trouble and disturbances of the circulation system are the field of this method. High blood pressure decreases on the average by 20 mm/Hg. The training is applied not only in rheumatism of all kinds, but as well for infective diseases like tuberculosis of all forms. Prof. Burger, M.D., in Paris has examined the considerable changes of the blood in Autogenic Training and its increased resistance against different germs.

In gynecology there are not only the many functional sufferings of the patient like dysmenorrhoa, but in obstetrics the "natural childbirth" with the decrease of anxiety and spasms (often in addition to the bodily exercises of Read) and Training is reported to be of a decisive support.

Even in fields where no effect may be expected serious research work has proved excellent results. In surgery fractures heal far quicker, if by the Training the circulation in the damaged limbs is improved. In ophthalmology at the university of Berlin e. g. all patients with glaucoma have been treated for some years with Autogenic Training (Vogelsang), and for the blind this method proved to have an especially high value (Thomas).

In psychiatry neurotic anxieties, some compulsions, light or decreasing depressions, epilepsy, some forms - mainly of alcohol and nicotine and drug - addictions, and chiefly with all kinds and forms of neurotic illnesses and symptoms: These are some few of the main indications for the Autogenic Training.

5. Autogenic Training and Hypnosis

There is no contradiction nor even a competition between both methods, ordinary hypnosis and self-hypnosis of the Autogenic Training. In the contrary, both methods are supporting each other.

Whenever immediate and/or strong effects are needed (e. g. in pain-relief in addiction, in overcoming fear or tensions), hypnosis brings therapeutic results within a short time.

The Autogenic Training will become effective only after several weeks of regular training, but then it brings the advantage of being independent from regular visits at the doctor's. At any time and any place the patient then will be able to help himself to become calm and relaxed and free from his disturbances. Especially working at own character will take a long time of patient Autogenic Training over a period of months.

One example may be given of how hypnosis and Autogenic Training can work together: For 35 years we have been hypnotizing alcoholics (and likewise tobacco- and drug-dependants) by giving series of hypnotic treatments (four in the first week, three in the second week and then less and less frequent treatments). At the same time the patients learnt the Autogenic Training and had their exercises at least twice daily, using the same formulas as in hypnosis. Thus a treatment of 15 sessions will do, showing an average of 60 to : 80 % good results.

But - we find it necessary to apply one further hypnosis once a month for at least one year. And here are the negative results: After four to six months the patients, happy about their freedom from alcohol or drugs donot show up to the dates of the further hypnoses as they donot think them to be necessary any longer. Also Autogenic Training is not exercised regulary. Then relapses are frequent.

6. Rules for effective "intending formulas" (post-hypnotic suggestions)

For thirty years we have been following and observing the conditions under which post-hypnotic suggestions (in Autogenic Training called "intending formulas") proved to be more successful or not. Seven rules were found which at the same time correspond to the findings and laws of poetry:

a) They should be short and impressive e. g. : "I do succeéd"

b) They should be positive:"I am calm, relaxed and free"
    ("I feel no anxiety" mostly increases fear)

c) They should follow a rhythm, which is to be combined with the heartbeat:
    "My wórk is my jóy"

    "At nigĥt my sleép
     is cálm and deép"

d) They should, if possible, include an end-rhyme or alliterations (see last example):"I wáke up at threé
               aleŕt and quite freé"

    alliteration: "I feel free from frustation and fright"

               "I love my life"

               "I like to learn"

e) They should correspond to the individuality and the situation of the personality: "I stand up for my rights". It follows the form of an encouraging, double-stressed statement, while "I shall stay sheltered" shows a calming trochaic rhythm.

f) They should always realize the present:
               "The arms are heavy", not "... will be";
    but the future may be included: "I aḿ and shall bé

               sure, steády and freé".

At the end of all formulas or suggestions one sentence helps them to go on in their effectivity: "The words go on working".

g) They should be reasonable, understandable and clear.

> A woman in vain used the formula: "Singultus is indifferent".
> She had not been told that her hiccup was named "singultus".

> A man, grinding his teeth, was not helped by the general words:
> "I am relaxed", but by the definite: "The jaws are heavy".

> A school-class was trained without success: "school-work is joyful".
> This was not felt to be true. Then they used: "school-work is done",
> and it worked.

An altogether of 1000 formulas, following these seven conditions were found, applied, proved to be more reliable than others and very finally published. (in Klaus Thomas, Praxis der Selbsthypnose des Autogenen Trainings [5] Thieme Verlag Stuttgart 1979)

7. Autogenic Training for Children

For 20 years we have been training children in self-hypnosis either in groups of six to ten children (mostly aged 8 to 11) or rarely whole school classes of any age.

In the courses we have six times (once a week) one hour for the training and a following hour for personal medical examination and psychological counselling, in which always the parents are included and several tests are applied (e. g. Staabs-Sceno and TAT). Thus the Autogenic Training is not the only therapy.

Though we use the same text for the formulas of relaxation, the whole language is adapted to the understanding of the children, and the method is far more activating: the children are drawing and using blackboard and models They are talking freely about their experiences, write down their needs and are telling jokes and stories in connection to the exercises.

Instead of four minutes training time three times within 90 minutes for the adults, we use twice three minutes for the children.

Any kind of psychosomatic diseases, e. g. asthma, disturbances of the intestinal tract, but also enuresis, headaches are described as well responding to the Autogenic Training. Furthermore disturbances of behaviour like aggressions, restlessness, stammering, tics, nail-biting, states of anxiety, especially at school, and more neurotic symptoms are to be treated with Autogenic Training.

We found it extremely necessary to look after depressive symptoms in childhood, as we constantly have to deal with children and adolescents in danger of suicide. In case of depressions always antidepressive drugs have to be applied.

In our special type of work we had to apply Autogenic Training with all children of a school for physically handicapped children, to work with blind children, with alcohol- and drug-dependent children and juveniles, with children suffering from guiltfeelings on account of masturbation and in special troubles of love and sex.

Altogether Autogenic Training as a self-hypnotic method of high value proved to be extremely helpful not only for healthy and sick adults in dozens of indications, but also in pediatrics.

8. Advanced level of the Autogenic Training

Some months after the basic exercises are mastered, the trainee may start the "advanced level" of the Training.
It begins with inner visualizations of a person's "own colour", moreover with experiences of any colour which may be wanted. A second group of exercises brings inner images of concrete objects, e. g. the house of ones own childhood, so that former psychic violations can be worked out.
In a third group abstract values (e. g. joy or justice or happiness) can be visualized and realized, bringing further experiences of self-knowledge.

A deeper insight into the "true self" is brought by imagining answers to most important questions: "How am I wrong? " "What should I do? " etc.

After years of systematic research Schultz and myself combined the "autogenic" and "hypnotic visualizations" following the experiences of Desoille, of Berta and Leuner introducing the "vertical direction" into the images of a hypnotized person. In the Advanced Autogenic Training thus a patient is guided (carefully instructed by a physician) "into the very depth of an ocean". Here the majority of the patients are able to meet in symbols their "deepest problems". (The German word for "soul" = "Seele" means ethymologically "deep sea")

These deep inner insights may be interpreted by psychoanalysis, but even without it they lead to an inner clarification and at last transformation. The doctor, occasionally discussing the results with the patient and accompanying him, keeps the patient independent and needs not spend too many hours to bring an inner freedom and health to the patient.

Another experience of the opposite vertical direction makes the patient "climb a high mountain... step by step, ... higher and higher". Experiences of an inner light, of clarity, of a hermit as a symbolization of the "superego, of the conscience help to overcome the frequent splitting up between the forces of the instincts and of the conscience, thus creating an inner peace.

Many patients, even and especially the so-called "agnostics" will find religious experiences in this exercise (e. g. visualizing heaven, Christ, paradise etc) without being influenced from any other side. Thus not too few of them recognize their own repressed religious longings.
On the other side the Autogenic Training itself stays a purely medical and innerworldly method, never passing over to any religious attitude.

Patients suffering from deeper neuroses and other people who are longing for a deeper self-knowledge and self-realization will find in the Advanced Autogenic Training a way of self-hypnosis which shows highes importance to win inner freedom and to build a strong and true personality.

© 1979 Elsevier/North-Holland Biomedical Press
Hypnosis 1979
G.D. Burrows, D.R. Collison and L. Dennerstein

AUDIO-VIDEO-POLYGRAPHY DURING HYPNOSIS:

A CONTRIBUTION TO THE VERIFICATION OF HYPNOTIC STATES

UROS J. JOVANOVIC

Psychiatric Clinic, University of Würzburg and Center for Chronomedicine, Theaterstr. 24,

8700 Würzburg, W-Germany

INTRODUCTION

To objectify hypnosis and its individual symptoms is not easy. The methodology is very
complicated, time-consuming and expensive. This fact must be one of the main reasons
that relatively few scientists have dealt with this problem. In recent years certain advances
have been made, however, only to a small extent[2].

EQUIPMENT

Our methodology is very comprehensive. For this purpose, a special building of the
Center for Chronomedicine Würzburg was technically equipped.

In the basement of this building there is a recording-laboratory, a doctor's office, the
secretariat with a switchboard, a room for the nurses and a room for two patients. The ward
is situated on the second floor. There are only rooms for one and two patients. In the attic
of the building there are additional rooms for group- and individual therapy.

In the recording-laboratory 10 polygraphs, one Bioprocessor 16 (BIO 16) with the XY-
Displayer, Magnetic Tape Analog Accumulator (AMPEX), Magnetic Tape Digital Accumulator (MTDA), Teletypewriter (TY), TV-Set, Telephone and Audio-Video-Monitors are
located, making an Audio-Video-Polygraphy-Computer-Studio (AVPCS). The doctor's office has his own monitors (Fig. 1). Special TV cameras, a TV-set, devices for the measurement of temperature and air humidity and telephone are installed in every patient's room.
The physician and assistants are able to communicate with the patients through the AVPCS.
Each patient has its own monitoring system enabling the making of ten simultaneous poly-
graphic recordings day and night. Autogenous training, bio-feed-back-therapy and hypnosis can be administered from the recording-laboratory. The AVPCS with control monitors
enables different on-line and off-line recordings and reproductions.

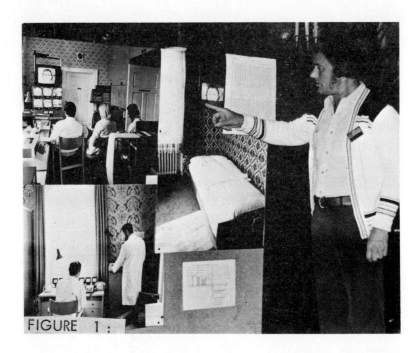

FIGURE 1 :

Fig. 1. This photograph was made by the use of two mirrors showing the rooms of the building of the Center for Chronomedicine, in which hypnosis is being performed and objectified.
In the left upper corner of the photograph you can see six TV-monItors which make possible
a simultaneous visual observation of 10 patients. The picture on the screen of the big TV-
set above the monitors can be seen by the patients in their own rooms. To the left of the 3
people watching TV, you can see the tele-typewriter giving access to the computer (BIO 16)
The polygraphs are located to the right, one of which is visible in the picture. The little
monitors which are to be seen on the doctor's desk (left lower corner of the photograph) show
the same pictures as large screen monitors shown in the upper quadrant of the photograph.
A section of a two-bed patient's room is shown in the center of the photograph in which the
connections for the polygraph can be recognized. Underneath, to the right side of the post-
er, tables and displays are attached.

TECHNIQUE

Polygraphy entails: The Electroencephalogram (EEG). The electrodes for the EEG are

attached to eight points of the head (frontal, pariental, precentral and occipital brain re-

gions bilaterally). Simultaneous with an on-line conversion of data from eight EEG channels

a recording of brain waves can be made on the AMPEX. Besides the bioelectrical signals

can be demonstrated graphically (Fig. 2 and 3) via Long-Term EEG-Monitoring-Program

(LEM) and the XY-Displayer.

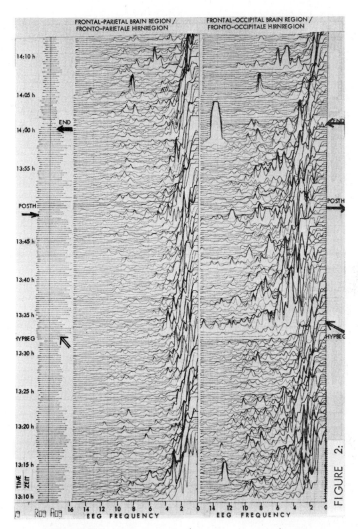

Fig. 2. Long-time electroencephalographic monitoring (LEM) display of a 21 year old female patient before, during and after hypnosis. Vertically, to the left, the frequency of brain-waves is entered in seconds (cycle per second = cps). From the left to the right, above, time divisions are indicated in units of 5 minutes each. Each line of the spectrogram, according to Fourier's Transformation, points out the mean of an epoch of EEG-waves of a duration of 20 seconds. The upper line with vertical straight lines demonstrates fluctuations of EEG parameters on the control channels. E.g. Ro9 = relative pronunciation of α-waves on channel 9; Ao9 = absolute pronunciation of α-waves on channel 9. At the beginning of hypnosis (HYPBEG, arrow to top and to right), the pronunciation of relative and above all, absolute pronunciation of brain-waves (α-waves) increase. The whole EEG-spectrum (spectral analysis) changes. The EEG spectrum changes again right at the beginning of the post hypnotic state (POSTH, arrow downwards towards the reader) so that the absolute pronunciation of α-waves decrease significantly. After additional 10 minutes, an abrupt deviation of wave-frequency in direction of slow wave trains becomes evident (END).

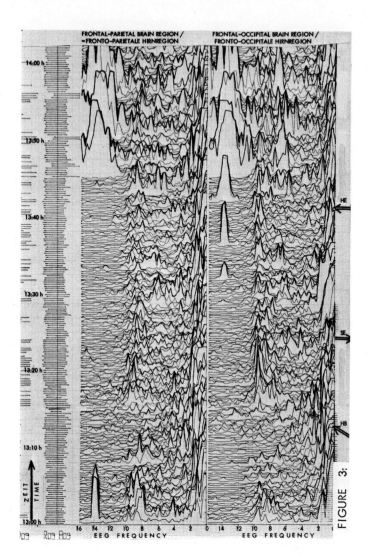

FIGURE 3:

Fig. 3. LEM (for abbreviations see Legend to Figure 2) of the female patient of Fig. 2. During the 8th session of hypnosis the hypnotist makes an attempt to reach a diagnosis. From case history it was known that the patient, in the past year, suffered from irregular episodes of somnolence lasting for 2-3 days. The hypnotist suggests a somnoleptic attack after hypnosis with the aim to determine if it was a hysterical or an epileptic reaction. At the edge of the picture on the left side, the patient is still awake. Slowly, she becomes sleepy, so that the EEG fluctuations are in favor of α-waves. The α-wave-peaks decrease. After the beginning of hypnosis via TV (HB = beginning of hypnosis, arrow to the top right), α-waves increase within a few minutes. We can see predominant α-waves in deep hypnosis. The highest frequency of the EEG is at 10 cps. During hypnosis, the hypnotist makes a suggestion that the patient "wake up" 20 minutes after he has stopped speaking (SE = end of suggestion, arrow downward towards the reader). Thereafter one attack is to follow. She should not be frightened, everything would soon be over. The patient wakes up shortly before the 20 minutes have elapsed since the suggestion (HE = end of hypnotic state, arrow to the top, seen from the reader).

The first attack sets in within a few minutes. (Prior to the attack, brain waves of high frequency, that increase from one moment to the next, are observed at three places of the spectrogram: see the first three peaks in the range of 14 cps increasing rapidly). The attack lasts for 10 seconds. Two minutes thereafter the next attack occurs which lasts for 14 seconds. The third attack, in the length of 30 seconds sets in during the next three minutes. The fourth attack occurs 6 minutes later and takes more than 30 seconds. Thereupon the patient became somnolent (after 14:00h) and complained of diffused headaches after a spontaneous awakening in the evening. All the while, a series of spikes could be observed in the original curve of the EEG during the individual attacks (epileptic reaction). The hypnosis decided the diagnosis. One attack had been suggested. As the attack had an organic (epileptic) and not a psychic (hysterical) nature, the hypnotist lost control over it in that several attacks followed, instead only one.

The Electrooculogram (EOG) is conducted over two channels from the polygraph. The electrodes are attached supra-orbitally, infra-orbitally and bitemporally in order to record the vertical as well as horizontal eye movements. During suggestions, in the course of hypnosis, the direction as well as the velocity and amplitude of eye movements are being recorded.

The Electromyogram (EMG) is conducted from both lower arms and in specific cases from the lower legs. Side differences of the movements and of the muscle tonus are simultaneously recorded and evaluated. E.g. after a suggestion: "....your right arm is heavy and relaxed; your left arm is stiff...".

The Positogram (Pos.) makes it possible to record the position of the body of the hypnotized person. Any changes of the position of the body are recorded with a General Recorder (GR) and demonstrated in degrees of position.

The Electrocardiogram (EKG) is being lead from the precardial points. Attachment of electrodes: In the axillary line left in the height of the apex beat and in the second intercostal area on the right side of the breastbone. One channel of the polygraph is reserved for the EKG.

Respiration (Resp.) can be checked in several ways by means of the respirogram: By means of a rubber tube, of only 5 mm diameter which is attached to the ribcage, bilaterally, over the epigastrium. This does not have to be wrapped around the whole ribcage but only the small front part. Graphite-dust is inserted in the rubber tube. This dust connects two electrodes located at both ends of the rubber tube. The inner resistance between the graphite electrodes is increased due to an expansion of the tube when inhaling and is decreased when exhaling. This change of resistance is observed through a channel of the polygraph (fluctuation of amplitude). The other method is applying another rubber tube which is tied around the whole chest and which is adapted to the size of the chest without being glued to the skin.

The bioelectrical skin-activity (BHA) (Electrodermatogram = EDG) has been recorded by us in two different ways from beginning on. One method records the changes of the galvanic skin resistance (GSR) by means of a mirror galvanometer, which is acting independently of other recording instruments. The electrodes are attached to the palm and the back of the left hand. Two wires lead to the mirror galvanometer. A source of light is directed to the mirror of the galvanometer which comes from a special tube through a narrow vertical gap. From there the light is reflected to a gauge which is suspended horizontally from the wall in

semidarkness. The gauge has 100 graduation marks to the right and to the left. The galvanometer is connected in such a way that the fluctuations of the bar of light to the left of the
zero mark will indicate an increase and to the right a decrease of the galvanic skin resistance. The second method records the bioelectrical skin potentials (BSP) on a channel of
the polygraph.

The Electrogastrography (EGG) is only applied in special cases, as due to principles we
only work with those methods which would not disturb hypnosis. A duodenum probe with two
openings at the end (electrodes) is swallowed. Both openings come in contact with the mu-
cous membrane and smooth muscles of the stomach and transfer the potentials on to a channel
of the polygraph during contractions.

Phallography (PLG) is applied with two methods. More information can be obtained
from our special contributions[4].

Clitorography (CLG) can only be applied indirectly because of technical reasons. Here-
by a thermistor is used on whose inner side a change of temperature with a sensitivity of
$1/100^{\circ}C$ can be recorded. The backside of the thermistor, which is approximately in the
size of a little finger nail, is temperature resistent through a good isolation. It is attached
close to the clitoris. During suggestion, on the erection of the clitoris, the temperature
will rise by 0.3 to $0.6^{\circ}C$.

Kolpography (KLG) was introduced in 1969. In the case of our instrument we are dealing with a 6-9 cm long rubber baloon, 0.8-2 cm in diameter[4]. It can be made larger by inflation. This small baloon is inserted into the vaginal canal like a tampoo before inflation.
A fine plastic tube (3 mm inner diameter and 4-5 m in length) leads to a specially constructed EEG-channel. A pressure chamber is installed between the two. A receptacle
filled with water (10-20 ccm) is located in the pressure chamber. The inflated rubber balloon in the vagina has an air connection with the water receptacle over the plastic tube.
During vaginal contractions a change of air pressure will occur in the pressure chamber resulting in a change of the water-level in the tube leading from the pressure chamber. This
change of the water-level can be seen on the recording trace of the polygraph-channel
which is to be evaluated afterwards. Additionally, the vaginal contractions can be demonstrated by means of acoustical and/or optical signals.

In order to measure the temperature (Temp.) we are using temperature measuring equipment with two to six channels. Side differences in temperature taken from the arms by
means of suggestion: "...your right arm is cold.... your left arm is warm...." can be
easily obtained.

The Urosensor (recording of bed wetting) which has been constructed by us has the task to record the enuretic episodes of bed wetters. This type of recording is quite important in therepeutic attempts to cure the enuresis nocturna with the help of hypnosis.

Acoustic arousal stimuli (AS) (85 $\pm$ 5 dB/A; distance from the head 100 $\pm$ 10 cm) are applied in order to determine to what extent the patient/test subject can be distracted through the stimuli.

Bio-Feed-Back-Methodology is applicable for diagnostics as well as for therapy.

In order to establish the personal characteristics of the control persons we use the personal characteristics questionnaire according to Fahrenberg and Selg[3] (Freiburg Personality Inventory = FPI); to examine feelings of anxiety in patients we apply the Manifesting Anxiety Scale according to Taylor and the Hamilton Rating Scale for depressions etc; to determine different symptoms lists for complaints were applied as well as questionnaires for the examination of psychic efficiency[4].

RESULTS

The verification of hypnosis was accomplished in more than 50% of the 60 test subjects/patients. The neuro-physiological parameters correlate with the degree of hypnosis. According to these findings the control persons and patients could be divided into three groups: good responders; moderate responders and non-responders. Due to lack of space we will only demonstrate electroencephalographic changes during hypnosis in one patient in Fig. 2 and 3. At a later date we will present statistical details of the results.

DISCUSSION

It is still a long way towards the final verification of symptoms of hypnosis. Our own results are just at the beginning of this long trail.

REFERENCES

1. Brickenkamp, R.: Handweisungen zum Aufmerksamkeitsbelastungstest. 2. Auflage, Hogrefe, Göttingen, 1962.

2. Emrich, H.: EEG bei hypnotischer Blindheit. Arch. Psychiat. Neurol., (1965), 207: 52-65.

3. Fahrenberg, J., und Selg, H.: Das Freiburger Persönlichkeitsinventar (FPI). Handweisung. Hogrefe, Göttingen, 1970.

4. Jovanovit, U.J.: Zur Methodik der Chronopsychologie. Psychometrische, polygraphische, klinische und Persönlichkeitsuntersuchungen. Inaug. Diss., Universität Würzburg, 1978.

Hypnosis 1979
G.D. Burrows, D.R. Collison and L. Dennerstein

HYPNOSIS IN THE MANAGEMENT OF CHRONIC PAIN

DIANA ELTON, GRAHAM D. BURROWS AND GORDON V. STANLEY
Departments of Psychiatry and Psychology, University of Melbourne, Parkville,
Victoria 3052, Australia.

INTRODUCTION

Treatment of chronic pain by psychological methods is gaining favour among
members of the medical profession. Methods include hypnosis, biofeedback,
placebo, psychotherapy, conditioning, relaxation and medication. In contrast
with the more traditional methods of treatment of pain by the use of medication
or surgery, these self regulation approaches are based upon active participation
of the patient in therapy.

It has been shown[1] that psychological processing plays a major part in the
total experience of pain. This 'reaction component' of pain is based both upon
the predisposition and the past learning of the individual, and is probably
associated with the vast individual differences in reactivity to pain. These
differences may be intercultural, intracultural and contextual.[2] Some stable
personality characteristics, such as anxiety[3] and low self-esteem[4] may also
show a close relationship to the pain experience. A highly anxious person, who
has a low self esteem might be inclined to augment pain and cling to it beyond
pathological expectancy. Personality difficulties, the outcome of faulty childhood learning are antecedents of chronic pain.[5] In comparison, a previously
well coping individual may experience pain due to factors such as secondary
gain, lack of support at home or at work, or some transient difficulties which
appear insurmountable at the time pain occurs.

Studies of 'sick role behaviour'[6,7] have suggested that sickness may be a
'way out' for some individuals. It may also produce a cognitive reorientation
involving dependency and passive aggression, hopelessness and helplessness.
Cumulative adverse experiences in life may provide a state of 'learned helplessness'.[8] Such a state may be characterized as a virtually static state of
cognitive immobility, where the individuals do not attempt to help themselves
believing that any such attempts will result in failure.[9] They may create
'self-fulfilling prophesies', and 'play pain games',[10] which consist of proving
to themselves and to the doctors how futile the medical profession is in solving
their problems. In the process their anxiety, feeling of worthlessness and
helplessness increase, and these feelings potentiate the pain experience.

Psychological treatment of chronic pain must aim beyond the removal of presenting symptoms. A re-education of the patients is needed with training to cope more adequately with pain and with life, accepting responsibility for personal progress. The present study examined four psychological approaches to treatment of chronic pain; hypnosis, biofeedback, placebo and psychotherapy. A comparison of relative effectiveness and value in behavioural modification was made.

METHOD

Subjects were 50 patients referred to the Department of Psychiatry, University of Melbourne. There were 30 females and 20 males with mean age 43.1 years (range 21 to 69 yr.). They suffered from a variety of complaints including tension headaches, migraine, arthritis, abdominal pain, causalgia, dental pains, and phantom limb pain. Average duration of pain was 14.3 yr. (range 3 to 30 yr.). All patients had previously received multiple treatments, (including medications, surgery, acupuncture, physiotherapy). Some had received multiple surgical procedures, and injested many pain tablets. All were rated on the Standard Hypnotic Clinical Scale (SHCS).[11]

DESIGN

Patients were randomly assigned to five groups. The four treatment groups were hypnosis, biofeedback, placebo and behavioural psychotherapy. The control group consisted of waiting list patients. Each person initially had two assessment sessions of one hour each. They were instructed in keeping pain charts, and completed a number of personality and mood questionnaires. A contractual relationship was established. Patients were informed of the nature of the study and agreed to attend for 12 weeks, to keep pain charts accurately and to offer maximal cooperation. If they did not do well in any treatment group, they could be re-assigned to another group at the termination of the 12-week period.

Treatment consisted of 12 weekly sessions of half hour each. Following this block there were a number of reassessment sessions. The initial two assessment weeks provided 'base-line' of pain and weeks 11 and 12 of treatment provided the 'final' scores. Basic principles of therapy were applied to all groups:
1. An attempt was made to establish a relationship of empathy, rapport and positive regard with all patients.
2. It was stressed that a high motivation to improve was crucial to the outcome of the therapy.
3. Inter and intrapersonal problems were discussed. Alternative methods of

dealing with their problems were suggested.

4. The therapy concentrated on the 'here and now' approach. Each patient had to write a short biography, to acquaint the therapist with the possible causes of the presenting condition. The emphasis was on what they were experiencing at present, and how that could be altered.

5. The patients were introduced to the rational-emotive approach of Ellis and Harper,[12] and were encouraged to apply these principles to themselves. This general conceptual outline was constant for all patients, but the actual practical applications were adapted to the needs of each individual.

6. Patients were given training in increased self-esteem and assertiveness.

7. Patients were required to produce written homework for each therapy session and to keep weekly pain charts.

8. They were not asked directly to discontinue their medication, this was to occur spontaneously.

9. The training followed a learning curve gradient, where simple tasks were attempted before the patients progressed to complex behavioural modifications. The rate of progress was adapted individually to each patient.

10. Spouses and other members of family were seen at least once during the treatment. This enabled an assessment of the social situation of the patient, and some possible precipitants of pain. The relatives' cooperation and reports of progress were asked for. There were some differences between the treatment groups:

Hypnosis group received 30 minutes of intensive interaction per session. The rapport was augmented by a heightened suggestibility of the patient, who was often more willing to attempt new approaches to pain relief and to self. The patients were trained in relaxation, and specific techniques of pain relief which included individually designed use of imagery, diversion of attention, amnesia of pain.

EMG Biofeedback group received 15-20 minutes of training on the biofeedback machine, with electrodes attached over the frontalis muscle. They learned to decrease the recording of the action potentials in that muscle. Relaxation was taught as one of the useful methods of lowering the tension in the muscle, but the patients were encouraged to find their own optimal ways of changing the feedback. The machine provided the patients with immediate information of their progress. It demonstrated the possibility of self-control. After the biofeedback training the patients had approximately 15 minutes of interaction with the therapist.

Both hypnosis and biofeedback were considered the active therapy group.

They emphasized autonomy, self-control, and responsibility for the therapeutic outcome. They also offered specific training in pain relief, which could be used firstly in the clinic, and then in the more stressful conditions at home and at work.

Placebo (non-specific drug therapy) group received tablets represented as a new pain drug, which was of benefit to many sufferers, in a double-blind trial. The treatment consisted of 15 minutes of discussion of their pharmacotherapy. This was followed by 15 minutes discussion of their inter and intrapersonal problems. The emphasis of the treatment was on the effects of the 'drug' on the patients' pain experience. If the patients reported no change, the dosage was gradually increased, and the patients were reassured that the effects were often cumulative, and may not manifest themselves for a few weeks.

Interaction (behavioural psychotherapy). These patients received 30 minutes of discussion of their inter and intrapersonal problems. Pain was hardly discussed. Relaxation was mentioned, but not taught. The emphasis of the treatment was on the inter and intrapersonal change. The patients were taught new coping strategies, they were asked to consider their past maladaptive behaviours and ways of altering these.

Control Group of waiting list patients attended the initial two assessment sessions, to determine their base-line scores of pain. Then they waited for 12 weeks, keeping their weekly pain charts. The weeks 11 and 12 of the waiting chart provided the final scores of pain, and also the base line scores for the treatment sessions. After 12 weeks they were randomly assigned to one of the two active therapy sessions, of hypnosis or biofeedback.

STUDY DESIGN

The hypnosis and biofeedback groups received training in relaxation, autogenic principles and specific techniques for pain relief. They were considered the active treatment groups. The placebo group acted as a control for the non-specific elements in therapy. An interaction group was included to compare effectiveness of a 'talking' therapy. The control group was included in order to examine the effects of time on the experience of pain of the patients, such as a possible spontaneous recovery, and the effects of keeping records.

Assessment included pain charts, visual analogue scales, the Melzack Pain Assessment Questionnaire, Tension Thermometers, and written assessments.

RESULTS

Three parameters will be discussed.

1. <u>Visual analogue scale</u> - which is a global assessment of pain on a 100 mm.
linear scale. The patient marked the pain experience for the week.

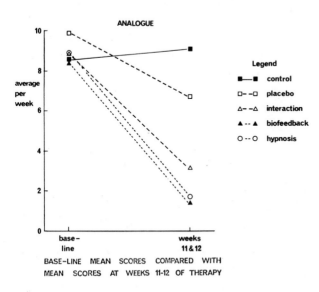

Fig. 1

Figure 1 indicates that the patients in the hypnosis group showed 89%
improvement on their global self-assessment of pain, the biofeedback group 82%,
the interaction group 65% and the placebo group 32% improvement. In contrast,
the control patients showed a slight deterioration.
2. <u>Duration of pain</u> (hours of pain per week). Figure 2 indicates that patients
in the hypnosis group showed 72% improvement in duration of pain, whereas
patients in the biofeedback group showed only 37%, the interaction group 22%,
the placebo group 9% improvement. The control group again showed reversed
symptomatology.
3. <u>Medication</u> (tablets per week). Figure 3 indicates that patients in the
hypnosis group showed 81 per cent improvement on this variable, and in the
biofeedback group 84%. The interaction group showed 71% improvement, and the
placebo group -48%. The control group patients deteriorated by 10%.
4. Transfer Control Group into hypnosis and biofeedback. Figure 4 indicates
that the control group showed a significant improvement after they have been
transferred into hypnosis and biofeedback group.

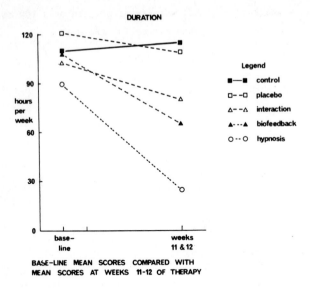

DURATION

BASE-LINE MEAN SCORES COMPARED WITH MEAN SCORES AT WEEKS 11-12 OF THERAPY

Fig. 2

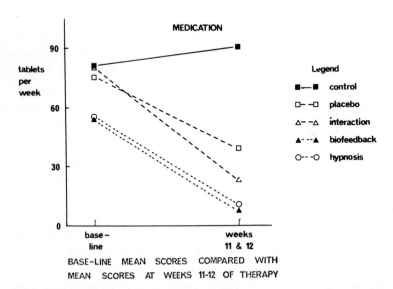

MEDICATION

BASE-LINE MEAN SCORES COMPARED WITH MEAN SCORES AT WEEKS 11-12 OF THERAPY

Fig. 3

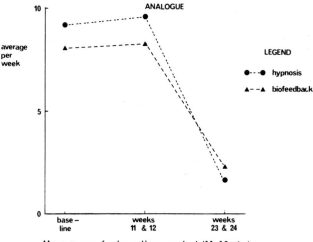

Mean scores for base-line, control (11-12 wks)
and crossover (23-24 wks) conditions

Fig. 4

DISCUSSION

The results of this study indicate that these psychological treatments were
successful in the treatment of chronic pain in these 50 patients. The patients
in hypnosis and biofeedback groups showed significant improvements. The
results were marginally higher for the hypnosis group, particularly in the
duration of pain. A three year follow-up has showed that the results appeared
lasting for the majority of patients. Hypnosis appeared the method of choice.
It did not require expensive apparatus to administer the treatment, and the
transfer of training appeared easier. Seven of the interaction group patients
showed significant gains, but three regressed. These were transferred into
biofeedback and hypnosis, and their symptoms were controlled. The placebo
group did not improve significantly. Possibly the use of another tablet had
less effect on the chronic pain patients, for whom many medications have failed
previously. All patients in the placebo group were randomly allocated into the
hypnosis and biofeedback groups, where they have shown further improvements.
The control group deteriorated. This showed that time alone and keeping of
records was insufficient to attain pain relief in this group of patients. These

patients were randomly allocated into biofeedback and hypnosis groups, and they have shown significant gains.

Training a patient to assume ones own control over life and personal pain, needs cooperation and motivation. Learning to cope with pain lessened the patients' feeling of helplessness, and enabled them to deal more effectively with other areas of life. Conversely, training a person to feel less helpless in dealing with any aspect of their existence may also be generalized to produce pain relief.

This study showed that behavioural techniques were effective in attaining pain relief in chronic pain patients, but their effect was greatly augmented if hypnosis and biofeedback were used in conjunction with behavioural modification.

REFERENCES

1. Beecher, H.K. (1959) The measurement of subjective responses. New York. Oxford.

2. Melzack, R. (1973) The Puzzle of Pain. Middlesex, Penguin Edition.

3. Elton, Diana & Stanley, G.V. (1976) Relaxation as a means of pain control. Australian Journal of Physiotherapy, 22, 3, 121-123.

4. Elton, Diana, Stanley, G.V. & Burrows, G.D. (1978) Self-esteem and chronic pain. Journal of Psychosomatic Research, 22, 25-33.

5. Engel, G.L. (1959) "Psychogenic" pain and the pain prone patient. American Journal of Medicine, 26, 899-918.

6. Poulsons, C.M. (1957) The Social System, Free Press, New York.

7. Mechanic, D. (1968) Medical Sociology, Free Press, New York.

8. Seligman, M.H.P. (1975) Helplessness, Depression, Development and Death. W.H. Freeman & Co., San Francisco.

9. Elton, Diana, Burrows, G.D. & Stanley, G.V. (1979) Hypnosis, chronic pain and the pain-prone patient. In Handbook of Hypnosis and Psychosomatic Medicine. Burrows, G.D. & Dennerstein, L. (Eds). Excerpta Medica, Elsevier North Holland, Biomedical Press of Amsterdam.

10. Sternbach, R.A. (1968) Pain - A Psychophysiological Analysis. New York. Academic Press.

11. Hilgard, E.R. (1975) Stanford hypnotic clinical scale. In Ernest R. Hilgard and Jospehine R. Hilgard, Hypnosis in the Relief of Pain. William Kaufman Inc., Los Altos, California, 209-221.

12. Ellis, A. & Harper, R.A. (1975) A New Guide to Rational Living. Wilshire, Hollywood, California.

© 1979 Elsevier/North-Holland Biomedical Press
Hypnosis 1979
G.D. Burrows, D.R. Collison and L. Dennerstein

HYPNO-ANALYTIC THERAPY OF HYSTERIC HEMIPLEGIA BY MEANS OF SECOND-
ARY PERSONALITIES

REIMA KAMPMAN, REIJO HIRVENOJA AND OLLI IHALAINEN
University of Tampere (Finland)

CASE REPORT

A 20-year-old woman was admitted into the Department of Neurology of a University Central Hospital for examinations of headache,
fugue episodes and right hemiplegic symptoms. Anamnestically it
appeared that the first episode had taken place two years previously. On that occasion the subject had lost consciousness for
about a minute. Thereafter she had had two similar episodes over
two months. During these episodes she had seen spots of light
before her eyes, after which an intense headache developed. The
headache made the subject non-functional; she was unable to speak
or understand the words spoken to her. During some of the episodes she had acted strangely: at school, for example, she had
tried to walk out of the classroom halfway through a lesson.

The subject also complained of different episodes with high
fever and intense flickering in her eyes without disorders ofcon-
sciousness. During these episodes she felt her limbs very weak,
particularly the right arm and leg seemed clumsy. The right side
of the tongue was also insensible. The everyday activities of the
subject were disturbed sufficiently to warrant hospital examinations.

The anamnestic symptoms gave rise to a suspicion of brain tu-
mour. In the neurological examination the patient appeared very
grave and strained. Skin sensibility was found to be depressed
over the entire right side of her body. Head torque to the right
was impaired. The lifting and compressive force of the right hand
was similarly impaired, as was also the muscular force of the
right leg. Pain and tactile sense was impaired over the entire
right side of the body. Vibratory sense was absent in the right
arm and below the thigh in the right leg. The peripheral tendon
reflexes were poorer on the right than on the left.

RESULTS OF EXAMINATIONS

The scanning examination yielded a normal finding. EEG, carotid angiography and PEG were similarly normal. Ophthalmologic consultation revealed nothing abnormal. Psychological tests were indicative of mild dyslexia and -graphia.

Since the patient's symptoms and the objective results of examinations were clearly disproportionate, a psychiatric consultation was decided upon.

PSYCHIATRIC EXAMINATION

The psychiatrist meets a young woman who has a slight limp when walking. She appears shy and inhibited. The patient tells of her symptoms, which agree with the above description. However, the phenomenon of "la belle indifference" is clearly observable in the patient's story.

CHILDHOOD BACKGROUND

The patient is the third of five children. The two eldest children are from the father's first marriage. The father's first spouse had died. Soon after her death, the father remarried. The patient is the eldest child from this marriage. She also has two siblings junior to her. The patient says her relationship with the younger siblings is very poor.

The patient tells of having had very many difficulties at puberty. After puberty she has had two intimate dating relationships, which, however, ended in her difficulties in sexual matters. She considered them completely disgusting and was unwilling to have any sexual intercourse.

No disorders of the reality level are apparent in the status. Since, moreover, the patient's symptom is restricted to a relatively narrow section of the personality, hypnosis is considered the method of choice.

It is easy to bring the patient into deep hypnosis. During the hypnosis she is brought back in time to the moment when she first had a fugue episode. She trembles violently, breathes heavily and seems to re-live some situation. When asked about it, she tells of a feeling of being separated from her body, which becomes insensible and non-functional. She is then asked to tell the

therapist what she feels and sees. She merely shakes her head
unable to say anything. The patient is given a dissociative suggestion to leave her body and sit down on the near-by chair. Her
body is then asked to speak automatically and relate what is happening. The patient now tells of a raping episode: her 13-year-
old stepbrother tried to have sexual intercourse with her when
she was six years old. At the same time, the two younger siblings stood by watching. During the hypnosis the event is then
discussed at the rational level. The patient is explained that
the 2- and 3-year-old sisters did not understand the incident and
can no longer remember it. An effort is also made to alleviate
the subject's own superego guilt by stressing that she was too
small to understand the matter at that time. The situation is
thus worked through. To the astonishment of both the therapist
and the subject, all the parts of her body become normal. The
previously insensible right side also becomes normal and the force
of the right hand is restored almost completely. In addition, the
subject no longer limps while walking. While in hypnosis, the
patient had also been given a suggestion that the matters experienced and discussed by her while in hypnosis are like a dream.
The patient's ego can thus be prepared to accept the things it
had previously repressed and to use as a defence the projection
into dream; after all, anything is possible in a dream. Having
waked from the hypnosis, the subject is highly astonished at her
recovery. Nevertheless, she immediately begins to doubt that the
symptoms may return.

SECOND THERAPEUTIC SESSION
    A week later the patient comes for another session. After the
first session she had been asymptomatic for a long time. The
symptoms gradually began to re-appear, however, as she approached
her home locality. Not all of the symptoms returned, and she retained her ability to walk. At the beginning of the session the
therapist converses with the patient. Some of the background
data are clarified. The subject says she suddenly remembered
that the stepbrother made use of her on several occasions over
about a week's time, until the younger sisters happened to see the
incident. This brought the sex play to an end. The subject had

completely forgotten this incident, until at the age of 15 she
read a guidebook on sexual matters. Only then did she remember
what had been done to her as a little girl, and she developed an
intense anxiety reaction. She repressed this reaction, however.
The problem agoin became topical when the patient began dating.
The relationship became intimate and intercourse was attempted.
During this attempt, the raping episode of her childhood was de-
picted before the patients eyes as if on a screen, which gave her
a forcible feeling of anxiety and disgust. The intercourses were
complete failures.

Since the patient's repression had been very effective, a
search for secondary personalities is undertaken. She is brought
back to the time preceding her birth. She says she is somewhere
in Egypt. She is a 23-year-old woman called Isabel Abdul. She
is married and has two children aged 2 and 3 years. The children
are called Ismael and Maria. The patient tells she is about to
fill a jar with water out of a basin and then to carry the jar
home on her head. The patient also has another secondary personality. She is an 18-year-old Briitta, who lives in Karelia. She
is living the year 1864. She cannot pronounce her surname, but
says it is a Russian name ending in v. Briitta also has a fiance,
whom she describes as a little odd. They have been associating
for about a year. Briitta, too, is at a well drawing up water.
There is a lever system of some kind for drawing the water out of
the well. Briitta complains, however, that one side of the lever
system is broken. After this, the patient is again given a dissociative suggestion, as on the previous occasion. She is aware
of this as well as the older and more recent experiences associated with her secondary personality and waking personality. The
therapist and the subject together analyze the secondary personalities in relation to the subject's illness and experiences. The
first secondary personality, Isabel Abdul, is a 23-year-old woman.
She has two children, aged two and three. These children symbolically represent the 2- and 3-year-old sisters who witnessed the
raping of the subject at the age of 6. Isabel is aged 23, which
is an obvious synthesis of the ages of the sisters. It appears,
moreover, that Isabel's husband closely resembles the stepbrother
who raped the subject when she was six years old.

It is also worth noting that Isabel Abdul is taking water out of a basin. The drawing of water out of a basin is somehow symbolic of a child's notion of the sexual organ. A six-year-old has no more accurate idea of the depth and dimensions of the female sexual organ. Subconsciously, she merely recognizes it as a basin-like depression.

The second secondary personality, the 18-year-old Karelian Briitta, is also drawing water from a well, this time really a well, not merely a basin. The Egyptian shallow basin is now replaced by a well, which may reflect the subject's altered notion of her own sexuality. When reading information on sexual matters, she has realized the significance of what her stepbrother had tried to do.

While drawing up the water, she says that the hauling system is broken. The subject associates this lever system symbolically with her own body. Her body is also broken. Also, she associates the scooping of water symbolically with her own illness. The causes of the illness must be scooped up deep out of childhood, deep out of a well and deep out of sexuality.

Hypnoanalysis shows how the two secondary personalities of the subject have come out. She has projected the raping episode of her childhood on to her Egyptian secondary personality. The second secondary personality, which lived in the 19th century, is symbolic of her current problems. The broken lever of a well represents a broken body. It cannot be used for drawing up water out of a well. Having waked after the analysis of secondary personalities, the subject feels herself completely free from symptoms. All the symptoms of insensibility and lack of strength are absent.

For years later, the subject continues to be asymptomatic.

DISCUSSION

Hypnosis is frequently used in the treatment of conversion hysteria, particularly when the symptom occurs in a restricted area and has not persisted very long. The results obtained in chronic cases have also been relatively good[1]. Hypnosis has also been used successfully in the treatment of spontaneous secondary personalities[2,3,4,5]. The most recent studies utilizing hypnosis

have altered our conceptions of the etiology of secondary personalities. Grunevald suggests that the splitting phenomenon may
be similar to the phenomenon noted in narcissistic disorders[6].
Kampman[7] investigated secondary personalities induced hypnotically, noting that they are characteristic of a functionally flexible and adaptive ego. Prior to that, Zolic[8] found that secondary personalities may also be centered around oedipal conflicts.
Leavitt[9] similarly found secondary personalities in hemiplegic
patients. It can thus be postulated that there are, in principle,
secondary personalities of three kinds. Healthy subjects have
ego-syntonic secondary personalities which enrich the ego. Subjects with clinical symptoms use secondary personalities as defences of the ego in their attempts to deal with an earlier conflict. In their case the ego is still well functional. The third
group would consist of spontaneous secondary personalities, which
belong to the category of narcissistic disorders. In those cases
the splitting phenomenon completely separates certain components
of the personality, yet retaining the difference between external
and internal reality.

REFERENCES
1. Kampman, R. and Kuha, S. (1975) Hypnoanalytic case study of
   conversion symptoms, Psychiatria Fennica, pp. 173-176.
2. Thigpen, C.H. and Cleckley, H.M. (1957) The three faces of Eve,
   New York McGraw Hill.
3. Ludwig, A.M., Brandsma, J.M., Wilbur, C.B., Benfelt, F. and
   Jameson, D.H. (1972) The objective study of a multiple personality. Or, are four heads better than one? Arch. Gen. Psychiat
   26, 298-310.
4. Schreiber, F. (1974) Sybil. Fletcher & Son Ltd., Norwich.
5. Prince, M. (1930) Dissociation of a Personality. London, Longmans Green & Co Ltd.
6. Gruenewald, D. (1977) Multiple personalitu anf splitting phenomena: a reconceptualization. J. Nerv. and Ment. Dis. 164,
   385-393.
7. Kampman, R. (1973) Hypnotically induced personality. Acta Uni-
   versitatis Ouluensis, Series d, Medica no 6, Psychiatrica no 3.
8. Zolik, E. (1958) An Experimental Investigation of the Psychodynamic Implication of the Hypnotic "Previous Existence" Fantasy, J. Clin. Psychology, 14, 179-183.
9. Leavitt, M.H.C. (1947) A case of hypnotically produced secondary and tertiary personalities. Hypnoanalytic Rev. 34, 274.

© 1979 Elsevier/North-Holland Biomedical Press
Hypnosis 1979
G.D. Burrows, D.R. Collison and L. Dennerstein

GROUP MEDITATION THERAPY

SCOTT INGLIS
Perth, Western Australia

INTRODUCTION

Studies such as those of Anand, Chhina and Baldev Singh (1961) have demonstrated the ability of subjects trained in yoga to produce a voluntary reduction
of the metabolic rate even below basal levels[1]. Since then Benson and his
associates (1974) have carried out extensive investigations in practitioners of
transcendental meditation, and have found that a hypometabolic state can be
produced also by this method. This led them to develop what they describe as a
'non-cultic' method of producing the same result. This 'relaxation reponse'
was used by them in attempts to control hypertension[2].

Carrington and Ephron (1975) found that the practice of transcendental meditation had benefits for both patients and therapists during psychotherapy[3].

The meditation state ('relaxation response') resembles the hypnagogic state,
which is the intermediate state between wakefulness and full sleep. During the
process of falling asleep the subject progressively withdraws his attention from
the environment. In meditation attention is withdrawn from the environment by
attending to a monotonous source of sensory stimulation. A commón procedure is
to repeat a word or phrase mentally ('mantra' or 'mantram'). Other sources of
sensory stimulation are reduced by closing the eyes and avoiding unnecessary
movement.

Elson, Hauri and Cunis (1977) investigated meditators who employed Ananda
Marga Yoga techniques and found that both the hypnagogic state and the meditative state had similar EEG criteria[4]. The hypnagogic state, however, soon
descends into unequivocal sleep whereas the meditation state can be indefinitely
prolonged. The 'deepest' meditation state appears to be close to Stage 2 Sleep.
It may represent the state of 'no mind' sought after by traditional meditation.

Silverman (1968) listed some characteristics of altered states of consciousness including: subjective feelings of timelessness and other disturbances of
time sense; changes in emotional tone; changes of body image including dis-
solution of boundaries between self and the world; perceptual distortions and
increases in visual imagery or a subjectively felt hyper-acuteness of perception;
perception of unusual meanings or significances in ideas and experiences
possibly with feelings of profound insight[5].

It was thought that the meditative state offered possibilities for a very undirected type of psychotherapy by lowering anxiety levels, increasing communication and offering unusual experiences of self. It was also thought that the personal participation of the therapist would be of significance in making the therapy a shared experience rather than a treatment to be delivered.

STRUCTURE

Two series of patients were treated clinically using meditative methods for relief of anxiety. There were 41 patients in the first series and 56 in the second. Each subject was asked to attend on three occasions at weekly intervals. It was found that subjects who defaulted were in general those who were unable to use the technique and therefore opted out of further treatment.

It was found useful for membership of the groups to overlap so that each session contained untrained and trained subjects if possible. The presence of those who had already made some progress was found to be strongly reassuring to beginners who frequently felt self-conscious and conspicuous. The group setting appeared to affect the quality of the experience. Certainly at first, subjects found that they achieved a much deeper level of relaxation when meditating in the group than they did when on their own.

Preliminary screening was carried out. Possible grounds of rejection would have been significant depression and psychotic and prepsychotic illness. No patient was in fact rejected.

During screening past and current problems were explored, and some discussion of the nature of anxiety was undertaken, together with an explanation of the basis of the proposed treatment.

Sessions were timed to take place late in the afternoons. All subjects were warned not to eat before attending. It has been found that inducing the relaxation response after heavy meals tends to produce indigestion or nausea. At the beginning of the session each subject was asked to describe progress since the last attendance. Then a brief account was given for newcomers of the nature of the meditative process and of what was to be aimed at.

Following this there was a meditation session lasting twenty minutes, timed by myself. After the session those who had taken part discussed their experiences. They were then asked to carry out the exercise twice daily at home, preferably before breakfast and before the evening meal.

TECHNIQUE

It was explained that the object was to acquire a feeling of passivity and acceptance. There was to be no conscious effort of any sort, in particular no effort to 'try to relax'. Closing the eyes and keeping quite still would reduce the number of messages to the nervous system, just as happens naturally when one is preparing for sleep. In this way a natural relaxation would be produced without effort.

In order to reduce the tendency to analyze what was happening, a 'code word' was to be repeated mentally. This term was used instead of the term 'mantra'. It was explained that the actual meaning of the code word was of no significance as it was merely a distracting device to interrupt 'active thinking' and permit 'passive thinking'. (This, of course, is not what is taught in systems of yoga, where the meaning and pronunciation of the mantra are considered to be of great importance.) The subjects were instructed that a code word should be selected which had no particular significance and which was easy to remember.

The following code words were used:

First Series (based on Sanskrit words)	Second Series (Greek letters)
Atma	Alpha
Dhyana	Theta
Karma	
Dharma	
Om	

Words based on Sanskrit were used at first, but it was found that the letters of the Greek alphabet were equally effective and less 'cultic'.

INSTRUCTIONS

'Sit in a comfortable position in an ordinary chair with your hands loosely curled up in your lap. Do not cross your knees or your ankles. You may find it more comfortable to remove your shoes. You have selected a code word. All that you have to do is to close your eyes and repeat the code word every time you breathe out.

'Remember that it is not necessary to change your breathing in any way. However, every time that you breathe out simply say the code word in your mind. After a few minutes you may find that you forget to say the code word. This does not matter. It simply indicates that you are becoming more relaxed. In fact, you may find that your mind may go completely blank at times. This is a sign of a very good level of relaxation. It does not mean that you have fallen asleep. In fact, if you were to start falling asleep your head would fall forward and this would wake you.

'Do not make any unnecessary movements. Do not try to direct your thoughts in any way. If you find yourself thinking about something, simply keep repeating the code word in your mind. If you notice outside sounds, do not make any conscious attempt to ignore them. Just accept them and they will bother you less and less as time goes on.

'Don't worry about the time. We will be relaxing together for twenty minutes. I will tell you when to open your eyes, so there is no need for you to worry about how much time has passed. When you carry out the relaxation at home you may sit in front of a clock. You may open your eyes from time to time without disturbing the relaxed state.

'You can use an electric timer if you wish, provided that it is not too noisy. The timer on an electric oven is usually very satisfactory.

'Get rid of flies in the room before you start, and try to avoid any interruptions such as from children, pets, and telephone callers. It may be unpleasant to be forcibly interrupted in the middle of your relaxation session. When the twenty minutes is over slowly open your eyes. Open and shut your hands and move your limbs a few times before getting up.

'You will find that the relaxed state is more easily produced after some practice. After a while you may find that only a few minutes a day may be enough and this may be taken at odd moments. Some people get most benefit from a single daily session of half an hour.'

RESULTS

	First Series	Second Series	Total
Unknown	5	3	8
Unsuccessful	10	16	26
Useful anxiety relief	22	22	44
Very good relief	4	15	19
	41	56	97

In 26 patients the results were regarded as unsuccessful, because of failure to produce the subjective sensations of the relaxation response, or of failure to produce therapeutic benefit. Another 8 patients who were lost sight of must be regarded as failures. Of the known failures it was assessed that 14 were unable to carry out the technique because of such factors as being unable to accept a passive role or of feeling foolish or self conscious. There was often the feeling that it was 'a waste of time'. This was also a common difficulty with successful meditators in the early stages, and was regarded as part of the neurotic difficulty in dealing with 'here and now' experiences. It was one of the areas frequently raised in group discussion.

Depression was present in 3 unsuccessful patients. Meditation tended to produce unpleasant imagery (for example, 'whirling black spirals') and to mobilise feelings of sadness.

The technique was unsuccessful in 2 patients with obsessional neurosis. One commented: 'That was horrible. I felt unreal'.

Of 2 anxious patients who failed to respond, one responded to a form ot autogenic training and the other to hypnosis.

In 44 patients there was useful relief of anxiety, in the sense of 'getting over a bad patch' or of learning to cope better with stressful situations. In 3 of these patients there was relief of neurotic depression.

3 patients in this group unexpectedly had relief of phobic anxiety of mild degree. However 1 patient had relief of general anxiety but not of phobic anxiety of heights and enclosed spaces. This patient was subsequently successfully desensitised using the autogenic state as a relaxation procedure.

The 19 patients described as having 'very good relief' had rather better results than might have been anticipated. This appears to have been due to the meditative process having more personal significance to them as an experience. This group tended to continue the practice on a long-term basis.

A patient with aortic valve replacement reduced his very heavy alcohol consumption and was able to stop taking tranquillisers.

A husband and wife who had been on the verge of a marital breakdown established much better communications and the marriage has continued.

A female patient who had been taking tranquillisers for many years for free-floating anxiety has completely ceased medications. The husband of this patient also participated in the series and had considerable relief of work-related stress and of dyspepsia.

A young housewife had problems of hostility towards her difficult four year old child. She had been raped just before the pregnancy and had many unresolved problems. She had rapid relief of anxiety following therapy. She reported that the behaviour of the child had improved, presumably due to the lowered level of maternal anxiety and irritability.

The results of the two series have been presented compositely. Although an attempt was made in the second series to obtain better selection of patients, the results were substantially the same. Some patients who initially seemed unlikely to benefit had good results.

SUMMARY

What has been called 'group meditation therapy' appears to have a place in the management of anxiety. For those who are able to produce the state, it has the advantage that the patient controls his own treatment.

For some subjects at least there are meaningful subjective experiences which are not found in other relaxation methods.

It is necessary to have other strategies (other relaxation methods, autogenic training, hypnosis, etc.) for the significant numbers of patients who are unable to benefit from this particular approach.

REFERENCES

1. Anand, B.K., Chhina, G.S. and Singh, Baldev. (1961) *Ind. Jour. Med. Res.*, 49, 1.

2. Benson, H., Marzetta, R.M., Rosner, B.A. and Klemchuk, H.M. (1974) *Lancet* i, 289-291.

3. Carrington, P. and Ephron, H.S. (1975) Clinical Use of Meditation. Grune and Stratton, New York, pp. 101-108.

4. Elson, Barry D., Hauri, Peter and Kunis, David. (1977) *Psychophysiology* 14, 52-57.

5. Silverman, Julian. (1968) *Brit. J. Psychiat.* 114, 1201-1218.

HYPNOSIS - A DIAGNOSTIC TOOL IN EPILEPSY

Meir Gross, M.D.
Head, Section of Child and Adolescent Psychiatry

CLEVELAND CLINIC FOUNDATION
9500 Euclid Avenue
Cleveland, Ohio 44106 U.S.A.

Evaluations of the patient who suffers from seizures presents a problem
for the clinician, if the type of seizure is epileptic, which is purely
an organic disorder, or functional which has its origin in the emotional
condition of the patient. Epilepsy is caused by a lesion in the brain
which in turn causes a breakdown in electrical brain wave activity and leads
to seizures. Functional seizures are called pseudoepilepsy, or hysterical
seizures; they are exclusively psychological and are rooted in severe
emotional problems. They result from an unconscious effort of the victim
to escape long periods of stress, depression or anxiety. Since the results
of only limited studies on hysterical seizures have been reported, there are
physicians who are not fully aware of this disorder and mistake these seizures
as being epileptic. In many patients, misdiagnosis results in a loss of time
and money on ineffective treatment over the years, a wide range of side
effects of anti-epileptic medications, and the social stigma of being labeled
an epileptic.

Hysterical seizures have two components. The first is the change in the
level of awareness of the patient; this situation is similar to a trance. The
patient might not respond to his surroundings and concentrate on himself, a
condition which seems similar to absences of epileptic seizures. This
phenomenon of change in the level of awareness is actually a dissociative
reaction. The second component is the motor activity of the muscles that
might be seen in certain patients, a convulsion of the muscles that might seem
like real epileptic convulsions. This motor activity is a conversion reaction
and it represents a body symptom that might be a symbol of an expression of
an underlying conflict that the patient is suffering. The patient is able to
release his high level of tension and anxiety. The dissociative reaction as
part of the hysterical seizures might not only be seen as absences but also as
amnesia. The patient might get into amnestic episodes in which he functions
differently, and when he comes back he might not remember what he did during
the episode. He may show some personality changes. During the amnestic
period his behavior could be considered strange or untypical, similar to the
temporal lobe automotism in psychomotor epilepsy. At times the presenting

symptoms might resemble a fugue reaction which could be part of the dissociative reaction or of temporal lobe epilepsy.

The conflicts that the hysterical seizures represent could be past traumatic events such as child abuse, sexual abuse, conflicts or problems with parents, boyfriend or girlfriend, and at times even catastrophic traumas such as fire and auto accidents. Electroencephalography (EEG) would not always be helpful in differentiating between the two conditions, since it is rather inconclusive. In other words, patients with real epilepsy might have completely normal EEG's whereas patients who suffer from functional seizures might show some non-specific abnormality in the EEG recording. The EEG is not reliable since the results can be false positive and, or false negative. The clinician can rely upon other clinical symptoms for differentiating between the two conditions, but they are as inconclusive as the EEG. Usually during a seizure a person with epilepsy has temporary loss of consciousness in which he might experience a loss of bowel and bladder control and bite his tongue; the patient with hysterical seizures has none of these signs during an attack. The hysterical patient sometimes looks as though he is losing consciousness, but is completely aware of his surroundings even though he is not responsive. The epileptic patient might have a positive Babinski sign during the seizure whereas the hysterical patient might not. Hypnosis is an additional and effective tool in the diagnostic armamentarium that might help in the differential diagnosis of the above two conditions.

Patients suffering from hysterical seizures are more hypnotizable and can quickly get into hypnotic trance. This is seen most often if the hand levitation test that was described by Spiegel [1] is used. In fact, any ideomotor activity suggested to the hysterical patient will initiate the hypnotic trance. Patients who are prone to get into dissociative reaction might respond to any ideomotor activity by getting into a dissociative state of the hypnotic trance. An important question arises, and it deals with why the hysterical patient will choose dissociative reaction as a symptom. The reason is probably that whenever the patient is faced with any stressful situation he cannot cope with in a rather healthy defense mechanism, he chooses to withdraw from the situation into a different level of awareness. Why is it that certain patients will use this symptom and not any other? The author believes that these patients are prone to get into spontaneous hypnotic trances and also that they have the innate mechanism to get into hypnotic trance very easily. Once they unconsciously realize that they easily shift their level of awareness, they might decide to use this ability to go into trance as a coping mechanism. In other words, the hypnotic trance becomes the coping skill of the patient.

This might be the reason that whenever a situation becomes stressful, the patient uses this pathological coping skill by going into a dissociative state that at times might seem similar to real epilepsy. Patients who might have muscle convulsions might be more sensitive to ideomotor activity and, for this reason, they have both factors of the dissociative reaction and conversion reaction, and their seizures seem similar to grand mal epilepsy.

Some investigators have noted [2,3] that when patients with hysterical seizures are under hypnosis they are able to recall what occured during their most recent seizures, unlike persons with epilepsy; but when aroused from the hypnotic state they might not remember what transpired during the trance and usually claim instead to have had another seizure. Schneck[4] suggested the use of hypnosis for the differential diagnosis of psychomotor epilepsy. He claimed that convulsions could be induced in a patient with organic psychomotor epilepsy under hypnotic trance, and that once the convulsions began the patient could not stop them under suggestion. Convulsions could be induced in the patient with psychogenic epilepsy during hypnotic trance, and they could be stopped at the operator's suggestion.

PRESENTATION OF CASES

CASE 1. A 16 year old white girl was seen in consultation because of passing out spells and convulsions. She was diagnosed as epileptic even though the EEG was normal, and was treated for about 7 months with anticonvulsant medications. Her parents had been divorced about three years previously, but during the past year she had been rejected by her father. When she called him on the phone he refused to talk to her. Her symptoms had begun about 8 months previously. Hand levitation technique was used in which the patient went into spontaneous trance. During the trance she remembered the previous seizures. She was completely amnestic to the trance and did not remember the other seizures as well when she came out of the trance. Anticonvulsant medications were discontinued when the patient was given hypnotherapy about four times a week for 1½ months. She was seen in follow-up thereafter on a monthly basis. She was free of any seizures from the first hypnotic session. Only one seizure recurred 2 months later after she had an argument with her sister. It was pointed out to her that the stress during the argument with her sister might have caused this seizure. No other seizures were observed thereafter during the 1½ year follow up.

CASE 2. A 15 year old white girl was admitted to the Adolescent Psychiatry Unit after consultation was requested by the neurologist. The patient was evaluated for epilepsy. She had been diagnosed as an epileptic earlier and had been treated with anticonvulsant medications with no response. The EEG was normal except for 14 - 6 positive spikes with no evidence for paroxysmal activity. From her history it was clear that this girl was under stress. She had separated from her boyfriend before the onset of her convulsions, and became depressed to the point of having suicidal intentions. Seizures enabled her to regain some of the attention from the boyfriend and more attention from her parents. The hand levitation technique was used. The patient went into hypnotic trance with no direct suggestion to do so. She was able to remember what had transpired during the seizures while under trance. Hypnotherapy was begun, four sessions a week for about five weeks and monthly thereafter. Anticonvulsant medications were discontinued when hypnotherapy started. The seizures stopped after one week of therapy; there was only one episode of seizures that recurred after 2 weeks of therapy, and that occurred after the patient realized that her boyfriend had decided to separate completely and stopped coming to visit her in the hospital. In follow up for about 2 years she was free of any seizures.

CONCLUSION

From these 2 cases it is obvious that the episodes of seizures were dissociative reaction rather than real epilepsy. The patients had the innate mechanisms to shift easily from one level of consciousness to another and resorted to that whenever they had to face stress, anxiety or severe depression. The change in the level of awareness was a coping mechanism that helped to solve the immediate stressful situation, but was pathological in origin. They were able to get into the hypnotic state easily and spontaneously with the use of the hand levitation technique or any ideomotor activity. Hypnosis as an integral part of the psychotherapeutic process was used to help the patients explore and abreact the past traumatic experiences, to resolve conflicts by interpretation of transference reactions and to suggest the ability of the self to control this dissociative episodes. Hypnosis was used to help the patient gain more insight into the underlying unconscious conflict that triggered the dissociative reaction in the first place. Besides getting insight into the dynamics of the underlying conflicts, and the use of suggestion to have complete control over their ability to stay in one level of consciousness, they could also be helped by getting to know the innate

mechanisms of their ability to go easily into trance and by knowing that
they were able to have better control over it. It is possible that because
of their high level of hypnotizability they were choosing the dissociative
mechanisms as the presenting symptom. This was the way to deal with the
underlying unresolved conflict. At the Cleveland Clinic in the Section of
Child Psychiatry, 30 such patients were diagnosed as suffering from
pseudoepilepsy in a period of three years. The degree of hypnotizability
was high in all patients, and all except three were found to have five points
on the Stanford Hypnotic Clinical Scale; these three patients had four points.
It is suggested that any patient who has negative results of the EEG tests
and no clinical evidence for epilepsy, with no response to anticonvulsant
medications should be evaluated by hypnosis. The test should include the
use of any ideomotor activity that is suggested to the patient, and if the
patient will easily go into hypnotic trance with high level of hypnotizability and if he will remember what transpired during previous seizures
while under trance, that could be evidence for dissociative reaction rather
than epilepsy.

REFERENCES

1. Spiegel, H., (1974) Manual for Hypnotic Induction Profile. Soni
   Medica, New York.

2. Schwartz, B.E., et al. (1955) Hypnotic Phenomena, Including Hypnotically
   Activated Seizures, Studied With the Electroencephalogram, J. Nerv.
   Ment. Dis., 122:564:574.

3. Peterson, D.B., et al., (1950) Role of Hypnosis in Differentiation of
   Epileptic From Convulsive-like Seizures. Am. J. Psychiat., 107:428-433.

4. Schneck, J.M. (1963) Hypnosis in Modern Medicine. Charles C. Thomas,
   Springfield.

© 1979 Elsevier/North-Holland Biomedical Press
Hypnosis 1979
G.D. Burrows, D.R. Collison and L. Dennerstein

HYPNOSIS IN THE TREATMENT OF PROLONGED GRIEVANCE OVER A DEATH

G. SCOTT JENNINGS, D. O.

41 Hawthorne Avenue, Medford, Oregon 97501, United States of America

The patient presented with complaints of; "arms aching like an ear ache, nightmares, waking up screaming, no social life, little sense of humor, lack of tolerance, and a lack of ambition." These symptoms occured after a jeep accident three years ago in which her daughter, age 18, fractured her neck and was killed instantly.

The patient felt guilty because she did not want "J" to go with this boy. The boy lied about getting the brakes repaired, which failed and caused the accident.

Her arms ached daily and kept her awake at night. A nurse, at the scene of the accident, would not let her hold "J" as she wanted. She would lie on her arms all night to ease the pain.

The patient had the same dream frequently and would wake up screaming. She sees "J" laying there with dirt in her nostrils, tan face, black hair, and a curl of hair along the side of her ear.

Under hypnosis she age regressed back and viewed the whole accident, and this time I had her hold "J" the way she had wanted to originally. She held her in her imagination, for an actual ten minutes. She felt immediate relief in her arms and most symptoms were relieved after this one visit.

In the death of loved ones I have noticed that people tend to blame themselves for an accident or have difficulty accepting a sudden death. My procedure is to hypnotize the patient and have them age regress back to the time of death and have them hold and hug the deceased for as long as they wish.

© 1979 Elsevier/North-Holland Biomedical Press
Hypnosis 1979
G.D. Burrows, D.R. Collison and L. Dennerstein

HYPNOTHERAPY FOR RAYNAUD'S DISEASE

BENNETT G. BRAUN, M.D., M.S., A.B.M.H.
Associated Mental Health Services, 180 North Michigan Avenue,
Chicago, Illinois 60601 U.S.A.

In 1862 Maurice Raynaud described a syndrome of digital cyanosis, pallor, and coldness, often accompanied by pain. He observed that these symptoms could be precipitated by cold, stress, and other external events and on occasion could lead to small areas of necrosis, gangrene, or even finger loss. He felt that it was due to overactivity of the sympathetic nervous system.

In 1896 Hutchinson differentiated between primary and secondary Raynaud's Disease. The criteria for primary Raynaud's Disease are discussed below. Secondary Raynaud's Disease is often found only after years of observation of a case of primary Raynaud's Disease, when a good diagnosis is made of the underlying disease such as scleroderma, lupus erythematosis, arteriosclerosis, vibration white finger syndrome, nerve lesions, allergies, thoracic outlet syndrome, and drug intoxication (e.g., ergot, methysergide, beta-adrenergic blockers).

Allen and Brown (1932) set forth the following criteria for primary Raynaud's Disease in their article "Raynaud's Disease: Minimal requirements for diagnosis": 1), episodes of Raynaud's phenomenon are precipitated by cold or emotion; 2), phenomenon is bilateral; 3), normal pulses are present; 4) gangrene, if any, is minimal and limited to the finger tips; 5), symptoms cannot be accounted for by any other systemic diseases; 6), symptoms are present for at least two years. Unfortunately, the diagnosis is often made without observing all the criteria. In reviewing 756 cases at the Mayo Clinic, Gifford and Hines (1957) found these criteria met in only 53 per cent of the cases diagnosed as Raynaud's Disease.

Lewis (1929, 1949) thought that local factors such as spasm, hypertrophy, and thrombosis of the digital arteries were due to an abnormal sensitivity to stimuli. Mishima (1978) showed that both the central factors of Raynaud and the local factors of Lewis are important in bringing about an attack of Raynaud's phenomenon. He also showed that the season of the year (not necessarily absolute temperature) may be a facilitating factor. Mishima, McGrath, et al. (1978) and Neilsen et al. (1977, 1978) have shown change in digital temperature with decreased room temperature and arteriole occlusion at as high as $23.5^{\circ}C$ to as low as $17^{\circ}C$ in sufferers from Raynaud's phenomenon and no occlusion in controls.

Increased viscosity of the blood has been reported by several authors. Hansen and Faber (1947) thought that the ischemia was due to the precipitation of proteins upon exposure to cold. Patients with cryoglobulinaemia show vascular sludging and occlusion with levels of 5-30 mg/dl (Holbrow, p. 952, 1977). These patients show symptoms of Raynaud's Disease. Marshall and Malone (1954) also found purpura and hemorrhages on retinoscopy and brain autopsy in these patients. Other factors have been implicated. These include cryofibrinogen, increased vasoactive peptides, increased catecholamines, and serotinin. Imhof et al. (1959) found occular erythocyte aggregations using the split lamp and reported that these started 30 seconds after cooling but did not reduce for five minutes after the cessation of cooling. Pringle and Walden (1965) found both an increase in blood viscosity and increase in plasma fibrinogin concentration, but normal packed cells in patients with Raynaud's Disease, as compared to controls. Goyle and Dormandy (1976) confirmed the increased viscosity. Jamieson et al. (1971) and McGrath et al. (1978) did not confirm these results.

Raynaud's Disease is usually diagnosed before the age of forty, but it is rarely seen before puberty. The incidence is almost five times greater in females than in males. This is especially prominent in females who are emotionally labile, however a vasospastic reflex can be elicited by a pinprick, loud noise, or even doing mental mathematics. Most all authors state that though some minor morbidity can occur in Raynaud's phenomenon, no mortalities occur. A recent article by Bulkley et al. (1978) casts serious doubts on this issue. They report on nine cases with progressive systemic sclerosis in which myocardial infarction or sudden cardiac death occured with normal coronary arteries; they all suffered from angina-like symptoms (with ST-T depression) prior to and at the time of death (patient age range, 12-71 years).

There have been many treatments suggested for Raynaud's Disease over the years based on the theoretical perspective of the experimenters. The major categories of approaches are sympathectomy, drug therapy, plasmapheresis, biofeedback, and hypnosis.

Sympathectomy for Raynaud's Disease has been suggested since 1925. At first the results were quite promising, but it now appears that they are short lived. Johnson (1965) reports over one half of his cases regressed. Dale (1978) questions its use except as a last resort. It appears to be more effective in secondary Raynaud's Disease than in primary.

Medical approaches to Raynaud's phenomenon must be divided into two areas, symptomatic relief and pharmacological approaches. Patients are often told to dress warmer and to wear gloves even inside and especially while handling ice trays, etc. They are also told to move to warmer climates. These ideas are not always practical or possible. The drugs that have been used include reserpine (orally and intra-arterially) which seems to be of short term benefit by depleting the catecholamine supplies. However, the Boston Collaborative Drug

Surveillance Program reported an increased incidence of breast cancer among hypertensive women taking reserpine. Guanthidine suppresses alpha and beta andrenergic receptors. Alpha-methyldopa interferes with the formation of dopamine, a precursor of norepinephrine and inhibits serotonin formation. General vasodilators have been tried without significant positive results. They may even have the potential for having a reverse effect because they dilate all vessels and the greater resistance in the fingers may cause the blood to pool elsewhere. Even pit-vipor venom (ancrod) is being tried to lower the blood viscosity. Another new way of lowering viscosity was reported by Talpos et al. (1977, 1978) who are doing plasmaphoresis for severe Raynaud's Disease.

Biofeedback has been used for Raynaud's Disesase since 1973. Surwitt, Jacobson et al. compiled five cases with positive results. Surwitt et al. (1976 a&b) reported more positive results. Greenspan (1978) reviews the area of biofeedback in cardiovascular disease and presents a theoretical concept for its use.

Hypnosis was compared with relaxation and suggestion in the control of skin temperature by Maslach et al. (1972), and they found no significance between the groups but did document an increase in skin temperature. Hypnosis was tried for Raynaud's Disease in 1973 by Jacobson et al. but was ultimately combined with biofeedback. Hilgard (1975) in his book on hypnosis and pain control showed that an ice water bath could be better tolerated with hypnosis.

CASE STUDIES

This paper reports on three cases of Raynaud's Disease which met the criteria of Allen and Brown and were successfully treated with hypnotherapy. The treatment methods for all three cases were similar and will be discussed in conjunction with Case 3 which was the most complicated. Cases 1 and 2 were treated during the cold months, and contact was lost after approximately one and two years of follow-up, respectively. Suggestions for stopping smoking as a part of the treatment were unsuccessful in all cases, probably because they did not come in wanting this.

Case 1. A 27-year old single Caucasian female had experienced a four year history of Raynaud's phenomenon with normal pulses. No evidence of local damage was observed, and her physician could find no underying reason for the problem. She was self-referred for hypnotherapy. No significant psychopathology was found. Therapy lasted for 12 sessions and incorporated autohypnosis with heterohypnosis, using ice water challenges. Attacks gradually became shorter in duration and farther apart. At follow-up the next winter she had to be encouraged to practice more regularly, as she was experiencing occasional short periods of pain which were completely absent at termination of therapy. These soon ceased, though she did get occasional short bouts of digital cyanosis which were easily controlled with hypnosis.

Case 2. A 28-year old divorced Caucasion female reported a three year history of bilateral Raynaud's phenomenon. She also had normal pulses bilaterally and no local damage. Communication with her physician was not possible. She was referred for hypnotherapy by a friend who was in hypnotherapy with me. In this case it turned out that the hypnotherapy was an entree to psychotherapy, as she was depressed since her divorce three years earlier (the time of the onset of Raynaud's Disease). She reported that she experienced very cold hands and feet since the age of 16. Auto- and heterohypnotherapy were used in conjunction with psychotherapy for the divorce issues to produce a successful result. On two year follow-up the patient had continued to use autohypnosis and was symptom free. She had changed jobs and moved to Seattle, Washington.

Case 3. A 34-year old married Latin female presented an eight year history of bilateral Raynaud's phenomenon. She experienced cyanosis, pallor, pain, and rebound rubor. She lived in Wisconsin and had fairly extreme problems during the winter but also suffered in the summertime. She would have to wear gloves to handle things taken from the refrigerator or freezer; even holding a drink at a summer picnic could precipitate an attack. The attacks could last for three to five hours or might subside in one hour, only to return in half an hour and last all day. She denied any problem in swallowing. Physical examination revealed a thin woman with shiny skin on all finger tips, and, except for her thumbs, several had scars from old necrotic areas. The rest of the examination was within normal limits, including neurological examination. The laboratory findings were within normal limits, including sedrate and Rf factor. She did have a cryoglobulinaemia of 6.3 mg/dl. X-ray was within normal limits. The patient came in during the summer months, and a good result was obtained in eight weekly sessions at which time she was able to keep her right hand in crushed ice for 14½ minutes and her left for 16 minutes without pain. There was an appropriate reactive rubor after this challenge. On follow-up during the winter she was reporting some trouble when outside and was seen for three more sessions. On four year follow-up she reported that she still had occasional attacks with pain while living in Wisconsin, but with autohypnosis she could alleviate them in a few minutes. She stopped practicing when she moved to Texas and is only rarely bothered now.

THERAPY

After the first session during which the problem was discussed and an evaluation of the patient's psychological and physical status were made, a discussion of hypnosis and its values in altering bodily physiology ensued, ending with the first heterohypnotic experience. A progressive relaxation tape, which the patient was instructed to play and memorize, was made in the second session. She was instructed to use the tape four times a day for 10 minutes with each practice session separated by at least one hour to allow for some tension to build up.

During the third session the patient was asked to do the autohypnotic technique out loud so I could hear and help her improve and shorten her patter. She was also trained in a technique of scaling, from zero to ten, her depth of relaxation. She was told to use the tape only one time a day and to shorten the technique in certain ways, provided she could still get to at least the same depth of relaxation she had previously attained. She was also taught to visualize her hands under a sun lamp and feel the warmth or to feel them in a bucket of warm water. She was to add these suggestions to her practice session. Warmth was chosen because it comes automatically with relaxation, thus increasing chances for mastery.

She entered the fourth session with cyanotic fingers bilaterally. She responded to warming with the left hand, and this was then used in the next series of suggestions which were ultimately successful bilaterally. She was taught to imagine that she was at a beach and was lying so that one hand would be in the warm sand with the sun beating down on it and the other hand would be in the cool water or imagining her one hand in a bucket of warm water and the other in cold water. This was done to obtain a differential in the hands to allow the patient to reinforce the learning. I would touch her hands and would give encouragement. When I felt the slightest difference I asked her to touch them together and feel the difference, further reinforcing her behavior. At this time if I felt the patient was ready I introduced the crushed ice and timed her tolerance (10 seconds) to pain. This was then repeated after suggestions of bilateral warmth. Since the patient was a radiology technician, she knew the meaning of vasodilation and that an increased speed and volume of circulating bloods yields warmth. This suggestion seemed to work the best, as she could picture the vessels and their getting larger.

The rest of the weekly sessions proceeded similarly, with changing, improving, and heightening of the suggestions and control, yielding a gradually increased tolerance for crushed ice until the eighth session (which was two weeks after the seventh) to check for retention of the skill without the hetero-hypnotic support. The patient could withstand 14½ minutes on the right hand and 16 minutes on the left with pain. She was terminated from therapy with instructions to continue to practice at least two to three times a day and once a week to challenge herself with ice to be sure she maintained the ability and to report her status in the late fall or early winter. If she had any troubles she was to call for an appointment.

In November she called and reported that she was having occasional bouts of Raynaud's phenomenon with pain when she would go outside. She was seen for three more sessions. During this time I suspected she was having reflexive digital vasospasm from cooling of the face. Reflexive vasospasm has been reported by Jamieson et al. (1971) and McGrath et al. (1978). I challenged with ice to her hands first, but she could bring warmth to them, and they did not turn blue. However, when ice was applied to her cheeks and forehead for one minutes she responded with digital cyanosis. She was instructed to warm her hands using autohypnosis. After completing this I suggested that she was wearing an imaginary ski mask which would keep her nice and warm when cold was applied to her face. This time when she did not respond to the ice challenge when applied to either face or hands or both, the imagery and challenge were increased in small steps. This was continued in the second session, and again two weeks were allowed between the second and third sessions. Therapy was terminated after the third session, during which a suggestion was given that the mask would automatically be donned as she opened any exterior door during cool times. She continued practicing two times daily and reported no further bouts of pain and was the same as she was after the previous series of therapy sessions.

DISCUSSION

The hypnotic approach was tailored to the patient's needs and experiences, always keeping in mind the psychology and physiology. Techniques from learning theory reinforcement and knowledge of results were combined with biofeedback, using the therapist as the instrumentation.

The relaxation and imagery were built to counteract the assumed pathophysiologic process by: 1) relaxing autonomic and vascular tone; 2) increasing vessel diameter to allow for more blood to move faster through the hands and return to the body for warming. This would decrease any sludging because the rapid return to the body would redisolve any cryoprecipitates that might form, and the larger vessels would be less likely to be occluded by any precipitate aggregation that might form, thus avoiding the ischemic pain. This also brought more warmth to the hands and increased the protection.

The reflexive digital vasospasm was seen only in one case, and luckily the first image tried was successful in protecting her. The automatic donning of the ski mask was suggested using heterohypnosis with the hope that even should she stop practicing this suggestion would hold and protect her when she opened the door, even to let someone in.

CONCLUSION

The technique discussed might even be improved upon by the use of actual bio-feedback equipment, though this experience shows that hypnosis can be called the "poor man's" biofeedback, because for some people all the expensive equipment is not needed. However, Western society is geared to external instrumentation, and many people need to experience actual dials, lights, sounds, etc., to believe that they can get results. It is unfortunate that the major review article on Raynaud's Disease (Coffman and Davies, 1977) doesn't mention either of these approaches. Hypnosis appears to be of value in selected cases of primary Raynaud's Disease (all patients were good hypnotic subjects). Biofeedback appears to be useful. Also, it is recommended that these approaches be tried before more drastic measures are taken, including medication with its side effects and especially surgery.

SUMMARY

A review of the history, diagnosis, theory, and therapy of Raynaud's Disease was elaborated. Three cases of primary Raynaud's Disease that were successfully treated with hypnotherapy were presented, and the method of treatment was discussed in some detail, keeping in mind psychology and pathophysiology.

BIBLIOGRAPHY

Acevedo, A., et al., "Effect of intra-arterial reserpine in patients suffering from Raynaud's phenomenon", J. Cardiovasc. Surg., 19:77, 1978

Adair, J. R., and Theobald, D. E., "Raynaud's phenomenon: treatment of a severe case with biofeedback", J. Ind. State Med. Assn., 71:990, 1978

Allen, E. V., and Brown, G. E., "Raynaud's Disease: a critical review of minimal requirements for diagnosis", Am. J. Med. Sci., 183:187, 1932

Arnot, R. S., et al., "Pathophysiology of capillary circulation: Raynaud's Disease", Angiology, 29:48, 1978

Boston Collaborative Drug Surveillance Program, "Reserpine and breast cancer" Lancet, 2:669, 1974

Bulkley, B. H., et al., "Angina pectoris, myocardial infarction, and sudden cardiac death with normal coronary arteries: a clinicopathologic study of nine patients with progressive systemic sclerosis", Am. Heart J., 95:563, 1978

Chamberlin, J., and Macpherson, A., "Cervico-dorsal sympathectomy for Raynaud's Syndrome", J. R. Coll. Surg., Edinburgh, 19:228, 1974

Coffman, J. D., and Davies, W. T., "Vasospastic diseases: a revew", Prog. Cardiovasc. D., 18:123, 1975

Dale, W. A., "Differential management of Raynaud's syndrome based on angiograms", Conn. Med., 42:447, 1978

Eastcott, H., "Dead fingers", The Practicioner, 218:662, 1977

148

Goyle, K. B., and Dormandy, J. A., "Abnormal blood viscosity in Raynaud's phenomenon", Lancet, 1:1317, 1976

Greenspan, K., "Biologic feedback and cardiovascular diseases", Psychosomatics, 19:725, 1978

Hansen, P. F., and Faber, M., "Raynaud's syndrome orginating from reversable precipitation of protein", Acta Med. Scand., 129:81, 1947

Hilgard, E. R., and Hilgard, J. R., Hypnosis in the Relief of Pain, LosAltos, Cal., Wm. Kaufman, Inc., 1975

Holborow, E. J., and Reeves, W. G., Immunology in Medicine, London, Academic Press, 1977

Imhof, J. W., et al., "Clinical and haematologic aspects of macroglobulinaemia Walden-strom", Act. Med. Scan., 163:349, 1959

Jacobson, A. M., et al., "Raynaud's phenomenon: treatment with hypnotic and operant techniques", J. AMA, 225:739, 1973

Jahnsen, T., et al., "Blood viscosity and local response to cold in primary Raynaud's phenomenon", Lancet, 2:1001, 1977

Jamieson, G. G, et al., "Cold hypersensitivity in Raynaud's phenomenon", Circulation, 44:254, 1971

Jarrett, Peter, et al., "Treatment of Raynaud's phenomenon by fibronolytic enhancement", Brit. Med. J., 2:525, 1978

Lewis, T., "Experiments relating to the peripheral mechanisms involved in the spasmodic arrest of circulation in the fingers, a variety of Raynaud's Disease", Heart, 15:7, 1929

Lewis T., Vascular Disorders of the Limbs, (2nd ed.), London, Macmillan, 1949

Marshall, R. J., and Malone, R. G. S., "Cryoglobulinaemia with cerebral purpura", Brit. Med. J., 2:279, 1954

McGrath, M. A., et al., "Raynaud's Disease: reduced hand blood flows with normal blood viscosity", Aust. N. Z. J. Med., 19:521, 1978

Mishima, Y., "Pathophysiology of Raynaud's phenomenon", J. Cardiovasc. Surg., 12:105, 1978

Nielsen, S. L., and Lassen, N. A., "Measurement of digital blood pressure after cooling", J. Appl. Physiol., 43:907, 1977

Nielsen, S. L., et al., "Raynaud's phenomenon in arterial obstructive disease of the hand demonstrated by locally provoked cooling", Scand. J. Thor. Cardiovasc. Surg., 12:105, 1978

Peters, J. E., and Sterne, R. M., "Peripheral skin temperature and vasomotor responses during hypnotic induction", Internat. J. Clin. Exp. Hyp., 21"102, 1973

Pringle, R., and Walden, D. N., "Blood viscosity and Raynaud's Disease", Lancet, 1:1086, 1965

Raynaud, M., "De l'asphyxic locale et de la gangrene symetrique des extremites", Paris, Rigoux, 6, 1962

Raynaud, M. "New research on the nature and treatment of local asphyxia of the extremities", (T. Barbour, trans.) (selected monographs), London, New Sydenham Soc., 1888

Surwitt, R. S., "Biofeedback: a possible treatment for Raynaud's Disease", Seminars in Psychiat, 5:483, 1973

Surwitt, R. S., et al., "Digital temperature autoregulation and associated cardiovascular changes", Psychophsyiol., 13:242, 1976

Talpos, G., et al., "Plasmaphresis in Raynaud's Disease", Lancet, 1:416, 1977

Talpos, G., et al., ibid., 1:672, 1977

(unsigned editorial) "Episodic digital vasospasms: the legacy of Maurice Raynaud", Lancet, 1:1039, 1977

© 1979 Elsevier/North-Holland Biomedical Press
Hypnosis 1979
G.D. Burrows, D.R. Collison and L. Dennerstein

L'ABBE DE FARIA: HIS LIFE AND CONTRIBUTION.

SHRIDHAR SHARMA

Professor and Head, Department of Psychiatry and Human Behavior,
Goa Medical College, Panaji-Goa. 403 001. INDIA.

The history of hypnosis is a fascinating subject; a tale of a
search for truth and a chase to grasp the illusive. It is a nar-
ration of progress which, according to William Osler "is a series
of negations, the denial today of what was accepted yesterday, the
contradiction by each generation of some part at least of the philosophy of the last; but all is not lost; ther germ plasma remains
a nucleus of truth to be fertilized by man, often ignorant even of
the body from which it has come. Knowledge evolves but in such a
way that its possessors are never in sure possession". Kutumbiah
(1969).

The present knowledge about this ancient art of hypnosis is still clouded in the mist of misconception, prejudices and neglect,
especially in its understanding. Traditionally the history of
hypnosis begins with Franz Mesmer (1734-1815) a Viennese Physician
who in 1779 propounded the theory of animal magnetism. He is most
popularly considered "The Father of Modern Hypnosis" Mesmer believed hypnosis to be a form of magnetism which flowed from the hypnotist to the patient; a force analogous to physical magnetism.
Unfortunately, he fell into disfavour in 1784, after an adverse
report from a Commission of the French Academy consisting of
Benjamin Franklin, Then the American Ambassador to France, Dr.
Guillotine, the inventor of the merciful machine of execution and
the Chemist, Lavoisier. These facts are well documented.

Regretably, the contribution of various philosophers and thinkers from the East is not well recorded. Hypnotic suggestion has
been practised for centuries in Hindu temples where it is used to
cure mental illnesses or as part of a penance. For example it
allows devotees to lay on beds of nails or walk barefooted over
glowing coals. Some of these scenes can be witnessed in temples
even today.

Much before, James Braid (1785-1860) who first coined the word
'hypnosis' and James Esdaile, a British Surgeon who practised in

Calcutta, India and operated from 1840-1849 with hypnoanaesthesia, a priest named Abbe de Faria, from Goa, India, arrived in Paris. It was in 1788, four years after the departure from there of Mesmer but mesmerism was still very fashionable.

The object of this paper is limited to explain the contribution of Faria in the field of hypnosis and to unfold his purposeful life and achievement.

LIFE

Jose Custodio de Faria, the future celebrated Abbe Faria, was born at Candolim, a village of Bardez, Goa, on 31st May 1756.

His father, Caetano Victorino de Faria, was a native of the village of Colvale, Bardez, and he was a descendant of Antu Sinai (Ananta Sinai) a Saraswat Brahmin by caste, and Patil (a powerful official) of the same village at the time of his conversion to Christianity at the end of 16th century.

Faria's noble birth is not only confirmed by his Brahmin (priest class) origin from an illustrious Hindu family but also by the fact that his family was the recipient of a rare privilege at the time, having a private chapel in his home, a privilege which was granted only to distinguished and noble families.

It may be interesting to add here that Goa is one of the ancient gateways of India and through its open and hospitable portals have passed many a prince and a potentate, merchant and mendicant, saint and soldier. The interplay of cultures brought to Goa from Hindu culture in the East and from across the Arabian Sea in the West has left an indelible impress on the various aspect of Goa. (Government of Goa, 1970).

Even at this stage, one can witness a unique mixture of East and West in this territory. When Goa passed into the hands of Portuguese in 1510, the propagation of the Christian religion was one of their main objects and the Portuguese made great efforts to convert natives and high class Hindus alike on a massive scale. However the powerful Hindu background of these converts allowed them to maintain their social distance and many of their social customs despite their conversion.

It was a part of this cultural background which prompted many of the Hindu priests, later to become Catholic priests on thier conversion. The pursuit of knowledge was the main mission of such

Brahmins and as a part of this mission, Faria sailed on 21st February 1771, from Goa in the ship, S. Jose and arrived at Lisbon on 23rd November 1771.

In 1772, Faria went to Rome via Genova with letters of recommendation from the Papal Nuncio to various personalities of Rome.

Jose Custodio Faria continued his studies in Rome as an Internee in the College of "Propaganda Fíde" upto 1780, when he took the degree of doctor in Theology on a profound subject, "about God's existence:- about one God and Divine Revelation". He was later ordained on 12th March 1780.

After completion of his studies, Abbe Faria returned to Lisbon where he was received in the court. The fact that his father was a priest and his mother a nun caused a certain interest, mainly in the eyes of the aristocratic public of Lisbon. Astute Faria soon realised that there was no chance for his advancement in an ecclesiastical career, in Portugal. He decided to seek elsewhere an appropriate field for his intellectual activity, aspiring to gain a certain "celebrity in arts or in the sciences", to fulfill his ambitions, he left for Paris in the Spring of 1788.

The first trace to be found of his presence in Paris is curiously recorded in the "Register of Denunciation" (1792) of the section of Ponceau. This register was better known after 1793, as of "the friends of the motherland" in the National Archives. He took an active part in the French Revolution.

One is interested to know how Abbe Faria became involved in mesmerism. There is a positive suggestion that he brought the basic knowledge and skill from India. As a philosopher by temperament and by studies and gifted with a spirit of fine observation and with a passion for all the novelties, and with the touch of mysticism, he was greatly attracted by this mystic science of mesmerism As such, it is not difficult to imagine, that Faria's attention was immediately attracted by this new phenomenon and that he dedicated himself to the studies of the magnetism. (Delgado 1906).

It is not easy to fix the date at which he began his public demonstrations of magnetism. The first time, that one sees the references to Faria, as a "magnetiseur" is in the "Memoir of Chateaubriand" published after the latter's death in 1843. The passage which refers to Faria was probably written in 1802 as it deals with the events which took place in that year. (Chateaubriand 1843)

Faria continued his experiments and practice in Paris upto the year 1811, when he went to Marseille as a Professor of Philosophy in the academy "Lyceum" of that city. During his stay there he was elected member of the medical society of Marseille, it was a distinct honour that a priest should be elected to a Medical Society.

From Marseille, Faria went to the Academy of Nimes as a Professor of Philosophy in 1812. He was discontended with his new position which was inferior to the one he held at Marseilles and returned to Paris in 1813.

After his return to Paris he decided to open a public course on hypnosis. With the permission from the Prefect of Police, he started on August eleventh, 1813 to conduct courses every thursday at no. 49, Clichy street. The price of entrance was five francs for each meeting. These courses attracted the best society of the city.

These public demonstrations on hypnotism, first of its kind during those days, not only made a history but also made them a subject matter of criticism. In this mixed atmosphere of praise and criticism, he continued his conference for few years.

It was during the publication of the first volume of his work that he succumbed to an attack of apoplexy, on September 20th, 1819 at the age of 63 years. He was buried in the cemetery of montmarte which was the burial place of the Parish of Saint Roche since 1798.

CONTRIBUTION

His work: "De la cause du Sommeil lucide" was divided into four volumes, out of which only one was published after his death.

I believe, (Sharma 1974) Faria brought the basic nucleus of his knowledge in the field from India and this was further nurtured by his philosophical temperament and astute observational ability. As such it is not difficult to comprehend that Faria's attention was attracted by this mystic phenomenon of mesmerism. He is the founder of the modern doctrine of suggestion. According to Professor Bernheim "Abbe Faria's doctrine is true and his approach is an outstanding development". (Delgado 1906). To evaluate his co-

ntributions, it is essential to compare his ideas with those of
his contemporaries. His contribution can be examined under the
following headings:-

1. The nature of lucid sleep.
2. Explanation on the cause of hypnosis (lucid sleep).
3. The procedure to provoke lucid sleep.
4. The theory to explain the phenomenon.

1. The nature of lucid sleep:

Faria believed that what he called lucid sleep was a pathological aberation of natural sleep. It is interesting, when so little
was known about the nature of sleep that he believed in different
degrees of sleep, and that lucidity is always proportional in its
intensity to the deepness. He divided sleep into light sleep and
deep sleep or somnabulism, He thought that the light sleep has
four stages and the deep sleep two. The latter differentiation
depending upon the degree of amnesia.

He introduced the further highly original idea that hypnotic
states may be "neurosis provoked". In other words, he drew attention to the relationship between hypnosis and hysteria.

During hypnosis he observed some common symptoms like transpir-
ation, palpitation, crisis of laughter or fit, tears, especially
among women, vomiting and headaches etc, which could be provoked
during lucid sleep. These observations were unique in his time.

2. Cause of Hypnosis (Lucid Sleep).

According to mesmer, whose views were prevalent in Paris at tha-
t time, animal magnetism was analogous with physical magnetism in
that certain bodies influenced the individual i.e. that this force
originated from physical objects and not in the mind of the subject. Many of the contemporaries of mesmer believed in this theory
and the minority of spiritualists like Barbarin and his disciples
considered animal magnetism to be a manifestation of the power of
the soul on matter.

In such an atmosphere, charged with emotion, Faria had the courage to contradict his contemporaries and refute their views by
saying "I can't conceive that all the human species were so foolish as to go in search of the cause of this phenomenon in a tub or
tree. Referring to mesmer's conviction that a particular tub or

tree was a potent source of "animal magnetism".

He also contradicted those who attributed the phenomenon of magnetism to 'imagination'. He explained 'imagination' as a common faculty of every man and asked why every man is not fit to develop the phenomenon of mesmerism. According to Faria the immediate cause of 'lucid sleep' lies on the 'concentration' and not imagination of hypnotised persons. He believed, one could be hypnotised by suggestion, however mental peace and calmness are prerequisites and further stressed that one cannot be put to sleep as long as the mind is occupied either by the agitation of blood or by worries, and troubles. He also explained that suggestion alone could not explain the whole phenomenon. According to him 'lucid sleep' is an "abstraction of senses provoked" according to the wish, with the restriction of freedom but with the reason of a motive given by an external influence - the suggestion.

After having examined all the arguments of Mesmer and his disciples he concluded his volume with these words "I think it is already clear that the supposition of magnetic fluid is completely absurd whether you consider its nature, whether you consider its application and finally whether you consider its results". (Delgado 1906).

According to Faria the hypnotiser is of no importance. It is the hypnotized person who is the active agent.

3. Procedure.

Mesmer magnetised his patients either directly by movements or indirectly by his tub, his magic wands or by a tree which he had magnetised in the suburbs of san Martin. The basis of his system was basically physical and consisted in the communication of the magnetic fluid to other persons. He was a magnetiseur who dispensed the fluid in the same manner as the pharmacist dispensed the medicines.

Faria denied not only magnetic fluid, a remarkable departure from the theory of mesmer but also showed the absurdity of other magnetic objects in the following demonstration. To quote Dalgado (1906) "A certain number of people were placed near the tree of Mesmer and Puysegur unknown to them but nothing happened. The same people were placed near another tree and were convinced that that tree was magnetised without it actually being so; it was observed that many fell into deep sleep". By this simple experiment he demonstrated that the supposition of magnetic fluid suggested by mesmer was absurd, whether one considers its nature, its application or its results". On the contrary Faria employed three broad processes to induce lucid sleep.

A) First Method:

His first method is completely different from the techniques of his contemporaries. After having chosen subjects who had the necessary disposition, he placed them on a bench and told them to close their eyes, to concentrate their attention and to think of sleep. When they were calm and waiting for an order Faria would exclaim, in a loud voice, "DORMEZ" (Sleep) and the person would fall into lucid sleep. If the first trial failed, he submitted the subject to a second one or sometimes to a third trial. This procedure is entirely suggestive and psychic. In order to stop the lucid sleep or dehypnotise a person Faria also used verbal suggestions like 'Get up'.

B) Second Method:

When his patients resisted his first procedure Faria used another technique. In this method Faria used to ask the person to fix his gaze on his (Faria's) hand. From a distance he would slowly approach until his hand was close to the eyes of the person, who would thereupon fall into lucid sleep. In this procedure the psychic element is connected with the sensorial. The main point is to fix gaze and to concentrate on one particular point. While describing this technique in his book Faria said "he did not know the procedure used by his ancestors" in India but this statement of his clearly shows he was aware that hypnosis was a traditional technique in India.

C) Third Method:

If these two preceding procedures did not produce any results, Faria used to touch the patients' forehead, the bridge of the nose the chest upto epigastrium, the knees and the feet. He believed that a slight pressure on any of these parts would provoke sufficient concentration to allow lucid sleep to be induced.

From these observations it is clear that Faria rejected the magnetic field theory. For him all these procedures worked by suggestion.

4. Theory.

According to Faria a man is composed of two substances - material and spiritual. The latter in the free state enjoys complete intuition i.e. it unveils the present past and future. It knows all the truth but when it unites to the body it only knows the truth by the senses of body and so its knowledge is limited.

When a person enters a lucid sleep the soul (the psyche) separates - 'in degrees' from the body and enjoys mixed intuition that is to say, ideas or memory can be real or false, and it can also unveil, in very rare cases, past, or future, but there are always subjective elements. According to Faria, in a lucid sleep man is in an intermediate state.

In the present scientific age not, all of Faria's ideas can be accepted but it is evident, that he was first in shifting the idea of hypnosis from external forces to the psychic procedure. He had the courage and conviction to deny the existence of the magnetic fluid by giving an alternative scientific explanation of hypnosis based on the theory of suggestion.

Despite his profession as a priest, his approach was more scientific and his logic more effective in explaining the phenomena of hypnosis, when compared to the views expressed by contemporary workers. Yet history has given him scant acknowledgement.

REFERENCES

1. Chateaubriand, (1843) Memorias de Alem Tumule, Paris.

2. Dalgado, D.G. (1906) Memoire sur la vie de L'Abbe de Faria, Paris, Henri Jouve, Editeur.

3. Government of Goa, Daman and Diu, publication department, Temples of Goa. (1970).

4. Kutumbiah P. (1969) Ancient Indian Medicine, Orient Longmans, Madras.

5. Sharma, Shridhar. (1974) Abbe de Faria - first to explain hypnotism". Indian Jour. Psychiat. 16, 307-301.

© 1979 Elsevier/North-Holland Biomedical Press
Hypnosis 1979
G.D. Burrows, D.R. Collison and L. Dennerstein

TENSION HEADACHE TREATED WITH HYPNOSIS
Ann M. Damsbo Ph. D.

One hundred and eighty-four patients (89 women and 95 men) were diagnosed as having tension headache and referred from the Neurology Clinic, Naval Regional Medical Center, San Diego, California to the headache clinic established in the department of Psychiatry in the same hospital. Prior to the first of three planned treatment sessions the patients were asked to complete a questionnaire indicating the frequency, duration and intensity of headaches with a brief description of the type of pain and the measures used for control in the past. At each subsequent session and with a mail back follow-up subjects were asked to complete the same questionnaire.

Patients were seen at two week intervals. New patients were put in one group and follow-up patients in another group.

During the first visit emphasis was placed on the organic component of the headache with particular emphasis on the physiology of a tension headache. Patients were reassured that the pain was "real" to them and while possible psychological contributions to the headache were mentioned, indepth discussion was deferred to follow-up, visits.

Typically, the first visit consisted of a discussion of the myths of hypnosis, question and answer period and explaining the nature of hypnosis and discussion of patients' concerns about possible organic etiology. Patients were then taught to go into the hypnotic state and taught to use a modification of the Stein Clenched Fist Technique (Stein 1969:130-135). Patients were asked to remember a time when they felt comfortable and confident, to imagine themselves in a place of their own choosing, and when they had done so, to clasp their dominant fist and relive the comfort and enjoy the place with all their senses. They were given a post-hypnotic suggestion that they could return to this place anytime it was appropriate to do so simply by squeezing the fist as they made themselves comfortable. The only restriction of the imaginary place was that only comfortable thoughts and feelings were permitted there—another place and time was to be designated for dealing with other than comfortable feelings and thoughts. After the comfortable retreat was established, the patients were invited to step out of that place by unclasping the dominant hand and attending to their pain. It was suggested that their pain had a color and that any negative thoughts or emotions were also represented somewhere in the body by the same or a different color. Next they were asked to imagine their body to be transparent so that if they were sitting in a chair opposite themselves they would be able to see the colors representing the pain and negative emotions and watch them melt and flow by an imaginary circulatory system into the non-dominant hand. As the colors collected there the patient could squeeze the non-dominant hand into a tight fist--the tighter they squeezed, the more relaxed and comfortable the rest of the body would become. When all of the colored material (or as much as they wished to rid themselves of at that moment), was visualized in the non-dominant fist they could symbolically drop it on the floor and squeeze the dominant fist and return to their place of comfort, healing, safety and security. It was also suggested that if they squeezed the non-dominant fist long enough and hard enought it would become the most uncomfortable area in the body as they could feel the tension and pain from the ischemia. Upon relaxing the fist they could feel the comfort as the circulation returned to normal.

While squeezing the comfortable dominant fist patients were given suggestions for time distortion so that seconds could seem like minutes or hours and a few minutes could become a miniature vacation.

Patients were then asked to rouse themselves at their own pace. Most patients reported some relief of symptoms at this point, however if one person in the group reported no relief of symptoms, before others reported relief, the group leader noticed that there tended to be fewer successes than when the first reporters indicated they had been successful. Thereafter, an attempt was made to reinforce the successful reports and suggest that some who had not been successful would probably be more successful on the next effort with more practice.

One lady expressed her resentment at this attempt to incorporate a bit of behavior modification by the following comment:

> "I'm not trying to knock the program or anything, but my third and last time I came there you held a mass discussion; only it seemed more like 'lets all embarrass, confuse and irritate those that don't know why they still have headaches after three visits to the program'. Like I said before, I'm not trying to knock this program because it has helped most people. I'm just one of those few that it hasn't."

The second and subsequent sessions were devoted to exploring the psychodynamics of the headache in a group therapy process. Ideomotor questioning techniques as described by Cheek and LeCron (1968:93-105) were used to uncover possible psychological etiology of headaches. Hypnosis was employed to effect physiological changes including change of blood pressure, hand temperature, suggestions for utilizing body chemicals such as endorphins (Goldstein 1978:33-34) and attaining the optimum balance of such emotionally stimulated body chemicals as adrenalin. There was also discussion of the life stresses of which the individuals in the group were consciously aware.

Patients who did not benefit from this treatment were referred to appropriate group therapy and/or for further medical work-up. Even though the precaution had been invoked to utilize only patients who had been diagnosed as having tension headaches by a neurologist, the assumption was kept in mind that there might also be an underlying organic etiology. Two cases evidenced this--one with a self-report of low blood sugar and one whose internist indicated the patient's headache was a complication of Premarin therapy.

To utilize ideomotor techniques, the concept of the "Hidden Observer" as described by Hilgard and Hilgard (1975:166-169) was employed. The Hilgards described the hidden observer after an experiment with hypnotic deafness proved that some part of the individual could hear through at the conscious level the subject was unable to hear. This led to later experiments with automatic writing, which indicated that at a deep level, an individual was able to experience stimuli not availalbe to the conscious level. Viktor Frankl (1975:31-32) in talking about the spiritual unconscious, states ". . . that which has to decide whether something is to be conscious or unconscious is itself unconscious." He refers to this aspect of the personality as a guard which awakens the sleeping mother when the breathing of her child becomes irregular even though it permits her to sleep through loud noises." Frankl further states that only in deeper states of narcosis is this guard itself put to sleep. The author had one case which suggests that even then this guard may be on duty. A patient was left for dead with skull fractures after being attacked in her barracks following a party. She later described herself as "stoned" on marijuana. Upon recovery some weeks later she was able, in deep hypnosis, to recall events that had taken place after she had been rendered unconscious by blows to the head severe enough to fracture the skull.

Cheek and LeCron (1968:84-85) describe the use of automatic writing and ideomotor movements (finger signals and Chevral pendulum) as methods of communicating with the unconscious or hidden observer. Through the use of the indicators and the concept of the hidden observer, it is possible to communicate with the subconscious mind and learn more about the underlying causes of psychosomatic illness. They describe seven keys: conflict, motivation, identification, masochism, imprints, organ language and past experience which account for much of psychosomatic illness.

Patients with psychosomatic problems seem to be much more receptive to investigation of the psychological aspect of the problem if the therapist first assures the patient that he believes in the somatic aspect. Patients often equate "psychosomatic" with "psychogenic". When the word "psychosomatic" was used it was carefully defined as the effect of both organic and psychological input to a symptom and the patient reminded that one cannot exist without the other. Often a patient after receiving hypnotherapy for a psychosomatic condition with relief of symptoms will ascribe his cure to physical therapy or environmental changes, since in our culture it is more acceptable to admit to a physical or environmental cause for a problem than to admit to a psychological cause. In the author's opinion, if the cure is actually a cure and not a flight into health or a symptom substitution, it is quite satisfactory and even desirable to permit the patient to save face in this manner.

The patient can work out the underlying etiology in the hypnotic state using the Clenched Fist Technique (Stein 1969:130-135). After subconscious recognitition of the underlying dynamics of the illness, perhaps accompanied by an abreaction, the patient is advised to put the painful material symbolically in the non-dominant hand or toes and drop it on the floor. Subsequently he clenches the dominant hand to neutralize the unpleasant experience and re-experience the feelings of confidence and strength. A positive suggestion for amnesia is offered with the arousal suggestion to "remember what you need to remember, the rest will come to you a little at a time as you are ready for it . . "

RESULTS:

Of the 184 subjects 52 came only one time and supplied no follow-up data for comparison. The remaining 132 subjects are grouped in the accompanying table.

TABLE OF REPORTING SUBJECTS

Category	N	Total Subjects (%)	Reporting (%)
I	41	22.3	31.1
II	48	26.0	36.4
III	23	12.5	17.4
IV	20	10.9	15.1
Not reporting	52	28.3	
Total	184	100.0	100.0

I Report total or marked improvement

II Report improvement

III Uninterpretable or ambiguous responses

IV No change or worsening

Of the twenty people (12 men and 8 women) who reported no relief or worsening of symptoms only six returned the final questionaire and all six of these reported that they were not attempting to use hypnosis for relief of symptoms. Five of the people who weren't helped by the group therapy felt that they could have benefitted from individual therapy. Even though three people in this group stated that it wasn't helping them, they requested and received at least two series of treatments with six or more total visits. Seven of the twelve active duty people in this group expressed strong dissatisfaction with the Navy. Typical comments from the four categories follow:

Category I: "No headaches since first visit. Hypnosis completely effective." "Since I attended the group I have had only one headache and hypnosis relieved it." "My headaches seem to be completely gone." "I learned how to relax my neck muscles and clench my left fist instead." "I still have the short piercing pains occasionally, lasting only seconds and not in the same place, but nothing like before." "Hypnosis works on less severe headaches." "By concentrating on an object I can allow my entire body to relax. Using this I 'let' the tension flow until it is dispelled from my body." "I use displacement (Stein clenched fist)."

Category II "Should use hypnosis more." "I cannot make the self-hypnosis work. Main benefit from sessions seems to be education of causes and muscles affected." "It (hypnosis) helps to relax and concentrate on other things. In other words it helps you take your mind off your headache." "It helped at first, but I have forgotten how to do it and have not been able to keep my other appointments." "It would help more to have individual sessions. I'm too shy to work in a group." "It would be more helpful if you had night sessions." "It has helped, but not enough." "Hypnosis doesn't help but relaxing on the carpet after lunch does."

Category III "Occasionally I find the pain too severe to concentrate enough to use hypnosis. It helped at first, but not anymore." "Hypnosis helped at first, now can't concentrate enough to get into it." "It helped at first. Nothing helps now--not even medications." "Sometimes it works, sometimes not." "Leaving my job in the pharmacy cured my headaches." "Now that I'm off the submarine I no longer have headaches." "My family problems have resolved and I am looking forward to my vacation. My headaches have stopped." "I have not suffered from the headache since I was at sea. I don't need a cure, but prevention. The prevention should be not going to sea on submarines. The Navy disagrees, therefore I must think positive and keep myself going until I can get #&* out of this #&* outfit and regain my health." "My fiance and I have settled our differences and I no longer have headaches." "Self hypnosis helps only when I'm doing it. The headache comes back immediately." :It helps at the time of the session, but that is it." "The tone of your voice was soothing. It helped to eliminate the tension, but it doesn't always work when I tried the hypnosis at home." "Hypnosis relaxes me but does not help headache." "Been able to deal better with day to day problems." "Headache feels as if a nail has been driven into my head. It moves from right to left temple. I have taken all medications with no relief, when I stopped taking Premarin my headaches stopped." "Weight lifting is more helpful in relieving my tension."

"I was treated for low blood sugar and have had no headaches since."

Category IV: "There has been no change in my headache since using hypnosis. I don't use it anymore." "My headache is worse since the session I attended in self-hypnosis so I did not return."

The mobile nature of the population from which this sample was drawn made it difficult for completion of the series for some patients. The treatment plan was for patients to attend three sessions at two week intervals, however ship's deployments, changes of station and terminations of active duty or eligibility for military care necessitated modification of the program.

Eighty of the 184 patients in this study came for only the first session. Of these 22 reported improvement, six reported no improvement and 52 did not return the mailed questionnaire. Some of these 52 had moved and left no forwarding address and did not receive the questionnaire. Others wished to repeat the series, coming for six or more sessions without reporting any relief of symptoms. Five of the people reporting no improvement wanted more therapy, preferably individual and 22 of the people reporting improvement indicated that they would like more therapy. The possibility that patients were denying improvement in order to continue the therapy had to be entertained. Twenty-one of the people reporting decreased symptoms wanted more therapy. Only two of the people involved in the study reported symptoms substitution. Both of these reported increased backache with elimination of headache.

SAMPLE VERBATION SUGGESTIONS FOR 1ST SESSION:

Remember a time when you were completely comfortable, when you felt the best both physically and emotionally and spiritually. As you recapture these feelings imagine yourself stepping onto an elevator on the 10th floor of a building and as you do so squeeze your dominant fist. As the doors close look at the number ten above the door and watch it turn to a nine as you double your relaxation and double your comfort with each floor you descend. When you arrive at the ground floor or descend as far as you choose to go, the doors will open on a very special place. This can be a real or imaginary place, indoors or out, a place you have been before or one you would like to visit or any combination of the above. As you continue to squeeze your dominant fist you can experience this place with all your senses. See the beauty, notice the details and colors. Observe the lighting whether it is sunlight, moonlight, starlight or artificial light. It might even be a safe comfortable dark place. Hear the sounds or if it is a quiet place, enjoy the silence, smell the fragrances--perhaps there is a favorite flower or an especially meaningful perfume which you enjoy in this place.

Perhaps you can even taste the salt air of the seashore or a particular food you associate with this place. Most important of all feel the comfort. Since this place is your own mental creation the temperature should be ideal, the humidity as brisk or as balmy as you choose. It can be any season of the year, any climate, any type of weather and you can change any of the details of your own private sanctuary to suit your mood of the moment. You can come to this place anytime it is appropriate for you to do so simply by making yourself comfortable, squeezing your dominant hand and remembering how you feel right now. The only restriction for this place is that you bring only comfortable thoughts and feelings here-- reserving another place and a different time for dealing with uncomfortable thoughts and feelings. After a few moments the patient is then asked to remain in hypnosis, but to step out of the special place by opening the dominant fist. Now I would like to have you focus your attention on your pain--imagine you can see it in color. Imagine also that you can see the physical tension that is contributing to your discomfort also in color--it can be the same or a different color. Imagine your emotional tension is also represented by a color, your fear, your uncertainty, your anger, frustrations, and any other negative emotions can also be represented by a color. Next imagine that your body is transparent and that if you were sitting opposite yourself you could look at yourself and watch the color representing your pain and unpleasant emotions melt and flow by its own imaginary circulatory system into your non-dominant hand. As it begins to collect there squeeze that fist tightly. The tighter you squeeze your non-dominant fist the more relaxed and comfortable the rest of your body will become. If you squeeze that fist hard enough, long enough and steady enough, it will begin to be painful due to lack of circulation, just as your head begins to hurt when you hold your neck muscles too tensely. When all of the colored material, or as much as you choose to put there right now, is in your fist or when your fist hurts more than any other part of your body you can symbolically drop the discomfort on the floor and go back to your place of comfort, tranquility and healing by squeezing your dominant fist. Because you are so completely relaxed now, take your time rousing yourself. You blood pressure is lower than normal and you can allow yourself to let it return to the optimal level for you right now as you slowly count from one to five, opening your eyes on the count of four, being wide awake, alert and comfortable on the count of five.

ACKNOWLEDGEMENT

Appreciation to Gale W. Bach, Ph. D., Commander, Medical Service Corp, United States Naval Reserve, whose clinical facility provided the opportunity for the study to be done.

164

BIBLIOGRAPHY:

1. Cheek, David B. and LeCron, Leslie M., Clinical Hypnotherapy, Grune & Stratton New York and London 1968

2. Frankl, Viktor E., The Unconscious God, Simon and Schuster, New York 1975

3. Goldstein, Avram, "The Endorphins and Pain--What We have Learned" Current Concepts in Postoperative Pain, January 1978; A special report prepared for Pfizer Laboratories by Hospital Practice based on a symposium held in conjunction with the Annual Meeting of the American Society of Anesthesiologists, New Orleans, October 1977

4. Hilgard, Ernest R. & Hilgard, Josephine R., Hypnosis in the Relief of Pain, William Kaufmann Inc., Los Altos, CA 1975

5. Stein, Calvert, Practical Psychotherapy in Non-psychiatric Specialties, Springfield, ILL, Charles C. Thomas, 1969.

© 1979 Elsevier/North-Holland Biomedical Press
Hypnosis 1979
G.D. Burrows, D.R. Collison and L. Dennerstein

MUTUALLY-INDUCED TRANCE AS A THERAPEUTIC MODE

James C. Hancock, M.D. and Edwina Hackett, M.S.W., Memphis, Tennessee*.

INTRODUCTION

The purpose of this paper is to explore the role of the transference/counter-transference relationship in therapy and to discuss the utilization of mutually-induced trance as a means of working the resistance in a very direct, productive and healthy manner.

In the process of evolving and refining this technique, we were well aware that we were challenging tenets basic to psychoanalytic psychotherapy. Reik[9] has suggested, however, that the critical area of research in psychoanalysis is the psychology of interpersonal relations, the study of how ".... the unconscious of one person react(s) upon the unconscious of another" (p.462).

We believe that mutual trance enhanced our therapy, hastened the process and made for a more productive experience than could have occurred with conventional methodology. We suggest that mutual hypnosis enhances direct communication at a level not ordinarily accessible to consciousness.

REVIEW OF THE LITERATURE

In a search of the literature through November 1976, we found no description of a therapeutic relationship such as we had experienced. There were, however, several articles tangentially relevant.

The only instance in which the therapist entered trance was in an instructional setting. Morris[6] utilized dual trance with those students who "could not" enter trance due to severe problems with control. She had the student place her in trance and instruct her as to how best she might use her skills to enable the student to experience trance. While in a hypnotic state, she then induced the student and brought him out thus allowing him the final control of bringing her out of trance last. She found this to be a helpful technique and states further a belief in the therapeutic potential of mutual hypnosis.

Another author, Sanders,[10] utilized hypnosis with a problem-solving group and found that blocks to creativity were diminished on the three levels identified for study: emotional, cultural, and cognitive.

Both Tart[12] and O'Hare' et al[8] utilized mutual hypnosis with the experimenter, "remaining in ordinary awareness while the subjects were in trance".

One particular statement by Tart[12] to the effect that during trance the subjects sometimes felt a "sense of merging identities, partial blending of themselves quite beyond the degree of contact human beings expect to share with others" (p.74) is striking. This description parallels quite well the unique sense of relatedness we experienced from time to time.

Although the techniques of Tart and O'Hare differ, findings were similar in that 1) strong rapport and intimacy developed between the hypnotized individuals; 2) at times, the intimacy though pleasurable was anxiety-provoking; 3) on occasion the hypnotized individuals resisted efforts by the experimenter or control to intrude upon their experience.

Finally, an article by Morris and Pastor[7] described mutual hypnotherapy in which one would induce trance in the other, the one in trance functioning as the patient to the other's therapist in an intensive psychotherapy hour. After some working through in a waking state of the hypnotic material, they would switch roles for another hour's session.

PROCEDURE

An on-going therapeutic relationship had been established with good rapport and mutual trust. On two occasions the client had experienced trance prior to the decision to attempt mutual induction. The therapist had had considerable experience in utilizing hypnosis both as a personal and as a clinical tool.

Initially the therapist took full responsibility for the structure of the induction itself. Soon responsibility for induction was shared so that cooperation and mutuality were high. This segment of the process utilized basic principles of hypnosis: relaxation, attention to breathing, receptivity and concentration and focusing of attention.

As visual-imagery, a seashore with lapping waves is utilized. The sun is warm; a slight breeze may be felt. In the distance we can see a buoy floating gently. Together we wade into the water and feel the waves lapping at our bodies--ankles, knees, hips. Lifted by the waves, we swim with strong, easy strokes towards the buoy. We swim well and are capable of remaining under water safely for long periods.

Reaching the buoy, we dive together swimming down the line to the depths. Our progress is measured by counting knots in the line.

At this point we have reached a moderately deep state of trance where various tasks, questions or fantasies are explored. It is also at this point that we begin to utilize the technique of the magic fluid which will become useful in many ways.

TECHNIQUE

We are at the bottom of the sea; there is the hulk of an ancient ship laden with treasure. We find a flask which contains shimmering golden fluid imbued with the powers of relaxation, understanding, sensuousness; of melding mind to mind.

The therapist continues the process by further describing the fluid in whatever way might best fit the current need (e.g., strength, peace, et cetera). He describes pouring the glistening fluid into his palm. He describes with care how he massages, strokes the fluid over the client's body. Consideration of detail is important here and would, of course, vary depending upon the relationship of the pair. At any point suggestions may be made as to the benefits to be gained from the fluid: e.g., over the chest the fluid may penetrate and heal "heartbreak"; regeneration may be visualized; feather strokes on the eyelids may wash away the clouds of distortion through which the world is seen providing a clear view; a small amount of fluid may be encouraged to enter an appropriate orifice and move through the body strengthening it against organic distress.

Upon completion the client further relaxes and absorbs the wished for amount of comfort and knowledge. The suggestion is made that when ready, the client may give the therapist a portion of the fluid if he wishes.

This technique has the advantage of deepening trance and increasing intimacy simultaneously. Any material stemming from the technique may be worked immediately as a part of that trance session. Furthermore, the utilization of dual trance minimized tremendously the time necessary for dreamwork. In trance we produced our own dream, more vivid for its immediacy. Both latent and manifest content being present, we could rapidly bring the unconscious into conscious awareness.

SYMBOLISM IN THIS HYPNOTIC STATE

Entering the ocean itself may be seen as floating upon the surface of the unconscious while the buoy and knotted line serve as markers in the deepening of trance and concurrently signify the entry and descent into the unconscious. The dive may best be seen as a commitment to and trust in the process. The line remains in place as a lifeline to the surface (back to conscious awareness). The ship becomes the self and a passage for exploration of the many facets of psychosomatic existence.

On a still deeper level, the salinity of the ocean suggests amniotic fluid with the line becoming the umbilical cord leading to the placenta of the ship placidly lying in the deep.

Thus this particular imagery lends itself to the active seeking of the self, a return home at whatever level the individual might seek.

UTILIZATION OF AUTOHYPNOSIS AS A THERAPEUTIC ADJUNCT

After working for sometime with dual trance, there was one area in particular which we had been unable to work through. That area was the locus of fear
and dread which was experienced as a drumming in the hollow of the client's rib
cage and from which flowed self-destructive energy.

On occasion, the client had utilized autohypnosis as an adjunct to the therapy hour. It had been used primarily for relaxation and the prevention of insomnia.

Frequently the perceived locus of stress came to mind as it continued to be
troublesome. One night, spontaneously, the client began to work with the
pendulum,[4] seeking an answer.

Beginning with LeCron's recommended manner of questioning[4] to determine the
temporal origin of the symptom, she was led by exclusion to the date of her
birth. Pursuing the matter with specific questions led to the response that
someone in the delivery room had stated that she was "too weak to live". With
confirmation by the pendulum of the accuracy of the last bit of information to
supply this answer came cessation of the internal drumbeat and the dread. The
symptom has never recurred regardless of stress.

"Cheek believes that birth experiences may be similar to imprinting which
makes a permanent behavior characteristic with one stimulus".[2] (p.90) Cases
are cited by Cheek where such a memory seemed to have an effect later in life.

Our experience is similar and we believe corroborates the value of Cheek's
studies of birth trauma and the atmosphere he recommends to welcome the new-
born. We conjecture that when feeling tones acquire a verbal expression they
consequently nullify the impact of the experience. Certainly, much more research is indicated in this area.

CONSIDERATIONS

Resistance occurs in both client and therapist as a natural and normal concomitant of ego involvement in any relationship. Encroachment upon the privacy
of the self stimulates a defense regardless of whether a traumatized self has
developed neurotic patterns or whether an essentially healthy self seeks to
avoid intimacy as a (possibly) temporary expedient. In therapy, these quite
normal uncertainties may hamper progress.

A real danger of transference/counter-transference, being hypothetical con-
structs, is that the feelings involved may not be recognized and even when
recognized are not owned or verbalized. Transference/counter-transference are
not considered real in the sense that other affective responses are considered
to be real. By relegating honest feelings to a sub rosa role, there is auto-

matically established a fertile fantasy field in which the feelings thrive on an unconscious level and may burst forth in inappropriate ways.

The unconscious drives towards its fulfillment and freedom. Denial or other means of thwarting its wishes generally succeed only in making it more devious in its expression. By verbalizing and owning these parts of ourselves, we not only expand in self-knowledge but also we de-fuse their intensity and decrease the likelihood of internal sabotage.

In our work together we discovered that our resistances came from different sorts of fears. Fairly early in therapy, one session ended with a spontaneous hug as a response to severe stress the client was experiencing at the time. The hugs continued, becoming a ritual of parting. For the client they served a crucial nurturant function at a point when there were no other options for warmth and contact. The therapist was not always comfortable with the situation. His resistances derived from expectation that physical touching might lead to sexual behavior which would then become in itself a resistance to therapy. For the client, resistance centered upon maintaining control and clinging to her anger without owning it out of fear that such rage would lead to rejection and abandonment by the therapist.

Various schools of analytic thought might interpret the resistances in different ways. We found it more effective to deal with our interpersonal issues than to attempt to identify the historical landmarks of our individual developmental struggles.

Later, as mutual trance evolved, considerable sensuality was evoked and could be experienced directly in the ritual hugs. The perceived change was more pronounced for the client who had not previously attached sexual meaning to the hugs. Because of the strong mutuality developed in trance, we were able to accept our sexual feelings as real and present and to discuss their impact upon our relationship. Dealing openly and realistically with the sexual issue enabled us to progress in therapy without the hindrance of hidden agenda.

In the therapeutic situation, the mutual trance heightened intimacy as it increased our ability to relate directly, with immediacy. The sense of psychic intimacy was and continues to be unique.

CONCLUSION

In these pages we have described what we have found to be a unique and effective psychotherapeutic tool. The mutuality of the relationship produced an I-Thou[1] sense of sharing and of responsibility towards both ourselves as individuals and towards the "usness" of the relationship itself.

170

Guided visual imagery[5] such as presented in this paper has proved to be a useful and valid technique in the management of various psychosomatic problems. The therapist and his colleague[3] have been successful in many cases in their private practices utilizing visual imagery as one of the tools of therapy. Sexual disorders,[3] management of hypertension, tachycardia, respiratory disorders, pain control and alteration of pathologic life style have all responded favorably to management utilizing guided visual imagery.

As mentioned earlier we had developed a strong sense of trust prior to the initiation of dual trance. This would seem essential. Further, as described by all authors of related experiences, dual trance is a powerful tool and will be best utilized only by therapists and with clients who have sufficient strengths to work through critical material in an intense way.

BIBLIOGRAPHY

1. Buber, Martin. I and Thou, N.Y., Scribners, 1958 (2nd edition).

2. Cheek, David V., M.D., and LeCron, Leslie, B.A., Clinical Hyponotherapy, Grune & Stratton, N.Y. & London, 1968, p. 90, 127, 200.

3. Hancock, James C., M.D. & Jacobson, H.A., PhD., Videotape presentation, 6th World Congress of Psychiatry, Honolulu, Hawaii, July 1977, Physiology of Female Orgasm Induced by Hypnosis.

4. LeCron, Leslie, B.A., Self-Hypnotism. Englewood Cliffs, N.J., Prentice-Hall, 1964.

5. Leuner, H., "Guided Affective Imagery: a Method Psychotherapy", American Journal of Psychotherapy, 1969, 23, 4-22.

6. Morris, F., "Mutual Hypnosis: a Specialized Hypnotic Induction Technique", American Journal of Clinical Hypnosis, 13:2 pp. 90-94, Oct. 1970.

7. Morris, F. and Pastor, M., "Mutual Hypnotherapy", Voices, 1973, 9, 13-18.

8. O'Hare, C., White, G., Lunden, B., Mac, Phillamy D., "An Experiment in Step-wise Mutual Hypnosis and Shared Guided Fantasy", American Journal of Clinical Hypnosis, 17:4 pp. 239-46, April 1975.

9. Reik, Theodor. Listening with the Third Ear, N.Y., Farrar, Straus and Giroux, 1948.

10. Sanders, Shirley, PhD., "Mutual Group Hypnosis as a Catalyst in Fostering Creative Problem-Solving", American Journal of Clinical Hypnosis, 19:1 pp. 62-66, July 1976.

11. Smith, Edward W. L., The Growing Edge of Gestalt Therapy, "Combining Hypnosis with Gestalt Therapy", N.Y., Brunner/Mazel, Inc., 1976.

12. Tart, Charles, T., PhD., "Psychedelic Experiences Associated with a Novel Hypnotic Procedure, Mutual Hypnosis", American Journal of Clinical Hypnosis, 10:2 pp. 65-78, October 1967.

GENERAL REFERENCES

1. Erickson, Milton. Advanced Techniques of Hypnosis and Therapy - Selected

Papers of Milton H. Erickson, ed. Jay Haley, N.Y., Grune and Stratton, 1967.

2. Frank, Jerome D., "Psychotherapy: the Restoration of Morale". <u>Weekly Psychiatry Update</u>, Series 19.

3. Fromm, Erika, "Altered States of Consciousness and Hypnosis: a Discussion", <u>International Journal of Clinical and Experimental Hypnosis,</u> 1977, Volume XXV, #4, 325-334.

* Address request for Reprints to: James C. Hancock, M.D., Director - Positive Alternatives to Addictions, Stress & Anxiety, Lakewood General Hospital, 1600 Abrams Road, Dallas, Texas 75214.

© 1979 Elsevier/North-Holland Biomedical Press
Hypnosis 1979
G.D. Burrows, D.R. Collison and L. Dennerstein

INSOMNIA AND HYPNOTHERAPY

Maurice A. Basker

Leigh-on-Sea, Essex, England.

John A.D. Anderson and Rosemary Dalton

Guy's Hospital Medical School, London, England.

Abstract: A method of investigating the value of autohypnosis in insomnia in patients in their own homes by means of a controlled trial with nitrazepam and placebo is described. Eighteen patients were randomly allocated to receive nitrazepam for 2 weeks followed by placebo for 2 weeks, or placebo followed by nitrazepam. During weeks 5 to 8, patients continued to receive the same tablets as they had during weeks 1 to 4 and were taught autohypnosis during weeks 5 and 6. Patients continued with autohypnosis in weeks 7 and 8, also in weeks 9 and 10 by which time all tablets had been withdrawn. Both doctor and patient were "blind" as to the exact nature of the tablets which a patient was receiving at a particular time.

The results, with discussion are presented. Patients slept significantly longer when on autohypnosis alone than when they received placebo, and significantly more patients had a normal night's sleep when on autohypnosis alone than when they received the placebo or nitrazepam.

Since 1918 barbiturates have been used to treat insomnia, but in more recent years have been misused and are dangerous in overdosage. Most deaths from barbiturates are the results from determined attempts at self destruction, and in 80% of such cases the victims never reach hospital. Although newer and safer hypnotic drugs have arrived, many people are prejudiced over even the limited use of these. The clinical use of hypnosis in insomnia has been demonstrated by hypnotists since Bramwell[1] (1906). It has been assumed that a subject making autohypnotic suggestions to himself that he should go to sleep might well do so. It was decided therefore to compare the treatment of insomnia with placebo, nitrazepam and autohypnosis.

Method

Practitioners were invited to participate on the agreement that they would prescribe placebo, nitrazepam and hypnosis to each patient admitted to the trial. It was stipulated that patients would be between 16 and 70 years of age, and that they considered they had suffered from insomnia of at least 1 months duration. It was agreed to exclude patients with pain, obvious endogenous depression and those with more serious nervous disorder, including psychopaths.

The trial was designed so that the first four weeks constituted a double blind trial of nitrazepam and placebo. Within blocks of ten patients, half were randomly selected to receive 5 mgm nitrazepam tablets for the first two weeks and placebo tablets of identical appearance for the third and fourth weeks. The other patients received placebo in weeks one and two and nitrazepam in weeks three and four. Patients were then given further supplies of the same preparation they were having during weeks three and four, for a further four weeks. During the first half of this further four weeks, i.e. weeks five and six, all patients were instructed in the use of autohypnosis for insomnia, so that they were using this with either nitrazepam or placebo until the end of the eighth week. At the end of week eight, all tablets were withdrawn, it being anticipated that full use of autohypnosis alone would be effective. Each practitioner was sent three bottles for each patient numbered serially for weeks one and two, three and four, and weeks five to eight of the ten week trial period. Neither doctor nor patients knew whether a particular bottle contained placebo or nitrazepam.

At the initial interview, patients were asked whether their insomnia was early, or whether middle with restlessness and waking, or late, i.e. early waking and difficulty in getting to sleep again. Causes of insomnia were sought as far as possible. Each patient was given simple advice in addition, as having adequate physical exercise, avoiding tea and coffee in the late evening and mental overactivity.

Patients were also asked about four aspects of their sleeping during the last week:

(a) Average time to go to sleep, categorised as –

0 – 30 mins,   31 – 60 mins,   over 60 mins.

(b) Average sleep duration, categorised as –

Under 2 hours,   2 – 6 hours   over 6 hours

(c) Quality of sleep, categorised as –

Restless,   heavy,   normal

In the analysis restless was considered the worst, normal as the best with heavy occupying an intermediate position.

(d) Waking state, categorised in order of decreasing desirability as –

Bright   Average   Tired

Patients were issued with diary cards every two weeks and every morning they classified their sleep into one of the above categories on each of these four aspects of their sleeping. At the end of weeks two, four, eight and ten and before seeing their diary cards, the practitioner concerned questioned the

patients on these same aspects and made his own observations and assessment of
the average during the past week. He also made sure that patients were carrying
out their instructions correctly. He then sent off his own notes with the
patient's diary cards for each two weeks period to those monitoring the trial,
so that any defaulters were noticed immediately, and an opportunity given to
continue follow-up.

Hypnosis/Autohypnosis.

It was stipulated that only experienced hypnotists would participate, that at
least four sessions of treatment would be given, and that although a more extensive neurosis might be uncovered, a short term approach only would be used,
but with ego-strengthening suggestions and the use of autohypnosis. No specific
trance induction or deepening techniques were stipulated as long as they were
suitable for the individual patient.

Results.

One patient had to be withdrawn from the trial because she had taken an over-
dose. Of the remaining eighteen patients who took part in this trial, all but
two were female. The ages ranged from 29 to 60 years with a mean of 46.1 years.
Duration of insomnia prior to the trial varied between three months to twenty
two years, with half being two to three years. Four patients suffered only early
insomnia, seven suffered early and middle insomnia, two middle and late insomnia
one early and late insomnia, and four early, middle and late insomnia. There
were no significant differences between the group who received placebo first,
and the group who received nitrazepam first on any of the above variables. Most
of the patients treated were those who had not attended previously complaining
of insomnia, or who had not had treatment for a considerable time.

Four patients were excluded from parts of the analysis because their treatment did not conform exactly to the protocol. For each measure of sleep there
were three possible categories, as already given and these were scored 1, 2 or
3 with 1 being the least, and 3 the most desirable.

On each of the four measures of sleep, patients who received the regime
starting with placebo alone were compared at the end of weeks 2, 4, 8 and 10
with those patients who received nitrazepam first using Mann-Whitney U-tests
and Fisher's exact test (Siegel, 1956)[2] for the difference between 2 independent
samples. At weeks 2 and 4 the effect of the placebo was not significantly different from that of nitrazepam on any of the measures. Similarly, at week 8
there was no significant difference between autohypnosis and placebo and autohypnosis and nitrazepam. At week 10 the effect of autohypnosis was similar
regardless of the previous treatment schedules.

The effects of the placebo, nitrazepam and autohypnosis and either the placebo or nitrazepam, and autohypnosis alone were compared for the group who received the placebo first and similarly for the group who received nitrazepam first. These comparisons of treatments within patients should be more sensitive than those between patients. Friedman's 2-way analysis of variance with allowanc for ties (Winer, 1971)[3] was used as this is appropriate for testing the differences between several treatments when each of these have been received by the same patients. (The test would have been inapplicable if each treatment had been given to a different group of patients). For a particular measure of sleep, each patient had a score for each treatment and these scores were ranked in order of preference for each patient. Friedman's 2-way analysis of variance assessed whether or not the differences between the sum of these ranks for each treatment were likely to be due to chance alone if the treatments were equally effective.

There was no significant difference between the 4 possible treatments in the group which received placebo first with respect to the average time to go to sleep (Friedman 2-way analysis of variance, $x^2 = 1.93$, d.f. = 3, N.S.). However there was a significant difference amongst those receiving nitrazepam first ($x^2 = 9.08$, d.f. = 3, $p < 0.05$); the time taken to go to sleep was less while receiving autohypnosis than when receiving either nitrazepam or placebo; it made no difference whether or not a tablet was being taken as well. Overall the proportion of patients taking more than 60 minutes to go to sleep were 3/17 and 4/17 while receiving the placebo and nitrazepam respectively and 0/16 while receiving autohypnosis and a tablet, and 0/17 while receiving autohypnosis on it's own. The numbers taking less than 30 minutes to go to sleep were 7, 10, 11 and 12 respectively.

There were significant differences in the time spent asleep between the 4 possible treatments in the group receiving the placebo first (Friedman 2-way analysis of variance, $X^2 = 9.00$, d.f = 3, $p < 0.05$). The placebo was the worst and the other 3 regimes similar with autohypnosis on it's own just the best. There were no significant differences between the treatments for those who received Nitrazepam first (Friedman 2-way analysis of variance, $X^2 = 4.80$, d.f. = 3, N.S.) but there was a tendency for the two regimes including autohypnosis to result in longer periods of sleep. It was not possible to detect any effect in the order of administration of the placebo and nitrazepam and if this possibility is ignored and weeks on placebo, nitrazepam and autohypnosis are compared there is a significant difference between the three treatments with autohypnosis being the best and placebo the worst (Friedman 2-way analysis of variance, $X^2 = 7.71$, d.f. = 2, $p < 0.025$). Amongst 17 patients on autohypnosis alone, 3 patients obtained less than 6 hours sleep a night, whereas amongst 17

receiving Nitrazepam it was 5, and 10 amongst 17 receiving the placebo. The
sleep duration varied between the 4 treatments in only 9 patients; 7 patients
slept longer on autohypnosis and none less when compared with the placebo
(binomial test, 2 tailed. p = 0.016) (Siegel, 1956).

The quality of sleep between the 4 weeks considered in table 1, was not quite
significantly different in the group receiving the placebo first but was significant for the nitrazepam first. Friedman 2-way analysis of variance, d.f.=3;
placebo first, X^2 = 7.40, 0.05 $<$ p $<$ 0.10; nitrazepam first, X^2 = 10.67, p $<$ 0.025.
In both groups there was a tendency for more patient's sleep to be normal in
weeks 8 and 10 than in weeks 2 and 4. It was not possible to detect any effect
of the order of administration of the placebo and nitrazepam and if this possibility is ignored and weeks on placebo, nitrazepam and autohypnosis are
compared, there is a significant difference between the 3 treatments with autohypnosis being the best and placebo the worst (Friedman 2-way analysis of
variance; X^2 = 13.17, d.f. = 2, p $<$ 0.005). On autohypnosis alone only one
patient out of 17 was not having normal sleep whereas the numbers were 12 and
10 for 17 patients when on the placebo and nitrazepam respectively. When
comparing autohypnosis and the placebo for the group who received the placebo
first, all 6 whose quality of sleep changed, has significantly improved sleep
with autohypnosis compared with the placebo (p = 0.032 (2 tailed binomial test)
and similarly all 4 whose quality of sleep changed in the other group had
improved sleep on autohypnosis. When the 2 groups are combined p = 0.002 (2 tailed
binomial test). Similarly when comparing autohypnosis and nitrazepam, all 4 in
each group who had a changed quality of sleep were better on autohypnosis and
when the results are combined the difference between nitrazepam and autohypnosis
is significant (p = 0.008 (2 tailed binomial test)). Eight had a change in
quality of sleep between nitrazepam and the placebo and nitrazepam was preferred
in 6 instances (N.S.).

With respect to waking state, there was no significant difference between the
4 weeks in either group (Friedman 2-way anslysis of variance, placebo first,
X^2 = 2.23, nitrazepam first X^2 = 4.24, d.f. = 3, N.S.). There was a slight
tendency for autohypnosis to produce a slightly better waking state than either
the placebo or nitrazepam. Autohypnosis alone resulted in 15 out of 17 patients
waking up in an average state and only 2 waking up tired, whereas after the
placebo 8/17 were tired and 7/17 were tired after receiving nitrazepam. Only 2
patients gave the answer "bright" on 3 occasions between them.

Discussion

The trial should have included more patients. However many difficulties are obvious in conducting such a complex trial. It was difficult to enlist hypnotists to give a drug or placebo when they had already decided hypnotherapy was the treatment of choice – an ethical consideration which cannot be ignored. A large number of patients were thought to be depressed, but many more were suspicious of hypnotherapy and declined to participate.

Many patients thought they would be deprived of their one consolation making life tolerable, and refused to have their usual prescription for a hypnotic with-held. The patients treated included all those who were suitable and willing to participate in a ten week period including autohypnosis.

Ideally the three treatments, nitrazepam, placebo and autohypnosis should have been rotated at random, but it was obviously impossible to prevent a patient using autohypnosis once this had been learnt and so only placebo and nitrazepam could be rotated. Only the placebo and nitrazepam part of the trial could be made double blind. The effect of treatment in week 8 might have been better than that in week 4 due to a beneficial effect of being taught autohypnosis in conjunction with a tablet. The fact that there were no significant differences between weeks 8 and 10 suggests that by the end of the trial, tablets could be withdrawn without any deleterious effect among patients who are willing to participate in such a trial and hence accept treatment by autohypnosis.

The apparent success of autohypnosis in the last week could be due to the effect of participating in such a trial and the discussion that some form of tablet would be unnecessary by the end of the trial rather than due to autohypnosis. However the net result is that patients appeared to do as well or better without tablets by the end of the trial as with tablets and this is obviously beneficial.

Summary

Patients slept significantly longer when on autohypnosis alone than when they received the placebo. Significantly more patients had a normal night's sleep when on autohypnosis alone than when they received the placebo or nitrazepam. There was a tendency for autohypnosis to reduce the time taken to go to sleep. With respect to the waking state, no significant differences were found between the placebo, nitrazepam and autohypnosis, although there was a slight tendency for autohypnosis to produce a better waking state.

Table I
Quality of sleep during the last week.

Treatment regime	Quality	week			
		2 Placebo/ nitrazepam	4 Placebo/ nitrazepam (note a)	8 Placebo/ nitrazepam and A/H (note b)	10 A/H (note c)
Placebo week 2 nitrazepam week 4/8	Restless	5	1	1	0
	Heavy	2	4	1	1
	Normal	3	4	7	9
nitrazepam week 2 Placebo week 4/8	Restless	3	4	0	0
	Heavy	2	1	0	0
	Normal	3	2	7	7

note a. Two patients (one on each regime) have been excluded since autohypnosis was taught in week three.

note b. One patient has been excluded since autohypnosis was not taught until week seven.

note c. One patient has been excluded because autohypnosis was not taught until week nine.

References

1. Bramwell, J.M (1906) Hypnosis, It's History, Practice and Theory 2nd. Ed. London, Alexander Moring Ltd, De La More Press.

2. Siegel, S (1956) Nonparametric Statistics for the Behavioral Sciences. New York. McGraw-Hill Book Co., 1956.

3. Winer, B.J. (1971), Statistical Principles in Experimental Design. McGraw-Hill Kogakusha.

Hypnosis 1979
G.D. Burrows, D.R. Collison and L. Dennerstein

HYPNOTIC SUSCEPTIBILITY, EEG THETA AND ALPHA WAVES, AND HEMISPHERIC SPECIFICITY

CRISETTA MacLEOD MORGAN

Psychology Department, Flinders University of S.A., Bedford Park, South Australia, 5042.

INTRODUCTION

Theta

Two studies on EEG and hypnosis have found significances in the theta waveband.

Galbraith et al.[1] performed a stepwise multiple regression analysis on the entire spectrum, in resting eyes-open and eyes-shut conditions for the full range of hypnotisability as measured by the Harvard Group Scale (HGS)[2]. Five correlations with HGS were found, all in the 5 – 8 Hz range; all but one of these were in the eyes-open condition.

Tebēcis et al.[3] compared waking, imagination, and hypnotic conditions in Ss experienced in hypnosis, to waking and imagination conditions in naive Ss. The only unequivocal finding was that experienced Ss had more theta than naive ones in all conditions.

Alpha

Baselines. It has been shown that high hypnotisables have higher baseline amounts of alpha than lows.[4,5] (Not all studies replicated this[6,7]). It has also been shown that susceptibility is enhanced by alpha biofeedback training[8,9,10]

Alpha ratios. Alpha abundance has been used as a measure of brain lateralisation, alpha being more suppressed in the activated hemisphere.[11,12] There is evidence to suggest that Ss who show bias towards activating their right hemisphere, are more hypnotisable.[11,13,14,15] Morgan et al.[15] also compared interhemispheric alpha ratios during the performance of spatial (R.Hem.) and analytic (L.Hem.) tasks but found no significant difference between HI and LO hypnotisables.

Tellegen Absorption Scale[16]

The TAS shows a consistent correlation with hypnotisability. Davidson et al.[17] also found that high scorers on the TAS showed more cortical specificity on certain tasks than did low scorers.

AIMS OF THE PRESENT STUDY

This study investigates whether:

(a) amount of theta in the EEG is correlated to HGS scores.

(b) experienced hypnotic subjects show more EEG theta than naive ones.

(c) amount of alpha in the EEG is correlated to HGS score.

(d) highly susceptible subjects show "right hemisphere bias".

(e) HS is correlated with HGS.

(f) TAS is correlated with HGS.

(g) TAS is correlated with HS.

METHOD

50 subjects (mean age 33.15 years) took part in the EEG study, 22 being experienced in hypnosis, and 28 naive. Both subgroups had approximately the same distribution of scores on HGS, which had previously been administered. None had experience of meditation, or had recently taken any psychotropic substance. Each subject also completed the TAS.

Tasks

There were six tasks, three of which were intended as left hemisphere tasks – Random Number Generation (RNG), Verbal Categories (VC) and Mental Arithmetic (MA); and three as right hemisphere tasks – Spatial Orientation (SO), Listening to Music (LM), and Tonal Memory (TM).

SO involved Ss pointing in the direction of various landmarks while seated in the windowless experimental room, and while visualising themselves standing at a familiar location in Adelaide.

RNG is a task devised by Graham and Evans[18] and involves saying the numbers between 1 and 10 randomly at the rate of one per second until 100 random numbers have been generated. Speed was fixed by a metronome. Output was scored for randomness as described in Knuth.[19] Graham and Evans found that success in generating numbers randomly was related to hypnotisability.

LM involved listening to part of the Andante movement from Mozart's Divertimento K563. Subjects were told that they would not be questioned about it but to signal lapses in concentration.

VC involved selecting one word in a set of five that did not belong to the same category as the others, and saying why. (adapted from ACER Test[20]).

TM used part of Seashore's Test[21] in which Ss had to signal which note of a short melody had been altered on a second playing, by counting on their fingers.

MA Ss attempted addition, multiplication, and division sums with only ten seconds in which to respond verbally to each.

Each task took on average 90 seconds; each was performed first with eyes
open, and then with eyes shut; right hemisphere and left hemisphere tasks were
alternated; a baseline recording (1¼ mins. eyes open, 1¼ mins. eyes shut)
preceded each task.

Apparatus

EEG recordings were made with a Devices Ltd., Type M3 physiological recorder,
measuring integrated amplitude alpha and theta waves from alternate hemispheres
for ten second epochs throughout the testing session. (Theta = 4-8 Hz; alpha =
7.25 - 12.25 Hz). EEG output consisted of a raw trace plus four sets of histograms, the heights of which were proportional to the amounts of right and left
hemisphere theta, and right and left hemisphere alpha present in each ten-second
epoch. These histograms were scored in arbitrary units, the scorer being blind
to subject identity to avoid possible bias.

Electrodes were shallow, cup-shaped, silver 1 cm. in diameter. Placements
were O1 - P3 for bipolar recording in the left hemisphere, and O2 - P4 for the
right (10-20 system[22]). Earth electrode was on the right mastoid bone. Grass
Electrocream was used to affix electrodes after thorough preparation of the
sites.

Procedure

Subjects were seated in an upright chair facing a blank wall. All experimental instructions were administered by tape recorder. E remained in the
experimental room throughout to ensure that these were followed and to operate
a second recorder for subject's responses. Experimental time for each subject
including affixing of electrodes was 1½ hours.

RESULTS

When dichotomising of HGS scale was necessary for ANOVA or diagrammatic
purposes, 8 and over = HI, 7 and under = LO.

Theta

Significant Pearson correlations between eyes-open theta and hypnotisability
(HGS) were found. (Baselines, r = 0.264, p = .032; tasks, r = 0.295, p =
.041). Eyes-shut correlations were not significant.

A repeated measures ANOVA on mean amount of theta for experienced and naive
subgroups showed no significant differences.

Alpha

Baselines. A repeated measures ANOVA between HI and LO groups across six
baselines in the eyes-shut condition found significant differences between the
groups (F = 4.146, df = 1, p = .045); a strongly significant difference between

baselines (F = 6.072, df = 5, p =.0001); and an interaction between these two
factors (F = 2.236, df = 5, p = .051).

A similar ANOVA for eyes-open alpha found no significant differences.

Alpha ratios. Alpha ratios were calculated:- $\dfrac{\text{R.Hem Alpha} - \text{L.Hem. Alpha}}{\text{R.Hem Alpha} + \text{L.Hem. Alpha}}$

Mean alpha ratios were computed for left hemisphere tasks (RNG, VC, MA) and
for right hemisphere tasks (SO,LM,TM). These will be referred to as LAR and RAR.

The correlation between HGS and LAR was 0.311 (p = .014) with eyes open and
0.349 (p = .007) with eyes shut. In other words, the higher the hypnotisability
score, the greater the positive alpha ratio during left hemisphere tasks. The
correlation between HGS and RAR was not significant.

LAR minus RAR was computed as a measure of hemispheric specificity (HS - the
extent to which a subject's alpha ratios differed for the two kinds of tasks).
The correlation between HS and HGS was significant in the eyes-shut condition
(r = 0.305, p = .016). In simpler terms, the higher the S's hypnotisability,
the greater the difference between his alpha ratio while performing a left hemisphere task, and his alpha ratio when performing a right hemisphere task. In
confirmation of this, t-tests between LAR and RAR for the HI hypnotisable
group were significant (eyes-open, t = 1.84, df = 28, p = .038; eyes-shut,
t = 3.47, df = 28, p = .001 (One-tailed tests)). Similar t-tests for the LO
group were not significant.

Fig. 1 illustrates the zig-zag effect as HI hypnotisables' ratio shifts in
the task-specific direction, especially in the eyes-shut condition. It can also
be seen that HIs perform R. Hem. tasks (SO, LM, TM) with alpha ratios roughly
equivalent to their baseline mean. For L. Hem. tasks their ratios become
significantly more positive. The LO group, on the other hand, shows a task
mean roughly equivalent to their baseline mean; ratios do not show task-
specific changes.   There was no significant difference between HI and LO
groups' performance on any of the scorable tasks.

Variance of α-ratios over 6 tasks, eyes-open, correlated negatively with
HGS (r = -0.417, p = .001). This was also true of eyes-shut baseline
(r = - 0.282, p = .024).

Tellegen Absorption Scale

There was a significant correlation between TAS and HGS. (r = 0.271,
p = .029). However there was no significant correlation between TAS and HS.

Random Number Generation

The correlation between HGS and RNG found by Graham and Evans was not
replicated.

Summary

To summarise the relationship between variables in this study and HGS, a stepwise multiple regression/correlation was carried out (Table 1). The final R^2 value was 0.428, i.e. almost half the variance of hypnotisability is explained.

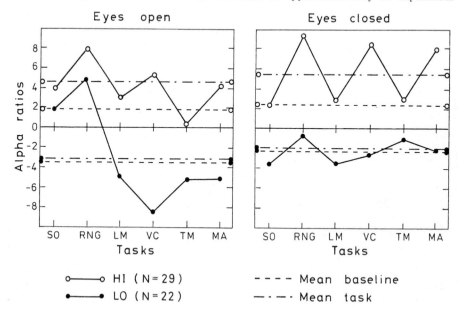

Fig. 1

Mean alpha ratios for baselines combined, and tasks separate and combined, illustrating HI and LO hypnotisables separately.

TABLE 1

MULTIPLE REGRESSION/CORRELATION ON HGS

Variable	Multiple R	R^2	R^2 change	Simple R
Variance of alpha ratios, tasks, eyes-open	0.417	0.174	0.174	-0.417
TAS	0.505	0.255	0.082	0.288
LAR, eyes-open	0.566	0.320	0.065	0.311
Mean baseline alpha, eyes-shut	0.605	0.366	0.046	0.214
HS, eyes-shut	0.641	0.411	0.045	0.305
Experience of hypnosis	0.651	0.423	0.012	0.130
LAR, eyes-shut	0.652	0.425	0.002	0.349
Theta, eyes-open	0.653	0.427	0.001	0.259
Variance of alpha ratios, baselines, eyes-shut	0.655	0.428	0.002	-0.282

DISCUSSION

Theta

Schacter[23] in reviewing theta research, discussed low arousal (eg sleep, meditation) and cognitive processing (e.g. problem-solving, memory). The HI group's theta was significantly greater than the LO's during tasks as well as baselines, so it is difficult to say which of these "kinds" of theta this may be, or what it means. A corollary to the present study which requires to be carried out too is whether increasing the amount of theta in the EEG by bio-feedback training (cf alpha studies[8,9,10]) would increase hypnotisability.

No relationship between theta and experience in hypnosis was found, so alternative explanations for the Tebēcis et al. findings should perhaps be sought. It is possible that susceptibility rather than experience was implicated - the study may have been looking at experienced HIs and naive LOs. Hypnosis per se cannot be excluded, since every session with the experienced group included hypnosis, and no session with the naives did. A definitive study on the experience issue would require control of both the quantity and quality of experience, which neither Tebēcis nor the present study attempted.

Alpha Baselines

The HI group's baseline amounts of alpha rose as the experimental session progressed (hence the significant difference between baselines in the eyes-shut ANOVA), but the LO hypnotisables' did not. If this effect proved to be replicable, it might explain conflicting results in the past, as an early baseline measure would show little difference between groups. Reviews by Evans[24] and Dumas[7] did not consider the eyes-open/shut dimension; it seems intuitively plausible that only the eyes-shut condition, when visual processing is at a minimum, would give a true comparative picture of amounts of alpha.

Alpha Ratios

It can be seen from Fig.1 that although the HI group does not show right hemisphere bias, and indeed seems to have more positive alpha ratios both for mean baseline and mean task (this difference was not significant) nevertheless, to perform R.Hem. tasks they do not have to shift from their baseline ratios, and so might be said to be "at home" with right hemisphere tasks. Left hemisphere tasks would seem to be better differentiators between HIs and LOs, however, since there was a clear correlation between LAR and HGS.

On hemispheric specificity, two apparently conflicting pieces of information were found.

(1) The correlation between hypnotisability and HS (i.e., the difference in alpha ratio between the two kinds of tasks).

(2) The negative correlation between hypnotisability and the amount of variance in both eyes-open tasks, and eyes-shut baselines.

What would appear to be happening, is that HIs make large, task-specific shifts in ratio, whereas LOs are more labile in general. (There was no significant difference in *performance* between the groups). This could be explained as HIs processing only relevent information, while LOs also process irrelevant environmental stimuli; in the eyes-open task condition, perhaps they survey the visual environment, and in the eyes-closed baselines – when task and visual processing demands are at a minimum – they "hunt" to and fro for information. This corresponds well with the Evoked Potential findings of Galbraith et al.[25] who found that in a selective attention task, HIs had enhanced EPs for attended stimuli, and attenuated ones for the stimuli to be ignored, whereas LOs showed quite the opposite effect.

RNG was the only task requiring continuous response from Ss in the present set of tasks, and in the eyes-open condition at least, there is little difference between HIs and LOs on this. Possibly the "lability" of the LOs has less opportunity to show itself on continuous tasks. An experiment is currently being carried out to investigate this.

James Braid, who gave hypnosis its original misnomer relating it to sleep, and later tried to change the name of the phenomenon to "monoideism", may have been on the right track. Since HIs do seem to "focus" their brains physiologically, hypnosis itself may prove to be an extreme form of this.

Meanwhile, until more information is to hand, the MRC R^2 figure of 0.428 is encouraging since all variables except the TAS were physiological ones. Bowers[26] and Hilgard[27] both wish to see hypnotic research domesticated within the psychology discipline, but popular misconceptions about it continue to make this a slow business. Therefore significant physiological findings with such hardware as EEG – unlikely to be susceptible to either fraud or magic – can only help to enhance the respectability of hypnosis as a serious research topic.

ACKNOWLEDGEMENTS

I wish to acknowledge the unfailing helpfulness and wisdom of Dr. Leon Lack. All electronic circuitry was designed and built by Leon Snigg, laboratory technician extraordinary (Flinders Psychology Department).

REFERENCES

1. Galbraith, G.C., London, P., Leibovitz, M.P., Cooper, L.M. and Hart, J.T. EEG and Hypnotic Susceptibility. *J.Comp.Phys.Psych.*,1970,72,125-131.

2. *Harvard Group Scale of Hypnotic Susceptibility*. Shor, R.E. and Orne, E.C. Palo Alto, California: Consulting Psychologists Press, 1962.

3. Tebēcis, A.K., Provins, K.A., Farnbach, R.W., and Pentony, P. Hypnosis and the EEG. *J.Nerv.Ment.Disease*, 1975,161,1-17.

4. London, P., Hart,J.T., and Leibovitz, M.P. EEG alpha rhythms and susceptibility to hypnosis. *Nature*, 1968, 219,71-72.

5. Nowlis, D.P., and Rhead, J.C. Relation of eyes-closed alpha activity to hypnotic susceptibility. *Percept.and Motor Skills*,1968,27,1047-50.

6. Edmonston, W.E. and Grotevant, W.R. Hypnosis and alpha density. *Am. J. Clin.Hyp*, 1975,17,221-232.

7. Dumas, R.A. EEG alpha-hypnotisability correlations: a review. *Psychophysiology*, 1977,14,431-438.

8. Engstrom, D.R., London, P., and Hart, J.T. EEG alpha feedback training and hypnotic susceptibility. *Proceedings of 78th Ann.Conv. of APA.*

9. London, P., Cooper, L.M. and Engstrom,D.R. Increasing hypnotic suscepti-bility by brain wave feedback. *J.Ab.Psych.*,1974,83,554-60.

10. Crosson, B., Meinz, R., Laur, E., Williams, D., and Andreychuk, T. EEG alpha training, hypnotic susceptibility, and baseline techniques.

11. Morgan, A.H., McDonald, P.J. and Macdonald, H. Differences in bilateral alpha activity as a function of experimental task, with a note on lateral eye movements and hypnotic ability. *Neuropsychologia*,1971,9,459-469.

12. Doyle, J.C., Ornstein, R., and Galin, D. Lateral specialisation of cognitive mode: II. EEG Frequency analysis. *Psychophysiology*, 1977,14, 431-438.

13. Bakan, P. The eyes have it. *Psychology Today*, 1971,4,64.

14. Gur, R.C., and Gur, R.E. Handedness, sex and eyedness as moderating variables in the relation between hypnotic susceptibility and functional brain asymmetry. *J.Ab.Psych.*,1974,83,635-643.

15. Morgan, A.H., McDonald, P.J. and Hilgard, E.R. EEG alpha and lateral asymmetry related to task and hypnotisability. *Psychophysiology*, 1974,11,275-282.

16. Tellegen,A., and Atkinson, G. Openness to absorbing and self-altering experiences ("absorption"), a trait related to hypnotic susceptibility. *J.Ab.Psych.*,1974,83,268-277.

17. Davidson, R.J., Schwartz, G.E. and Rothman, C.P. Attentional style and the self-regulation of mode-specific attention: an EEG study. *J.Ab.Psych.*, 1976,85,611-621.

18. Graham,C., and Evans, F.J. Hypnotisability and the deployment of waking attention. *J.Ab.Psych.*,1977,86,631-638.

19. Knuth,D.E. *The Art of Computer Programming, Vol. 2*. Reading,Mass.: Addison-Wesley, 1969.

20. ACER *Higher Test, Form M, Section L.* Victoria: Australian Council for Education Research, 1967.

21. *Seashore Measures of Musical Talents*, 1975 Revision. Seashore, C.E., Lewis, D., and Saetveit, J.G. NY: The Psychological Corporation, 1975.

22. Cooper, R., Osselton, J.W. and Shaw, J.C. *EEG Technology, 2nd Edn.* London: Butterworth, 1974.

23. Schacter, D.L. EEG theta waves and psychological phenomena: a review and analysis. *Biological Psychology*, 1977,5,47-82.

24. Evans, F.J. Hypnosis and sleep: techniques for exploring cognitive activity during sleep. In Fromm, E., and Shor, R.E. (Eds.) *Hypnosis: Research developments and perspectives.* Chicago: Aldine-Atherton, 1972.

25. Galbraith,G.D., Cooper, L.M., and London, P. Hypnotic susceptibility and the sensory evoked response. *J.Comp.Phys.Psych.*,1972,80,509-514.

26. Bowers, K.S. *Hypnosis for the seriously curious.* Belmont, Calif.: Wadsworth, 1976.

27. Hilgard, E.R. *Divided Consciousness.* NY.: John Wiley and Sons, 1977.

© 1979 Elsevier/North-Holland Biomedical Press
Hypnosis 1979
G.D. Burrows, D.R. Collison and L. Dennerstein

PAIN CONTROL THROUGH HYPNOSIS By Dr. Albert Rappaport

   The roots of clinical hypnosis are obscure and probably more closely tied to
religion and magic than to science. It may be that maraculous cures accomplished by the priests of Egypt and Greece were accomplished hypnotically. The
power to heal by suggestion or by "laying on of hands" was generally ascribed
to devine innervention until the 17th century when Athanasius Kircher, a German
scholar, came up with the idea that a natural force called animal magnetism was
at work.

   In the next century a physician, Franz Mesmer, practicing in Vienna took the
idea of animal magnetism and turned it into a household word. He believed that
sickness and health were controlled by the balance of a universal invisible
fluid in the human body, and that when illness occurred this fluid could be
returned to its proper harmonius function by use of magnets. With these magnets, Mesmer cured a number of patients with a variety of complaints. Strangely enough, they would usually go into convulsions during the treatment which
Mesmer took as a sign that magnetism was working. His explanation for his
failures were that some people had a mysterious force in their body that defied
his magnets. Mesmer's real contribution to hypnosis was that he learned how
to induce a trance, but his outlandish claims for this power caused the medical
profession to drive him out of Vienna. He arrived in Paris during the period
of the French Revolution and set up a clinic that became the rage among the
wealthy people. Soon Mesmerism was being practiced all over France. The
French Medical Association was as quick to cry freud as their Austrian counterparts had done. In 1784, a government committee of which one of its members
was Benjamin Franklin, American Ambassador to France, pronounced Mesmers cures
to be figments of his patients imagination. By this time, there were Mesmer-
ists all over Europe. Some of them were respectable physicians and some of
them were quacks who made wild claims for the powers of animal magnetism. In
1837 the Commission of the French Academy of Medicine delt Mesmerism a blow by
proclaiming that there was no such thing as animal magnetism. Any cures
affected by mesmerism were brought about entirely by suggestion. Hypnotism
fell into disrepute in medical circles.

At about the same time as English physician, James Braid, was experimenting with animal magnetism on his own. He decided it was a psychological effect and not a physical phenomenon as Mesmer had thought. He coined the word Hypnosis from the Greek root meaning "to put to sleep". Braid was the first to make credible use of hypnosis in surgery. Hypnosis might well have gained wide use in anesthetics, but chloroform then coming into general use was more reliable. The spiritualists of the day took up hypnosis and by doing so, hypnosis once again fell into disgrace among scientists.

But this did not keep Jean Charcot, the famous French neurologist, from trying out hypnosis with some of his patients. At the same time, there was another group of scientists by the name of Lee Bolt and Burnhein, and they were called the Nancy School. They felt hypnosis was achieved through suggestion and did not have to be hysterical or pathelogical to achieve that state of hypnosis as the Charcot School felt at that time.

An early colleague of Freuds by the name of Joseph Breuer, used hypnosis to treat hysterical paralysis. It was Breuer's work that inspired Freud to try it. Unable at one point to hypnotize one of his patients, Freud simply placed his hand on her head and asked her to repeat whatever came into her mind. In this way without hypnosis, Freud was able to get the critical early trauma that was causing her depression. Thus, the technique of free association was born.

Hypnosis never became a common tool of the psychoanlytic movement. Few phychiatrists learned to practice it and hardly anyone was willing to defend it. Again, hypnosis took a dip. Most of the psychiatrists were using Freud's free association method as a tool. This took longer to get at repressed memories but was easier for the average psychiatrist to put to use.

In World War I and II we see a resurgence of interest in hypnosis. It was then used specially to treat shellshock and battle fatigued soldiers. But it was not until 1956 that the American Medical Association pronounced that hypnosis was a valuable and theraputic adjunct to be used in medical treatment. This meant that hypnosis was no longer a bastard, but a legitimate offspring of the medical world. It also meant that monies for research grants would be available. At this point, hypnosis had definitely arrived and was here to stay.

My motivation in practicing hypnosis is to relieve anxiety and tension in my patients, so that the dental procedures may be accomplished with minimal discomfort. People who are hypnotized for the first time are frequently dissappointed to find that they are experiencing nothing overwhelming. They feel mildly relaxed but remain in touch with reality and in control of their thoughts. They may discover that hypnotist's suggestions are quite resistable. Contrary to what most people believe, a person under hypnosis may need not fall asleep nor lose contact with his surroundings nor relinquish his will. He is often able to recall everything that has happened during the trance and acts perfectly normal.

Before turning to hypnosis for the control of pain, we have to understand that pain is made up of two components. Pain is really two kinds of signals that blend into one: 1) the physical sensation registered by the brain and 2) the psychological reaction to the sensation. Hypnosis will rarely cure the malady that is causing the pain. What it will do is to alter the patients perception of the pain.

The prevalence of pain in our society can be readily attested by the attention the pain killers receive in our advertising media. Millions of dollars are spent by the public to prevent pain. So in modern day practice of dentistry with the efficient tools, high speed drills, background music, everything is done in an effort to relax the patients. So it seems that pain reduction is now one of the primary tasks of dentists. Anxiety can serve to exaggerate pain, and hynosis can be effective in reducing anxiety and raising the pain threshold.

What is hypnosis? The hypnotic trance is undoubtedly an extension of common states of mind. My definition of hypnosis is a deprevation of sensory stimuli where the attention is limited or funneled on one positive thought or a series of positive thoughts. Just as you are listening to me right now, some of you may be funneling in on just my talk, you may be thinking about what you're going to do tonight, or whom you're going to see. So you are really being bombarded with alot of stimulation. Through hypnosis you can eliminate all of that and function on one channel. Somehow the mind and the brain when functioning on one thing is able to produce maximum results.

We all undergo everyday trances from time to time when we are deeply absorbed and preoccupied with whatever we are doing. At these moments, we are fully focused and completely oblivious to whatever is happening around us. The ability to be absorbed in this way is called response attentiveness. It marks one as a good candidate for hypnosis. This brings us to the point of who can and cannot be hypnotized. Three traits mark one as a potentially good hypnotic subject. The ability to focus attention and concentrate, an openness to new experience, and a willingness to comply with suggestion.

There are three procedures that I use to control pain once the patient is in a hypnotic trance. One is called direct suggestion. For example, I suggest to the patient to relax and close his eyes and breathe deeply, thereby reducing the tention and anxiety inherent in dental procedures. What you are doing is focusing in on your breathing, and as you breathe you feel the air pass through your mouth, your teeth, and out through your lips. As your mind functions and concentrates on one thing it eliminiates all extra sensory stimulization. This helps produce relaxation and lessens anxiety.

The second procedure is called altering the experience of pain. For example, the patient may be told that his jaw is numb by producing analgesia in a hand and transferring it to the jaw. This is called glove analgesia. I use this on patients who cannot use a chemical anesthetic either because they are allergic to it or are afraid of the injection. By using hypnosis you can anesthesize the hand and transfer it to the jaw, thus producing sufficient analgesia so you can do surgical preparation of the tooth.

The third method is directing the patients attention away from the pain and its source. For example, as in the phantom limb pain where the patient is told that his tooth is detached from his body, and he can watch it as an interested spectator while the tooth is surgically prepared. This is a good method to use on patients who have a great imagination.

In dentistry we use direct suggestions approximately 80% of the time and altering of pain the balance of the time. These are the two methods that I use when patients cannot be managed readily by local anesthetics and premedication. Hypnosis is most useful with these problem patients who cannot be managed due to being nervous and frightened. As Dr. A. A. Moss says, "the primary use of hypnosis in dentistry is to normalize the patient so we can manage him as we do our other patients".[1] The word normalize is the important word here because all we are really trying to do is re-educate the patient. The fact is, one of the advantages of hypnosis over other methods is that we can re-educate the patient through post hypnotic suggestion. When I have a very nervous patient who cannot tolerate anesthetics, after they go into the initial hypnotic trance, I give them the post hypnotic suggestion that the next time they come to the office they will feel very comfortable and relaxed. They will also look forward to further dental work without any discomfort.

This is one of the great advantages of hypnosis because it cuts down time. Many people do not use hypnosis because they feel it takes too much time. This is wrong because after the initial trance is induced, by post hypnotic suggestion you can cut your time down to 5 seconds to put a patient into a trance.

Primary, we don't want the patient to become dependent on the hypnotist as a father figure. We want them to be the master of themselves. In fact, another thing about the hynotic trance that people misunderstand is that you're not under the influence of the hypnotist. This is because when a person is in a trance there are 2 ego factors working. One, where he sees himself at center stage, and another person sitting in the wings watching what is happening. Now if anything is suggested that the patient thinks is detrimental to him, that ego factor in the wings will say, "stop this, I'm going to wake up". I have seen this happen where a person is given a suggestion they don't like and will just wake up.

So this is what it is all about. We want to re-educate the people we see in the office, and we don't want them to become dependent upon it like a drug. It is used mainly to facilitate dental procedures and help to relax our patients.

So after 200 years of using hypnosis, we still cannot say with all certainty what hypnosis is nor exactly how it works, but it does work and is here to stay.

1. Moss, Dr. A. A. (1963) Journal of Dental Medicine - Hypnosis for Pain Management in Dentistry.

Hypnosis 1979
G.D. Burrows, D.R. Collison and L. Dennerstein

HYPNOTIC STRATEGIES IN THE DAILY PRACTICE OF ANESTHESIA

JAMES C. ERICKSON, III, M.D.

Professor of Anesthesiology, Jefferson Medical College of Thomas Jefferson
University, Philadelphia, Pennsylvania   19107

INTRODUCTION

Hypnotic techniques should be applied to all patients undergoing surgical
and obstetrical operative procedures. These patients are universally anxious.
They often fear pain, death, mutilation, the diagnosis of an incurable disease,
or the possibility of a dreadful experience. They are sometimes afraid of
being awake and aware of pain and the sights and sounds of the operating room
and conversely are often fearful of the anesthetic sleep, equating it with
death. Many anesthetists inform their patients that they are about "to put
them to sleep" prior to administering thiopental sodium, only to see the
patients become wide-eyed with fear, with increases in pulse rate and blood
pressure. This phrase is a familiar euphemism for putting an aged or sick pet
dog out of its misery! Thus, our patients are highly responsive to suggestions
of all sorts, both careless comments and the carefully planned positive phrases
of covert hypnosis.

COVERT HYPNOSIS AND GENERAL ANESTHESIA

Covert hypnosis is applicable to all patients, especially those in the operating theater. Suggestions for ease, relaxation, comfort, safety and ego-
strengthening praises are liberally offered without hypnotic induction cere-
monies or discussions about hypnosis per se. Eye contact is unnecessary and is
often nearly impossible to achieve. Their anxieties prepare them to be highly
motivated and very receptive to the calming phrases of an empathetic physician •
or attendant which aids in achieving a state or depth of hypnosis that fulfills
their needs[1]. Pre-anesthetic sedation and the strategic intravenous administration of small doses of barbiturates, tranquilizers and opiates seem to
enhance the receptivity to positive suggestion. This occurs partially because
of decreased critical thinking and also because the intravenous medication is
given to cause drowsiness at the very moment that suggestions for deep breathing and increased sense of a comfort and sleepiness are given. Thus, the
pharmacologic effects of the drugs seem to synergize covert hypnosis, rather
than lessening the impact of hypnotic suggestion, enabling us to achieve

induction of general anesthesia with smaller doses of thiopental than usual. These maneuvers often cause a distinct slowing of tachycardias and a decrease of elevated blood pressures of overtly anxious patients. Further suggestion to alleviate anxiety by "allowing all fears and apprehensions to flow out with the stale air during the next exhalation" (avoiding the word expiration) has been particularly effective. As the induction continues, the patient is continuously given quiet suggestions for a calm, relaxed nap, with the anticipation of "awakening in the recovery room feeling comfortable and very pleased that the operation and anesthetic have gone so well, so smoothly, so pleasantly." Realizing the persistance of auditory perception during general anesthesia, suggestions are given to our patients throughout the procedure[2]. Of course, all the aforementioned suggestions are reiterated during the period of arousal from anesthesia, with additional emphasis on postoperative concerns such as: comfortable breathing, easy voiding and a pleasant feeling of hunger. In addition, they are told that they "will probably notice a feeling of pressure beneath the bandages covering their operation when the anesthetic effect wanes." This pressure is explained as a natural muscle spasm response, which they can control by taking deep breaths and exhaling completely, "allowing all the muscles to become pleasantly, smoothly, comfortably relaxed." This phrasing has been extremely successful, with patients offering little or no complaints of pain while in the recovery room. When questioned, they respond that the pressure is very mild and that they are ready to be escorted back to their room.

COVERT HYPNOSIS AND REGIONAL ANESTHESIA

The induction and maintenance phases of regional anesthetic techniques lend themselves especially well to the use of covert hypnosis begun in the operating room or during a pre-anesthetic visit. Patients are lightly sedated and are warned of each impending manuever (needle prick, blood pressure checkup) during the early portion of the proceedings. These warnings of potentially noxious stimuli are always phrased in innocuous terms, conceived to minimize the patient's perception of the pain. As an example, an intravenous administration of diazepam (Valium) usually causes burning pain along the course of the vein through which it is introduced. It is quite effective to tell the patient to expect "a warm, pleasing sensation flowing up your arm....and when it fades away you will become relaxed and sleepy, feeling warm and comfortable." Such verbal preparation enhances the sedative effect of the drug so that small doses are as effective as larger quantities, thus avoiding unwanted effects on circulation and respiration. Patients who are operated upon under spinal, epidural and peripheral nerve block techniques also respond well to the post-operative metaphor of "pressure beneath the bandage which is mostly muscle spasm" and which is controllable by progressive relaxation triggered by deep breathing. These patients too, enjoy an easy relaxed state in the recovery room and rarely require analgesic drugs.

DISCUSSION

When patients return to the post-operative ward or floor, they may become victims of the expectations, fears and prejudices of family members, other visitors, the nurses and physicians. The majority of these well-meaning individuals frequently voice their expectations that terrible pain is to be expected, and thereby enhance the patients' perception of his or her discomfort. Of course, this means that all these non-patients can perform in their own way to treat the patient, by applying cold or warm clothes to their brows, or by offering injections of analgesics or by inspecting and palpating the site of surgery. Thus, each one indulges in their own ego-strengthening exercise, but to the detriment of the poor victim. Too often, the control of post-operative pain gained with overt or covert hypnosis is lost, due to a bombardment of pain-emphasizing suggestions when patients return to their rooms.

Optimum benefits from covert hypnosis can be expected if the anesthetist meets patients a day or two prior to surgery, and along with the assessment of his physical state and discussion of the anesthetic management, includes a description of the gentle, smooth manner in which the induction will be accomplished. One can rehearse the entire surgical experience bringing the patient back to his room "just as you are now." All this conversation is conducted in a quiet, confident, easy manner with the physician maintaining steady eye contact with the patient. The post-operative course of patients undergoing hemorrhoidectomy has been far more satisfactory when this approach is used. They received either low spinal or caudal epidural anesthesia with a generous accompaniment of suggestion and minimal pharmacologic sedation. Their recuperation was marked with comfort, minimal analgesic requirement, very little pain with the first bowel movement, and discharge from the hospital a day or two sooner than anticipated.

As implied throughout this paper, a constant flow of positive suggestion is offered to the patient to flood their thoughts and attention. Thus, covert hypnosis resembles a symphonic accompaniment to the solo instrument or voice (the pharmacologic anesthetic method), each enriching the effect of the other. This method has proven to be universally acceptable and applicable. It is a non-authoritarian, permissive approach and resembles Barber's method[3] in many ways. The efficacy of this mode of psychological management plus the safety of modern anesthetic drugs and techniques should relegate hypnoanesthesia to a niche in history. Indeed, the use of hypnoanesthesia without drugs of any sort for major surgery is little more than an ego-strengthening exploit for the hypnotist. Covert hypnosis, on the other hand, is applicable to all patients and can be administered by any thoughtful anesthetist or surgeon. Patients seem to arrive at the depth of hypnosis necessary for them to attain emotional and physical relaxation[1]. There is rarely an obvious trance state.

The semantics of positive hypnotic suggestions for surgical patients are of utmost importance. A person with excellent intentions but thoughtless emphasis on pain and the clinical details of surgery and anesthesia will frighten patients rather than create a calm confident state. Fears are often inflammed by careless remarks made within the patients' hearing, of the malignant diseases or complications of persons other than themselves. We must be constantly on guard to protect our patients from such influences lest they become the victims of their own apprehensions which are so easily triggered by such thoughtlessness.

The lessened consumption of analgesics in the immediate post-operative period and the increase in patient satisfaction for their anesthetic management has become obvious in our daily observations of recipients of covert hypnosis. One can only speculate as to other benefits, such as a greatly diminished incidence of cardiac arrhythmias and bronchospasm during anesthetics which are accompanied by covert hypnotic suggestions. Both complications occur far less frequently in the author's practice than in the experiences of many colleagues. It can be postulated that the neurohumoral responses of the autonomic nervous system's reaction to stress and anxiety are kept in abeyance by the constant hypnotic commentary even during the unconscious state of light or deep general anesthesia.

In summary, one must simply reiterate that covert hypnosis should be applied to all surgical and obstetrical patients to achieve relaxation, and freedom from anxiety during the surgical experience. It is a non-authoritarian approach and requires a physician or therapist who carefully selects his words and phrases, using those suggesting the desired relaxed comfortable state, with scrupulous avoidance of all comments with a frightening connotation.

REFERENCES

1. Schafer, D.W. and Hernandez, A. (1978) Hypnosis, Pain and the Context of Therapy. Int. J. Clin. Exp. Hypnosis, 26, 143-153.

2. Scott, D.L. (1974) Modern Hospital Hypnosis. Year Book Medical Publishers, Chicago, 1-202

3. Barber, J.(1977) Rapid Induction Analgesia. Amer. J. Clin. Hypnosis, 19, 138-147

© 1979 Elsevier/North-Holland Biomedical Press
Hypnosis 1979
G.D. Burrows, D.R. Collison and L. Dennerstein

HYPNOTHERAPY OF A PSYCHOGENIC SEIZURE DISORDER IN AN ADOLESCENT

T. J. GLENN, M.D. AND J. F. SIMONDS, M.D.
University of Missouri Medical School

A clinical case study of a 13-year-old girl admitted to a mental health center because of psychogenic seizures is presented. Hypnoanalysis and posthypnotic suggestions were helpful in managing the girl's seizure episodes.

INTRODUCTION

Psychogenic seizures, also referred to as hysterical seizures, are rare but dramatic symptoms that can simulate true seizure disorders. These seizures are called psychogenic because emotional conflicts are prominent precipitating factors. Sometimes an underlying neurotic disorder manifested by conversion or hysterical symptoms can be demonstrated. This paper will examine the literature reports of psychogenic seizures and then present a case history of a girl who was treated by the authors for such a disorder.

REVIEW OF LITERATURE ON PSYCHOGENIC SEIZURES

Reports of convulsions as symptoms of conversion reactions are rare in children and adolescents. In 1888 Charcot (Kanner, 1972) demonstrated a 14-year-old boy with grand mal hysteria. Many cases were reported during the 1890's. During the 1900's fewer and fewer cases were observed. Keith (1963), a neurologist at the Mayo Clinic, did not remember seeing one case of a hysterical convulsion in a child during a 21 year period. Two patients ages 15 years and 36 years were diagnosed as having hysterical convulsions by Lindner (1973). He used hypnosis to regress his patients to the time of the convulsive experience and was able to get the patients to respond with a seizure on cue. Lindner (1973) theorized that the consciousness could not accept aggressive impulses and the seizure served as a safety valve mechanism. Bernstein (1969) reported on three patients with psychogenic seizures manifested by fainting, dissociation, tremors and writhing movements. All patients were adolescent girls in situational crises involving sexual activity with boy friends. The violent motor response according to Bernstein (1969) seemed to discharge the girls' anger and frustration. When the situation was resolved the seizures ceased.

Epidemics of hysterical convulsions have been reported (Moss and McEvedy,

1966,; Schuler and Parenton, 1943; Trainor 1974). In 1892 a 10-year-old girl
who lived in Silesia developed tremor of the hand which spread to the rest of
her body (Kanner, 1972). Eventually 20 girls were experiencing convulsive-
like movement. When school ended the convulsion ceased but with the start of
the school year the convulsions returned in the girls but not in the boys. A
recent epidemic in a remote village in Canada involved 25 children and
adolescents who attempted to fly and when restrained they would flail and
fight for hours (Trainor, 1974). Each youth's fit was preceded by a period of
fatigue, irritability, headaches and boredom.

The manifestation of a psychogenic convulsion approximates the idea or
concept that the youth has about the convulsion. Unless the youth has observed convulsions in the past, his concept will be that of a bizarre, gross
motor movement. In cases where family members have epilepsy, the youth's
concept will be closer to reality. An even closer approximation occurs in
youth who also have apilepsy and for one reason or another imitate their own
convulsions.

Charcot (Kanner, 1972) classified the various stages of a hysterical
seizure. The first stage or prodromal stage is characterized by visual or
auditory experiences, spells of unchecked laughing or crying and pelvic or
abdominal pain. The epileptoid or second stage is marked by rigidity,
twitching and clonic or tonic convulsions. During the third stage the youth
may assume peculiar postures such as the "arc de cercle" (the back is bent so
that the occiput may touch the heels). Uncoordinated kicking movements also
occur. The stage of affective attitudes is manifested by features and postures that express terror, rapture, hatred. A fifth or delirious stage is
marked by impaired orientation but no amnesia.

The differential diagnosis of a "hysterical" convulsion includes (1) true
epilepsy, (2) conversion seizure, (3) a combination of true epilepsy and conversion seizure.

The following are historical or observational characteristics of a seizure
which would be indicative of a psychogenic origin (Kanner, 1972; Bakwin and
Bakwin, 1973; Grinker and Sahs, 1966):

(1) dramatic, theatrical quality

(2) occurrence in the presence of others

(3) emotional episodes precede the onset of the seizures

(4) the individual rarely injures himself

(5) postures are bizarre

(6) individual is easily roused by painful stimuli

(7) incontinence does not occur

(8) during the seizure there is no unconsciousness

(9) stupor does not follow the seizure

(10) pupils react normally and corneal reflex is present

(11) attempts to open the eyes are resisted.

The EEG should not contain spike and wave forms diagnostic of epilepsy if one is to consider a diagnosis of conversion seizure alone. Of course in a patient who is a known epileptic, the diagnosis of conversion seizures must rest on historical and observational criteria.

Hypnosis may activate the clinical conversion seizure without a corresponding EEG abnormality. In the Schwarz et al. (1955) study hypnosis failed to activate seizures either clinically or in the EEG in 16 true epileptics. On the other hand hypnosis reproduced clinical seizures without EEG findings in 10 patients who were not presumed to be true epileptics.

The following case history demonstrates many of the characteristics of the hysterical convulsive reaction.

CASE HISTORY

The patient, Ann, was a 13-year-old Caucasian girl who was referred to a mental health center children's ward because of recurrent seizures which were suggestive of a psychogenic conversion reaction. The seizures were manifested by violent thrashing movements, banging of the head, excessive salivation, and a prodrome characterized by dizziness. The episodes lasted from 30 minutes to 90 minutes and were followed by amnesia, sleepiness, weakness, headaches. There were no symptoms of incontinence, tonic-clonic movements or unconsciousness.

The mother dated the onset of problems to approximately four years prior to admission when the girl became nervous and tense following the death of her father who had treated her as a favorite child. However, neurological symptoms did not develop until about six months prior to admission when she hit the back of her head on some bedsprings and became dazed for several hours. About one month prior to admission she fainted while running during a physical education class. Shortly after the fainting episode she lost her voice and was only able to speak in a whisper for several weeks. Two weeks before admission she again accidently hit her head on a porch beam. Allegedly she was unconscious for several hours. She was seen by a physician who did not take x-rays but recommended bed rest for a day. The seizures began a few days after the injury. Coincidentally with the onset of the seizures she regained the ability to speak. A physician hospitalized the patient in a local hospital and started her on Dilantin. Despite this treatment the seizures became almost continuous especially following her discharge home. A second hospitalization and a psychiatric consultation eventuated in her referral to the mental health center.

Ann was born into a poor family. Her natural father was an alcoholic who was moderately retarded and quite dependent. Father and mother were separated when Ann was five years old. A divorce occurred after a few years. Nevertheless father continued to visit Ann intermittently until his death. Mother remarried three years prior to admission but again the husband turned out to be alcoholic. The second husband periodically would desert the family.

Mother's pregnancy and delivery were uneventful. Growth and development were normal except for a tendency to be obese. Ann was never completely toilet trained and she continued to wet her bed at night four times per week. When Ann's menstrual periods started three months before admission she gained 25 lbs. Menarche seemed to be a frightening experience.

In her early school years, Ann had been slow in speech development but this responded to speech therapy. In later years she experienced increasing peer ridicule because of her obesity. She was called vulgar names which insinuated that she was sexually promiscuous. This led to a loss of motivation in academic performance, attempts to buy friends with gifts and many absent days. Her marks in the eighth grade averaged D+. She had to repeat the eighth grade because of 96 absent days.

At the time of admission Ann had a body odor which suggested poor hygenic practices. The physical examination was normal except for obesity. She talked with a slight lisp. Although confused regarding specific events prior to admission, she was not disoriented. She tended to repress sad and angry feelings. Activity level was low due to cautiousness and inhibition. Her self image was poor as a consequence of peer ridicule.

On the Wide Range Achievement Tests she scored at seventh grade level in reading, fifth grade level in spelling and third grade level in mathematics. Low scores in mathematics seemed more related to motivation than to low skills. The WISC scores were Full Scale 83, Verbal 79, Performance 92.

Initial EEG, skull x-rays and a two hour post prandial blood sugar were normal. A second EEG done one month after admission showed right temporal lobe slowing. During hypnoanalysis the girl experienced a seizure similar to previous seizures and she described a scene in which she was raped by three boys in a woods and later was lying next to her dead father while snakes crawled over her body. Previous medical examinations including a pelvic examination indicated that Ann had never experienced sexual intercourse. It was hypothesized that the rape fantasy suggested conflicts relative to emerging sexual desires.

For several days after admission Ann complained of dizziness and nausea. On three occasions she was unresponsive for periods of one minute to eight minutes. She would stare without falling to the ground. On several occasions she thrashed in her bed and fell to the floor but denied remembering the event. After each episode she slept for one hour and complained of headaches and an upset stomach. These seizures at times seemed to be of temporal lobe origin and at other times hysterical features were prominent. Dilantin was gradually discontinued over a five day period after admission. No seizures were observed after the first week of hospitalization which lasted four months. There were also no seizures reported during a two year post discharge period.

Ann was started on a 1000 calorie diet which resulted in a 22 lb. weight loss. She was given Tofranil 50 mg. at bedtime which reduced bedwetting from 4 nights in 7 to 1 night in 7. Tofranil was continued throughout hospitalization. She participated in hypnotherapy sessions three times weekly during the first two weeks of hospitalization. The ward program focused on a behavior modification approach while individual therapy was psychoanalytically oriented. Ann was able to express her angry feelings appropriately to staff members and peers. She gradually developed a closer relationship with her mother and stepfather who came twice a month for counseling sessions.

On the ward Ann was able to participate in all activities including swimming and trampoline. The nursing staff worked on improving her personal hygiene which helped with the girl's increased self image. After two months of hospitalization she was able to attend the local public school in the ninth grade. She worked independently and over a two month period improved her academic skills by one year. Ann returned to live with her mother and stepfather and after two years her adjustment was good with no recurrence of seizures.

Since the patient manifested a high degree of suggestibility, one of the authors used hypnosis for the diagnosis and treatment of psychogenic components of the seizure disorder. The patient experienced hypnoidal, light and medium states but she did not develop a plenary trance state. Posthypnotic suggestions were given so that she would be able to prevent the seizures by pressing her right thumb and forefinger together. She was taught how to stop hypnotically induced seizures on cue and to verbalize her fantasies instead of acting out the fantasies that accompanied the seizures. Eventually Ann was able to verbalize her feelings and fantasies at times other than during the hypnotic sessions.

DISCUSSION

The patient presented a diagnostic dilemma because some symptoms such as amnesia and postseizure sleepiness and the finding of slow waves in the EEG, suggested a psychomotor seizure disorder. Nevertheless a diagnosis of conversion reaction, manifested by seizure-like symptoms, was made. The motor component of the seizure was an uncoordinated thrashing rather than a tonic or clonic movement or automatic motion. At no time was the patient observed to lose consciousness except by mother immediately after the head injury. Perhaps she did experience a mild concussion at that time. Yet the treating physician did not think the condition was serious and the mother's story was vague. It should be noted that the seizures had a dramatic flair and always occurred in the presence of other persons. Usually the seizures were preceded by an emotional stimulus and at no time was the patient ever hurt. Her fainting episode was probably related to hyperventilation. The loss of ability to speak above a whisper, often a classical conversion symptom, was further evidence that the symptoms were related to psychological factors. In addition the seizures seemed to start almost as a substitute symptom after the patient was able to speak with normal intensity. The frequency of seizures increased when the girl returned home and this seemed to indicate that the secondary gain might have been related to a desire to return to a hospital setting and escape from a stressful home environment. This idea was further supported when the frequency of seizures dramatically decreased from 20 per day to only three during the first week of psychiatric hospitalization. Dilantin had no effect on the frequency of seizures prior to psychiatric hospitalization and there was not a return of seizure activity after Dilantin was discontinued. The three seizure-like episodes during the first week of hospitalization could be explained on the basis of a psychological reaction to stress created by peers on the ward who teased her. Other evidence which suggested a psychogenic conversion reaction was the high degree of suggestibility, the ability to experience seizures on cue during hypnosis and to respond dramatically to posthypnotic suggestions. An EEG recording during a hypnotically induced seizure would have been very useful and perhaps diagnostic as Schwarz et al. (1955) mentioned. The EEG which showed temporal lobe slow waves did not disprove the psychogenic diagnosis since such a recording can be found in emotionally disturbed children as well as normal children.

There was evidence that the patient was experiencing stress in her home and school environments. Her father was dead, her mother seemed preoccupied with her own problems and the girl was ostracized by peers. With the onset of menstruation she gained a great deal of weight which aggravated an already low self concept. No doubt she had conflict with sexual urges and desires of adolescence. Thus the patient was a prime candidate for developing further psychiatric symptoms which provided an opportunity to escape from an intolerable situation.

Hypnosis can be used to clarify a diagnosis of conversion reaction since it is likely to activate only a conversion seizure and rarely a true seizure disorder. An EEG done during a hypnotically induced seizure should not contain spike waves characteristic of a true seizure disorder. Hypnotherapy can help a person gain a sense of control over psychogenic seizures by enabling him to initiate and end the seizure on cue. As with most behavioral and emotional disorders hypnosis can only provide lasting benefits when combined with other techniques such as behavior modification, individual psychotherapy, group therapy, family therapy, parent counseling, environmental manipulation and drug therapy.

REFERENCES

1. Bakwin, H., Bakwin, R., Behavior Disorders in Children, 4th edition, Philadelphia: W. B. Saunders Co., 1972.

2. Bernstein, N., Psychogenic Seizures in Adolescent Girls, Behavioral Neuropsychiatry, 1969, 1, 31-34.

3. Grinker, R., Sahs, A. L., Neurology, 6th Ed. Springfield, Illinois: Charles Thomas Co., 1966.

4. Kanner, L., Child Psychiatry, 4th Ed. Springfield, Illinois: Charles Thomas Co., 1972.

5. Keith, H., Convulsive Disorders in Children. Boston: Little Brown Co., 1963, p. 114-115.

6. Lindner, H., Psychogenic Seizure States: a Psychodynamic Study. International Journal of Clinical and Experimental Hypnosis 1973, 21, 261-271.

7. Moss, P., McEvedy, C., An Epidemic of Overbreathing Among School Girls. British Medical Journal Nov. 26, 1966, #5525, 1295-1300.

8. Schuler, E. A., & Parenton, V. J., Recent Epidemic of Hysteria in a Louisiana High School, Journal of Sociological Psychology, 1943, 17, 221-235.

9. Schwarz, B. E., Bickford, R. G., & Rasmussen, W. C., Hypnotic Phenomena Including Hypnotically activated Seizures Studied with Electroencephalogram. Journal of Nervous Mental Disorders, 1955, 122, 564-574.

208

10. Trainor, D., Seizure Epidemic Reported in Remote Canadian Village, Psychiatric News, Dec. 4, 1975, 17.

© 1979 Elsevier/North-Holland Biomedical Press
Hypnosis 1979
G.D. Burrows, D.R. Collison and L. Dennerstein

HYPNOSIS IN THE TREATMENT OF LONG TERM SEQUELAE OF SEXUAL ASSAULT ON CHILDREN

NEILL MALCOLM M.B.,B.S.
P.O. Box 400, Leduc, Alberta, Canada.

The year 1979 has been designated by the United Nations as the Year of the Child. One aspect of this that has received much publicity is the problem of child abuse, one form of which is sexual abuse.

In the 1890s Freud and Breuer suggested that sexual assaults on children could be the origin of hysteria in adults[1]. Such assaults horrify the general public and this stirred up opposition to their theories, so that with time Freud came to consider these assaults to be fantasies. As a result of this the possible damaging effects of sexual assault on children was overlooked for about seventy-five years.

However, sexual assaults are common[2] but statistics vary. Two retrospective surveys suggest that as many as one child in three in the United States is sexually assaulted[3,4]. On the other hand a recent survey from the Georgia Child Abuse Registry on confirmed cases indicated an incidence of about 0.2%[5]. In England and Wales in 1960 there were about three and a half thousand cases known to the police of interference with adolescent girls. Only 232 cases were known in children under the age of thirteen[6]. These widely varying figures suggest that the majority of cases never become known to the author-ities, particularly in the case of younger children. It is possible, therefore, that up to half a million children may be sexually assaulted each year in the United States. This is equivalent to about fifty thousand in Canada, thirty thousand in Australia and a hundred and twenty thousand in England and Wales. About ninety percent of assaulted children are girls. It is rare for the assaulter to be female[3,5]. About eighty percent of cases are confined to such acts as exposure or digital manipulation. The remaining twenty percent are cases of rape, incest, sodomy and intercourse[7].

The effects of sexual abuse may not become evident for many years and may require reinforcement by subsequent events before symptoms arise. The Sexual Information and Education Council of the United States stated in 1970 that "the evidence suggests that the long term consequences of victimisation are quite mild..... Indeed there is evidence even among children who were the victims of father-daughter incest that the long term outcomes were not, at least in terms of gross measures of functioning, any worse than for a controlled population from the same social level[3]." I do not have a control group but I have only treated one person with symptoms similar to those to be described and who admits to having been assaulted whose symptoms could not be ascribed to the assault.

Peters, from the Philadelphia Sex Offenders and Rape Victim Center, states that the repression of a sexual assault may cause serious psychological problems for the victim as an adult[8]. I suspect that the reason that people have failed to find a relationship between sexual assault and later emotional dysfunction is that the assault has been repressed or that the victim is extremely reluctant to talk about it even many years later. Without reference to the subconscious mind, the connection between the assault and the symptom may be totally overlooked.

This paper deals with eight cases, all female, that I have treated in the past few years in which the patients' symptoms have been caused to a large extent by the fact that they have been sexually assaulted as a child.

The presenting symptoms, while differing from case to case, can all be classified as psychosomatic and in only three of them was there a sexual dysfunction. Some patients had more than one main presenting symptom. Five had symptoms of depression; one could be classified as post-partum depression and in two there was dependence on tricyclic anti-depressant drugs. One patient had a phobic anxiety state. Six had been assaulted by members of their family, the father in four cases, brothers in one and father and brothers in the other. One had been assaulted by the father of a school friend and the last had been kissed by a father figure. In two cases the assault appears to have been an isolated incident but in the remaining six the child appears to have been victimised on several or many occasions.

The first case is one that presented with superficial dyspareunia. During treatment it was found that she had been subjected to several incestuous attacks by her father when a teenager. In particular the last attack made when she was three months pregnant in her first pregnancy was important as this reinforced her guilt feelings from previous episodes and left her with the irrational fear that he could be the father of her child. She was given strong reassurance about the impossibility of this and about her innocent role. After review of the information obtained and of the traumatic episodes she was desensitised to the memories that caused her symptom and was relieved of it.

The second case presented with recurrent headaches from the age of thirteen at which age she had been assaulted by her father. Initial treatment was by symptom removal and was successful for a year. On the second occasion an analytical approach was used and the traumatic events discovered. Her role was shown to be an innocent one and she was then desensitised to the memories by repeated review of them while in hypnosis. She was symptom free when last seen two years later.

The third case presented as post-partum depression following the birth of her second child. This had not been significantly helped by anti-depressant drugs. In hypnosis, ideomotor responses confirmed the role of her father who had molested her on three occasions between the ages of three and five. The birth of her second child was by an extremely difficult breech extraction which required much intra-vaginal manipulation. This had reinforced the memories of genital manipulation as a child. Understanding the psycho-dynamics of her depression brought about a lasting relief from her symptoms.

The fourth case presented with depression, migraine and phobic anxiety. She had been subjected to repeated intercourse with her father from the age of eight until she became pregnant by him ten years later. Her innocent role was established with difficulty after it was explained to her that her behaviour had become a matter of habit and that she was afraid of possible consequences if she resisted. She was relieved of her guilt feelings and she was free of headaches and depression but returned a year later because of a long standing fear of travelling by boat and plane which she had not mentioned before. Her boat phobia was related to an incident with her father in a rowing boat while her flying phobia was not connected to her sexual traumas but was related to an episode when she was caught in turbulence in a light plane. This had re-inforced childhood memories of nausea on a roundabout. She was easily de-sensitised to these phobias once their origin was understood.

The fifth case is one of depression and lack of libido. This could be traced to repeated assaults on her by her brothers at the age of eight. She was given reassurance about her innocence and the consequent relief of guilt feelings quickly brought about a dispersal of her depression and a marked improvement in her marital relationship.

The sixth case is one of depression with habituation to anti-depressant drugs. This was traced back to a kiss that she had been given by a father figure when she was sixteen years old. She described this kiss as not being an avuncular one and it caused her to say something which was the crux of the matter. It was never possible to find out just what was said but during treatment her ideomotor responses changed to indicate that it was no longer of importance to her. Following this it was easy to wean her off her amitryptilene which she had been unable to do on several previous occasions.

The seventh case is one of depression of very long standing with habituation to amitryptilene and perfenazine. She is a reformed alcoholic. Her depression was traced to multiple assaults by her brothers and her father when she was eight years old. Discussion and review of what had happened started an improvement but it was apparant that other factors were at play here. With very much difficulty she admitted to assaulting her own eighteen month old daughter when nineteen years old. She felt very guilty about this and it was never possible to remove this guilt, nor was it possible to explain her action, except to state that she was an alcoholic by that time. However, following this her depression lifted but she remained obstinately dependant on amitriptilene although in two thirds of the original dosage. She had given up perfenazine easily. She is now much happier and is able to lead a much more comfortable life.

The last case, like the seventh, remains a relative failure. She presented as a sexual dysfunction having no desire for intercourse with her husband on account of pain although she had had several painless extra-marital affairs. She had a history of many suicidal gestures. Her symptom had first occurred during strenuous intercourse during her first pregnancy which had been started out of wedlock. Search for an original cause quickly lead to her indicating that something had happened when she was six years old. But it was never possible to find out what. Automatic writing while watching a scene of "someone just like her" produced the sentence "She was raped!" It seems that she had been molested by the father of a school friend. The severe pain during intercourse probably revived the memory of what had happened when she was young. Treatment continued intermittently for about two years without any improvement in her presenting symptom. Since then she has only had one more affair and has not attempted to commit suicide. Although her husband works for an airline, she refuses the offer of help for a phobia of flying. It seems that she is punishing her husband in lieu of the original attacker. She seems to gain much satisfaction from her unsatisfactory state of affairs and I expect that she will continue to enjoy a state of "Unholy Deadlock" for a long time to come.

In conclusion, then, eight cases of psychosomatic illness are presented in which sexual assault on the patient as a child has played an important role aetiologically. There seems to be little doubt that sexual assault on children is common, although the more severe forms, which seem more likely to cause trouble in later life, are rarer. Hypnosis has proved to be an invaluable tool in establishing the aetiology of the patients' symptoms. It has also proved to be of great help in assisting the patients to overcome their complaints.

So was Freud so very wrong when he said that sexual assault was important in the genesis of illness later in life?

REFERENCES

1. Strachey, J. Ed. (1955) The Complete Works of Sigmund Freud. Hogarth Press, London.

2. Rosenfeld, Alvin A. (1978) Sexual Assault of Children. JAMA, 240, p.43.

3. Sexual Encounters Between Adults and Children. (1970) Sexual Information and Education Council of the United States.

4. Daily Express. 12th. November 1977. London, England.

5. Alley, J. et al. (1979) Morbidity and Mortality Weekly Report, Center for Disease Control, Atlanta, Georgia. Vol 28, No. 3.

6. Henriques, Sir Basil. (1961) BMJ, Vol 2, p.1629.

7. Jaffe, Arthur C. et al. (1975) Sexual Abuse of Children. Amer. J. Dis. Child. Vol 129, pp.689 - 692.

8. Peters, Joseph J. (1976) Children Who Are Victims of Sexual Assault and the Psychology of Offenders. Amer. J. Psychotherapy. Vol 30, p.398.

© 1979 Elsevier/North-Holland Biomedical Press
Hypnosis 1979
G.D. Burrows, D.R. Collison and L. Dennerstein

THE HYPNOTHERAPEUTIC PLACEBO

Dr. H.E. Stanton

Director. Higher Education
Research and Advisory Centre
University of Tasmania.

Webster's dictionary defines a placebo as: "an inert medication given for its psychological effect especially to satisfy the patient" and as: "something tending to soothe and gratify". This definition would seem to fit the practice of psychotherapy rather well, particularly if one adopts the view advanced by Torrey[1].

Torrey suggests that there are four components of psychotherapy which are reflected in the procedures of all successful practitioners of the art. The first of these is a view of the world which is shared by both client and therapist. This means that the therapist is able to put a label on whatever it is that is troubling the patient. Once the patient's illness can be named, the first step in effecting a cure has been taken, for the therapist has been able to identify an offending agent. By so doing, he demonstrates to the client that he understands what is wrong and thus helps to reduce the latter's anxiety. Whether the label is correct or not is totally irrelevant. It simply must be plausible and acceptable to the patient. As Torrey has pointed out, the witch doctor might suggest that the client's problem is caused by a spirit which has taken possession of his soul, whereas the modern psychiatrist might apply the label of childhood trauma.

Naming the illness helps to soothe and gratify the patient. It works as a placebo. So, too, does Torrey's second factor, which encompasses certain personal qualities of the therapist which seem to promote "healing" in the patient. Following the view of Carl Rogers, he stresses the importance of genuiness, unconditional acceptance, and empathic understanding. The therapist who can be a human being in his own right rather than a remote professional, who can accept the patient as he is rather than as he would like him to be, and who can share the viewpoint of the patient, is the one best able to help a person change in the ways in which he wishes to change. As Ellis[2] has pointed out:

"The personality of the therapist is the most important factor in psycho-therapy ... The therapist's deepest inner self, as well as his more external characteristics and manner are, whether or not he is conscious of the fact, inevitably used in his therapeutic relationships; and it is by the use of himself as an instrument that he usually ... helps effect significant changes in the self of the client."

Torrey's third factor involves belief and expectancy. He would argue that a patient has certain expectations about getting well, these being increased by such things as the journey involved in actually getting to the therapist (the pilgrimage to Lourdes idea), the impressiveness of the place of therapy, the therapist's belief in himself, special paraphanalia (such as degrees hanging on the wall), and the therapist's reputation. Warren[3] stresses the same points in a specifically hypnotic context when he suggests that a patient's response depends on the presence of three factors. The first of these is "aura", the public respect given to the therapist, his degrees and expertise. Motivation is the second, the patient's desire to get well which has driven him to seek help. Finally, Warren sees probability of success as most important. The patient has heard of <u>you</u> as an effective healer and feels <u>you</u> are capable of helping him. Perhaps he has been recommended by a previous patient or a general practitioner. However it may happen, if the patient believes a therapist can help him he is already well on the way to a "cure". If the therapist, too, believes in his own healing effectiveness and can communicate this belief to the patient, perhaps little else is required to achieve a successful outcome. Fish[4] puts this rather neatly when he says: "Effective faith-healing is a process which takes place between two believers". I feel the word "faith" could be removed from this statement without detracting from its validity.

The belief-expectancy factor discussed above would seem to be the very essence of placebo therapy. Oyle[5], speaking as a physician, has commented that:

"If the patient believes I know what I'm doing and I firmly believe in my therapeutic ritual, healing usually takes place ... Apparently some kind of ritual is necessary ... some patients decide that only the proper herbs can heal while others put childlike faith in the power of the pill; still others insist that salvation can only be achieved by mastering a particular yoga position or by repeating a mantra. *Whatever you put your trust in can be the precipitating agent for your cure.*"

Ritual is important, and this is Torrey's fourth factor. He calls it technique, and feels it really doesn't matter at all which particular one is used, be it behaviour modification, psycho-analysis, hypnosis, or anything else, as long as both therapist and patient believe in its healing power. Hypnosis is a very much a ritual procedure, invoking long established ideas of magic. Much as we might decry such connotations, we benefit greatly from our patient's belief in the power of the technique we choose to use. It is this belief, this placebo effect, which seems to be the chief reason for using a hypnotic

induction for it appears that its actual effectiveness in creating a state
known as "trance" is rather doubtful.

The work of Barber and his associates[6] would suggest very strongly that
hypnotic induction procedures are unnecessary for eliciting the behaviours
usually described as "hypnotic". These behaviours, such as amnesia, analgesia,
catalepsy, hallucination, and hyperesthesia, have conventionally been associated
with the concept of an "altered state of consciousness", but Barber's
experiments have demonstrated that they may be produced equally effectively
through the use of short instructions designed to motivate subjects' performance. However, although Barber would deny the necessity of using a hypnotic
induction to produce "hypnotic" behaviours, he would not dismiss this ritual
as useless:

"When hypnotic induction procedures are helpful, it is not because the
subject is in a 'trance' or 'hypnotized' in the popular sense of these
terms. Instead, the evidence indicates that they are helpful when they
reduce the subject's critical attitudes towards the suggestions and thus
help them accept the suggestions as believable and harmonious with their own
ongoing cognitions."

If it is the believed-in efficacy of the suggestions which is the critical
factor rather than the hypnotic trance, our hypnotic technique would seem to
fall under the placebo rubric even more completely. However, there is, of
course, some difficulty in talking about hypnotic technique so glibly.
Hypnotherapists are individuals and, as such, work in different ways. The
specific methods they use for inducing relaxation, encouraging age regression,
helping patients overcome phobias, and engendering confidence do vary. Yet
these differences are probably far less important than the similarities of
approach.

Most of us use relaxation, suggestion and imagery as our basic tools and,
for the purpose of this paper, I propose to operationally define hypnotherapy
in this way. When I refer to hypnotherapy I mean a technique which makes use
of these three elements rather than the invocation of some mystical state of
"altered consciousness". The occasional therapist, and Milton Erickson is one
who immediately springs to mind, does seem able to engender a "trance state"
with some patients. However, more commonly, our patients simply relax to a
greater or lesser extent. In this relaxed state they would seem to experience
what Baudouin[7] has described as "an outcropping of the unconscious" and be
both more accepting of suggestion and more able to engage in goal-directed
imagery.

This technique, of using a hypnotic induction to guide the patient into relaxation and to then use suggestion and imagery to help him change in ways he desires, can be tremendously effective. Although I have described it as a placebo, I do not mean to thus imply that I am denigrating the approach. Rather, my argument is that we should recognize hypnotherapy as a placebo, accept it as such, and deliberately work to maximize its placebo effect.

In his book, *Placebo Therapy*, Fish[8] offers guidelines which help us to do this. Beginning with an overview, he suggests that the patient must be persuaded that it is what *he* does, not what the therapist does, which results in his being cured. Fish regards this as crucial because it implies that the patient is the master of his behaviour rather than its servant. This does seem a vital point for we cannot really cure any one. What we can do is establish an environment within which the patient is helped to cure himself.

Hypnotherapeutic procedures are ideally suited to create such an environment for they are, I believe, basically oriented towards helping a patient to feel more confident about his own power to help himself, to take control of his own life, to transcend the limitations he has placed upon himself. This confidence building aspect of hypnotherapy is reflected in the ego-enhancement approach of Hartland[9]. It is also very much a part of my own approach[10] which blends suggestions from Coue, Ellis, and Hartland to help patients feel more assurance in their own value and worth as human beings.

Fish's emphasis on a patient taking responsibility for himself and for his own healing is at the heart of much hypnotherapeutic practice. I'm sure many hypnotherapists would agree with Ellis[11] when he claims that most human un-happiness is self-inflicted, a result of the negative, depressing things we tell ourselves and the negative images we put into our minds. It seems so easy to tell ourselves we are inadequate, unattractive, stupid, ill, and to constantly imagine the worst about outselves. As Emerson put it, "Most of the shadows of this world are caused by standing in our own sunshine".

This internal talk is reflected in our behaviour. Negative self-talk results in negative behaviour, depression, misery and inadequacy. But a patient does not have to talk to himself in this way. He chooses to do so. Accordingly, he can choose to change the things he says to himself. Instead of seeing himself as he fears he is, imagining the worst, he can use his self-talk and imagination constructively, seeing himself as he wants to be. He has tremendous power to change himself by putting into his mind the image of how he wants to be. Through our positive ego-enhancing suggestions we can help him do so, and thus hekp him change the things he tells himself. Through our use of guided imagery we can help him see himself as he wants to be. Frankl[12] has claimed that man's greatest freedom is that of deciding the attitude he will take to something.

Through hypnotherapy we can help patients adopt a positive attitude so that they feel they are curing themselves. This re-programming of the mind carried out by the patient with the therapist acting as a catalyst is the very essence of placebo therapy.

The placebo must be carefully prepared. Fish places great store on specificity. In the initial stages of therapy it is necessary, he affirms to encourage the patient to be quite precise. For example, instead of accepting the statement: "My wife worries me", the therapist probes further: "What is it that your wife does which worries you?" By working in this way, the therapist helps the patient define clear cut goals, communicating to him the belief that he can attain these goals, reassuring him that he isn't crazy or pityfully weak. Similarly, in the preparation of the placebo, emphasis is placed on actions as well as feelings. As Fish states:

"the answer to 'what did you feel then?' is as important as the answer to 'what did you do then?' The world responds to one's actions, not one's feelings."

Once the placebo is prepared, the healing ritual takes place. Whatever form it may take, everything within it should be defined as progress. In the first session, the therapist establishes that the patient may improve, stay the same, or become worse, yet all three possibilities are seen as signs of improvement. If the patient reports progress, the therapist can say that the treatment has begun to work and that the rate of improvement will accelerate. Should the patient report an unchanged condition, the therapist might sympathize with his disappointment over slow progress but point out that as soon as the current stage of therapy has ended, improvement will be far more rapid. If the patient gets worse, the therapist can point out that occasionally people regress if they reach a point where such regression can help them cope with current problems.

To protect the patient from over-reaction to future bad periods, the therapist, in the last session, talks about life's ups and downs, reassuring the client that he will be able to handle the difficult times and recover quickly. Also, so as not to remove support entirely, he indicates his availability should any future problems develop. Still, he suggests that such an occurrence is unlikely as the patient now has the ability to cope successfully with his environment.

This point is stressed as treatment is terminated in order to maintain the placebo's effect. The patient is congratulated on his self-cure and is reassured that he can cope with life without therapy. With the experience of therapy, he is now equipped to think up self-mastery techniques of his own, for further difficulties are to be attributed to life's ups and downs, not to the patient's "mental illness".

These ideas of preparing the placebo, conducting the healing ritual, and maintaining the cure have applicability to therapy in general. However, there are, as Fish points out, certain additional things the hypnotherapist can do to enhance the power of his placebo. Giving the patient a signal he can use to justify labelling himself as "hypnotized" is one of these. So, too, is congratulating the client upon his hypnotizability which will enable him to achieve his goals effectively. Emphasis in this way on the patients status as a good hypnotic subject normally results in increased receptivity to suggestion and increased facilitation in goal-directed imagining. As a good hypnotic subject, the patient obviously has the ability to hypnotize himself to continue his self-cure. Possessing the tool of self hypnosis, he feels further reassured of his ability to cope with life more successfully. Confidence is what it is all about - confidence, belief and expectancy. Hypnotherapy may be a placebo but it is certainly a most powerful one. As Wolberg[13] has expressed it:

"...people like to be comforted, like to feel safe, like to feel as if they are being treated by a magically wise and powerful person."

We as hypnotherapists can do this for our patients and by doing so help them to help themselves.

REFERENCES

1. Torrey, E.F. (1972) The Mind Game: Witchdoctors and Psychiatrists, New York, Emerson Hall.

2. Ellis, A. (1955) New approaches in psychotherapy techniques. Journal of Clinical Psychology. 11, p.7.

3. Warren, F.Z. (1976) Handbook of Medical Acupuncture. New York, Van Nostrand Reinhold.

4. Fish, J.H. (1973) Placebo Therapy. San Francisco, Jossey-Bass.

5. Oyle, I. (1975) The Healing Mind. Millbrae, Calif., Celestial Arts, pp.20, 25.

6. Barber, T.X. (1978) Hypnosis, suggestions and psychosomatic phenomena: A new look from the standpoint of recent experimental studies. In, J.L. Fossage and P. Olsen (Eds.) Healing: Implications for Psychotherapy. New York, Human Sciences Press.

7. Baudouin, C. (1970) Suggestion and auto-suggestion. London, Allen and Unwin.

8. Fish, J.M. (1973) Placebo Therapy. San Francisco, Jossey-Bass.

9. Hartland, J. (1971) Medical and Dental Hypnosis, 2nd ed., London, Balliere Tindall.

10. Stanton, H.E. (1975) Ego Enhancement Through Positive Suggestion. Australian Journal of Clinical Hypnosis, 3, 32-36.

11. Ellis, A. (1971) Growth Through Reason. Palo Alto, Calif., Institute for Rational Living.

12. Frankel, V.E. (1963) Mans Search for Meaning. New York, Basic Books.

13. Wolberg, L.R. (1965) Short-term Psychotherapy. New York, Grune and Stratton.

© 1979 Elsevier/North-Holland Biomedical Press
Hypnosis 1979
G.D. Burrows, D.R. Collison and L. Dennerstein

THE USE OF HYPNOLOGY AS AN ADJUNCT IN CURBING SMOKING, OBESITY AND HYPERTENSION

C.A.D. RINGROSE, M.D., F.R.C.S.(C)

1160 - 10830 Jasper Avenue, Edmonton, Alberta Canada

Cardiovascular diseases account for over one million deaths yearly in North America.[1] The "big three" that contribute to this death toll as well as the great morbidity for victims with non-lethal forms are: smoking, obesity and hypertension. This paper appraises the impact that the ancient art of hypnosis can have on the management of these conditions.

SMOKING

Smoking is a major public health problem throughout the world. Three leading causes of death for both sexes in Canada are; coronary disease, stroke and lung cancer and all are more prevalent in smokers. Cigarette smoking is also productive of morbidity due to chronic bronchitis, emphysema, cancer of the bladder, pancreas, lung, mouth, larynx, and esophagus. As well, peptic ulcers and peripheral vascular diseases are more common in smokers. Cigarette smoking retards fetal growth and increases the risk of still birth and neonatal death.[2,3] The reasons given for smoking are: to allay nervousness and promote relaxation, to be sociable, to assert independence, to imitate an idol and later, because of physiologic and psychologic dependence. If therapy is to be effective, the motivation to quit must overcome the "attributes" mentioned above.

MATERIAL AND METHODS

A. Smoking. My approach to curbing smoking initially presents basic information to the consumer on the health problems associated with smoking. This is coupled with the teaching of self hypnosis and the utilization of four techniques. Firstly, transference therapy to replace the psychological craving for a smoke with a benign alternative such as a warm finger is useful. Secondly, aversion therapy is used to magnify the natural obnoxious attributes of cigarette smoke. Thirdly, some of the end results possible to heavy smokers are fantasized and used to motivate the person to resist the habit in the future. Finally, age regression is employed to recapture attitudes towards cigarette smoking before the habit started. These attitudes can be transferred to the present and the future and help in overcoming the psychologic and physiologic dependence

that exist. As well, the relaxed composure the subject can achieve through
self hypnosis and the increasing realization of self worth, makes the continuing consumption of cigarettes distasteful and unnecessary.

Three initial sessions are suggested to learn self hypnosis. The first two
should be just a few days apart and the third can be a week or so later. Therapy
can be individualized and subsequent sessions can be utilized as desired. The
office education and therapy is supplemented by the use of cassette tapes to
reinforce the suggestions between visits. Before trance induction and during
trance, the advantages of not smoking and disadvantages of smoking are stressed.
Disadvantages include an increased incidence of cancer of the lung, lip, tongue,
esophagus, pancreas and bladder. Crippling lung diseases such as emphysema are
increased. Heart disease, strokes, ulcers and circulatory ailments are increased.[3] The pollution of the blood with carbon monoxide gas produces headaches, fatigues and detrimental changes in cells throughout the body. It also
ties up hemogloben and makes it unable to carry oxygen. The air is polluted
for others when smoking and the breath of the smoker is fouled and the fingers
stained. There is an increased fire hazard from smoking and it is a costly
habit representing an investment in ones own destruction.

The advantages of not smoking include: decreased risk of disease, cleaner
lungs, less cough, greater endurance and a better sense of taste and smell with
fresher breath and unstained fingers.

Hypnosis is then induced and a team effort between subject and therapist is
stressed while the technique is learned. It is helpful to stress that the
therapist cares about the results achieved. As hypnotic relaxation is learned
many of the tensions and fears that induced the need for cigarettes are completely replaced by confidence, contentment, creativity and courage. The
trance is deepened using visual imagery and employing an ultra sonic device to
make the subject's heart beat audible. This greatly enhances deepening of the
trance state and the learning of self hypnosis. On arousal from the trance,
the subject is given a cigarette consumption graph to record termination or
decline in consumption as this is achieved. Figure I.

CIGARETTE CONSUMPTION GRAPH

NAME		AGE		DURATION OF HABIT		
DATE						
NUMBER PER DAY	0	1	2	3	4	etc.
30						
25						
0						

The subject also records the circumstances of each future cigarette on a form illustrated in figure II. A suitable award for successful subjects curbing the habit is a great motivator.

Figure II

CIGARETTE CONSUMPTION RECORD

DATE	OCCASION	CIGS. NO.	NO. OF PUFFS
		first	
		second	
		third	
		etc.	

RESULTS

Table I outlines the duration of the smoking habit in 50 hypnotherapy subjects with approximately 3/4 of the subjects in the 10 to 30 year range.

TABLE I

DURATION OF SMOKING HABIT - 50 SUBJECTS

Years	Percent of Total Group
0 - 10	14%
11 - 30	72%
31+	14%

Table II outlines our results. 86% had a significant reduction in one week and 75% of the group achieved a further reduction of greater than 50% in the number smoked in the second week. Special cassette tapes to reinforce the hypnotherapy are available to sustain and enhance improvement on an ongoing basis. With this adjunct it is felt that most of the "cures" will be permanent.

TABLE II

PERFORMANCE IN CURBING SMOKING - 50 SUBJECTS

Percent Reduction In Amount Smoked	After One Week	After Two Weeks
0 - 25	14	13
26 - 50	28	12
51 - 75	16	25
76 - 100	42	50

B. Obesity. Obesity is a major health problem confronting the developed
countries with about one third of the population in North America being overweight. This is defined as more than ten percent above normal weight for the
age and height as determined by actuarial tables. The problem is increasing.
Obesity jeapordizes a persons health in many ways. It increases the incidence
of heart disease, high blood pressure, diabetes, gall stones, varicose veins,
back problems and arthritis. It is commoner in the lower socio-economic groups
and more prevalent in females.[4,5] Reasons for obesity in descending order of
importance include using food as an emotional reward or tranquillizer, bad
eating habits, excessive gain with pregnancy and change in life style.

MATERIAL AND METHODS

Basic nutritional information is presented along with information on the
consequences of obesity. A well balanced diet of 500 calories daily is suggested and periods of fasting for two or three days a week are encouraged until
the weight goal is achieved. An increase in the amount of exercise is endorsed
and good dietary principles are outlined. These include the avoidance of food
and fattening beverages between meals, in the evening and through the night,
eating slowly at mealtime, chewing the food meticulously, moving it around in
the mouth so that every taste bud is saturated and pausing frequently between
bites of food. It is also suggested that the subject eat only at a formal
place setting at the table, preferably in the company of another person. Shop-
ping for food should be done from a list when the person is not hungry. A
dietary diary sheet is suggested to record every calorie before it is eaten.

Figure III

DIETARY DIARY

Date	Occasion	Emotional State	Foods &/or Beverages	Calories

A weight control sheet (Figure IV) is used to graphically depict the return
to normal weight.

Figure IV

WEIGHT RECORD

Name	Age	Height	Current Weight	Ideal Weight	Excess

Date										
Current Weight										
200										
175 etc.										

Self hypnosis is then presented using eye fixation and visual imagery and deepening is achieved once again with the ultra sonic device. All the hazards of obesity and the behaviour modifications suggested are reiterated while the subject is in trance. The benefits of a normal weight are stressed and a thin, svelte stature visualized to become the subject's self image. Possible future complications are fantasized and these can then "come to mind" in the future waking state if excercise is forgotten or if any dietary indiscretion is entertained. Age regression can be used to recapture pride in a thin, well toned figure before obesity occurred. The urge for inappropriate food can be transferred to a benign alternative. Anguish, apathy, anxiety and anger (4 A's) can be diminished and replaced by confidence, contentment, creativity and courage (4 C's). Three sessions are suggested at weekly intervals to learn self hypnosis followed by periodic refresher courses as desired until the weight goal is achieved and maintained. Cassette tapes to reiterate the format can reinforce the suggestion between visits.

RESULTS

159 consecutive patients with obesity underwent this regimen. Although three visits at seven day intervals were suggested to learn self hypnosis, it was not possible for all of the subjects to come in at precisely seven days. For purposes of comparison however, this interval has been surveyed and the percentage loss in body weight recorded. Table III outlines the degree of obesity in the subjects. It is apparent that approximately half the subjects are 10 to 30 percent overweight and the other half greater than 30 percent overweight.

TABLE III

DEGREE OF OBESITY - 159 SUBJECTS

Percentage Overweight	Percentage Of Total Subjects
10 - 30	49
31 - 60	34
61+	17

Table IV outlines the results achieved in this group of subjects. 87% were successful in losing weight.

TABLE IV

REDUCTION IN BODY WEIGHT

WITH HYPNOTHERAPY - 159 SUBJECTS

Change In Weight	First Week % Total (159)	Second Week % Total (63)	Third Week % Total (13)
0 - 2% gain	13%	24%	7.5%
1 - 2% loss	52%	59%	85%
3 - 4% loss	30%	17%	7.5%
5 - 6% loss	5%	--	--

After three sessions, further therapy is individualized and a certificate of achievement provided when the desired weight is reached. Interim progress memos are encouraging for the subjects.

The team effort between the subject and therapist is stressed at all times and ego strengthening is an important part of each session. The use of anorexiant drugs was discouraged because of the high incidence of side effects and the low incidence of beneficial effects.

C. Essential Hypertension. This disease of modern society afflicts one third of adults. 90% of cases are essential hypertension resulting from faulty adaptation to stress in susceptible persons. Along with obesity and smoking, hypertension is a frequent factor in over 200,000 stroke deaths each year in North America. It is commoner in obese people as well as blacks and males. Traditional therapy with chemicals is characterized by a poor compliance rate because of the frequent lack of symptoms and serious side effects to some of the medications.[6,7,8,] The cost of treating a case of hypertension averages $200.00 per year with an additional $125.00 required to treat the medication induced side effects.[9,10]

A hypnotic trance is frequently characterized by a drop in blood pressure. I recently calculated the effect of trance on blood pressure in 88 normotensive and 30 hypertensive subjects. Table V outlines the change in the blood pressure in the normo tensive group.

TABLE V

Blood Pressure Change in Trance

88 Normo Tensive Patients (100 observations)

Systolic Change	Percentage of Group
0 - 5	10%
Decline 5 - 15 mm hg.	75%
Decline 15+	15%

Diastolic Change	Percentage of Group
Increase 5 - 10 mm hg.	8%
No Change	40%
Decrease 5 - 15 mm hg.	50%
Decrease 15 mm hg.+	2%

90% manifested a drop of five to thirty millimeters of mercury in the systolic pressure and 52% experienced a drop in the diastolic pressure of from five to twenty-five millimeters of mercury. In the hypertensive group, defined as those with a blood pressure over 140 millimeters systolic and/or 90 millimeters of mercury diastolic, all subjects experienced a decline in the systolic pressure of between five and 50 millimeters of mercury. As well, 75% experienced a decline in the diastolic pressure of between five and twenty millimeters of mercury as outlined in table VI.

TABLE VI

Blood Pressure Change in Trance

30 Hypertensive Patients (40 observations)

Systolic Pressure Change	Percentage of Group
Same or Increase	0%
Decrease 5 - 15 mm hg.	25%
Decrease 15 mm hg.+	75%

Diastolic Pressure Change	Percentage of Group
No Change	25%
Decrease 5 - 15 mm hg.	62.5%
Decrease 15+ mm hg.	12.5%

The magnitude of the drop in the systolic pressure in the hypertensive group was far greater than the drop in the normo tensive group. 87.5% of the hypertensive group had a systolic pressure drop of 15 millimeters of mercury or more while in trance whereas in the normotensive group a drop of this magnitude was recorded by 31% of subjects. In the diastolic pressures the normotensive group had a drop of 15 millimeters of mercury or more in six percent whereas in the hypertensive group 22.5% had a drop of this magnitude. Hypnotic trance induction may also serve to distinguish between essential hypertension and endocrine, renal, or drug induced hypertension with an opportunity to save on the $2083.00 required to differentiate the type of hypertension with present methods of detection.[7] Hypnotherapy increases a subject's ability to cope with stress by using relaxation to prevent as well as dissipate tension, transferring it to a benign alternative.

SUMMATION

All of the subjects involved in these studies were motivated people that sought therapy with the author at their own expense. Stanton has previously indicated that financial responsibility for therapy encourages success.[11] There appears to be great cost effectiveness in using hypnotherapy in stress disorders due to the virtual freedom from side effects. The active involvement of the patient in the treatment encourages greater compliance with the therapeutic suggestions. Abandoning cigarettes, making exercise part of the life style, using a balanced nutritious low salt diet with the appropriate calories and occasional periodic fasting as required plus achieving a composed, relaxed outlook on life, can all contribute to better present and future health. It may well be that tax incentives by governments to encourage good health and discourage the ravages of cigarette smoking, obesity and hypertension will greatly curtail health care costs and result in a more productive, creative and contented society.

BIBLIOGRAPHY

1. Ca - A Cancer Journal for Clinicians, Vol. 29, #1, pp 7, 1979

2. Smoking & Health in Canada, pp 17, 7, 105, 101, March 1977

3. Holbrook J., Ca, Vol. 27, #6, pp 344-353, 1977

4. Insel & Moos, Social Factors in Obesity, Lexington Books, 2, 11, 1974

5. Stewart R.B., Health and Social Environment, pp 239, 1974

6. Eyer J., Hypertension in Modern Society, Int. J. of Health Services, Vol. 5 pp 539, 1975

7. Hypertension Detection Coop Group, JAMA 237, pp 2385, 1977

8. Stason W.B. and Weinstein M.C., Alleviation of Resources, NEGOM, Vol. 246, 732, 1977

9. Ferguson R.K. Cost & yield in Hypertension, Annals of Int. Med., 82,761,1975

10. Verrone F.A. & Mol M.F. Financial Expenditure for Cardiovascular Disease, Public Health Reports, 92, 272, 1977

11. Stanton H.E. Fee Paying and Weight Loss, Am. J. of Clin. Hypnosis, Vol. 19, #1, 47, July 1976

© 1979 Elsevier/North-Holland Biomedical Press
Hypnosis 1979
G.D. Burrows, D.R. Collison and L. Dennerstein

CLINICAL MEDICAL HYPNOTIC TREATMENT OF PHYSIOLOGICAL
DISEASE-A HOLISTIC APPROACH

J. ALAN JENSEN, Ph.D.
30611 El Sueno Drive, Malibu, California, 90265, U.S.A.

ABSTRACT OVERVIEW

1. PURPOSE AND OBJECTIVE

2. CLINICAL MEDICAL HYPNOSIS
   PSYCHOLOGICAL-PHYSIOLOGICAL

3. USE OF THE HYPNOTIC
   INDUCTION PROFILE

4. CLARIFICATION; HYPNOSIS,
   INDUCTION, TRANCE

5. HYPNOSIS: CLIENT CENTERED

6. TRANCE DEFINED

7. HYPNOTIC TRANCE: INCREASED
   SELF CONTROL

8. PSYCHOPHYSIOLOGICAL ENERGY:
   HYPNOSIS AND APPLIED THEORY

9. HYPNOTIC TRANCE AND
   MOTIVATION

10. SYMPTOMS REVIEWED AND
    DEFINED

11. TRANCE RATIFICATION

12. SUBJECTS

13. METHOD AND DATE: STATEMENT
    OF TREATMENT PREMISE:
    HOLISTIC PRINCIPLES

14. HYPOTHETICAL STATEMENTS

15. THEORETICAL APPROACH

16. OVERVIEW OF OBJECTIVES AND
    PROCESS

17. BIBLIOGRAPHY:
    A comprehensive, 376 biblio-
    graphical reference is avail-
    able. If copies are desired
    they can be obtained for the
    mailing fee. Address inquir-
    ies to:

    J. Alan Jensen,Ph.D.
    30611 El Sueno Dr.
    Malibu, California 90265,USA

PURPOSE AND OBJECTIVE

Determine if long term fibrocystic changes (tumors) of the
breast are of a psychophysiological nature; and if symptom management or remission is possible with the use of clinically applied
hypnosis.

Objectives: integrate a holistic treatment approach and concept; determine hypnotizability; secure patient's self esteem
and faith in themselves; suggest to each patient a realistic capacity for recovery; attempt to eliminate ideas that patient's are

victims of disease; point out how impulse reactions may have contributed to acquisition of symptom.

CLINICAL AND MEDICAL HYPNOSIS: PSYCHOLOGICAL-PHYSIOLOGICAL

Hypnotic trance relies on a relearning of sub-cortical activity in the brain. Symptoms are defined as pre-verbal, conditioned reflexes which at some sensate level makes sense to the person; symptoms are designed and used to prevent experienced stress; patient's dilemma is; a life survival defense system designed to solve problems may produce a health problem, eg: an ulcer may be a message of not being able to stomach something.

This treatment approach regards directness as moving quickly to the source and may contribute to a clinical, iatrogenic energy, commonly referred to as resistance or acting out. If the primary problem is pre-verbal or sub-cortical, as a neural-synaptic impulse, then this charged-combined emotional and pre-cognitive sensation becomes a volative bio-energetic resource and often conceals an imprint or engram which has been cortically encoded to produce a psychoneuromuscular mutation (symptom). Imprints or engrams are reciprocal, cortical events, related to interaction with a sub-cortical, negative stimulus which produces subconscious physical or emotional discomfort. Denial, repression or amnesia are models of the classical explanation of these intrapsychic phenomena.

USE OF THE HYPNOTIC INDUCTION PROFILE

Introduce hypnosis with Spiegel's Hypnotic Induction Profile; teach auto-hypnosis as a naturally superior means of coping with environmental demands; help patients to avoid the unsophisticated aberration of disease syndromes.

CLARIFICATION: HYPNOSIS, INDUCTION, TRANCE

Clinical hypnosis is defined as a permissive, coercive, transitory depotentiation of an earlier learned set of beliefs, which is often a learned limitation, generally a value imposed by another person's belief system and often only their prejudice.

Permissive/coercive is defined: permissive...allowing the patient's behavior to be acknowledged as acceptable, thereby depotentiating any negative set of learned limitations; coercive...subtle manipulating of the patient's abilities by gradually supporting each patient's actions, gently taking control and guiding them into a state of increased receptivity (trance).

HYPNOSIS: CLIENT CENTERED

Clinical Medical Hypnosis is a personal experience, bringing the doctor together with the patient to create a therapeutic relationship of trust. The essential outcome of treatment is the eventual realization that people tend to create their own world views, and when we change our perspective we seem to change the creation of our lives.

People are often not able to create this perspective of objectivity along. According to Kroger, 75 to 80% of all disease is stress-related. In the "non-verbal communication model", if cancer is a non-verbal form of dialogue, then it seems logical that a culture can teach patients to reverse the disease. When a cancer patient is free of disease we could say that he is "changed", or at least he is expressing himself differently.

TRANCE DEFINED

Rossi and Erickson refer to clinical hypnotic trance as an inner directive experience, free from some of the learned limitations of previous history and training; a natural free period of inner discovery, exploration, and realization of personal, natural potential.

Patient's motivations bind them to their task of inner focus when not interrupted by irrevelent stimuli. Personal motivation accounts for differences found between laboratory hypnosis and clinical hypnosis.

Fundamental to trance is that patient's have symptoms and problems or learned limitations. The objective is to relax these learned limitations, engrams, imprints, sets, of the patient's usual frames of reference and permit unrecognized potentialities to operate. Treatment assumes a state allowing patient's intrapsychic movement. Once freed from the common sets, biases and inhibitions of consciousness, learning can proceed on more of an autonomous, or what is conventionally called an unconscious, sub-cortical level (focus attention).

HYPNOTIC TRANCE: INCREASED SELF CONTROL

Trance attempts to accelerate a patient's ability to reorganize thinking, to have his or her own unique experience and simultaneously to learn the responsibility of personal health through self-involvement without guarantee.

Responsibility for understanding personal experience is unique and subjective. Trance helps patients to change their rigid, imprisoning mold another may have cast and to free them from this apparent, learned bondage. Symptoms provoke intrapsychic, directive perceptions and sensations into severely disturbed bio-chemical mutation. Trance is more direct and useful simply because it is a natural human capacity. Research has shown that "double bind" communications produce schizophrenic behavior. It is well

accepted that double binds are valid sources (causes) of severe
psychoneuromuscular change which may activate neurotic behavior.
Hypnotic induction provides similar double bind choice points,
only in the direction of health and harmony. **Trance** offers two
positive alternatives rather than negative behavior choices.

PSYCHOPHYSIOLOGICAL ENERGY: HYPNOSIS AND APPLIED THEORY

Symptoms are defined as spontaneous hypnosis; a natural, perceptual, real world event, causing a rigid psychoneuromuscular
set. This bio-energy pool establishes a functional cognitive limitation (symptom), which can be more easily depotentiated with a
direct involvement (trance) than indirect (insight).

Erickson and Kroger have cited hypnosis to be direct because a
person in trance is more easily approached and influenced to allow
a healtheir viewpoint to be considered rather than their symptom
or complaint as a solution.

HYPNOTIC TRANCE AND MOTIVATION

Rossi and Erickson refer to the work of Deese and Holse:
"trance is an active process of unconscious learning, somewhat
akin to the process of latent learning or learning without awareness". Trance can then be viewed as a motivated situation.

SYMPTOMS REVIEWED AND DEFINED

Research suggest symptoms are rooted in natural,critical life
events, resulting in an imprint or engram phenomena and seem to
relate to fixed, specific encoding of cerebral pathways in the
cortex as a measurable bio-energy; with a great deal of potential
to distort perception. Hypnotic revivication facilitates new re-
solutions by reevaluating old events for self discovery and acceptance of mistakes.

Therapeutic trance is conceptualized as a vivid example of the fundamental nature of all phenomenological experience being state-bound; ie., once an altered state is produced and the imprint or engram is fragmented, or opened, then symbolic associations alone can be sufficient to reinduce new experience. The earlier works reported by Kroger in physiology, referring to cognitive mapping or the idea of imprints and encoding can assist the doctor in approaching deep-seated problems.

Deep, or truly satisfactory trance experience, depends on the patient's ability to subordinate and eliminate waking patterns of behavior and to give up some of the learned limitations and habitual frameworks of one's characteristic pathogenisis.

Classification for depth of clinical trance:

State: Hypnoidal
Test: Fluttering of the eyelids, physical relaxation
      closing of the eyes, feeling of muscular lethargy

State: Light trance
Test: Inability to open the eyes, deep and slow breathing,
      progressive deepening of lethargy

State: Medium trance
Test: Glove anesthesia, partial amnesia, hallucinations

State: Deep trance, including somnambulism
Test: Ability to open the eyes without affecting the trance,
      virtually complete anesthesia, extensive amnesia,
      post hypnotic amnesia and allergenia, age regression,
      post hypnotic positive and negative hallucinations,
      and perhaps the most significant, lip pallor.

SUBJECTS

Treatment was applied to a population pool of 120 patients seeking private treatment. Each agreed to complete medical review and differential diagnosis.

METHOD AND DATA: STATEMENT OF TREATMENT PREMISE: HOLISTIC PRINCIPLES

Data researched involves the phenomenon of steady state behavior; specifically fibro-cystic changes of the breast. This disease is defined as a sub-vocal, abreactive psychoneuromuscular impulse. According to Sidman's research model for single subjects, disease is best defined for research as a descriptive-manipulative research problem presented by: (1) observation, (2) anecdotal reporting, (3) transcription of hypnotic, therapeutic dialogue (indirect and direct), (4) manipulation of steady state behavior through clinically applied hypnosis and auto-hypnosis. Disease modification toward control and cure is dependent on patient's desire and motivation to learn generalized health impulses, taught by combined holistic applications of empirical medicine and clinical hypnosis. Data was secured from a Center providing private treatment in Beverly Hills, California.

HYPOTHETICAL STATEMENTS: (1) symptom management; (2) symptom remission; (3) no change; (4) termination; (5) serious complication; (6) surgery.

THEORETICAL APPROACH: Assimilation of methods and philosophies developed by William S. Kroger, M.D., Raymond LaScola, M.D., Carl Simonton, M.D., Herbert Spiegel, M.D., and others in clinical medical hypnosis. (1) Daily events include altered states of consciousness, a natural hypnosis which may hold the etiology and remission core; (2) Symptoms are defined as spontaneous sub-cortical, real world events, which may, when trauma or life sustaining energy is commanded by the organism, produce psychophysiological, neuromuscular, imprint-engram as a factor in disease pathology; (3) Unrelated or event related stress may contribute a 70% - 80% loading factor of disease pathology toward symptom bound bio-energy; (4) Disease networks are sub-vocal, sub-cortical, intra-psychic, self-destructive, (emotionally) charged bio-energy masses,

inappropriately applied to life experience and when re-directed,
become a human resource capable of intelligent, creative, appropriate behavior; (6) Pathogenisis is a viable, useful, humanistic
bio-energy resource pool which can be redirected to accommodate
alternate strategies to life's problems; (7) Exploration of secondary gains of disease is essential; etiology is each patient's
responsibility; control, cure or remission is dependent on honest, genuine efforts toward health goals; (8) Holistic application of empirical medicine and clinical hypnosis to facilitate
and redirect human energy; (9) Primary goals:a) control and inhibit iatrogenic influence,b) symptom management,c) symptom remission.

OVERVIEW OF OBJECTIVES AND PROCESS

A. Develop a holistic treatment plan and apply Clinical Medical
Hypnosis;

B. Produce a satisfactory treatment prescription for symptom management and possible remission of the physical disease;

C. Determine whether manifestation of disease etiology may have a
psychoneuromuscular component. (1) determine hypnotizability;
(2) complete medical history;(3) introduce holistic health concepts; (4) carefully teach each patient auto-hypnosis; (5) facilitate patient faith in themselves; (6) determine how world
view, life experience, critical events, engrams or imprints contribute in psychophysiological-neuromuscular, symptom bound energy; (7) substantiate patient responsibility: more than a helpless
victim of disease; (8) facilitate patient's active, assertive, natural health; cure and symptom control is a joint effort.

© 1979 Elsevier/North-Holland Biomedical Press
Hypnosis 1979
G.D. Burrows, D.R. Collison and L. Dennerstein

NEUROPSYCHOLOGY, BIOETHICS AND HYPNOSIS.

MIROSLAV SENK, M.U.Dr.,
304 Old Northern Road, Castle Hill, N.S.W., 2154, Australia.

This paper deals with the application of bioethical laws to behaviour
and their utilization in hypnopsychotherapy. Neuropsychology is a branch of
psychology which attempts to explain behaviour on the basis of neuronal
structure of the central nervous system. Bioethics is a philosophy which
believes that man's moral, intellectual and aesthetic capacities are dependent
on biological principles.

The ontogeny of the central nervous system begins with primitive germinal
cells which multiply by mitotic division into cells called neuroblasts. These
lose their mitotic ability and grow eventually into nerve cells or neurones.[1]
Their importance is in that they carry genetic instructions to develop into
their appointed roles in the nervous system. Thus the function of any functional unit of the brain is determined already during the embryonic life. The
neurones organize themselves into pathways in a programmed manner so that
there is no random formation. Even the number of the cells is determined genetically so that there is no excess of unused or unwanted neurones. Genetic
coding decides the exact ontogeny not only of the structure but also the
timing at which a structure should become functional. The brain is programmed
to optimal performance under optimal conditions but, of course, illness, mal-
nutrition or injury can change the quality of development. This can happen
during the pre-natal as well as post-natal life because the functional development of the brain is not completed at the time of birth. As the proli-
feration of neural pathways continues the brain organizes itself into three
basic functional units[2]:

The unit for regulating tone and mental states, e.g. attention – organized
in the stem of brain and midbrain.

The unit for receiving, analyzing and storing of information, localized
in occipital, temporal and parietal regions of neocortex.

The unit for programming, regulation and verification of conscious activity, located in the anterior regions of the hemispheres in front of the
precentral gyrus.

Even the basic biological activity requires a certain tone of the orga-
nisms' nervous system. This tone is determined by the degree and quality of
stimulation to which the organism is subjected and that, of course, depends
on the situation in which the organism finds itself. Therefore, the situation
is the activating factor in exciting a response and comprises both extrinsic
and intrinsic influence. The extrinsic influence comes from sensory imput,
one of the functions of the second unit. The intrinsic influence depends on
the metabolic processes of the organism including the genetically determined
metabolic processes organized in inborn behavioural systems such as instincts
and drives. This part of the intrinsic influence comes from the reticular[3]
system of the first unit. There is also a second source of intrinsic influence and this comes from the third unit which is concerned with verification
of conscious activity and with plans, goals and intentions.

For any mental activity there exists a genetically determined neural
pathway into which a stimulus will be channelled when an appropriate situation develops. This, of course, means that the neural pathway is in so to
speak dormant or latent state as if waiting for the favourable situation to
take place. A typical example is the sexual drive : neural pathways no doubt
exist prior to puberty but are in a dormant state until that time. And
'that time' is genetically determined. It is the optimal time in which sexual
behaviour should begin its last stages of maturing process. We must remember
that the brain works as a whole system each unit interacting with the other
two units. Therefore, the genetic metabolic processes within the first unit
must proceed hand in hand with the sensory stimulation of the second unit
and be approved by the regulating and verifying activity of the third unit.
All three units must be in harmony. My own limited investigation suggests
that a girl sexually molested before puberty develops a tendency to sexual
unresponsiveness later in life whilst a raped mature woman suffers from fear
of violence but it does not seem to affect her sexual response.

The behavioural response, therefore, depends very much on the timing of
the first experience[4]. It is the first experience which secures the functioning of the genetic neural pathway and biologically correct response will develop only when the first experience takes place in genetically predetermined
optimal time. This from the practical point of view can lead to two possible
anomalies:
The first experience occurs before the optimal time : the central nervous

system as a whole system is unable to cope with it and random, usually adverse behavioural reaction occurs. Example : the above mentioned sexual anomaly.

The first experience misses the optimal time : no response is learned and when eventually a situation develops which emphatically requires a response an evasive reaction will take place. Example : pubertal obesity.

The emotional development of a child depends on the quality of mother-infant bondage, a relationahip of understanding, tolerance, trust and respect. The emotional bond becomes as important as the physiological needs, so closely tied together that they become synonymous. The need of, and therefore the drive for, bond is the first bioethical law[5,6]. In an experiment a small group of mothers were instructed to provide four more hours of close togetherness with their infants during the first three days of their life than the control group. Their children showed later less stranger anxiety, better emotional balance, earlier speech learning, better verbal communication and better school progress than the control group.

The expression of bond is affection which means physical contact. If an infant is not given the chance to learn this response it simply does not learn it though some degree of compensation may take place later. This, of course, may have far reaching consequences which can affect not only the personal life of that individual but also lives of following generations. No doubt many cases of frigidity belong to this category and seen from this point of view the Masters-Johnson's approach to therapy is very much an ersatz therapy. It can teach a sexual technique but it cannot provide understanding, tolerance, trust and respect which are of utmost importance in development of social responsibility in later life.

As already mentioned the brain works as a complete system and, therefore, the intellectual development goes hand in hand with any other development. The need for mobility at first purely physiological leads to inquisitiveness and through that it stimulates the drive for learning which covers not only the discovery of immediate environment but also the need for communication and socialization. It is interesting to note that this period in life is not reached until the age of 3 to $3\frac{1}{2}$ years, that is not before the control of bowels is achieved[7]. Only then the child is ready to accept another child, be it even its own sibbling. Exposure to socialization before the optimal time leads to feeling of rejection and subsequent envy and jealousy. Missing the optimal time leads to shyness and difficulty in communication[8].

The drive for mobility deserves another mention because it requires an
environmental condition without which it cannot express itself and that is the
freedom of space. And as the psychological consequence of the drive for mobility is inquisitiveness the freedom to enquire, to think, to experiment is
another bioethical law. Yet so many individuals are deprived or even voluntarily deprive themselves of this freedom. When a meaningless ritual replaces
independent thinking there is no chance of development of identity and identity
crisis is a major source of modern neuroticism. Values contrary to bioethical
laws lead to intrinsic conflict with resulting tension, neuroses and psychosomatic illness. Much of these displacements of values start in infancy and
early childhood and are caused by faulty or untimely first experience.

The trace left by the first experience is called engram and the character
of the engram determines the subsequent behavioural reaction. The engram is
of some durability but not necessarily of permanence. Its formation is not
restricted to infancy or early childhood though most engrams are formed in
this period of life. The word itself is not an abstract ; it is in close relation to memory. We know from recent research that long-term memory is based
on biochemical metabolism within the synaptic clefts which direct the flow of
transmission within the net of neural pathways in the central nervous system[9].
The synaptic cleft metabolism is genetically determined but its character can
be modified by pathological conditions during the gestation as well as in
post-natal life. The offsprings of a pregnant chimpanzee exposed artificially
to stressful situations will have tendency to neuroticism and it will take
three to four generation of ideal conditions before this tendency disappears[10].
Similarly the first experience in post-natal life can alter the direction of
transmission and deviate it from the genetically determined pathway. The
deviation, however, will create a conflict because the three main brain units
must work as a whole in harmony and the units not primarily involved will
receive coding which they cannot process. Hysterical reaction is a typical
example of such a confusion. Deviate behavioural reaction is a result of trans-
mitting the impulse into a shunt which takes it onto a track leading to inappropriate destination.

The main mechanism in formation of engrams is what the French psychologists
call 'mimesis d'appropriation' or adaptive mimicry. In infancy this process

is spontaneous[11]. Later, voluntary identification depending on cultural environment may often lead to assuming roles contrary to genetic endowment.

My conclusion is that the structure of the central nervous system is programmed according to the bioethical laws which are common to all living organism and which serve the purpose of survival of individual and his species[12]. The ontogeny of moral development has also been genetically assimilated and is now part of the automatically guided process of mental development[13]. According to Lawrence Kohlberg the moral development proceeds in the following steps :

1. Obedience to rules and authority to avoid punishment ;
2. Conformity to group behaviour ;
3. Prevention of being rejected or disliked by others ;
4. Prevention of being censured by authority ;
5. Acceptance of laws and values of society ;
6. Allegiance to principles of choice.

Stage four represents the morality reached by baboons and chimpanzee groups and most humans reach this stage and the stage five. It is, therefore, not the man who defines morality but morality which defines the man[14].

Hypnopsychotherapy appears to be the treatment of choice in those conditions which are the result of conflict between the genetic and acquired personality traits. It is a suggestion treatment and suggestion is a process of adopting a proposition in the absence of critical thought which would normally occur. This is achieved in hypnosis by gradual reduction of the tone of the central nervous system. This triggers off a chain reaction composed of four basic steps :

1. Inhibition of muscle tone leading to akinesia ;
2. Reduction of autonomic activity seen in slowing down of pulse, lowering of blood pressure and so on ;
3. Inhibition of cortical activity with diminished degree of alertness and therefore, volition;
4. Reduction of affective response characterized by detachment from emotional involvement;

The brain as a whole is involved in the induction of hypnotic trance and as a whole it must be involved in the therapeutic endeavour. Simple symptom removal without wholistic approach will have doubtful results. A suggestion will be accepted only when the three basic units of the brain are in harmony.

Genetic programming plays an important role in this process. In genetic engineering we can teach a microbe to produce, say, a human hormone in commercial quantities but this is possible only when the new genetic instructions are compatible with the microbe's standing order. A well-known substitution syndrome such as obesity following cessation of smoking, so frequent in hypnotherapy, is a typical example of unilateral approach.

The inclusion of bioethical laws into the hypnotherapeutic counselling helps the patient to find his own answer' within the frame of his genetic programming and removes the need for rationalization and intellectualization. The necessity of detailed psychoanalysis is eliminated and anamnesis can be reduced to what is essential for differential diagnosis. This not only saves the time but also frees the patient from disclosing his involvement in embarrassing incidents[15].

REFERENCES

1. Eccles, J.C. (1973) The Understanding of Brain, McGraw-Hill Book Co.

2. Luria, A.R. (1973) The Working Brain, Penguin Education.

3. Birkmayer, W., Pilleri, G. (1966) The Brainstem Reticular Formation and its Significance for Autonomic and Affective Behaviour. Roche Publication.

4. Lorenz, K. (1938) Ueber Tierisches und Menschliches Verhaltan, R. Piper Verlag, Munich.

5. Klaus, M. et al. (1970) Human Maternal Behaviour at the First Contact with her Young. Paed. 46, 187.

    Rosenbaum, P. (1975) Parent-Child Interaction in the First Year of Life. Canadian Family Physician, May, 63-66.

6. Bowlby, J. (1969) Psychopathology of Anxiety : The Role of Affectionate Bonds in Studies of Anxiety. Royal Medico-Physiological Assoc. and Headly Bros., ed. M.H. Lader, Kent.

7. Bower, T.G.R. (1974) Development in Infancy. Freeman, San Francisco.

    Ilf, F.L., Ames, L.B. (1971) Child Behaviour, Hamish Hamilton, London.

    Rheingold, J.L. (1956) The Modification of Social Responsiveness in Institutional Babies. Monogr. Soc. Res. Child Develop., 21, No. 63.

8. Harlow, G.F. (1960) Primary Affectional Patterns in Primates, A.J. Orthopsych. 30, 676-684.

    Harlow, G.F. (1959) The Development of Learning in the Rhesus Monkey. Amer. Sci., 47, 459-479.

    Kohlberg, L. (1969) Handbook of Socialization. Rand-McNally Co., Chicago.

9. Ketty, S.S. (1972) The Biogenic Amines in the CNS. Neurosciences, Rockfeller Univ. Press. N.Y.

10. Deneberg, V.H., Rosenberg, K.M. (1972) Nongenetic Transmission of Information, The Development of Behaviour, Sinauer Assoc. Inc.

   Addler, R., Conclin, P.M. (1963) Handling of Pregnant Rats, Sci. 142, 411-412.

11. Girard, R. (1978) Des Choses Cachees Depuis La Fondation du Monde, Grasset, Paris.

12. Wilson, E.O. (1978) On Human Nature, Harvard Univ. Press.

13. Peters, R.S. (1974) Psychology and Ethical Development, Allen & Unwin.

14. Patocka, J. (1968) Czechoslovak Human Rights Manifesto Suppressed document

15. Govinda L.A. (1977) Creative Meditation and Multi-dimensional Consciousness. Allen & Unwin Press.

Hypnosis 1979
G.D. Burrows, D.R. Collison and L. Dennerstein

A CASE OF HYSTERICAL BLINDNESS WITH SYMPTOM REMOVAL IN ONE SESSION

MICHAEL D. ZANNONI, M.D.

YORK SQUARE-SUITE 42-6285 PEARL ROAD-PARMA HEIGHTS, OHIO 44130 U.S.A.

PRESENT ILLNESS

On May 15, 1973 a forty-seven year old married female was admitted to a hospital
of her city by a neurosurgeon with the chief complaint of "I'm going blind." According
to the events recalled, six weeks prior to admission she bumped her head while getting
into her automobile striking the right fronto-parietal region. After several minutes
she experienced mild discomfort on the right side of the head and face which continued
an undetermined length of time. There was no loss of consciousness. About one week
after this incident, she began to experience persistent severe headaches localized primarily in the mid-frontal area and associated with intermittent blurred vision. No
drugs were taken or prescribed at this time. Gradually over a period of the next two
to three weeks, blurred vision became associated with dim double vision. At this time'
she made an appointment to see her family physician who referred her to a neurosurgeon who arranged for hospitalization.

THE NEUROLOGICAL EXAMINATION AND WORK-UP

The neurological clinical assessment reveals normal fundoscopic examination. The
patient is unable to count fingers. Her pupils react directly to light quite actively, but
consensually, they are somewhat reduced in activity. The left reacts consensually
when stimulated by light on the right; however, the right pupil less actively when stimulated by light on the left. Examination of the cranial nerves is normal. There is
no lateralized motor, sensory or reflex loss. Superficial reflexes are normal. There
is no Babinski. On May 19, 1973, bilateral carotid arteriograms and pneumoencepha-
lograms were performed and proved to be normal. Serology was non-reactive. Other
investigations showed a normal hemogram, urine analysis, SMA-12, electrocardiogram, electroencephalogram, chest film and brain scan.

OPTHALMOLOGICAL EXAMINATION AND CONSULTATION

The neurosurgeon at this point requested ophthalmological consultation. This spec-
ialist reported that he could not account for the inability to see, as a direct result of
any ocular pathology.

PSYCHIATRIC CONSULTATION

On May 26, 1973, the neurosurgeon referred this patient to me for psychiatric evaluation, recommendation and treatment. During the psychiatric interview she several times stated that she did not consider herself to be an unusually nervous person because, "I went through a period of extreme stress when my husband had open heart surgery and handled it O. K." Based on the history, the mental status examination, the symptom. the results of the total work-up, and an academic review[1] of theoretical[2] and clinical concepts[3] regarding the psychotherapeutic process[4] and hypnosis as from time to time appeared in the literature, a diagnosis of hysterical blindness was made. Again, at various times during the interview, the patient expressed her willingness to cooperate to the fullest extent of her ability.

TREATMENT: AGE REGRESSION AND SYMPTOM REMOVAL

A non-authoritative progressive relaxation induction procedure was selected and proved to be profitable and effective. In deep trance the subject was given two cue suggestions: one for eye closure, the other for eye opening. It was suggested that each time the therapist would touch the middle of her forehead her eyes would open. It was also suggested that each and every time the therapist would touch her eyelids simultaneously, she would close her eyes. This is accomplished easily using the thumb and index finger.

Hypnotic age regression[5] has been the focus of attention[6] of various researchers[7] and clinicians.[8] Touching the middle of the forehead gave an immediate response of opening both eyes. As the patient remained with her eyes open, she was questioned about her present age. How old are you? She answered forty-seven. She was questioned as to how it felt to be forty-seven years old and permitted to discuss any problems that she felt she wished to share. She spoke of the extreme differences in personalities between she and her husband and her great difficulties in meeting his needs and understanding him as a person. The cue for eye closure was given as the therapist simultaneously suggested she go back in time one year. The suggestion you are now forty-six years old; you are forty-six years old now was then given. After a few seconds the cue for opening the eyes was given, the patient responded adequately and appropriately remaining now with the eyes open. To the questions, "How old are you", she answered "Forty-six, and my husband is having open heart surgery." She was now questioned as to how it felt to be forty-six years old and again permitted to discuss any problems she wished to share with the therapist. She began to relate how she found it emotionally difficult and disturbing to deal with her own feelings of anger toward her husband but especially now during the period of his convalescence. She stated that her husband sees her role of wife as one of being subsurvient, to be efficient in meeting all of the needs of the master of the house; factual and without criticism or opinion. Now she was weeping as she expressed ideas that affectual exchange, sharing and recognition of emotional needs has no place or importance in marriage according to her husband. She continued to express her husband's outlook and attitudes and his childish demands. By this time she had composed herself and no longer was weeping. So the cue signal for the eye closure was given. Using the same described modalities, she was returned to her forty-seventh year of age.

In this manner the age regression had elicited a catharsis and abreaction regarding her intrinsic emotionality. A psychoanalytical resolution of her own repressed feelings was hypnotically achieved.[9] Interesting works[10] regarding this complex phenomenon[11] are discussed. At this point the psychotherapeutic process for effective symptom removal warranted adequately structured therapeutic intervention and resolution at the patient's own rate of progress and achievement. The patient was able to accomplish complete removal of the symptom in one setting of an hour and ten minutes duration. Four different hypnotic experiences were achieved each using the same clinically extablished and agreed upon suggested cues to be initiated voluntarily by the subject; one specific cue to indicate acceptance (nodding the head once); another for non-acceptance (shaking head no, once); and still another to convey the subject's intention not to become involved in the structured task (shaking head no, twice). These essential factors along with the previously established cues for eye closure and eye opening (the signal being given by the therapist at the appropriate therapeutic moment by touching the subjects forehead or eyelids) form the basis by means of which clinical effective communication from subject to therapist and therapist to subject is hypnotically, structurally and dynamically established.

Accordingly, each of the four hypnotic experiences was structured obtaining progressive visual acuity at the subject's own innate capacity of cue response (acceptance, non-acceptance or non-involvement); own innate ability of performance; and own recognition of actual achievements (from blurred shadows-hypnotic experience one); to (clear shadows-hypnotic experience two); to (outline of objects-hypnotic experience three); to (clear colored objects-hypnotic experience four). A positive voluntary innate cue signal of acceptance was communicated by the subject to the therapist in response to each of the four hypnotic experiences as suggested and structured. The therapist's cue signal for eye closure was given just before the therapeutic suggestive structuring of each hypnotic experience. The therapist's cue signal for the eyes to open was given five to ten seconds after each one of the four therapeutically structured suggestive hypnotic experiences. During and for each of the hypnotic experiences the subject's eyes remained open in response to the cue from the therapist and the subject encouraged to verbalize the innate achievement response obtained as well as to recognize and accept the corresponding psychophysiologic structured goal accomplished. At the end of the fourth hypnotic experience accomplishment (clear colored objects) again the cue signal for eye closure was given by the therapist.

The subject now was instructed to terminate her trance counting backwards from five. It was suggested that when she arrived at her count of one she would open her eyes, retain her visual achievements and accomplishments, would be relaxed and very alert and well in all respects. As she voiced the number one and opened her eyes she explained, Doctor, I can see you. She was smiling, content and thankful. She was asked if she would like to meet the nursing staff that had been caring for her during the hospital stay and responded appropriately and favorably. She was permitted to be up and about and to ambulate as tolerated with minimal supervision.

OUTCOME:

The patient was discharged improved on May 29, 1973. She was seen in follow-up care one week after discharge, one month after discharge, six months after discharge and yearly since. All of her visits were of from ten to twenty minutes duration and she was encouraged to relate any difficulties or problems. She reported feeling well in all respects and much happier now that her husband was treating her like a human being instead of a thing or possession. Hypnosis was never used again in any of the follow-up visits. She was last seen on August 31, 1977, at which time she had gained eight pounds, was well in all respects and had never during this period of time experienced substitution symptoms[12] nor a return of the original symptom which may be a manifestation of a "ripple effect"[13].

REFERENCES

1. Shor, R. E. (1962) Three Dimensions of Hypnotic Depth. International Journal of Clinical and Experimental Hypnosis, 10, 23-38.

2. Spiegel, H. (1959) Hypnosis and Transference. Archives of General Psychiatry, 634-639.

3. Spiegel, H. (June, 1960) Hypnosis and the Psychotherapeutic Process. Comprehensive Psychiatry, 174-185

4. Spiegel, H. and Shainess, N., (1963) Operational Spectrum of Psychotherapeutic Process. Archives of General Psychiatry, 477-488.

5. Barber, T. X., (1962) Hypnotic Age Regression: A Critical Review Psychosomatic Medicine, 286-299.

6. Gidro-Frank, L. and Bowersbuch, M. K. (1948) A Study of the Plantar Response in Hypnotic Age Regression. Journal of Nervous and Mental Disorders. 107, 443-458.

7. Gebhard, J. W. (1961) Hypnotic Age Regression: A Review. American Journal of Clinical Hypnosis, 3, 139-168.

8. Fiore, E. (1978) You Have Been Here Before, New York: Coward, Mc Cann & Geoghegan, Inc.

9. Watkins, J. G., (1975) Methods and Relationships in Hypnotism. Minerva Medica, 66, (6), 291-296.

10. Hollanda, L., Jr. (1975) The Logic and Cybernetics of Hypnosis. Minerva Medica 66, (6), 285-290.

   Kolb, L. C. (1973) Modern Clinical Psychiatry, Philadelphia: Saunders, pp. pp. 412-424.

   Major, R. (1974) The Revolution of Hysteria. International Journal of Psychoanalysis, 5513, 385-392.

11. Mastronardi, V. (1975) Hypnosis within the ambit of Psychotherapy. Minerva Medica, 66, (6), 298-301.

12. Reider, N. (1976) Symptom Substitution. Bulletin of The Mehninger Clinic, 40, (6), 629-639.

13. Spiegel, H. and Linn, L., (1969) The "Ripple Effect" Following Adjunct Hypnosis in Analytic Psychotherapy. American Journal of Psychiatry, 126, 53-58.

Hypnosis 1979
G.D. Burrows, D.R. Collison and L. Dennerstein

PAIN SENSITIVITY BIOLOGICAL TIMIDITY AND PSYCHOSOMATIC DISORDERS

ZBIGNIEW PLESZEWSKI
Institute of Psychology,The Adam Mickiewicz University,
ul.Szamarzewskiego 89., Poznań, Poland

INTRODUCTION

Generaly speaking a human being has two connected mechanisms
of defence towards biological threat: pain sensitivity and
biological timidity. These both mechanisms are a very complicated structure of sensory, cognitive, emotional and visceral
processes.
The first anxiety experienced by small baby has a biological
nature, i.e. his anxiety or fear concern the biological values
above all. On this basis only can develop the functional autonomy of non-biological, psychosocial anxiety and fear. The adult
can feel anxiety or fear in a social stressful situation more
intensive than in a presence of a biological threat. This is a
paradox, in regard to genesis of human anxiety.

Some people have very developed psychosocial timidity and
it prevails over the biological timidity. Particularly it can
be observed in some psychosomatic patients, which display significant discrepancy between developed mechanisms of "psychosocial ego" defence and undeveloped or suppressed mechanisms
of "biological ego" defence. In other words: the biological
timidity is connected with a question "how to live as an organism", and the psychosocial timidity is rather connected with
a question "how to live as a human being".

Biological timidity is a personality feature which signifies
a tendency to react with fear or anxiety towards these stimuli
which can be a signal of pain, illness or death.
On the contrary, psychosocial timidity means a personality
feature manifested in a tendency to react with fear or
anxiety towards these stimuli which are recognized as a signals
of social critique, competition, failure, ridicule, isolation etc.

These both features can be measured by WMK Scale /it is Polish inventory, MMPI-like, to assess the structure of needs and some features of emotional functioning/.

These two kinds of timidity derive from the common needs of self-preservation /cf.Ebrahim [3] /, but in the course of socialization one kind of timidity can prevails over another. In other words: different people take various values as a main component of their self.

CLINICAL INVESTIGATION OF EMOTIONS IN PSYCHOSOMATIC PATIENTS

The hypothesis presented above was confirmed in the clinical research of emotional functioning of patients with coronary heart disease [6] - see Table 1.

TABLE 1. Modal ranks of life plans in group of patients before myocardial infarction /M.I./ and in group of patients after M.I.

Plans	Ranks before M.I.	Ranks after M.I.	D_i	D_i^2
try to be useful	1	8	-7	49
achieve greater professional success	2	11	-9	81
gain higher professional qualifications	3	14	-11	121
obtain higher earning power	4	13	-9	81
improve education continuously	5	15	-10	100
improve the prosperity of own family	6	7	-1	1
perfect own character/personality/	7	9	-2	4
improve atmosphere in own family	8	5	+3	9
devote more time to wife and children	9	4	+5	25
behave quietly, calmly	10	3	+7	49
more recreational activities	11	10	+1	1
visit different countries	12	6	+6	36
increase social contacts	13	12	+1	1
avoid injurious /for health/ situations	14	2	+12	144
know own health status	15	1	+14	196

Total D_i^2 = 898

$$r_s = 1 - \frac{6 \sum D_i^2}{N \; /N^2 - 1/} = -0,60$$

In the period before M.I. patients were motivated by strong drives to achieve the social success, to raise professional and personal values. At the same time many aspects of health protection were ignored. The great part of this group appeared as people with high tolerance of weariness, low biological timidity, tendency to denial of illness symptoms and any trouble. Tibblin[11] called them as a "undercomplainers". These patients with decreased biological timidity/in period before M.I./ survived a more severe myocardial infarction, i.e.more extensive and complicated by rhythm disorders and also have had rather sudden onset of MI.

TABLE 2. Biological timidity before M.I. and sudden onset of M.I. / chi^2 and Kendall`s Q /.

Patients before M.I.	M.I.preceded by angina pectoris	Sudden onset of MI.	Total
High biological timidity	12	2	14
Low biological timidity	6	17	23
Total	18	19	37

df=1   chi^2= 13,06   p= 0,001   Kendall`s   Q= 0,89

TABLE 3. Relation between biological timidity and severity of MI. /very severe M.I. means more extensive and complicated by rhythm disorders/.

Biol.timid.before MI.	Not severe M.I.	Very severe MI.	Total
High biological timidity	14	6	20
Low biological timidity	14	23	37
Total	28	29	57

df= 1   chi^2= 5,38   p= 0,02

The other part of M.I.patients - people with increased biological timidity usually survived M.I. preceded by angina pectoris. What is more, in the period before M.I. they expressed and reported very easily their somatic and neurotic troubles.

These results could be explained as following: The low biological timidity had retarded a motivation to visit a physician earlier, enough in order to take preventive treatment. These people did not like to listen to, talk or think about biological symptoms

and troubles /so called "alexythymic structures of personality"/.
Doing their social and professional tasks they "had not time" to
avoid of weariness, pain symptoms etc. First painful signals from
cardiovascular system were reinterpreted as a "stomach or liver
disfunctions". Such somatic stimuli were not so threatening to
them in comparison with other psychosocial stressors.

On the contrary, people with high biological timidity have had
better motivation to preventive visitation in a health service
unit. They can be treated earlier and the course of their coronary heart disease can be better controlled by specialists.

Usually the high biological timidity is connected with neurotic features of personality. In the research carried out by Le-
bovitz it has been shown that patients with angina pectoris obtained high neurotic scores in the MMPI/ Hp,D,Hy,Pt/. It is appeared that neurotics perceive very easily their somatic sensations
as an unpleasant, painful and threatening. Probably it could be
confirmed that the more defensive attitudes and expectations
the higher the pain sensitivity. It would be supposed that pain
sensitiveness is a correlate of personal timidity.

THE LABORATORY INVESTIGATION OF PAIN

Recent studies on pain have highlighted the role of emotional
states as being responsible for the feeling of pain[3,5,7].
The phenomenon of pain is a disorder of emotional state rather
than a sensory sensation. Certainly, there is a specific nociceptive receptor system /unmyelinated nerve fibres found in all the
tissues of the body/. These receptors are activated by some
degree of chemical or mechanical abnormality of the tissue.
However, an activation of this nociceptive receptors not always
leads to feeling of pain. It depends on many peripheral and central neurological circumstances, determined by psychological
agents as well.

A conceptual model of pain mechanisms, presented by Melzack[5],
illustrates different ways of cooperation of sensory-discrimina-
tive, cognitive and emotional systems. In this model it is easy
to observe that the central control system is able to modify the
different stages of the process of pain sensation. This modification may occur either through the cognitive semantic processes

or through the emotional processes. It is of particular importance that emotional states may modify, i.e. facilitate or inhibit, the gate processes immediately or through the central control system. Melzack`s model allows us to foresee not only the
influence of attention, distraction, expectation and suggestion,
but also the influence of emotional state on sensitivity to
threshold stimuli.

In the research carried out by Pleszewski[7], it has been
presumed, that a basic function of emotion is isolated, specific
/adequately to content/ reorganization of central and local
neuronal processes in order to increase or decrease the contact
with an object of emotion. For example, a situation of fear can
provoke many changes in the organism: visceral, expressive, cognitive etc.,in order to facilitate a better recognition of a
threat, and to appropriate a behavior reducing the influence of
a threat. The author agrees with a concept such as Duffy`s[2] and
Schachters[9], that in an emotional arousal we can separate the
increase of general activation of the c.n.s. /state of alert/
and also specific pattern of activation of different centres of
the c.n.s. This specific pattern of neuronal activity leads to
some modification of perception: facilitation for one information and inhibition for another.
What is more, it leads to modification of cognitive processes
and behavioral programmes. Increased activity of some neuronal
structures and decreased activity of another give a mutable sensory sensitivity, i.e. preference for some information.

It was presummed that the principal function of anxiety and
fear is to increase a vigilance/expectancy for threat information. As pain stimuli are a threat information, so have the facilitated way to different neuronal systems. This hypothesis can
be also drown out from signal detection theory. Anxiety or fear
increase the input probability /expectancy/ for all threat information, and also for pain.
On the contrary, anger reorgaizes many sensory, cognitive and
behavioral processes in order not to receive an information
about threat, but rather to produce some threat for other outside
objects. Probably, the pain sensitivity in anger will be decreased, and in fear - increased.

The author has investigated the sensitivity threshold in a group of young students. The whole experiment had three phases. In the first phase /F=fear/ the subjects were provoked to feel fear or anxiety/test anxiety/. In the second phase /A=anger/ an emotion of anger was evoked. The third phase /N=neutral, non-emotional/ assured them of a state of peace, comfort and relaxation.

For the measurement of the pain threshold an algesimeter of radiating heat connected with electronic chronoscope was used /cf.Green[4]/. In order to control an effect of lateralisation, the algesimeter has been applied to the central part of the forehead.

Instruction: "On your forehead you have an apparatus, which allows to estimate your ability for precise self-observation. Your task is to press the switch precisely at the moment when your feeling of heat will just change to pain sensation".
The time of heat radiating /in sec./ has been regarded as a good measure of the pain sensitivity threshold.

Results: Emotional stressors have been brought in individually in order to keep similarly high level of general arousal. Three physiological parameters: systolic blood preasure, pulse and GSR have been measured continuously; as well some observerable behavior and verbal reactions have been estimated. It was noted that there were no significant differences in physiological parameters of general activation between phase F. and phase A. for group measures /average percentages of increasing of all parameters are similar in both phases in comparison with phase N./. Therefore, the differences between pain threshold in two various emotional states could not be determined by general activation.

Investigation carried out indicates that the emotion of fear lowers in a statistically significant manner the pain threshold. TABLE 4. Average pain threshold in fear, anger and relax.

Differences between phases	Pain threshold	Student"t"	p
Fear - Neutral	1,193 sec.	3,070	0,01
Fear - Anger	0,590 sec,	2,920	0,01
Anger - Neutral	0,603 sec.	2,849	0,05

It was shown that pain sensitivity in fear was notably increased
in comparison both with neutral state as well with anger.
However, pain sensitivity also increased in anger a little.Some
loweringof the pain threshold in anger could be explained by the
influence of general activation /common similar arousal/ or else
by the necessity of concentrating attention on pain stimuli -
- an experimental artefact, that need not take place in a natural
situation.

The dominating pattern of activation can be determined by not
only emotion, but also by different mental processes and features, e.g. expectancy, suggestion, distraction, style of perception etc.Sweeny et al.[10] showed that persons with analytic style
of perception complain of more intensive pain than the globals.

Suggestion in hypnosis as well as in waking states also decreases the pain sensitivity, probably through the disorganization
of the neuronal pattern of fear /cf.Barber[1]/.
What is more, a hierarchy of mental and somatic information can
be changed in a state of hypnosis. It can easily be shown in a
short/experiment,carried out by Pleszewski[8]. In the first stage
of the experiment a subject was informed that his left foot
would be in a state of hyperesthesia, while his right one in that
of hypoesthesia. Reactions of the subject were found to be con-
guent with the suggestion. In the next stage, the investigator
said:"now I am touching your left foot" /while stimulating the
subject`s right foot/. It was found that in such a situation
the subject was prone to react adequately to the verbal information and not to the somatic,sensory stimulation.
Probably, the same mechanisms occur during hypnotic analgesia,
when the verbal information "no pain,only touch" prevails over
the sensory one.

CONCLUSION
Usually the pain sensitivity is a relatively constant feature
of personality connected with biological timidity. But it can be
temporarily determined mainly by actual state of emotion, attitude, expectancy etc. However, in regard to etiology and course
of some psychosomatic disorders, more important seems to be
the relation between typical timidity and pain sensitivity.

260

It would be also very important to know, which neurotic features
of personality /e.g.tendency to depression or high level of
anxiety/ can disturb the process of the treatment and rehabilitation.

REFERENCES

1.Barber,T.K.and Hahn,K.W./1962/ Physiological and subjective
  responses to pain under hypnotically-suggested and waking-ima-
  gined analgesia. J.Abn.Soc.Psychol. Vol 65. No 6.
2.Duffy,E./1962/ Activation and Behaviour.,Wiley,NY.
3.Ebrahim,D.W./1979/ Hypnosis and the neurological model.Part III
  Swensk Tidskrift för Hypnos. No 1.
4.Green,L.C.and Hardy,J.D./1962/ Adaptation of thermal pain in
  the skin. J.Appl.Physiol., Vol.17. No 4.
5.Melzack,R.and Casey,K.L./1970/ The affective dimension of pain.
  in:M.Arnold,ed,Feelings and Emotions.,Acad.Press. NY,London.
6.Pleszewski,Z./1977/ Emotional functioning of patients before
  and after myocardial infarction.,in:Y.Ikemi,ed.Proceedings of
  4th Congress of International College of Psychosomatic Medicine
  in Kyoto,Japan.
7.Pleszewski,Z,/1979/ Pain sensitivity as a psychosomatic phenomenon., British J.of Psychol. /in press/.
8.Pleszewski,Z./1979/ Relation between verbal and sensory information in state of hypnosis.,/paper in Polish,unpubl.UAM Poznań
9.Schachter,S./1962/ Cognitive,social and physiological determi-
  nants of emotional state., Psychol.Rev. No 69.
10.Sweeney,D.R./1965/ Pain reactivity and field dependency.,
  Percept.and Motor Skills, Vol.21. No 3.
11.Tibblin,G.B./1972/ Emotions and heart diseases.,in:R.Porter and
  J.Knight,eds.,Physiology,Emotion and Psychosomatic Illness.,
  Elsevier/North-Holland Biomedical Press.

HYPNOTIC REGRESSION INTO PAST LIVES: A CASE OF RESISTANCE TO
HYPNOSIS

EDITH FIORE, Ph.D.

20688 Fourth Street, Saratoga, California 95070 (USA)

INTRODUCTION

Throughout the long history of hypnosis suggestion has played
a starring role. The role of suggestion to induce the hypnotic
trance has been a major one, but once the trance has been effected
suggestion has been the therapeutic agent sine qua non.

During the past several decades an increasing number of therapists have demonstrated that hypnotic regression to forgotten
traumas is a very effective treatment modality. The use of regression has been necessary when suggestions have been ineffectual
no matter how skillfully given. Until the past decade or so, only
a limited number of hypnotherapists searched for buried memories
beyond the patients' childhood years.

Recently others (Fiore, 1978;[1] Wambach, 1978;[2] Leonardi, 1975;[3]
Kelsey, 1976;[4] Iverson, 1976;[5] Netherton, 1978)[6] have extended the
frontier back before conception--back to former lives.

The purpose of this paper is not to prove or disprove the validity of the recalled experiences nor to explore the concept of reincarnation. I am interested only in presenting some of my findings with the hope that they may be of help in our efforts to
serve the needs of our patients. I also hope that this paper will
stimulate research into an area of investigation that has been
largely ignored by mental health professionals.

Four years ago, several of my patients under hypnosis spontaneously regressed to events in past lives. Following these experiences there was immediate and lasting removal of their symptoms
with no symptom substitution. At the time my private reaction was
that these were fantasied events. These regressions seemed to be
removing the symptoms involved, not differing in any way from a
regression in the patient's current life. For this reason I included past life regressions in my armamentarium. Since that time
I have conducted more than three thousand individual past life

regressions. My patients have regressed to all periods of history, even before recorded history. Many have spoken apparent ancient languages and more modern languages to which they had not been exposed.

A wide range of presenting problems and symptoms have had their origins in traumas from past existences and have been successfully dealt with through uncovering the causal events. In many cases, a symptom was due to more than one past life event, often many. All had to be dealt with before the symptom abated completely. With some patients, a symptom of many years' standing was removed in only one session by a regression to a past life and with others many sessions were necessary.

Obesity has been often traced to a death, or more than one death, from starvation. I have found four cases of hypoglycemia originating in slow deaths in prisons and dungeons where the prisoners were only fed one meal a day. Following these regressions, the symptoms were eliminated completely.

Insomnia and other sleep disorders have been found to stem from traumas occurring in former lifetimes. For example, many patients have remembered being murdered, killed or sexually molested during sleep. Nightmares, especially recurring ones, are often flashbacks to experiences that are later hypnotically recalled. Pleasant and neutral dreams have been found to be flashbacks as well.

Physiological disorders of many kinds, including hypertension, arthritis, cancer, asthma, epilepsy, have been traced to past lives. Tension headaches and migraines have been found to be due to the person being guillotined, clubbed, stoned, shot, hanged, scalped or in some way seriously, usually fatally, sustaining injury to the head or neck. Several patients with chronic abdominal pain regressed to events when their abdomens were run through with swords, bayonets or knives. Dysmenorrhea and menstrual tension have been found to be caused by forgotten former lifetime traumas, usually of a sexual nature. In general, many kinds of pain have been traced to past lives.

Depressions and the concomitant depressive emotional and physical symptoms often were traced to tragedies that occurred, usually with a strong carry-over of guilt.

A large variety of sexual problems, including homosexuality, have originated from experiences in past existences. One of the most dramatic cases, which I have described elsewhere[1] is of a woman in her early thirties who at the time she sought treatment had been married eight years and had never consummated her marriage. After regressing to six traumas in six past lives, she had intercourse with her husband and eliminated all her inhibitions, as well as the disruptive tensions in her marriage. Her premenstrual tension was also alleviated completely.

All sorts of phobias, fears and even aversions have been traced back to some traumatic event. Irrational fears, for example, of snakes, fire, being alone, flying, crowds, cataclysms such as earthquakes, volcanoes, tidal waves, have stemmed from some terrifying experience in a former lifetime.

RESISTANCE

In this paper, I shall discuss one type of fear that every hypnotherapist is frequently confronted with; namely the fear of hypnosis itself, manifested as resistance. Resistance to hypnosis can take a myriad of forms. It can range from getting dizzy while in a trance to terminating treatment.

As a result of using past life regressions in my work, I have found several main categories of the causes of resistance. The following are the most common:

First, "going under" hypnosis is subconsciously equated with going under anesthesia, going under the knife during surgery or going under water in the process of drowning. Each of these situations have resulted in the death of the person in a past life and has left an indelible fear. As an example, one woman was asked to go back to the event responsible for her fear of deep trance. She recalled falling off a rock into the sea. She described her death in the following words: "...like slipping down, going under deeper and deeper...the unconscious feeling slipping upon you--it's gradual, it's a gradual loss of consciousness, terror, fear!"

Second, the buried trauma that caused the symptom was so frightening that many patients subconsciously avoided re-experiencing it by becoming resistant. Sometimes the patient did not

1. Fiore, E. (1979) You Have Been Here Before. New York: Ballantine Books, pp. 99-147.

want to even remember or know what had happened.

Third, in a number of especially fascinating cases, patients actually experienced hypnosis, or were victims of mind control practiced in various forms or were drugged in order to be controlled mentally and/or physically. In each case there were disastrous consequences, usually death, the disclosure of important political or incriminating personal secrets, or the patient was forced to perform horrendous deeds. These people had a dread of losing control. An example is the case of a young woman who found herself on a hypnotist's couch in England in the early twentieth century. She repeated to me word for word his induction and just as she was about to succumb to his suggestions to sleep, she felt his hand on her breast. She sprang up and fled from his office.

Fourth, during past lives some patients were gifted psychically. Because they were unable to heal someone, a famine occurred for which they were held responsible, or because they accurately predicted someone's death, they were labeled witches or considered possessed and persecuted by the church. These people were subconsciously afraid that their present hypnotic treatment would reactivate these latent abilities. Since psychic talents had been conditioned to extreme anxiety or panic they were fearful of finding themselves as scapegoats again.

Fifth, hypnosis was sometimes subconsciously or consciously equated with sleep. Some patients responded with fear because in a past life they had been harmed, attacked and/or killed while asleep. These patients often had some kind of sleep disorder.

Sixth, patients often resisted going into anything but a light trance because they were afraid that hypnosis would bring to light the fact that they may have lived before. If the symptom originated from a past life event, then exposing that event would place them in a position of dealing with the concept of reincarnation. These patients had a conscious or subconscious conflict, usually because of religious training.

Seventh, sometimes patients were resistant because they did not want to face something they had done; for example, a crime committed, a murder, a betrayal, a suicide.

It is beyond the scope of this paper to discuss the manifestations of resistance. I shall illustrate the relationship of resistance to past lives by one case study in which the resistance took a familiar form--an incapacity to recover subconscious memories.

CASE STUDY

Mrs. A., a housewife in her mid-fifties, sought treatment after selecting my name from the telephone directory. She had decided that hypnosis might be helpful since nothing else had helped her. For the past 14 years she had suffered from depression, a host of persistent phobias, especially agoraphobia, and from many physical symptoms, including overwhelming dizziness and a spastic colon. Although she had been treated by various specialists including three psychiatrists, had taken many types of medications, and had had electroconvulsant treatments, her condition remained substantially unimproved. She saw hypnosis as her "last chance".

Mrs. A. stated during our first session that she had always been an overly fearful person, even as a small child she had many unusual fears. However, she had been able to cope with her anxieties during her first 40 years. Symptoms developed after she was subjected to tremendous stress due to her daughter's very prolonged and serious illness, nephrosis. At the same time her mother, with whom she had a very close and loving relationship, became ill and eventually died.

Mrs. A. expressed the fear that she could not be hypnotized even though she wanted it "desperately". At the end of our first session, I induced hypnosis by means of progressive relaxation, making a tape for her continued use. She seemed to achieve a light trance.

During our next session, a few days later, Mrs. A. again voiced concern that she could not utilize hypnosis. She said she felt relaxed by the tape which she played two or three times a day, but she did not feel she had really been hypnotized. Of course, I had given her the usual preinduction talk regarding the nature of hypnosis in terms of awareness, not being under the operator's control and so forth. Despite good finger signals and arm levitation she still maintained she was not hypnotized but was probably helping me by lifting her fingers and arm consciously. I gave her clear instructions to eliminate this possibility and the finger signals dropped out almost completely. While they were in operation she had used her "I don't want to answer" finger quite enough to give me a substantial clue as to the resistance with which we would have to deal.

I saw Mrs. A. biweekly for one year and since then she has been coming for treatment on an average of once a week, for a total of two years. During the early months of her treatment, she remained consistently cooperative at a conscious level and just as consistently uncooperative at a subconscious level! Although she faithfully listened to the tape at least twice daily, each time she felt herself letting go and slipping into a deeper state she would abruptly come up to a much lighter level, usually with a feeling of panic. Sometimes she even awakened spontaneously in the middle of the taped induction. She was very angry with herself when this happened because she would mentally chant to herself, "Go deeper, go deeper". Despite an explanation about the law of reversed effects, she still continued to try to go into a trance. We worked on her fear of failure before she could relax without making an effort. She told me from time to time that she could feel herself "fighting" me. She complained also that she was more relaxed at home while listening to the tape than in my office even though I used the same induction and she looked forward to our sessions. I tried various other techniques such as eye fixation, counting, visualizations, etc., but no one seemed more effective than the others and she preferred the progressive relaxation. During this period hypnosis would be induced and while relaxed she would discuss her current worries, feelings and the events from her daily life. Often, sometimes as a result of direction, sometimes spontaneously, she would discuss consciously remembered events from her childhood. During this period I made another tape for her with ego-strengthening suggestions and a visualization of her leaving her home, going to a department store and the market enjoying herself in a relaxed state. For the first nine months of her treatment under hypnosis, she dealt essentially with only conscious material. She recovered only one subconscious memory, that of her sister trying to smother her as an infant. Following this "breakthrough" there was no subsequent change in her ability to utilize hypnosis or allow herself to experience a deeper trance level. She seemed to stay within a light trance.

One day, under hypnosis, I suggested that she use an improvised "story telling" technique to find the origin of her resistance to hypnosis. Within a few minutes, she described seeing a young woman on an operating table surrounded by doctors and nurses who were futilly trying to stop her bleeding. Apparently slipping into a deeper trance. she continued to describe the blood, the emotions and the thoughts of the patient. I asked her to tell me more about what had happened just before this. Then she began describing the scene, using the first person. She went into detail about how it felt to "go under" anesthesia, how she felt more and more relaxed as she lost consciousness. Then she described the frontal lobotomy that was being performed on her as she watched in horror and anger from the side of the room. She became very emotional, crying and raging as she relived this traumatic experience.

Since that session, Mrs. A. has allowed herself to achieve a medium and at times deep trance. She has found herself in many past lives, recalling and reliving trauma after trauma. As a result she has let go of most of her symptoms. In addition to conquering her depression, she has eliminated almost all of her crippling emotional and physical complaints. Currently, Mrs. A. is much more assertive, happier and feels more in charge of her life. We still have work to do before she becomes the free and well-adjusted person that is her goal.

It was interesting to both of us to discover that the reason the lobotomy was performed was to relieve an agitated depression precipitated by the crib death of an infant daughter. Theoretically, the serious illness of her daughter in this life may have weakened the repression of that similar trauma in her past life. This may have disrupted her defensive structure in general with the result that many symptoms developed and old fears were exacerbated. The overall result was an inability to handle the anxieties in her life, which up to that point she had been able to cope with because her defenses were intact.

DISCUSSION

Past life therapy has been extremely helpful with a wide range of problems. It must be remembered that this technique was often not the only way with which the patient was helped. It was one tool among many.

Nor is past life therapy a panacea. There have been a few patients whom I consider treatment failures. With these cases, some were unwilling at one level to give up their symptoms despite regressions to the responsible events. With others, their resistance was too strong to permit exploration of the subconscious factors involved and they were not helped by hypnotic suggestion alone.

I have found that usually belief or disbelief in reincarnation makes no difference in the results obtained as long as the hypnotized patient is willing and able to report what comes to mind. Also it is not necessary for the therapist to believe in reincarnation in order to be effective. For several years I was quite skeptical myself and yet my patients were eliminating symptom upon symptom. Once we step out of the role of therapist, I believe that question of fantasy or reality is extremely important, intriguing and as of now still unanswered.

REFERENCES

1. Fiore, E. (1979) You Have Been Here Before. New York: Ballantine Books.

2. Wambach, H.S. (1978) Reliving Past Lives: The Evidence Under Hypnosis. New York: Harper & Row.

3. Leonardi, D. (1975) The Reincarnation of John Wilkes Booth. Old Greenwich, Connecticut: Devin-Adair Company.

4. Kelsey, D. & Grant, J. (1976) Many Lifetimes. London: Corgi.

5. Iverson, J. (1976) More Lives Than One? New York: Warner.

6. Netherton, M. & Shiffrin, N. (1978) Past Lives Therapy. New York: Morrow.

© 1979 Elsevier/North-Holland Biomedical Press
Hypnosis 1979
G.D. Burrows, D.R. Collison and L. Dennerstein

HYPNOSIS IN BURN THERAPY

DABNEY M. EWIN, M.D.
Tulane Medical School, 914 Union Street, New Orleans, Louisiana,
70112, U.S.A.

INTRODUCTION

The purpose of this paper is 1.) to review experimental work
showing that in a standard thermal burn the depth and severity
result not only from the heat applied, but also from the body's
inflammatory reaction to the stimulus; 2.) to present evidence
that negative attitudes can enhance and maintain inflammation,
thus interfering with healing; and 3.) to show that in the burned
patient early hypnosis can prevent the body's inflammatory reaction and thus attenuate the depth and severity of the burn.

BACKGROUND

Anyone who has had a significant sunburn knows that at the time
of leaving the sun there may be redness and some discomfort, but
it is only later that inflammation occurs, with the serious symptoms of burning pain, tenderness, swelling, fever, and blistering.
Very little morbidity would ensue if the inflammatory reaction
could be aborted and the process arrested at the time the stimulus
is withdrawn. Confirming Delboeuf's[1] experiment, Chapman, et al[2]
have done classic experiments demonstrating that the degree of
inflammatory response and tissue damage to a standard burn can be
augmented or diminished by hypnotic suggestion as well as by ther-
moregulatory reflexes induced by immersing the feet in hot or cold
water.

But what of the patient whose burn is severe and deep, who
has what we call a third degree or full-thickness burn? Can he be
helped? Brauer and Spira[3] have done a remarkable experiment showing that in a full thickness burn, the destruction of all skin
elements does not occur immediately. A standard and reproduceable
full-thickness burn was applied to young pigs (whose skin most
nearly resembles human skin in laboratory studies) and the burned
area was excised and transferred as a free skin graft to a viable
bed where the response of the body would be toward acceptance such
as occurs with any skin graft. Of 53 burn skin to normal beds
there was an estimated 73 per cent take, while 23 grafts of normal
skin to the same burn beds has an 80% take and 18 normal skin to
normal beds had 98% take. They noted that "a delay of hours
before removal of the burn graft materially influences graft survival in the new bed." This correlates with the evidence of
Chapman et al[4] that the bradykinin-like substance associated with

the inflammatory response is released within the first two hours of injury.

Entin and Baxter[5] using human volunteers plotted a graph showing temperature-time relations for different degrees of thermal injury (Fig. 1,) at temperatures up to 110 degrees Centigrade. Coagulation of skin occurs with two seconds of exposure at 110 degrees Centigrade. No studies are available going as high as 950 degrees Centigrade.

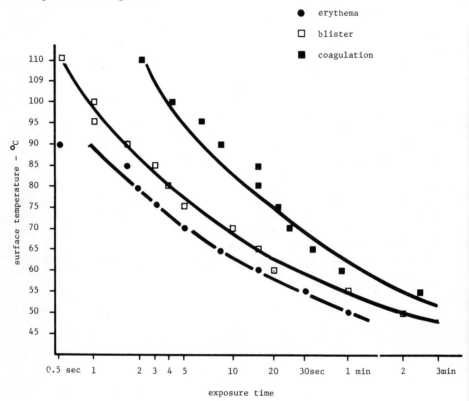

Figure 1 Surface temperature-time relation for different degrees of thermal injury to human skin. Entin and Baxter, 1950.

The author has used hypnosis in treatment of 14 significant burns of the face or extremities. One patient scoffed at the idea of hypnosis from the start, required skin grafts of his elbow and forearm, and had some permanent loss of motion of his fingers in spite of 6 months of physiotherapy. The others all healed repidly without scarring and only one developed signs of infection on the eighth day. Examples of both enhancement and attenuation follow.

CASE REPORT - Enhancement

S. L., 38 year old caucasian male was seen in the office complaining of one week of severe itching, pain, redness, and swelling in an area on the thigh exactly outlining the donor site of a previous skin graft. Ten years previously he had sustained deep second and third degree burns of 60% of his body surface including his trunk, head, and upper extremities. His major pain experience had been at the donor sites, since the nerve endings were destroyed in most of the burn area.

Color pictures were taken and in hypnosis the patient easily recalled that one week earlier he had read a front page story about a teen aged boy who sustained a 60% burn, had felt very sympathetic towards the boy, and had reactivated his old memories of his own burn (i.e. a spontaneous regression filled with emotion). He realized that he was identifying with the boy, and it was suggested that he could help more by writing a letter to tell the lad how well he had done and letting his own leg be well. He accepted this idea, and within 15 minutes color pictures showed a marked decrease in the inflammation, and he left the office feeling comfortable.

CASE REPORT - Attenuation

R. G., 28 year old white male anode worker in an aluminum plant slipped and fell on August 22, 1974, with his right leg as far as the knee going down into molten aluminum at 950 degrees Centigrade (approximately 1750 degrees Farenheit). He was holding on to a stud and extricated himself quickly. First-aid attendents at the plant applied ice packs immediately and transported him in the plant ambulance directly to the emergency room where he was met by the author. The outer layers of skin were cooked brown and peeling, while the inner layers were blanched white with no apparent blood supply. He had very little pain, and pin-prick testing produced no blood and only an occasional response of sensation. Using the example of how a thought produces a blush and dilates all the blood vessels in the face, his attention was directed to the idea that what he thought about could affect the healing of his burn. He was receptive to learning how to do this and went easily into trance with a simple request that he close his eyes and focus his attention entirely on what I was saying. He had had 50 mg of meperidine (Demerol) and the ice packs were still in place. He was given suggestions that his right leg was cool and comfortable, and he readily acknowledged that this was how he felt and that it was a pleasant sensation. He was then given the suggestion that his mind would lock itself to this feeling so that his leg would continue to feel cool and comfortable day and night until it healed. He was asked to let his index finger rise to signal when he had a sense of certainty that he could accomplish this, and when he did it the trance was terminated.

Color photos were taken and the burns dressed with cyclomethy-
caine (Surfacaine) antibiotic was given. The following morning
(21 hours post burn) his blood count showed 9300 white cells, with
70 segs, 25 lymphs, 5 monos. His temperature varied between 99
degrees and 100 degrees until his first dressing change on the
sixth post-burn day when there was a single spike to 102 degrees.
Photos were again taken. There was no clinical infection, no odor,
almost no drainage on the dressing, and no edema of the foot in
spite of the circumferential burn. He required one to three
tablets of aspirin, phenacetin and caffeine, propoxyphene, (Darvon
Compound 65) per day for relief, knowing that he could have meperidine if he requested it. On the 12th post-burn day the dressings
were removed and he was started on daily whirlpool baths which
were too vigorous for the delicate epithelium and caused some sub-
epithelial hemorrhage. He was ambulatory and discharged from the
hospital on the 19th post-burn day and returned to work on
November 4, 1974, ten and a half weeks post-burn. The skin on the
leg healed without scar tissue formation, with regrowth of hair,
and with some permanent bronzing of the skin still present 22
months later. The patient had returned to the same job and had
been promoted to foreman.

DISCUSSION
There are an estimated 2 million burns annually in the United
States (Salisbury and Pruitt[6]); it is possible that a great deal of
morbidity could be alleviated by early hypnosis. Since both brain
and skin have the same ectodermal origin in the embryo and the
skin is the most highly innervated organ in the body, it is not
surprising that the central nervous system exerts a profound control over physiological responses in the skin. Steiner and Clark[7]
report 65% of 35 hospitalized adult burn patients having psychiatric complications severe enough to interfere with treatment

Reporting their experiences, Chapman et al[4] conclude "that the
subject's perceptions and attitudes may be relevant to neural
activities that engender or enhance inflammatory reactions." There
are multiple reports of hypnotic recollections of a previous burn
(Ullman[8], Bellis[9], Johnson and Barber[10]) causing acute inflammation
and/or blister formations at the site of the previous burn. This
author has observed the same phenomenon on several occasions.
Since every burned patient has had the experience of a burn, it is
thus possible for his mind to maintain and enhance the inflammatory reaction by thinking about it.

One of the most damaging emotions is guilt (Cheek[11], Ewin[12]), and
if present it must be removed before a patient will accept good
suggestions of healing. The patient should not only avoid harmful
thoughts, he should develop a positive, optimistic attitude. Artz
is quoted (Dahinterova[13]) "that the well motivated, secure individual did extremely well after even the most severe burn injury

whereas individuals without these resourses had considerable difficulty adjusting to the result of a massive injury." A number of
clinical reports describe burn patients on a pitiful, hopeless,
downhill course, who, after being hypnotized and encouraged to be
optimistic, experienced a dramatic turn-around with rapid healing
(Crasilneck et al[14], Cheek[11], Bernstein[15], Dahinterova[13], LaBaw[16],
Schafer[17]).

Infection will deepen a second degree burn to third degree,
requiring a skin graft where primary healing might have occured.
The effect of hypnosis on infection is perplexing; the trance
state might be viewed as analogous to the dormant state in trees,
the cyst form on the amoeba, and the spore of the clostridium
which are resistant to assaults which would easily overwhelm them
in their active, vegetative existence. Esdaille [18]had a 50 per
cent mortality rate from surgical infection which dropped to 5 per
cent when he began using hypnotic anesthesia. Chong[19]describes
the Hindu firewalkers of Singapore on Thaipusam Day going into
somnambulistic trance, piercing thin steel shafts through their
skin, silver pins through the tongue and cheeks, and walking on
hot coals across a pit 20 by 30 feet. He says "Curiously enough,
with no aseptic preparation of the steel shafts and needles no
case of sepsis or tetanus of the multiple puncture wounds has ever
been reported. None of the fire-walkers suffer from pain or burns,
though as they walk across their feet may sink into the hot cin-
ders up to their ankles." Schafer[17] notes that in the patients
whom he hypnotized on the Burn Unit of Orange County Medical
Center "There was no infection of any burns"; he then attributes
this to good surgical care.
It is apparent in reviewing the case reports in the literature
that the hypnotist tends to be the last healer called in, and then
only in desperation. I find only one patient treated early, namely,
case 3 of Crasilneck et al[14]. "A 32 year old non-white man was
admitted to the hospital with a mixed superficial and deep dermal
burn over 35% of the body surface. He was subjected to hypnosis
after arriving at the hospital about four hours after the injury.
No narcotics were required during the acute phase of injury or at
any time during his 18 days of hospitalization. Complete alleviation of pain was obtained with hypnosis in this man throughout his
hospital course." I quote this case in its entirety because it describes the usual course of these patients in my experience as
treating surgeon and hypnotist. An occasional patient will laugh[17]
at the whole idea and have a poor response, as some of Schafer's
did. It should be noted that the work of Chapman et al[2] showed
that icing a burn holds the inflammatory process in check for several hours. Since icing is now standard emergency room care in
the U.S., there would be ample time to call a qualified hypnotist
if the primary physician is not skilled in the technique of
hypnosis.

SUMMARY

1. In burns, there is no substitute for prevention, but having been burned, nothing could be more desirable than to limit depth of the burn.

2. Experimental work shows that this can be done with <u>early</u> hypnosis, and clinically it has been my experience that these patients heal rapidly with increased resistance to infection,very little pain, and with an optimistic expectation of early return to normal activity.

3. Guilt and identification with other burned patients should be dealt with early, because they can maintain inflammation and delay healing.

4. Resistance to infection seems to be enhanced in patients who are hypnotized early.

5. It is emphasized that the suggestion "cool and comfortable", or suggestions of anesthesia are effective; the word "normal" is to be avoided because in experimental studies these subjects developed a "normal" burn.

6. A case is reported of a young man whose leg was immersed in molten aluminum at 950 degrees Centigrade; he was hypnotized within 30 minutes, developed only a second degree burn, and although antibiotics were not used, had no infection. He was discharged from the hospital on the nineteenth day and healed without scar tissue formation on the leg.

REFERENCES

1. Delboeuf, J. De L'origine des effets curatifs de l'hypnotisme. Bull. Acad. Royal Belgique, 1877. In Bernheim, H. <u>Suggestive Therapeutics</u>, N.Y.: London Book Co. 1947, 411.

2. Chapman, L. F., Goodell, H., Wolff, H.G. Augmentation of the inflammatory reaction by activity of the central nervous system. AMA Arch.Neurol., 1959, 1:557-72

3. Brauer, R. O. and Spira, M. Full-thickness burns as source for donor graft in the pig. Plastic and Reconstructive Surgery, 1966, 37:1, 21-30.

4. Chapman, L.F., Goodell, H. Wolff, H.G. Changes in tissue vulnerability induced during hypnotic suggestion. Journal Psychosomatic Res., 1959, 4:99-105

5. Entin, M.A. and Baxter, H. Experimental and clinical study of histopathology and pathogenesis of graduated thermal burns in man and their clinical implication. Plastic and Reconstructive Surgery, 1950, 6:352-373.

6. Salisbury, R. E. and Pruitt, B.C. <u>Burns of the Upper Extremity</u>, W. B. Saunders Co., Philadelphia, 1976.

7. Steiner, H. and Clark, W.R. Jr., Psychiatric complcations of burned adults: a classification. Journal of Trauma, 1977, 17, 134-143

8. Ullman, M. Herpes simplex and second degree burn induced under hypnosis. American Journal of Psychiatry, 1947, 103, 828-830.

9. Bellis, J. M. Hypnotic pseudo-sunburn. The American Journal of Clinical Hypnosis, 1966 8:4, 310-312.

10. Johnson, R.F.Q. and Barber, T. X. Hypnotic suggestions for blister formation: subjective and physiological effects. The American Journal of Clinical Hypnosis, 1976, 18:3, 172-180.

11. Cheek, D. B. Ideomotor questioning for investigation of subconscious "pain" and target organ vulnerability. American Journal of Clinical Hypnosis, 1962, 5:1, 30-41.

12. Ewin, D. M. Hypnosis in industrial practice. Journal of Occupational Medicine, 1973, 15, 586-589.

13. Dahinterova, J. Some experiences with the use of hypnosis in the treatment ob burns. International Journal of Clinical and Experimental Hypnosis, 1967, 15, 49-53.

14. Crasilneck, H. B., Stirman, J. A., Wilson, B.J., McCranie, E.J. & Fogelman, M.J. Use of hypnosis in the management of patients with burns. Journal of American Medical Association, 1955, 158, 103-106.

15. Bernstein, N.R. Observations on the use of hypnosis with burned children on a pediatric ward. International Journal of Clinical and Experimental Hypnosis, 1965, 13, 1-10.

16. LaBaw, W. L. Adjunctive trance therapy with severely burned children. International Journal of Child Psychotherapy, 1973, 2, 80-92.

17. Schafer, D. W. Hypnosis use on a burn unit. International Journal of Clinical and Experimental Hypnosis, 1975, 23:1, 1-14.

18. Esdaile, J. Hypnosis in Medicine and Surgery, originally titled Mesmerism in India, The Julian Press, Inc. New York, 1957.

© 1979 Elsevier/North-Holland Biomedical Press
Hypnosis 1979
G.D. Burrows, D.R. Collison and L. Dennerstein

CONTRACTUAL ASPECTS OF HYPNOSIS IN PSYCHOTHERAPY

NEIL PHILLIPS M.B.,B.S.   M.R.A.N.Z.C.P.
26A Marlborough Street, Drummoyne N.S.W. 2047, Australia.

The idea of regarding psychotherapeutic interactions in terms of a contract
between the therapist and the patient has been around for quite a while
and has been discussed with regard to hypnosis previously.[1] Some sort of
contract certainly seems to be operating in clinical hypnosis and it seems
that analysis and deliberate modification of the contract would be clinically
useful.

If the clinical hypnotist takes the time to ask himself what he is doing,
he is likely to become bewildered by the complexity of the interaction. It is
difficult enough to unravel the hypnotic process in the research laboratory
where, one hopes, motivations are more straightforward and emotions are
calmer. In the clinical hypnotherapist's office the patient comes with a
heavy emotional load and an extaordinary variety of intellectual attributes,
prejudices and beliefs. The clinician also has a complicated role. He may be
an omnipotent healer or a nervous beginner; he may be an erudite scholar
obsessing about theoretical minutiae, or a seat of the pants performer free
of theoretical restraints. Whatever he really is, the patient will probably
have an utterly different perception of him. To confuse the issue further,
both the clinician and the patient, while presenting with overt motivations
to heal, to be healed, to earn a living and so on, will bring hidden thoughts
and intentions into the situation and, furthermore, will harbour a host of
unconscious wishes and fantasies. Additionally nothing is static; these factors
in each person will begin to influence the other, generating new factors at
various levels of openess.

The experienced hypnotist will have a whole lot of techniques to induce
trances, overcome resistances and promote therapeutic results. Usually, after
some minor and often unconscious adjustments, the gears of the hypnotist
and patient mesh, a trance is induced and , with a bit of luck a therapeutic
result is achieved. The hypnotist and the subject part company in an
atmosphere of mutual satisfaction.

Unfortunately failure is quite common and makes it necessary to examine
the hypnotic interaction more carefully so that we can understand what is
happening, and repair the damage or do better next time.

The thing that appeals to me about examining the hypnotic interaction as a contract, is that it brings some order into chaos, while conveniently bypassing the problem of the existence or nonexistence of a trance state, and does not require a commitment to a particular theoretical model. I believe that it is important to see the hypnotic contract as occurring between individuals in a cultural and historical setting. We can learn from the past that we are not always doing what what we think we are doing, and that we are often doing what we are doing for its value as ritual rather than for some intrinsic value. We need to remain sceptical about the value of our most sacrosanct practices.

To illustrate these points we can look to the past. Mesmer did not develop mesmerism in a cultural vacuum; he worked and lived in a time of developing rationalism and was himself seeking an understanding of illness and new methods of treatment through the mechanistic theories of astrology. His treatment involved animal magnetism and touching and stroking the patient. These methods reflected the fascination that magnetism and the flow of mysterious fluids through the aether held for the thinkers of the time, and the practices of certain religious healers.[2] Paracelsus himself was responsible for some of the earlier theories about magnetism and health. Mesmer's use of the term "animal magnetism" derives from the concept of the anima or life spirit and is seen by Miller[3] as an attempt to reconcile the developing mechanistic science of the time with preservation of "some special spiritual value in human life."

Mesmer's detractors had a more sophisticated understanding of scientific method, but because of their own mechanistic bias failed to ponder the real wonder of his cures, dismissing them as being merely due to imagination.

Charcot, working in a hospital and gripped with the excitement of his work in pathology, could only see hypnosis as a pathological state and was accordingly presented with model neurotic symptoms and behaviour by his subjects. His contract with them demanded it, just as Mesmer's contract with his subjects demanded an epileptiform crisis.

Gradually changes occurred in hypnotic practice and, with the twentieth century, developments in experimental psychology provided systematic methods for the study of hypnosis. At the same time authoritarian values have fallen away in western society and these two factors have influenced modern hypnotic contracts. We now very often present hypnosis to our subjects in an egalitarian non-authoritarian way, calling on the mystical prestige of science to underwrite our authority.

The old authoritarian model of a hypnotist with special powers taking over the will of the subject is fading, and is proving to be only another way of dressing the hypnotic transaction up in the costume of its era. Reflecting on history makes one wonder how our methods will look in fifty years when they can be seen objectively in there cultural context.

There are problems in analysing the hypnotic interaction in terms of it being a contract. The greatest problem is the incredible complexity of the interaction and the fact that it is dynamic rather than static. Although some areas of psychiatry use written contracts to define rights and duties in the therapeutic situation, I am certainly not advocating such an unsubtle method in the finely tuned hypnotic communication. We can still, however, use a mental formulation of the contract to examine the needs and wishes and the give and take on each side.

There are three levels of openess in the hypnotic interaction, perhaps equivalent to large print clauses, small print clauses, and unwritten, secret and trick clauses. I have chosen to use the terms -- <u>Overt</u> agreements or understandings, mutually aknowledged by both parties. <u>Hidden</u> intentions or understandings - where only the party having them is aware of their existence, and completely <u>unconscious</u> wishes and fantasies which, nevertheless, influence the transaction.

TABLE 1

NETWORK OF INFLUENCES AFFECTING OUTCOME

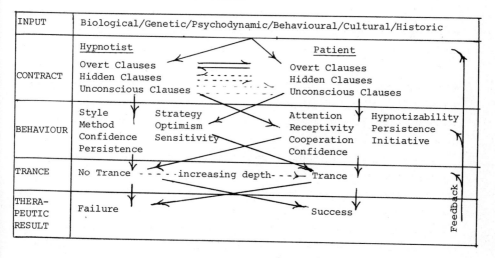

INPUT	Biological/Genetic/Psychodynamic/Behavioural/Cultural/Historic			
CONTRACT	Hypnotist Overt Clauses Hidden Clauses Unconscious Clauses		Patient Overt Clauses Hidden Clauses Unconscious Clauses	
BEHAVIOUR	Style Method Confidence Persistence	Strategy Optimism Sensitivity	Attention Receptivity Cooperation Confidence	Hypnotizability Persistence Initiative
TRANCE	No Trance ----increasing depth---> Trance			
THERA-PEUTIC RESULT	Failure		Success	

Feedback

I would now like to illustrate this method by presenting three cases.
I must aknowledge that access to hidden and unconscious material is difficult,
but sometimes the material is forthcoming as one gets to know the patient
and some of the hypnotist's own unconscious clauses become evident with a
bit of non-defensive self examination. Even when verification is not
available, I believe that some intuitive speculation can often throw some light
into dark and puzzling corners.

CASE A

Mr. A, aged twenty seven years was referred by a patient previously
successfully treated with hypnosis. He complained of a feeling of tightness
and tension in his face, he was unable to relax and suffered from insomnia.
He also had some relationship problems with the woman with whom he lived.
It is important to note that he was a dedicated socialist, deeply concerned
about the world and active in left wing politics. Apart from expressing
disapproval at the lack of suitable ideological content in the magazines
in my waiting room, he was well motivated, cooperative and friendly. He
achieved a score of four on the Hypnotic Induction Profile[4] and readily
went into a trance. During the second induction I used the phrase "take some
time off -- withdraw into yourself - let the world take care of itself";
this had the immediate effect of bringing him instantly out of the trance
glaring at me and demanding that I retract the political statement I had
just made. He was very annoyed that I had tried to interfere with his
political beliefs while he was under hypnosis. An apology from me and an
agreement to keep politics out of it, allowed the hypnosis to continue and
proceed to a successful outcome

The Contract in Case A

Hypnotist

Overt -- Wanted to do a good job.
        Presented an egalitarian scientific model of hypnosis.
        Interested in patient's ideas.

Hidden -- Wanted to impress patient.
        Wanted to reduce patient's critical faculties during
        the trance.

Unconscious -- The patient produced political guilt feelings in
        the hypnotist, made him feel old and corrupt.
        Identification with the patient.
        Anger at the patient.
        A wish to make the patient more moderate.

Patient

    Overt --   Wanted to get rid of tension.
                          Wanted to cooperate.
                          Wanted to convey his political message.

    Hidden --   Possible feelings about hypnotist as a private
                          doctor, member of the establishment, revisionist
                          or reactionary.
                          Possible discomfort at dependency feelings.
                          Alert for propaganda.

    Unconscious --   Ambivalence to the hypnotist, probably intensified
                          by transference feelings from his past experiences.
                          Rivalry, dependency needs and fears of his wish
                          for dependency.
                          An infantile view of the hypnotist as having
                          great powers.

Hidden and unconscious clauses in the patient's contract sensitized the interaction to any political message from the hypnotist, no matter how subtle. The hypnotist, also influenced by hidden and unconscious clauses, inadvertently supplied just the message the patient was looking for and blocked the hypnosis. When the contract was rewritten the hypnosis proceeded.

CASE B

Mrs. B, aged thirty years, recently separated from her husband. She was referred on an urgent basis and was still very upset after an emotional crisis the previous night. She had had a spontaneous abreactive outpouring of emotion while trying to deal with her estranged husband. Initially she had a great need to talk and we proceeded to insight oriented psychotherapy which progressed rapidly and effectively. One day Mrs. B commented on some hypnosis literature on my desk and, at that point I lost my therapeutic perspective. I talked enthusiastically about hypnosis and I suggested that I show her how to do self hypnosis. There were absolutely no indications for using hypnosis. Mrs. B agreed to try, but with hindsight I can see that it was without much enthusiasm. I tested her with the Hypnotic Induction Profile and found that she had a decrement profile, suggesting that something was interfering with her capacity to go into a trance. Fortunately I regained some therapeutic acumen at that point and gave up trying to do hypnosis and returned to the psychotherapy. The therapy continued to progress well and at the time of termination, I was able to get some feedback about the failed hypnosis, which allowed me to formulate some ideas as to what had happened. Shortly after the failed hypnosis deep issues of trust and transference emerged, and were satisfactorily dealt with.

The Contract in Case B

Hypnotist

Overt --
Presented hypnosis as something useful that patient should know about.
Obviously sharing intellectual enthusiasm with the patient.
Presented hypnosis in a non-threatening non-authoritarian way.

Hidden --
Wanted to impress patient.

Unconscious --
Positive countertransference.
Seductive manouver.
Omnipotent fantasies.

Patient

Overt --
Agreed to hypnosis.
Curious about hypnosis.
Had initiated discussion of hypnosis.

Hidden --
Surprised.
Did not want to be hypnotized.
Felt intruded upon.
Felt that she was already making good progress in psychotherapy and did not want to be rushed.

Unconscious --
The comment on the literature on the desk was possibly an expression of an unconscious wish to be hypnotized.
There was a fear of repeating the abreactive experience.
There was transference to the hypnotist as a parental figure with all the ambivalent feelings this involved.
Very strong conflicts regarding trust and dependence were present at the time.

In this case the hypnotist's attempt to hypnotize the patient was inapproriate and contraindicated. The patient's, possibly unconsciously motivated remark connected with the hypnotist's countertransference and pecipitated the attempt at hypnosis, which failed because the contract was quite inappropriate for the patient's needs.

CASE C

Miss C, a twenty three year old nurse, presented with a rapidly cycling depression and a habit of picking the skin off her face. Originally it seemed an unusual case of manic dpressive illness, but I decided to use hypnosis to help her to stop picking her face and postponed giving her medication. The first trance induction failed and I had a sense of great resistance. The second induction worked and the problem of the face picking was solved with a simple strategy. The depression also cleared and did not return. I thought I had finished with her , but she kept coming to see me. I continued to see her because I was aware of some contradictions in her relationships and I anticipated another crisis, and because she told me that her previous therapists had all regarded her as cured by the fifth or sixth session. The therapy stayed at a superficial level despite repeated attempts to draw from her whatever it was that was plainly troubling her.

One morning, at two a.m., I was called by her flatmate and informed that Miss C was trying to leap off the balcony, terribly upset and very drunk. When I arrived, I found that she was having a tremendous abreaction; recalling events of two years previously when her boyfriend had been killed in a car accident. He had been drinking before the accident because he was upset that Miss C had had a pregnancy terminated two days previously without telling him. I had heard nothing of this in several months of psychotherapy. In the next few sessions I was able to get her to share her feelings with me and I was then able to let her terminate therapy with some confidence that she would return and speak to me about the unspeakable if she needed to do so.

Incidently, her boyfriend suffered severe facial injuries in the accident and Miss C was with him for a while at the hospital before he died.

I have mentioned this case because I believe I have some understanding of the strong initial resistance to hypnosis and the subsequent good therapeutic response.

The Contract in Case C

Hypnotist

Overt --	Displayed confidence that hypnosis would be useful. Supportive, presenting hypnosis as something she could learn to do for herself.
Hidden --	Doubt about the appropriateness of hypnosis. Awareness of her fragility. Disturbed by the damage she was doing to her face. Confusion about her relationships, she had arrived nursing an infant which the hypnotist mistakenly thought was her own. The baby was very significant to her.
Unconscious --	Omnipotent fantasies. Rescue fantasies. Possibly a sense of rivalry with previous therapists. Intrigued by her relationships.

Patient

Overt --	I need help. I want to please you. I really am a strong and independent person. I feel terribly ashamed of my dreadful face.
Hidden --	I won't tell you about my terrible feelings. These things are best kept to oneself. I fear talking about them or even thinking about them. I must maintain an appearance of strength and independence. I want to avoid new relationships, particularly with men.
Unconscious --	If you know my terrible secret you will condemn and reject me. I need protection, I need to get close, I mustn't get close, I need to make sure I get rejected. I need to make myself ugly, to injure my own face. If I don't stop picking my face, and getting depressed I will have to keep coming and you will learn my secret.

The first attempt at hypnosis failed because her defences were fragile and she was close to abreaction. At the second attempt she faced a problem; if she failed to go into a trance I would be likely to explore her resistance, and she might spill the beans, if she became hypnotized she believed that she would have to give up her symptoms. She chose the latter course to keep me off her back, but was trapped by her own dependency needs and found herself continuing to come and see me.

REFERENCES

1. Hodge, J. R. (1976) The International Journal of Clinical and
   Experimental Hypnosis, Vol. XXIV, No. 4, pp. 391-399.

2. Owen, A. R. G. (1971) Hysteria, Hypnosis and Healing, the work of
   J. M. Charcot. Dobson, London, pp. 170-171.

3. Miller, Jonathan, (1976) Nervous Insights, Transcript published by
   the Australian Broadcasting Commission. p. 45.

4. Spiegel, H., and Bridger, A. A. Manual for Hypnotic Induction Profile:
   Eye-roll Levitation Method. New York: Soni Medica, 1970.

THE COGNITIVE PREREQUISITES OF POSTHYPNOTIC AMNESIA IN CHRONIC SCHIZOPHRENIA

LUCIE GIRARD-ROBIN & GERMAIN LAVOIE

Université de Montréal and Hôpital Louis-H. Lafontaine, Montréal, Canada

The experimental investigation of posthypnotic amnesia in schizophrenia can be traced back to Kramer and Brennan[1] who observed a very high incidence (80%) of recall amnesia in their schizophrenic sample, when compared with the 32% of Ss in the original normative sample of the SHSS:A[2] who were amnesic on the same item. In 1973, Lavoie et al.[3] published a study, based on an earlier communication by Lavoie & Sabourin[4] demonstrating that while recall amnesia was high in schizophrenic Ss, reversibility was far lower and residual amnesia higher, than what is observed in normal Ss.

A series of studies were then planned to investigate the nature of that phenomenon. A summary of these studies can be found in Lavoie & Sabourin's[5] review of experimental and clinical studies on hypnosis and schizophrenia. The main features of amnesia in unselected chronic schizophrenics are the following[6]: (a) high incidence of spontaneous "amnesia", 90% of Ss passing the amnesia item of SHSS:A before any suggestion of amnesia; (b) evidence of cognitive deficit, illustrated by the severe difficulty most patients experienced in active learning procedures; (c) high incidence of suggested amnesia (SHSS:A procedure) in spite of generally low or medium hypnotic susceptibility; (d) low reversibility and high residual amnesia; (e) no disruption of retrieval; (f) no difference in recall of passed and failed items; (g) best recall for the first items on the scale, and (h) lower IQs for Ss presenting a high recall amnesia and no reversibility. This last factor suggested that, in the absence of reversibility, high recall amnesia could probably be explained by the cognitive deficit of these patients.[3]

Furthermore, initial studies[3,4,7] were unable to show any evidence that either susceptibility or hypnotic induction had an effect on amnesia and reversibility. Lieberman et al.[8] were however able to show that, given a sufficient proportion of high susceptible Ss, reversibility does relate to hypnotizability in schizophrenics as in normals and suggested that hypnotic induction increased reversible amnesia. Since that study was not counterbalanced in the waking-hypnosis condition, the present study was designed to investigate the effect of hypnotic induction and suggestion on recall amnesia and reversibility, using a counterbalanced design.

Reversibility implies that the material that could not be recovered when the S was amnesic was nonetheless properly recorded, and the recording of material depends upon cognitive functions appropriate to the level of difficulty of the task. Nace et al.[9] insisted that posthypnotic amnesia is an _active_ psychic process. The cognitive process involved in reversible amnesia would require a sufficient degree of thinking organization.

Piaget's theory would appear to be a particularly appropriate theory to test the relationship between cognitive level and efficiency, and memory performance and reversible amnesia. Rapaport[10] asserted that the thought disorders in schizophrenia "involve all aspects of thought-organization including memory", and that "memory, that is registration, retention and reproduction, are dependant upon schemes, organized and activated by attitudes". The scheme is the primary unit of mental organization in Piaget's theory of development, and is defined as "the structure or organization of actions as they are transfered or generalized by repetition in similar or analogous circumstances"[11].

In their work on memory and intelligence, Piaget & Inhelder[12] provided an integrated method of investigation of the action of intellectual schemes on memory performance. They link their conception of memory to those of Pierre Janet[13] and of Bartlett[14]. Janet considered the recall of memory as a reconstruction which occurs in a manner comparable to that practiced by the historian (conduite du récit). Janet also characterized recall by its social function, because it is communication of information to someone, in the absence of the motivating event.

Lavoie[6] formulated the hypothesis that there would be a correlation between cognitive efficiency and the production of reversible amnesia in chronic schizophrenia. It was understood that cognitive "efficiency" meant (a) a sufficient strenght and stability of intellectual schemes and (b) a sufficient ability to resolve, in the reversibility process, the hypothesized conflict between schemes induced by the suggestion of amnesia. This led to a master degree thesis by Lucie Girard-Robin[15], who also investigated other aspects of the phenomenon.

METHOD

Subjects. Twenty-eight male chronic schizophrenics were matched across four experimental groups according to age (M = 42.5 years, range = 23-58), lenght of hospitalization (M = 10.6 years; range = 2-23), and hypnotic susceptibility (SHSS:A) (M = 4.5; range = 1-10).

General procedure. Two of these groups (groups 1 & 2) received a suggestion of amnesia, while the two others (groups 3 & 4) did not. Group 1 and group 3 were tested in the waking state on Day 1 and under hypnosis on Day 2. Groups 2

and 4 were tested in a reverse order. The sequence of the experiment for each
of the experimental conditions is presented in TABLE 1.

TABLE 1

GENERAL PROCEDURE

	Group with suggestion		Group without suggestion	
	Hypnosis	Waking	Hypnosis	Waking
1	Contact	Contact	Contact	Contact
2	Induction (SHSS:A)	———	Induction (SHSS:A)	———
3	Introduction to Piaget's tests	Introduction to Piaget's tests	Introduction to Piaget's tests	Introduction to Piaget's tests
4	Tests adminis-tration & imme-diate recall after each test	Tests adminis-tration & imme-mediate recall after each test	Tests adminis-tration & imme-mediate recall after each test	Tests adminis-tration & imme-diate recall after each test
5	First recall (R1) for the whole series	First recall (R1) for the whole series	First recall (R1) for the whole series	First recall (R1) for the whole series
6	Amnesia suggestion	Amnesia suggestion	———	———
7	Awakening	———	Awakening	———
8	Second recall (R2) for the whole series	Second recall (R2) for the whole series	Second recall (R2) for the whole series	Second recall (R2) for the whole series
9	Lifting of amnesia	Lifting of amnesia	———	———
10	Third recall (R3) for the whole series	Third recall (R3) for the whole series	Third recall (R3) for the whole series	Third recall (R3) for the whole series

For the $\underline{S}$s in the hypnosis condition, the instructions given were that it was
possible to open one's eyes while remaining in the trance and a comparison with
somnambulism was presented to the $\underline{S}$ to illustrate the point. The $\underline{S}$ was then
requested to open his eyes, to look at the figure before him as long as he
wished. The figure was then removed, and the $\underline{S}$ was asked to reproduce it. The
same procedure was repeated for each of the eight drawings of the series. Drawings 1 (serial configuration in the form of the letter "M") and 2 (divided
triangles) relate to additive logical structures; drawings 3 (corresponding
series) and 4 (intersection of classes) relate to multiplicative logical structures; drawings 5 (levers) and 6 (causal relationships) relate to causal structures; drawings 7 (geometrical transformation) and 8 (horizontal levels) relate
to spatial structures. These tests permitted a quantitative and qualitative

evaluation of memory as it is rooted in the cognitive structures. Three basic scores were obtained: R1 (first recall, step 5); R2 (second recall, step 8); and R3 (third recall, step 10). The total possible score on recall 1 is 32, compared to 12 in the SHSS:A.

"M" variation of a size graded seriation used as standard for memory reproduction.

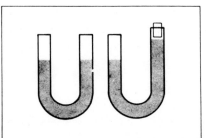

Figure used as standard for memory reproductions of water levels.

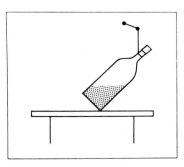

Figure used as standard for memory reproduction of water level orientation.

Fig. 1. Three figures used in the experiment (Reproduced from Inhelder & Chipman[16]).

Index of amnesia. Nace et al.[9] have proposed an index of amnesia which tries
to conteract the ceiling effect. This index was expressed as a proportion:

$$\frac{\text{N reversed items - recalled items}}{\text{N total items - recalled items}}$$

In this study, this proportion can be expressed as R3-R2/32-R2. For a S to be
considered amnesic, the difference R3-R2 should be positive. The importance of
his amnesia is given by the result of the division of that difference (R3-R2)
by (32-R2)

RESULTS

An analysis of variance confirmed the hypothesis of an effect of the amnesia
suggestion on recall, and of an effect of the lifting of amnesia on reversibility. However, these effects were not increased after an hypnotic induction,
when compared to the waking state.

Six Ss (out of 28) obtained a positive index of amnesia in the waking state
(5 in the suggestion condition and one, without suggestion). Four of these
were also amnesic in the hypnosis condition. Twelve Ss were amnesic in the
hypnosis condition (9 in the suggestion condition, and 3, without suggestion).
A rank order correlation was computed between the cognitive level of these
twelve Ss, as measured in the waking state and their index of amnesia, as computed in the hypnosis condition. The correlation was 0.76 (p < .01).

TABLE 2

PARTITIONING OF Ss ACCORDING TO (A) THE COGNITIVE LEVEL OF EFFICIENCY IN THE
WAKING STATE (USING PIAGET & INHELDER'S TESTS[11]) AND (B) REVERSIBLE AMNESIA
IN THE HYPNOSIS CONDITION (USING NACE et al.[9] INDEX)

	Reversible amnesia in hypnosis condition	
	Below median	Above median
Cognitive level in waking state		
Above median	1	5
Below median	5	1

Table 2 gives a clear representation of that relationship. Five of the six
Ss who had obtained higher scores of cognitive efficiency in the waking state
were among the more amnesic in the hypnosis condition. In contrast, five out
of the six Ss who had obtained lower scores of cognitive efficiency in the

waking state were among the less amnesic S̲s̲ in the hypnosis condition.

Hypnotic susceptibility co-determined amnesia and reversibility. The rank-order correlation between hypnotic susceptibility (SHSS:A) as measured prior to the experiment, and Nace et al. index of posthypnotic amnesia (adapted for Piaget's tests) was 0.58 (p < .05).

DISCUSSION

As far as the respective influence of suggestion and hypnotic induction on amnesia are concerned, this study essentially replicated Sabourin's[7] data. In both studies, there was a significant reversibility, resulting from the suggestion of amnesia, regardless of the presence or absence of hypnotic induction. It is worth noting that these two studies reached the same conclusions with somewhat different designs. Sabourin[7] used an independant group design where the S̲s̲ had to actively memorize a set of words later submitted to the amnesia-reversibility process. This study used a counterbalanced design with repeated measurement on the waking-hypnosis condition, where the S̲s̲ did not have to reach any pre-determined criterion before the amnesia-reversibility procedure.

The two studies, however, relied on an active learning procedure where the S̲ was requested to make a conscious effort to memorize the material, which is different from the usual passive incidental learning involved in standard SHSS: A administration. Lieberman et al.[8] demonstrated a significant effect of this modification of the procedure on recall amnesia, and on reversibility, especially in the hypnosis condition. They also suggest that the effect of hypnotic induction on amnesia and reversibility might be obscured with active learning procedures.

Two factors in posthypnotic amnesia. This study replicated Lieberman et al.[8] observation that reversible amnesia does relate to hypnotizability in schizophrenic patients, when the samples include enough high susceptible patients to make this comparison meaningful. Previous studies[3,4,7] used almost unselected samples, while Lieberman et al.[8] and this study carefully screened S̲s̲ with the HGSS:A and SHSS:A, to have an adequate representation of the low, medium and high susceptibility levels.

Table 2 indicates that reversible amnesia also depends upon the operation of intellectual schemes. It does not however provide information on the actual process that is taking place. Here we would suggest two areas of investigation. First the presence of a high recall amnesia with no reversibility would indicate either (a) an organic deterioration of the schemes and/or (b) a severe psychic conflict making impossible a proper encoding of the material. The deterioration of memory would indicate the schemes are not adequate or can not be used at the moment to support the memory-images. Second, the presence of a high recall amnesia with a high reversibility would be possible only for those Ss presenting a high level of cognitive effectiveness and structuration. On the recall amnesia test, two or more schemes would come in conflict, resulting in an actual temporary inability to recall. The material would be there, would be encoded (as shown by the pre-experimental recall), thus attesting the efficacy of the relevant schemes, but it would not be retrieved because of the stimulation of a competing attitude ("not remembering" or "forgetting") that would activate antagonistic schemes and operations. Later on, reversibility would follow a reactivation of the schemes involved in the encoding process beforehand, which would again become dominant. The S would then progressively reconstruct his memory, using (a) the actual cues (experimenter, place, situation, etc.) and (b) the schemes used when he was first exposed to the stimuli to be remembered.

An experiment could be devised that would study the interaction of hypnotic susceptibility and cognitive efficiency as they co-determine reversible amnesia. The joint use of Piaget's theory and methodology and of Nace et al. approach to the estimation of posthypnotic amnesia should lead to further significant progress in our understanding of posthypnotic amnesia.

REFERENCES

1. Kramer, E. and Brennan, E.P. (1964) J. Abn. Soc. Psychol., 69, 657-659.

2. Weitzenhoffer, A.M. and Hilgard, E.R. (1959) Stanford Hypnotic Susceptibility Scale, Form A, Palo Alto, California: Consulting Psychologists Press.

3. Lavoie, G., Sabourin, M. and Langlois, J. (1973) Int. J. Clin. Exp. Hypn., 21, 157-168.

4. Lavoie, G. and Sabourin, M. (1971) La susceptibilité hypnotique, l'amnésie post-hypnotique et le Q.I. chez les schizophrènes et autres psychotiques chroniques. Paper presented at the Annual meeting of ACFAS, Sherbrooke, Quebec.

5. Lavoie, G. and Sabourin, M. (1979) in Burrows, G.D. and Dennerstein, L., Handbook of hypnosis and psychosomatic medicine, North-Holland Biomedical Press, Amsterdam.

6. Lavoie, G. (1976) Some implications of posthypnotic amnesia in chronic schizophrenics. Paper presented at the 28th Annual meeting of the Society for Clinical and Experimental Hypnosis, Philadelphia.

7. Sabourin, M. (1971) Effets de l'induction hypnotique et de la suggestion sur l'amnésie dans la psychose chronique. Unpublished doctoral dissertation, Université de Montréal.

8. Lieberman, J., Lavoie, G., and Brisson, A. (1978). Int. J. Clin. Exp. Hypn., 26, 4, 268-280.

9. Nace, E.P., Orne, M.T. and Hammer, G.A. (1974) Arch. Gen. Psychiat., 31, 257-260.

10. Rapaport, D. (1951) Organization and pathology of thought. New York: Columbia University Press.

11. Piaget, J. and Inhelder, B. (1969) The psychology of the child. New York: Basic Books.

12. Piaget, J. and Inhelder, B. (1968) Mémoire et intelligence. Paris: P.U.F.

13. Janet, P. (1928) L'évolution de la mémoire et la notion de temps. Paris: Chahine.

14. Bartlett, F.C. (1932) Remembering: a study in experimental and social psychology. Cambridge: Cambridge University Press.

15. Girard-Robin, L. (1977) L'amnésie post-hypnotique et ses rapports avec les fonctions cognitives chez les schizophrènes chroniques. Unpublished master's thesis, Université de Montréal.

16. Inhelder, B., and Chipman, H.H. (1976) Piaget and his school: a reader in developmental psychology. New York: Springer-Verlag.

© 1979 Elsevier/North-Holland Biomedical Press
Hypnosis 1979
G.D. Burrows, D.R. Collison and L. Dennerstein

THE EFFECTS OF POST HYPNOTIC SUGGESTION ON MAXIMUM ENDURANCE PERFORMANCE AND RELATED METABOLIC VARIABLES

J. ARTHUR JACKSON,* AND GREGORY C. GASS

The Research Institute of Applied Physiology, Cumberland College of Health Sciences, Sydney, New South Wales, Australia

INTRODUCTION

Over the years, man has sought a variety of ways of increasing his strength and endurance, particularly in sports endeavour. One technique that has received a great deal of interest in this regard is that of hypnosis, and for this reason much research has gone into assessing the effectiveness of hypnosis in increasing a person's endurance performance.

A great many of these studies have proved conflicting in their findings. When evaluating the effects of hypnosis *per se*, some workers [1,2,3] found that hypnosis increased endurance performance, whilst others [4,5,6,7,8,9,10] were unable to substantiate these results.

Various workers have attempted to determine the combined effect of hypnosis and motivational suggestion, and here again there is a considerable divergence of opinion. Some researchers [4,7,11,12,13,14,15,16] have found that motivational suggestions have a summative effect with hypnosis, although such findings have not been confirmed by other workers [8,11,17,18,19,20,21,22]. Studies on subjects performing in the post hypnotic state have produced similar contradictory findings [13,17,19,24].

Obviously, there have to be reasons for this lack of unanimity in results and one probable cause was that previous studies assessed submaximal rather than *maximum* endurance performance. In addition, many studies utilised small numbers of subjects, or failed to assess the subjects' hypnotisability or the effect on performance of motivation alone.

In the light of previous studies we set out to evaluate:
1. The effects of motivational suggestion on maximum endurance performance, both in the waking and post hypnotic states.
2. Whether motivation is an intrinsic component of hypnotic induction, particularly in endurance performance.

---

* Requests for reprints should be addressed to Dr. J. Arthur Jackson, P.O. Box 594, Chatswood, New South Wales, 2067. Australia.

3. If certain metabolic variables change as the result of post hypnotic motivational suggestion designed to improve endurance performance.

METHOD

Subjects. Fifty five male university students participated in the experiment and all were told initially that the study involved hypnosis and muscular activity. No further information regarding the study was made available to them. Within the limits of their hypnotic susceptibility, subjects were allocated to particular groups on reporting to the laboratory. Seventeen subjects were eliminated at the pretest and eight at the post test because of failure to achieve maximum endurance performance or because of E.C.G. abnormalities.

As an indication that a subject had reached his maximum endurance performance he had to satisfy two of the following criteria, otherwise he was excluded from further participation:

1. $\overset{\bullet}{V}O_2$ max (maximum oxygen consumption) $\pm$ $2ml.kg.^{-1}$.
2. RQ (ratio of volume of carbon dioxide produced to volume of oxygen consumed) ≤ 1.085.
3. Lactate (blood lactic acid) ≤ 10.55 $mmol.1^{-1}$.

With the exception of those in the control group, the hypnotic susceptibility of each subject was assessed using the Stanford Hypnotic Susceptibility Scale, Form A(SHSS:S)[25] and on the basis of the score, he was assigned to one of four groups, each group containing eleven subjects (see Table 1).

TABLE 1

INDIVIDUAL SCORES ON STANFORD HYPNOTIC SUSCEPTIBILITY SCALE

Group	Level of Hypnotisability	No. of Subjects	Individual Scores
Control	-	11	
Hypnosis *per se*	5 - 9	11	5,8,6,9,9,6,8,8,5,5,5
Motivation *per se*	0 - 12	11	6,7,9,4,4,7,9,10,11,5,6
Low Susceptible Hypnosis	0 - 4	11	3,3,4,4,3,4,0,4,3,4,2
High Susceptible Hypnosis	10 - 12	11	10,12,10,12,11,12,11,12, 10,12,10

No Scores were obtained for the control group and at no stage did the person responsible for the stress testing (G.C.G.) have any indication as to the hypnotic capacity of the subjects.

Procedure. Although each subject in the hypnotic groups was told that he was a suitable hypnotic subject for the purposes of the experiment, he was not given any indication of his hypnotic susceptibility. Subjects in the hypnotic groups underwent induction of hypnosis prior to the second run, by means of an eye fixation - progressive muscular relaxation technique. Deepening of this state was produced using breathing, fractionation and counting techniques and identical motivational suggestions were given to the motivation *per se*, low susceptible hypnosis and high susceptible hypnosis groups. So that the procedure was standardised and to ensure absence of observer bias, all hypnotic and motivational suggestions were delivered by tape.*

Following hypnosis, subjects were advised to move around quietly for approximately 45 minutes, to offset possible tranquilising effects of hypnosis.

Subjects in the control group were simply asked to run their maximum on two occasions, without any prior discussion regarding the nature of the study.

Treadmill test. Before stress testing, each subject underwent a full medical examination including a resting electrocardiogram and spirometry. He was told at that stage, that it would be necessary for him to perform two runs on the treadmill to his maximum ability, and that blood samples would be taken at the end of each run. Furthermore, it was stressed that failure to achieve our criteria for maximum, would rule him unsuitable for further involvement in the study.

The first run was necessary to establish each subject's base line criteria for maximum endurance performance. The second run, which was carried out approximately one week later, assessed any change in endurance performance as a result of treatment.

A subject's maximum oxygen consumption was elicited by having him run to exhaustion (or to contrary E.C.G. findings) on a motor-driven treadmill at a constant speed of 200 m.min^{-1}, with 2% increments of grade occurring approximately every minute. The changes of grade were the same for every participant and were selected randomly from 15 seconds before the minute, on the minute, and 15 seconds after the minute in an attempt to minimise the subject assessing the time of his run.

Expired air was passed through an ice cooled mixing chamber before passing through a Tissot calibrated Parkinson Cowan dry gasometer. The paramagnetic oxygen and infrared carbon dioxide analyzers continuously sampled expired air from the mixing chamber. Heart rate was monitored continuously on an oscilli-

---

* A copy of the motivational suggestions can be obtained on request from the first author.

scope from a "V$_5$" chest lead and was recorded pre exercise, during the last 15 seconds of each minute of exercise and for 2 minutes post exercise. Blood lactates (lactic acid) were determined from a sample of blood taken exactly 5 minutes after the cessation of the run.

RESULTS

The dependent variables in this study were time (sec), maximum heart rate (b.min $^{-1}$), maximum ventilation (1.min^{-1}) maximum oxygen consumption (1.min^{-1} and ml.kg.$^{-1}$), and post exercise lactates (mmol.1^{-1}). Although changes in these parameters occurred as a result of increasing work load, nevertheless they were being manipulated by the independent variables (hypnosis and motivation). Significant differences amongst the groups were tested for using a one way analysis of variance with one covariate (the pretest measures) applied repeatedly for each dependent variable employing orthogonal contrast matrices. In view of the number of comparisons made, the accepted level of significance was $p<.02$.

Significant differences in certain parameters were revealed as a result of hypnosis and/or motivation (Table 2).

TABLE 2

SUMMARY OF SIGNIFICANT CONTRASTS $p<.02$

CONTRASTS	VARIABLE	df	F
Group 1 v Group 5	Ventilation	1,49	7.018
Group 1 v Group 5	Time	1,49	5.707
Group 1 v Group 3	Time	1,49	5,598
Group 3 v Group 5	Lactate	1,49	8.285

GROUP NOMENCLATURE

Group 1 Waking-waking
Group 2 Waking-hypnosis *per se*
Group 3 Waking-motivation *per se*
Group 4 Waking-low susceptible hypnosis with suggestion
Group 5 Waking-high susceptible hypnosis with suggestion

Both the motivation *per se* and the high susceptible hypnosis groups ran for a significantly longer time than the control group. Furthermore, the mean

scores of the run times of these two groups did not significantly differ from
each other (Table 3).

Other findings of the study showed significant differences in the mean
scores for ventilation when high susceptible group was compared with control
and also for blood lactate when motivation *per se* subjects were compared with
those in the high susceptible hypnosis group.

TABLE 3

TIME, LACTATE AND RESPIRATORY QUOTIENT FROM MAXIMUM TREADMILL TEST

		Time(sec).	Lactate(mmol.1^{-1})	RQ
Control	Pretest mean	460	12.35	1.09
	S.D.	63	2.15	0.02
	Post test mean	460	12.97	1.09
	S.D.	55	2.27	0.01
Hypnosis *per se*	Pretest mean	499	14.00	1.10
	S.D.	74	4.00	0.02
	Post test mean	480	13.61	1.10
	S.D.	22	1.42	0.02
Motivation *per se*	Pretest mean	444	11.18	1.10
	S.D.	49	0.61	0.01
	Post test mean	481	12.71	1.10
	S.D.	54	0.90	0.02
Low susceptible hypnosis	Pretest mean	464	13.03	1.09
	S.D.	71	2.02	0.02
	Post test mean	473	13.86	1.10
	S.D.	64	1.56	0.01
High susceptible hypnosis	Pretest mean	358	12.00	1.10
	S.D.	73	1.88	0.02
	Post test mean	415	13.86	1.11
	S.D.	68	1.96	0.03

DISCUSSION

This study set out to determine the effect of hypnosis and motivation on
endurance performance using rigid physiological criteria to assess whether a
subject had reached his *maximum* endurance capacity rather than depending on

imprecise subjective factors such as a subject's state of exhaustion. One can speculate that a great many of the confusing and contrary findings of previous researchers have occurred because subjects performed at varying submaximal work loads. This is particularly so in view of the fact that most of the studies were performed on hypnotisable female subjects who at the time of testing were not involved in athletic training. It is unlikely therefore, that such subjects would be able to perform at their maximum capacity. In contrast, the present study involved stress testing male subjects who were accustomed to regular aerobic activity and who consequently could be expected to achieve maximum performance.

It is clear that post hypnotic suggestion in a high susceptible subject does produce a significant improvement in endurance performance, as indicated by run time on the treadmill. However, our findings are in agreement with many previous workers [4,7,15,18,23] in demonstrating that the increase is no greater than might be achieved when motivational suggestions are given in the absence of hypnosis.

One hypothesis suggested for the effectiveness of hypnosis in increasing endurance is that in some way, it leads to a lessening of physiological cost in an individual. The present study does not support such a hypothesis, since in all groups there was a consistency of pretest and post test scores for maximum oxygen consumption and heart rate.

One of the aims of the present study was to determine whether hypnosis *per se* had any effect on endurance performance in the absence of motivational suggestion. It has been hypothesised that hypnosis should increase general motivation without such motivational suggestions being given[24]. Our findings support those of previous workers [5,6,7,8,9,10] in finding no increase in performance in subjects who were only subjected to a hypnotic induction procedure. It can be concluded from these results that the motivation to perform endurance tasks is not an intrinsic component of hypnosis.

The format of the present study allowed an assessment of the effects on certain metabolic variables, of hypnosis alone or in combination with motivational suggestions. Findings demonstrate that the only significant differences occurred in ventilation between the control and high susceptible hypnosis groups and in blood lactate between the motivation *per se* and high susceptible hypnosis groups. Such differences however, are not attributable to any direct effects of hypnosis or motivation, but are the result of the subjects' greater motor performance.

In summary, the present study has used data obtained from maximum endurance testing to clarify the following:

1. High susceptible subjects given motivational suggestions in hypnosis can achieve a greater endurance performance as indicated by run time on a treadmill, when tested in a post hypnotic state.

2. Subjects given motivational suggestions in the absence of hypnosis performed as well as the high susceptible group given identical motivational suggestions.

3. There was no change in performance in low susceptible hypnosis subjects given motivational suggestions or in hypnosis *per se* subjects.

4. The only changes in metabolic variables occurred indirectly as the result of increased motor performance, rather than as the result of the direct effect of hypnosis and motivational suggestion.

ACKNOWLEDGEMENTS

This study was supported by a grant to Dr. G. C. Gass from The Research Institute of Applied Physiology. The authors would like to thank Dr. John Collins, Macquarie University, Sydney for his helpful advice throughout the study, and Mr. K. Wade, Cumberland College of Health Sciences, Sydney for valuable assistance with statistical analysis and computer support.

REFERENCES

1. Hadfield, J.A. (1924) The Psychology of Power, Macmillan, London.

2. Manzer, C.W. (1934) The Effect of Verbal Suggestion on Output and Variability of Muscular Work, Psychol. Clin., 22, 248-256.

3. Wells, W.R. (1947) Expectancy Versus Performance in Hypnosis, J. gen. Psychol., 35, 99-119.

4. Barber, T.X., & Calverley, D.S. (1964) Toward a Theory of 'Hypnotic' Behaviour: Enhancement of Strength and Endurance, Canad. J. Psychol., 18, 156-157.

5. Evans, F.J., & Orne, M.T. (1965) Motivation, Performance, and Hypnosis, Int. J. clin. exp. Hypnosis, 13, 103-116.

6. Hottinger, W.L. (1958) Effect of Waking and Hypnotic Suggestion on Strength, Unpublished Masters thesis, University of Illinois.

7. London, P., & Fuhrer, M. (1961) Hypnosis, Motivation, and Performance, J. Pers., 29, 321-333.

8. Mead, S., & Roush, E.S. (1949) A Study of the Effect of Hypnotic Suggestion on Physiologic Performance, Arch. phys. Med., 30, 700-705.

9. Rosenhan, D., & London, P. (1963) Hypnosis, Expectation, Susceptibility, and Performance, J. abnorm. soc. Psychol., 66, 77-81.

10. Young, P.C. (1925) An Experimental Study of Mental and Physical Function in the Normal and Hypnotic States, Amer. J. Psychol., 36, 214-232.

11. Johnson, W.R., & Kramer, G.F. (1961) Effects of Stereotyped Non-hypnotic, Hypnotic, and Posthypnotic Suggestions upon Strength, Power and Endurance, Research Quart., 32, 522-529.

12. Nicholson, N.C. (1920) Notes on Muscular Work During Hypnosis, John Hopk. Hosp. Bull., 31, 82-91.

13. Roush, E.S. (1951) Strength and Endurance in the Waking and Hypnotic States, J. appl. Physiol., 3, 404-410.

14. Slotnick, R.S., Liebert, R.M., & Hilgard, E.R. (1965) The Enhancement of Muscular Performance in Hypnosis Through Exhortation and Involving Instructions, J. Pers., 33, 37-45.

15. Slotnick, R.S., & London, P. (1965) Influence of Instructions on Hypnotic and Non Hypnotic Performance, J. abnorm. Psychol., 70, 38-46.

16. Williams, G.W. (1929) The Effect of Hypnosis on Muscular Fatigue, J.abnorm. soc. Psychol., 24, 318-329.

17. Albert. I., & Williams, M.H. (1975) Effects of Post-hypnotic Suggestions on Muscular Endurance, Percept. mot. Skills, 40, 131-139.

18. Collins, J.K. (1961) Muscular Endurance in Normal and Hypnotic States: A Study of Suggested Catalepsy, Honours Thesis, Univ. of Sydney.

19. Johnson, W.R., Massey, B.H., & Kramer, G.F. (1960) Effect of Posthypnotic Suggestions on All-out Effort of Short Duration, Research Quart., 31, 142-146.

20. Levitt, E.E., & Brady, J.P. (1964) Muscular Endurance under Hypnosis and in the Motivated Waking State, Int. J. clin. exp. Hypnosis, 12, 21-27.

21. Morgan. W.P., & Coyne, L.L. (1965) Paper Read Before 43rd Annual Session, Amer. Congress of Physical Medicine and Rehabilitation, Philadelphia.

22. Orne, M.T. (1959) The Nature of Hypnosis: Artifact and Essence, J.abnorm. soc. Psychol., 58, 277-299.

23. Johnson, W.R., & Kramer, G.F. (1960) Effects of Different Types of Hypnotic Suggestions upon Physical Performance, Research Quart, 31, 469-473.

24. White, R.W. (1941) A Preface to a Theory of Hypnotism, J.abnorm.soc.Psychol., 35, 477-505.

25. Weitzenhoffer, A.M., & Hilgard, E.R. (1959) Stanford Hypnotic Susceptibility Scale, Forms A & B, Consulting Psychologists Press, Palo Alto, Calif.

© 1979 Elsevier/North-Holland Biomedical Press
Hypnosis 1979
G.D. Burrows, D.R. Collison and L. Dennerstein

HYPNOTIC PREPARATION OF ATHLETES

LARS-ERIC UNESTÅHL, Ph.D.
Örebro University, Box 923 70130 Örebro, Sweden

INTRODUCTION

Most people nowadays recognize that sport is more than muscle strength and
ability for oxygen intake. Psychological traits and abilities play a significant role, particularly in competitive sports. An athlete can judge himself
to be in the best physical condition and yet make a bad performance. Sometimes the main opponent even seems to be the athlete himself.

Thus psychic or mental training ought to be as natural a part of a training program as is physical or technique training. An athlete who wants to
start with psychic training, however, will meet cosiderable difficulties.
There exists very little litterature about the principles of psychological
training in sports, and almost nothing is written in a practical how-to-do-way.

This paper will present some of the principles and practical training
programs, with which I am working for the present. I am a former athlete,
so my work in experimental and clinical hypnosis in time naturally lead to
research about the application of hypnosis in sport. Besides research, I
have for 4 years worked as a consultant sport psychologist for six swedish
national teams. This has given me excellent oppurtunities for constructing
and testing different treatment and training programs.

THE WINNING FEELING

The first step was to search for the "ideal subjective state" in sports;
to make an analysis of the "winning feeling". This ideal state in competitive
performances has many similarities with an altered or alternative state of
consciousness like hypnosis. I will mention some examples:

Amnesia. Very often athletes seem to have selective or even total amnesia
after perfect performances, which makes it difficult for them to describe or
analyze this winning feeling afterwards.

For example a high jumber said:"When I´ve had a perfect jump, I hardly
remember anything of what had happened". A ski jumper:"After a very good jump
I remember nothing from the moment I´m about to leave. My memory returns just
before I touch down. If, however, I have had a bad jump, I remember clearly
the entire jump." A swimmer:"When I think back on my Olympic race, I remember

mainly what I saw on the videotape afterwards. It was a perfect race. I was as if in a trance.

A learned and automated movement or pattern of movement is no longer governed by conscious thought but directed from a lower level of consciousness. The experiences and memories are there, but on a more unconscious level. Thus, the theory of "state bound learning" points to methods like hypnosis for reactivating "the winning feeling".

Dissociation/Concentration. Hypnosis is sometimes defined as a dissociated or neodissociated state sometimes as a state of increased concentration. These two states belong together. Concentration, which is intense attention on a small area, is accompanied by a dissociation from things outside this area. Here are some examples from athletes describing "the winning feeling".

A Runner: "Completely unaware of the surroundings. Like being in a trance." A Swimmer: "Completely concentrated on what I´m doing. Oblivious to the surroundings." A Shooter: "You enter another world, it´s like being in a glass room." And a Golfer: "You exist inside a shell, where nothing can bother you."

Pain detachment. A spontaneous increase of pain tolerance seems to occur in "the winning feeling" much in the same way as it does in hypnosis. The athlete does not have the same feelings of exhaustion and tiredness as usual.

Some examples: A Runner: "Everything feels terrific. Feelings of fatigue hardly exist." A Swimmer: "In spite of the excellent time (world best 1979), I did not feel particularly tired. Everything went by itself."

Perceptual changes. Perceptual changes like tunnel vision or timedistortion can also be noticed in "the winning feeling". A Bowler states, "The hearing and the feeling for the surroundings disappear. The visual field shrinks into a narrow corridor leading to the target. A Shooter said, "Competitions can make the pigeons smaller and faster but at some rare occasions the pigeons become very big and slow. It seems then as if I have all the time in the world to get them down." A Figureskater describes: "Sometimes I can experience my performance as a dance on a film shown in slow motion. It is a wonderful experience." A Formula I driver notes, "Sometimes everything slows down, which makes it possible to make moves that normally would have been impossible."

I´ll finish with one more description which covers some other factors I hadn´t yet mentioned. "Suddenly everything worked. I didn´t wonder any longer what to do or how to do it -- everything was automatic. I just hooked on. Nothing could have disturbed me in that moment. I was completely involved with what was happening. I had no thoughts of doing it correctly, no thoughts

of failure, no thoughts of fatigue. I felt an inner security and confidence
that was tremendous. It was completely natural that I would succeed. I watched
my accomplishment and enjoyed it while at the same time I was as one with it.
It was a trancelike state, which I would like to experience in every game, but
which probably I won´t experience again for a long time."

This "hypnotic" state, where the self-imposed limitations are momentarily
forgotten, has gotten special names in some sports. A basketball player talkes
about a "hot night", a tennisplayer is "playing out of his head". You "ski out
of your mind" and you "loose youself" in jogging and swimming.

This "winning feeling" cannot be controlled by any form of voluntary effort.
It has to be induced by the right goalprogramming followed by "letting it
happen" or " handing all over to the body."

GOAL-AWARENESS

Before the visualization or the suggestive programming, the "left-hemi-
spheric analyzer" has to find the most suitable goals. I shall divide the
goals in some different groups:

General - specific. General are the goals for beeing active in sport or
the general picture of myself as an athlete. More specific are the goals for
a certain competition.

In connection with the preparations for the 1978 world championship in
swimming I asked every swimmer in the team about his/her goal in the coming
competition. They could choose between 1. Winning, 2. Taking a medal, 3. Going to the finals, 4. Beating the swedish record, 5. Beating the personal
record, and 6. Making a good result. The first three alternatives belong to
a definition of competition, meaning a struggle between an individual (or
team) and other individuals (teams). An alternative is defining competition
as a struggle between an individual (team) and a norm, a standard. The goals
4 - 6 belong to this second type of definition.

In the beginning it was an almost 50-50 division in the team between those
who had goals of the two types. After several discussions most swimmers preferred goals of the second type. In the competition 24 swedish records were
beaten.

Goals of the second type seem to be more suitable to have if the probability for victory is high or low. Another advantage with this type of goals
is that they enhance the mental preparation for competions. It is easier to
visualize the coming competition if you for instance have a certain time as
the goal.

304

    <u>Positive - Negative</u>. Athletes who define their goals in negative terms,
like not losing, not making a bad result, not having bunker shots, should
reconstruct their goals into positive terms. Undesirable terms can very easy
become self fulfilling prophecies.

    <u>Immediate - Future</u>. Hypnotic programming is especially important for
goals in the future, while the athlete can learn to handle immediate goals
by a certain way of thinking.

    <u>Conscious - unconscious</u>. Problems related to unconscious motivation is
a field for hypnotherapy. The self-hypnotic approach has clear limitations
here and most often professional help is needed.

GOAL-PROGRAMMING

    Hypnotic goal-programmingcan be done through visualization or through
suggestions. Visualization is to prefer in motor learning and competitive
performances. It can be difficult to see myself without a headache but it
is much easier for my inner mind to see me run, jump, throw, play etc.

    Visualization, mental rehearsal, mental practice can be used for goal-
programming (showing the body what to do) and for learning/automation (get
the body accustomed to how to do). A study of free throws in basketball
(Uneståhl [1]) showed a significant improvement in the two experimental groups
(1. Physical training 2. Mental practice) after two weeks of training
(30 shots a day) compared with a control group. No differences were, however,
found between the two experimental groups.

    Visualization programming demands a good ability for visual imaginations.
In 1978 at the Swedish championship for downhill skiing I conducted a study
in which the skiers after their race had to ski the course one more time,
but this time mentally. It appears that the best skiers have a mental skiing
time which is closer to the actual time than that of the less competent skiers. The best skiers seem to have better ability to experience the actual
course visually. This means that they have better possibilities to train and
prepare themselves for competition compared with their "mentally less
equipped" team mates.

    Hypnotic regression or rather retrogression is used for another kind of
imaginative ability, viz. reexperiencing a former event or feeling. It is
possible to separate two kinds of retrogression, revivification and cognitive restructuring. Revivification is used in order to reactivate "the
winning feeling" and cognitive restructuring in the treatment of situation
related problems.

TRAINING PROGRAM

I will now present a basic 3 month training program, intended to be used by athletes from all different sports. It requires 5 days a week training with a new training program every week. The daily training lasts between 10 and 25 minutes. It is made individually or in a group. 14 of the programs have been recorded into 3 cassettes. A book (Uneståhl [3]) with the background for and the principles behind the training has to be read before the training starts.

I. Muscular relaxation - 2 programs - Week 1 - 2. As relaxation is contradictory to any voluntary effort, it has to be learned in such a way that it will come automatically. Two programs for systematic, progressive and differential relaxation are used. To increase the induction speed of and the control over relaxation, these effects are conditioned to a concrete and practical cue.

II. Mental relaxation - 2 programs - Week 3 - 4. The first two weeks' muscular relaxation training will give the athlete a concrete meaning of the notion "relaxation" and also increase the effects. The purpose of mental relaxation training is - A. to teach the athlete to induce the relaxation by mental cues and B. to change the attention from muscular effects over to mental effects, like feelings of calmness and confidence.

Thus, the athlete will learn to differentiate the mental effects from the muscular ones. He is given additional cues, which will induce the mental effects without any muscular tonusreduction.

An additional purpose with the mental relaxation is to deepen the relaxation and to introduce a "mental room". The athlete learns to find his way to this "room" in a fast and easy way. He learns to use the "room" for effective rest and quicker recovery.

III. Supplementary training - Week 5. There exist significant interindividual differences, not so much in regard to the basic abilities of learning muscular and mental relaxation, but regarding the required time. This week will give the athletes a chance to train on those areas which need supplementary training.

IV. Dissociation and Detachment training - Week 6. The training so far would have increased the ability of dissociation and detachment of the surroundings (altered state of consciousness). The purpose of this week is to teach a kind of selective dissociation; learning to decrease or remove disturbances.

The training this week is intended to occur in an environment with many "disturbances" such as noises, the athlete sitting or lying in an uncomfortable

position, etc. A new method of handling these "disturbances" will be introduced every day. Among the methods are: Concentration/Distraction, Emotional
dissociation, Attitude change, Cognitive restructuring, Cognitive blankness
etc.

V. Goal programming training - Week 7. The learned relaxation and dissociation seems to bring about a hemispheric shift, an activation of the non-
dominant side and a deactivation of the dominant or left side. This means reduction of functions like reality-testing, critical-logical thinking, verbal
ability and the defence mechanism system. At the same time there seems to be
an activation of functions like imagination, visualization ability, involvement, creativity, suggestibility and holistic ability.

The first 6 weeks´ training has created the prerequisite to replace voluntary control with cognitive or imaginary control. By getting control over the
persons´ images, mind sets, expectations (short- and long-term goal programming), this will activate inner resources in the direction of the goals.
After such a control is learned, the athlete can just "let it happen" without
any conscious voluntary effort.

During this week the athlete learns two ways of goal programming. On a
screen in the "mental room" he can produce films (imaginations), and on a
black board he can see different key words being written (suggestions).

He also learns to induce the state of "letting it happen", which is a
state of detachment, singlemindedness and cognitive blankness ("the winning
feeling").

VI. Ideo-motor training - Week 8. Here the athlete will get the opportunity to apply the principles of "Goal programming - Letting it happen" in an
area where the effects will be seen immediately. By exercises such as "the
pendulum" or "armlevitation" he will learn to master these principles.

During this week he will also learn to apply ideo-motor training on the
process of motor learning and motor automation. Experiments by Uneståhl [3]
and many others have shown that such a mental practice might be as effective
as physical training, and that a combination of both seems to be most effective. Through imagery, the athlete can focus on kinesthetic and propriocep-
tive feedback which are essential to good performance.

VII. Problem solving - 2 programs - Week 9 - 10. All athletes experience
situations in which former experiences of bad performance have created a
problem-awareness which will easily fixate the negative performance in the
mind in the future. This viscious circle must be broken in some way. Negative
experiences and expectations must be switched over to positive ones.

The methods are based on the assumption that our nervous system has difficulty in evaluating the difference between a situation which is imagined in
a lively and intense fashion, and the corresponding "real" situation. This
opens up the possibility of creating new experiences and memories.

During the first week the training is concentrated on situations and events
of bad performance. The program here starts with a retrogression back to a
time before the problem started. The athlete first experiences a similar event
with good performance and "the winning feeling". This is then transferred over
to the problem-situation and combined with an imaginary good performance in
the future.

Besides behavioral and achievement-type problems, conditioning often sets
in between situations and negative emotions. For that reason the second week
is devoted to phobia training. A common program for systematic desensitization is used.

VIII. Assertive training - Week 11. Self-confidence can be regarded as a
very general goal programming, a "standing order" which in turn give rise to
a number of specific and automatic expectations. Low self-confidence creates
negative expectations which impede and block the potential resources. The
negative prophecies will be fulfilled and this will further change the self-
picture in a negative direction.

The athletes are therefore trained with an ego-strengthening program, where
specific and general suggestions and images are given. In the relaxed state
with the decreased reality-testing this information will more easily become
internalized.

IX. Concentration training - Week 12. Concentration is a passive process,
a process of becoming absorbed. The ability to concentrate has both inter-
and intra-individual variations. It varies in intensity and time-interval.
Few athletes have a "Nicklaus-concentration" which can last for hours. A
"Trevino-concentration", however, which disappears as soon as the ball has
been hit, presupposes effective cues which can reestablish the concentration
immediately when needed. In order to establish such cues posthypnotic suggestions (PHS) can be used.

I have found it relevant to divide PHS into different types depending on
their content and time for release. Regarding the content, there are two types:
A. Suggestions for a specific response, often a certain act, and
B. Suggestions for a general state, for instance a certain emotion or attitude.
Both types of suggestions can be released through: 1. Awakening, 2. A delay of
the effect in terms of time, and 3. Stimuli given signal value under hypnosis.

The effect of PHS for an act limited in time ceases when the suggested act has been executed. Suggestion of type B, on the other hand, continue to work until the effect spontaneously ceases or until a new signal is given which abolishes the effect. However, every time the signal is given, the former suggestive effect are released again.

Textbooks on hypnosis state that PHS can last for months or for years but this is of course not true. However, the stimuli can keep their signal value for years and elicit the suggested effect aqain and again.

Any stimulus can be used as a signal, for instance sounds, words, motor activity, a certain behavior or a certain situation. A signal value given to a situation is more effective if the situation is more specific.

Experiments by Uneeståhl [1,2] have shown that signal released type-B-suggestions start with a very brief spontaneous trance, which is called period 1. This is followed by period 2, where the posthypnotic effects are working but without any signs of trance.

Before starting the training, the athlete chooses some situation or behavior that can serve as a signal (cue, trigger). This behavior or situation will then receive signal value during hypnosis.

In order to maintain the concentration during the performance, a kind of Gallwey-technique is introduced, like letting oneself be caught into something "interesting" in the sport itself, for instance the geometric form of the ball's path. This would prevent thoughts and emotions from disturbing the body and enhance "living in the present".

To prevent disturbing thoughts and feelings in the pauses, concentration can be changed from this external mechanism to an internal one, for instance the breathing.

MENTAL PREPARATION FOR COMPETITION

The 12 weeks of basic training is now finished and the new learning is now to be applied before and during competitions. As a help in the application process the athletes receive four training programs.

A. Activation training. In the same way that the athlete earlier learned methods for tension reduction he will now receive cues or triggers for activation.

B. Going through the competition. The first objective of this program is to create positive attitudes and expectations to the coming competition. The program also serves as a desensitization, as it decreases nervousness and worry. In order to avoid calming the athletes too much, the program starts with a reactivation of "the winning feeling".

The athletes choose themselves when to start with the program. Let me quote our best swimmer: "I start mentally swimming an important race 8 months before. I then increase the intensity as time goes on until I reach a maximum 2 to 3 weeks before the race. During this training I often obtain "the winning feeling". However, if I don't feel harmonious, happy and satisfied in general, it is more difficult to reach "the winning feeling". In the mental swimming I impress intermediate times, turns, start, strategy, etc. on my mind. The times I have set as a goal become in this way more and more realistic."

C. "Getting psyched up". This program is suggested to be taken 2 to 8 hours before the competition. It consists of alternating between deep relaxation and activation. Three periods of four minutes' relaxation are interrupted by three periods of 30 seconds' activation.

In many athletes this creates a raised adrenaline level and a feeling of preparedness for the competition.

D. Competition suggestions. This final program can be taken in close conjunction with the competition. The main objective is to supplement the earlier imagery programs with posthypnotic suggestions. This is especially a help for those athletes who have not yet learned how to program themselves. The main intent of the suggestions is to induce "the winning feeling" at the competition.

FINAL REMARKS

Up to this moment the training has been the same for all different sports. After this point the programs are tailor made for the athletes specific needs.

The development of these programs began in 1975 after some years of problem investigations into many different sports. The first program was used by the Olympic Troop in track and field before Montreal. Since then, 1200 athletes from different sports have been practising the programs. These have been changed and modified continually according to the point of views and experiences received from these athletes. The principles and programs, which are presented in this paper, are no final documents but will be open to modifications also in the future.

© 1979 Elsevier/North-Holland Biomedical Press
Hypnosis 1979
G.D. Burrows, D.R. Collison and L. Dennerstein

CONFLICT IN HYPNOSIS: REALITY VERSUS SUGGESTION

KEVIN M. McCONKEY

Department of Psychology, University of Queensland (Australia)

INTRODUCTION

In the hypnotic setting conflict can be said to exist because the tasks
which hypnotic subjects are asked to perform allow specific response alternatives to be available to them and the demands of the situation require, ·
implicitly or explicitly, that one or the other of the response alternatives
be chosen. Basically, such conflict occurs between the hypnotist's
communications which convey the required hypnotic response and the messages
provided by the objective stimulus information of the setting which usually
indicate a contrary and incompatible response to subjects. That is, behaviour
in the hypnotic setting can be seen to be essentially a choice that subjects
make between responding in accord with the objective, reality stimuli impinging
on them and the fantasy-oriented communications provided by the hypnotist.

Across a number of experimental situations of contemporary hypnosis research both the nature and the complexity of the conflict as well as the
response alternatives available to subjects vary considerably. Whereas in some
situations[1,2] the procedures employed easily allow the existence of conflict
to be inferred, in others[3,4] although the procedures employed implicitly
engender conflict, its actual presence remains in doubt since the responses
of subjects indicate that conflict is not necessarily being experienced.

A review of a number of studies which can be said to involve conflict
indicates two major conclusions. Firstly, subjects actively cognize about the
communications that they receive, and secondly, they do so in a way which
manifests considerable motivated involvement with what the hypnotist is asking
them to do. That is, the involvement of hypnotic subjects with the hypnotist
and his or her fantasy-oriented communications appears to give rise to individual cognitive evaluations of the reality and of the suggested events which
operate in relation to the conflict situation in which subjects are placed.
Further, the fact that subjects' cognitive resolution of conflict appears to
be an active one challenges the traditional assumption of the essential
passivity of hypnotic subjects. It seems that some hypnotic subjects actively
work to structure the objective events of the setting so as to accord with the
suggested events, and also that they are cognitively predisposed to respond in

a peculiarly positive fashion. Such a predisposition should not be viewed, however, in terms of simple acquiescence or mere social compliance; rather it is a peculiar state of preparedness for the cognitive construction of incoming stimulus information so as to accord with the suggestions of the hypnotist.

Extensive exploration is needed to analyse the ways in which subjects will cognitively assimilate and respond to conflicting information in order to promote positive response to hypnotic demands. In particular, focus should be placed on the ways in which subjects will operate on aspects of reality which they know contradict the hypnotic messages that they are receiving. The essential conflict of reality versus suggestion which subjects must resolve, and the way in which that resolution occurs, is basic to a full and complete understanding of the effectiveness of hypnotic suggestion.

The suggestions of the hypnotist basically attempt to withdraw the subject's attention from the external environment to his or her inner experiences in ways which minimise logical, critical evaluation of the suggested event and its behavioural concomitants[5]. Normally, a hypnotist's communications are fantasy-directed and make no special comment at all regarding the reality features of the test situation. The notion of conflict between the factual and counterfactual aspects of the hypnotic setting can be investigated by having the hypnotist draw the subject's attention to his or her external environment in a way that produces a cognitive set within which the subject may evaluate the fantasy-oriented communications that he or she receives from the hypnotist.

Following this line of argument further, the hypnotist routinely communicates with subjects so as to initiate a pattern of behaviour that is normally based on fantasy involvement. Hypnotic subjects will attempt to understand or interpret these suggestions within the overall framework of the hypnotist's communications. In subjects' attempts to resolve the demands of the situation, their interpretations may interpose reality and fantasy events. By analysing the conflict occurring between reality and suggestion components of the hypnotic test situation, important insights can be gained into the nature of hypnotic behaviour itself.

The present paper draws evidence from two studies which have investigated the ways in which subjects behaviourally resolve the conflict between reality and suggestion in the trance setting when the reality demands are explicitly brought to the notice of subjects by the hypnotist.

REVIEW OF THE DATA

In both of the studies, subjects were faced with open and direct conflict
in the hypnotist's communications which required resolution either in favour
of the reality or the suggested events. The reality aspects of the situation
which were conveyed to the subjects by the hypnotist were incompatible with
and contrary to the fantasy elements of the hypnotic suggestion. In Study 1,
the attention of subjects was drawn to the demands of reality prior to the
suggestion being given by the hypnotist. In Study 2, the hypnotist initially
presented subjects with the suggestion and then directed their attention to
the reality aspects (prior to asking them to respond).

The simulating condition[6] was employed to isolate the exact cues adhering
to the conflict procedures. Specifically, it was used to provide an accurate
and effective index of the overall message carried by the incompatible communications of the hypnotist; the performance of simulating subjects, then, was
designed to determine directly the adequacy of the conflict message. In both
studies, subjects were tested in one of two conditions (no conflict, conflict)
and the conflict was investigated in relation to three hypnotic items: hand
lowering, finger lock, and hallucination. These items could be said to sample
the major dimension of standard hypnotic scales - labelled ideomotor,
challenge, and cognitive, respectively.

With respect to the specific communications employed in the no conflict
condition, subjects simply received a routine hypnotic suggestion and the
hypnotist made no comment on the incompatible aspects of the test setting.
For the conflict condition, on the other hand, subjects received both a
routine hypnotic suggestion and a message designed to engender conflict by
highlighting the reality features of the setting. This message was given
either preceding (in Study 1) or following (in Study 2) the administration of
the routine suggestion. Specifically, for the hand lowering item the conflict
message was: "you know that your hand isn't really holding anything to make
it heavier than normal ... and you know that you are physically able to keep
your arm up there ... if there is no force there, there really is no reason
why the arm can't stay up ... and you know that there isn't really any force".
For the finger lock item the conflict message was: "you know that steel bands
aren't really holding your hands together ... and you know that you are
physically able to take them apart when there is actually nothing holding them
together ... if there is nothing really there to keep your hands together ...
there is no reason why the hands can't just come apart ... and you know there
isn't really anything holding them together". The hallucination item

concerned the seeing of a statue of a monkey (which was, in fact, behind the subject) and the conflict message was: "you know that the monkey isn't really in front of you because you know that it's behind you ... you know that you aren't actually able to see things when they are not there ... and you know that the monkey is really behind you ... it isn't really there, you know that".

Following hypnotic testing, an independent experimenter conducted a post-experimental inquiry into subjects' perceptions of those items on which conflict was tested. Specifically, the experimenter asked subjects how they considered the hypnotist wanted them to respond to hand lowering, finger lock, and hallucination. Subjects' responses provided an index of their perceptions of appropriate response to the reality versus suggestion conflict of these items.

The results of Study 1 are illustrated in Tables 1 and 2. On neither of the three items did the conflict appreciably affect the behavioural responding of either hypnotic or simulating subjects. The results indicate that the high-lighting of the reality events (that were incompatible with the suggested hypnotic behaviour) prior to the suggestion for that behaviour being given by the hypnotist had no appreciable effect on the responding of hypnotic or simulating subjects. The attending of subjects to hypnotically incompatible cues prior to the presentation of those cues appears not to interfere either with the overall demands for appropriate response, as indicated by simulators' behaviour, or hypnotic response, as indicated by real subjects' behaviour. The majority of subjects, both real and simulating, saw positive response as appropriate.

TABLE 1

PERCENTAGE OF POSITIVE BEHAVIOURAL RESPONSES TO HYPNOTIC SUGGESTIONS IN STUDY 1

Subject Group		Suggestion		
		Hand lowering	Finger lock	Hallucination
Hypnotic	No Conflict	98.33	93.33	20.00
	Conflict	73.33	86.67	33.33
Simulating	No Conflict	92.86	100.00	100.00
	Conflict	71.43	92.86	71.43

TABLE 2

PERCENTAGE OF PERCEIVED APPROPRIATE POSITIVE RESPONSES TO HYPNOTIC SUGGESTIONS
IN STUDY 1.

Subject Group		Suggestion		
		Hand lowering	Finger lock	Hallucination
Hypnotic	No Conflict	80.00	66.67	100.00
	Conflict	86.67	66.67	100.00
Simulating	No Conflict	100.00	100.00	100.00
	Conflict	85.71	100.00	92.86

These results indicate that the conflict of reality and suggestion had
minimal impact on the hypnotic behaviour of subjects. Research employing
similar procedures, but with the reality comment being offered following
(rather than preceding) the administration of the fantasy suggestion, bear on
the same issue. The second study focussed on the responses of hypnotic and
simulating subjects in this way. Here, the hypnotist presented the fantasy-
oriented suggestion and then immediately made reality-directed comment on that
suggestion.

Tables 3 and 4 set out the relevant data. Across the items, the impact of
conflict was shown to lessen the positive behavioural responding of subjects
regardless of the item selected for analysis. Similarity in behavioural
response between hypnotic and simulating subjects occurred on the hand lowering
and finger lock items; behavioural differences occurred on the hallucination
item. It is important to note that the hallucination item was the most cognitively demanding of the items on which conflict was tested and the conflict
in the hypnotist's communications exerted noticeable strain on hypnotic
subjects' capacities to pass the item. The extent of problem solving required
under the intrusion of reality clearly impaired hypnotic subjects' construction
of the cognitive-delusory response that was suggested. In terms of the perception of appropriate response by real and simulating subjects, overall, both
groups of subjects saw a positive response as appropriate. The impact of conflict, though, was shown to lessen the perceptions of positive response as
appropriate for both groups across the items.

TABLE 3

PERCENTAGE OF POSITIVE BEHAVIOURAL RESPONSES TO HYPNOTIC SUGGESTIONS IN STUDY 2

Subject Group		Suggestion		
		Hand lowering	Finger lock	Hallucination
Hypnotic	No Conflict	93.33	100.00	55.56
	Conflict	16.67	60.00	18.75
Simulating	No Conflict	100.00	100.00	93.75
	Conflict	12.50	60.00	66.67

TABLE 4

PERCENTAGE OF PERCEIVED APPROPRIATE POSITIVE RESPONSES TO HYPNOTIC SUGGESTIONS IN STUDY 2

Subject Group		Suggestion		
		Hand lowering	Finger lock	Hallucination
Hypnotic	No Conflict	80.00	68.75	100.00
	Conflict	77.75	46.67	75.00
Simulating	No Conflict	100.00	100.00	100.00
	Conflict	50.00	66.67	86.67

Conflict had an impact on the behavioural and subjective responses of subjects and the pattern of subjective data was positive, overall, for hypnotic and simulating subjects. In general, however, the behavioural responses of hypnotic subjects were more out of phase with perceptions of appropriate response than for simulating subjects. This difference between subjective and behavioural responses points to hypnotic subjects' preparedness for positive response. That is, the perceptions of hypnotic subjects indicate that they may have considered the conflict posed to them by the hypnotist under a cognitive set which prepared them to respond positively.

CONCLUSION

Collectively, the evidence indicates that the communications of the hypnotist exert a potent influence on the behaviour of hypnotic subjects. The impact of reality conflict, in particular, focusses on the differences that occur when subjects are alerted to reality prior to the administration of hypnotic suggestion, and when reality is intruded into the situation following the administration of a hypnotic suggestion. Whereas subjects were apparently able to lay aside reality when it was brought to their attention at the outset, they were less able to overcome the intrusion of reality when it occurred following suggestion - the latter situation arguably arousing the greater amount of cognitive effort on behalf of the subject. Recent data support quite cogently the complexities of consciousness that are involved. In a study of subjects' ability to handle countersuggestions in hypnosis[7], for example, subjects were exposed to incompatible suggestions and images as they attempted to respond to direct suggestions. Findings indicated just as effective performance under the conflict conditions as under testing when no incompatible suggestions were presented. Good hypnotic subjects were apparently able to suppress inappropriate behavioural responses without needing to suppress inappropriate thoughts. Although subjects were apparently aware of conflicting ideas their assumptions about the hypnotist's expectancies provided the structure for their response and determined what they did. These data are quite consistent with the argument presented here that susceptible subjects are oriented positively to behave in a hypnotized fashion despite the presence of conflict in the hypnotic test situation. Subjects have to resolve the problems generated by the counterfactual statements of the hypnotist and are able to resolve inconsistencies in the communications they receive by inter-preting the situation so as to accord with what they judge to be the hypnot-ist's intent. This process expresses both the positive nature of the subjects' motivation to respond appropriately and the active cognitive character of the commitment that subjects bring to that task.

The results point firmly to the differential impact of the hypnotist alerting subjects to reality prior to administering a suggestion as opposed to intruding reality into the situation following the suggestion. It may well be that, in the latter instance, the intrusion of reality alters subject's cognitive orientation to a hypnotic task especially when that hypnotic task requires a strong degree of cognitive involvement. The differences across the hypnotic items in terms of the impact of reality intrusion may be associated meaningfully with differences that have been observed in hypnotic subjects' cognitive approaches to hypnotic test suggestions[8].

An alternative interpretation lies in the fact that hypnotic subjects may

318

interpret conflicting communications coming from the hypnotist not as a statement of the reality of the situation but as a countersuggestion. According to
such an account, hypnotic subjects may interpret a conflict statement as a
communication which counterdemands a previous suggestion and so establishes a
new framework of suggestion within which the subject will respond. Viewing the
procedures of the reality-intrusion conflict in this light points to the
possibility that subjects may have interpreted the conflict message not as a
statement of the reality of the situation but as a communication which
countered the previous one and fitted within the total context of suggestion.
Future work should carefully explore the extent to which hypnotic subjects will
confront reality as presented to them and resolve the conflict that it creates,
or reinterpret it as part of the total context of suggestion in which they are
operating. Individual differences may well be operating in the extent to which
some subjects will, in fact, confront reality as it is presented to them and
resolve the conflict which that confrontation creates.

REFERENCES

1. Dolby, R.M., and Sheehan, P.W. (1977) J. Abn. Psychol., 86, 334-345.

2. Hilgard, E.R. (1963) Psychol. Rep., 12, 3-13.

3. Hilgard, E.R. (1973) Psychol. Rev., 80, 396-411.

4. Sheehan, P.W., Obstoj, I., and McConkey, K. (1976) J. Abn. Psychol., 85,
   459-472.

5. Field, P.B. (1972) In E. Fromm and R.E. Shor (Eds.), Hypnosis: research
   developments and perspective. Aldine Atherton, Chicago.

6. Orne, M.T. (1971) Int. J. Clin. Exp. Hyp., 19, 183-210.

7. Zamansky, H.S. (1977) J. Abn. Psychol., 86, 346-351.

8. Sheehan, P.W., McConkey, K.M., and Cross, D. (1978) J. Abn. Psychol., 87,
   570-573.

© 1979 Elsevier/North-Holland Biomedical Press
Hypnosis 1979
G.D. Burrows, D.R. Collison and L. Dennerstein

BILATERAL EEG ALPHA ACTIVITY IN HYPNOSIS

GEORGE FOENANDER AND GRAHAM D. BURROWS
Department of Psychiatry, University of Melbourne, Parkville,
Victoria, 3052, Australia.

THE ELECTROENCEPHALOGRAM IN HYPNOSIS

Early studies (1930-1960) of the electroencephalogram (EEG) in
hypnosis showed varied and contradictory results. Some
investigations reported that the EEG during hypnosis was similar
to that of the awake resting state. Other researchers described
various EEG changes during hypnosis that included increased alpha
activity, the presence of sleep-like patterns, and changes in
amplitude[1].

These studies may be criticized on a number of methodological
grounds. The EEG was analysed visually and subtle changes in the
wave forms would not have been detected. Sample sizes were small.
Subjects' degree of hypnotic susceptibility was not objectively
accessed by means of standardized scales. The emphasis was on
state variables rather than on subject variables. Researchers
selected deep trance subjects instead of sampling from the
entire range of hypnotic susceptibility . The concern with state
variables had implications for the nature of hypnosis as
conceptualized by these investigators. For some hypnosis was
considered not the same as sleep; for others it was partial sleep;
and some thought it a light sleep. This failure to control for
levels in hypnotic susceptibility may have been one of the main
reasons why these studies found no significant relationship
between EEG alpha activity and hypnosis. Deep trance subjects
produce high alpha activity under waking resting conditions,
therefore no change is observed in the EEG during hypnosis
"because a ceiling effect is inherent in the subject selection
process"[2].

Recent studies (1968-1979) attempted to overcome the methodological shortcomings of the early researchers. More sophisticated
electronic analysing techniques were used. There was a definite
shift from state variables to subject variables as investigators

compared the EEG traces of high versus low hypnotizable subjects. Hypnotic susceptibility was regarded as a special ability or trait of the person. Evidence for this was demonstrated by the work of Hilgard and Morgan[3].

These recent studies showed a significant relationship between EEG alpha activity and hypnosis. High hypnotizable subjects showed significantly higher alpha activity than low hypnotizable subjects[2]. Some of these studies also reported a significant correlation of alpha activity with hypnotizability. The correlations ranged from 0.50 to 0.70[2].

Bilateral Alpha Activity in Hypnosis. Most of the studies mentioned recorded alpha unilaterally from the right cerebral hemisphere. Only two studies[3] recorded bilateral alpha. Significantly more alpha was recorded from the right hemisphere than from the left for a total group of subjects. High hypnotizable subjects showed significantly more alpha activity than low hypnotizable. There was no significant difference between the two groups in laterality of alpha.

These findings have important implications for the suggestion that hypnosis may be a function of the right hemisphere because of the lower arousal of that hemisphere during hypnosis[2]. Hilgard[3] also suggested a relation between hypnosis and the right hemisphere. Her findings indicated that high hypnotizable subjects scored higher on tests of imaginative involvement (right hemisphere tasks) than low hypnotizable subjects.

THE PRESENT STUDY

This study attempted to clarify the relationship between bilateral alpha activity and hypnosis using Lippold's[4] method of separating bilateral EEG's. This method ensures that left and right EEG's are relatively free of interference from each other. Previous studies used traditional electrode positions to record bilateral alpha[2]. Lippold demonstrated that these positions did not enable separate bilateral EEG recordings. This may explain the findings of previous studied which showed no significant relationship of laterality of alpha activity with hypnosis or hypnotic susceptibility.

METHOD

The subjects were 26 volunteers (11 males and 15 females, age range 22 to 40 years) undertaking studies in psychology and psychiatry at Melbourne University. The subjects were chosen to cover the range of "low" and "high" hypnotic susceptibility and were right handed.

The experiment was carried out in a sleep laboratory. The subject sat in a comfortable chair in a quiet semi-darkened room. The EEG recordings were made in an adjacent room by the experimenter who was able to observe the subject by means of a window. Communication between the subject and the experimenter was possible by a two-way sound system. The hypnotic induction was administered by a tape recorder connected to a speaker in the subject's room. The tape recorder was situated in the experimenter's room. The EEG recordings were made by means of a Grass Model 7D 6 channel Polygraph. The electrodes were located in the occipital-parietal regions according to Lippold's criterion, in order to maximise the bilateral separation of the alpha waves from each cerebral hemisphere (Figure 1).

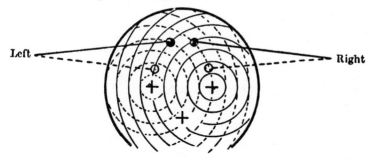

Inion

Method of electrode placement for bilaterally separate recording of alpha waves. With centre at a point 5 cm up from the inion and 5 cm lateral to the mid-line, two electrodes are placed 5 cm apart on an arc of radius of 10 cm. The lower of the two electrodes is 7 cm above the inion. The dotted lines are isopotential contours for the left alpha focus; continuous lines for the right

Fig. 1. Lippold's method of electrode placements.

A schematic diagram of the recording and playback system is shown in Figure 2.

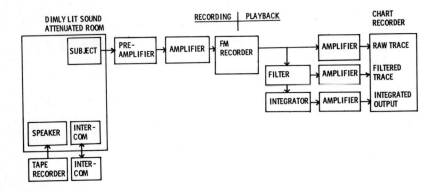

Fig. 2. Schematic diagram of recording and playback system

Each subject was seen once per week for 3 consecutive weekly sessions.

1. A brief interview with the subject in order to take a short history, establish rapport, and to explain the purpose of the study. Following this a brief induction using Barber's procedure[1].

2. Assessment of the subject's hypnotic susceptibility by means of the Barber Scale.

3. Bilateral EEG recordings were made under conditions of:

    a. Baseline 1 - eyes closed resting.

    b. Induction - a hypnotic induction by means of Barber's induction procedure.

    c. Baseline 2 - eyes closed resting.

During the baseline conditions the subject was instructed to "close your eyes and relax for a few minutes, do not fall asleep or go into hypnotic state. Keep your mind as blank as possible. Just enjoy being in a relaxed state".

The sessions 2 and 3 were administered by means of standardised tape recordings.

DESIGN

EEG alpha scores for each subject, recorded from the right and

left cerebral hemispheres separately, were calculated by averaging
the integrated alpha output over four minute periods. The alpha
scores were expressed for convenience in terms of integrator units.

In order to compare interhemisphere differences in alpha activity alpha laterality scores were calculated for each subject, for
each experimental condition, according to the formulae:
Laterality Score = 100 x $\frac{RH-LH}{RH+LH}$ where RH = Right Hemisphere alpha
Scores, LH = Left Hemisphere alpha Scores, and 100 scales the
difference ratio into a relative percent difference. A score of
zero indicated equal alpha activity recorded from both hemispheres
a positive score indicated higher alpha recorded from the right
hemisphere, and a negative score higher alpha recorded from the
left hemisphere.

The statistical analysis consisted of the following procedures:
t-tests comparing paired-mean alpha scores for the total group
in order to test for differences between the experimental conditions; t-tests comparing independent mean alpha scores in order to
test for differences between the experimental groups (high
hypnotizable vs low hypnotizable and males vs females) during the
experimental conditions. Similar analyses were carried out on the
laterality scores in order to compare interhemisphere differences
in alpha activity between the experimental groups during the
experimental conditions.

RESULTS

1.Bilateral alpha activity

a.Distribution of hypnotizability scores. Table 1 shows the mean
hypnotizability scores as measured by the Barber Scale for the
high and low hypnotizable groups and for males and females. The
high hypnotizable group scored significantly higher on this scale
than the low hypnotizable group (t=10.07, p<0.01). Of the high
hypnotizable group 13 were females and 3 were males. Of the low
hypnotizable group 2 were females and 8 were males. Female
subjects were significantly more hypnotizable than male subjects
(t=-3.35, p<0.05). These findings had no influence on the
relationship between alpha measures and hypnotizability since
there was no significant difference between sex and alpha
activity.

TABLE 1

HYPNOTIZABILITY SCORES FOR THE HIGH HYPNOTIZABLE AND LOW
HYPNOTIZABLE GROUPS AND FOR MALES AND FEMALES

Group	Hypnotizability scores: Barber Scale 1969		
	N	Mean	SD
High hypnotizable	16	7.25	0.77
Low hypnotizable	10	3.60	1.07
Males	11	4.55	2.07
Females	15	6.80	1.37
	Mean Difference		t
High vs Low	3.65		10.07**
Males vs Females	-2.35		-3.35*

*$p < 0.05$
**$p < 0.01$

b. <u>Group differences</u>. Figure 3 and Tables 2 and 3 show the mean
integrated alpha scores recorded from both cerebral hemispheres
for the high hypnotizable and low hypnotizable groups during the
different experimental conditions.   There were significant
differences between the groups in the absolute amount of alpha in
each hemisphere (Tables 2 and 3).   The high hypnotizable subjects
generated significantly higher alpha levels than the low hypnotizable subjects in both hemispheres during all the experimental
conditions with the exception of the right hemisphere baseline 1
measure.

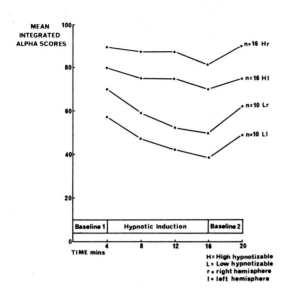

Fig. 3. Mean integrated alpha scores recorded from the right and left cerebral hemispheres for the high and low hypnotizable groups

TABLE 2

INTEGRATED ALPHA SCORES FOR HIGH AND LOW HYPNOTIZABLE GROUPS RECORDED FROM THE RIGHT CEREBRAL HEMISPHERE

Experimental Conditions	High Hypnotizable N=16		Low Hypnotizable N=10		Mean Difference	t
	Mean	SD	Mean	SD		
Baseline 1:						
Eyes-closed	88.38	28.57	70.77	33.85	17.61	1.43NS
Hypnosis 1	86.87	27.00	59.10	33.90	27.77	2.31*
Hypnosis 2	87.36	29.02	52.22	31.32	35.14	2.91**
Hypnosis 3	81.70	28.30	49.77	28.70	31.99	2.78**
Baseline 2:						
Eyes-closed	90.06	28.84	62.25	29.41	27.81	2.37*

NS = Not Significant
 *p<0.05
**p<0.01
One integrated alpha score unit = 0.82 microvolts

TABLE 3

INTEGRATED ALPHA SCORES FOR HIGH AND LOW HYPNOTIZABLE GROUPS
RECORDED FROM THE LEFT CEREBRAL HEMISPHERE

Experimental Conditions	High Hypnotizable N=16		Low Hypnotizable N=10		Mean Difference	t
	Mean	SD	Mean	SD		
Baseline 1:						
Eyes-closed	79.88	28.37	56.90	26.82	22.98	2.05*
Hypnosis 1	75.16	20.45	46.70	24.23	28.46	3.22**
Hypnosis 2	76.57	29.06	42.20	26.38	34.37	3.03**
Hypnosis 3	69.76	25.61	39.20	22.20	30.56	3.10**
Baseline 2:						
Eyes-closed	75.33	24.80	49.20	24.80	26.13	2.61**

NS = Not Significant
 *p<0.05
**p<0.01
One integrated alpha score unit = 0.82 microvolts

In general the bilateral EEG records of high hypnotizable
subjects showed higher amplitudes and more symmetry in the wave
forms than the low hypnotizable subjects.

c. Hemisphere differences   Figure 4 and Table 4 shows the mean
integrated alpha levels for the total group of subjects recorded
from the right and left hemispheres. More alpha was recorded from
the right hemisphere than from the left during all the experimental
conditions. This difference was not significant (Table 4). For
both hemispheres significantly more alpha was recorded generally
during the baseline conditions than during the hypnosis conditions.
Alpha levels furing baseline 2 were generally lower than those of
baseline 1 but these differences were not significant.

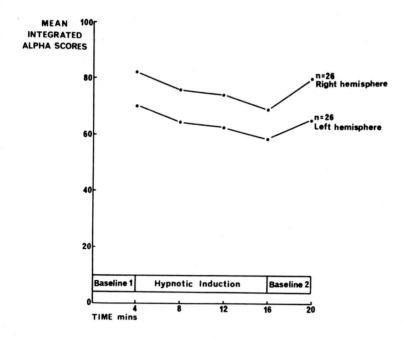

Fig. 4. Mean integrated alpha scores for the total group of subjects recorded from the right and left cerebral hemispheres

TABLE 4

INTEGRATED ALPHA MEASURES FOR THE TOTAL GROUP OF SUBJECTS RECORDED FROM THE RIGHT AND LEFT CEREBRAL HEMISPHERES

Experimental Conditions	Right Hemisphere N=26 Mean	SD	Left Hemisphere N=26 Mean	SD	Mean Difference	t
Baseline 1:						
Eyes-closed	81.61	31.28	71.04	29.53	10.57	1.25NS
Hypnosis 1	76.18	27.00	64.21	25.73	11.97	1.64NS
Hypnosis 2	73.85	34.10	63.35	32.37	10.50	1.14NS
Hypnosis 3	69.42	32.06	58.00	28.30	11.42	1.35NS
Baseline 2:						
Eyes-closed	79.36	31.63	65.28	27.54	14.08	1.70NS

NS = Not Significant

One integrated alpha score unit = 0.82 microvolts

328

2.Asymmetrical alpha activity

a.Hemisphere differences. Figure 5 and Table 5 show the mean alpha
laterality scores for the high hypnotizable and low hypnotizable
groups.   The positive values of the mean laterality scores indicated that more alpha was recorded from the right hemisphere than
from the left hemisphere.   The lower the laterality score (that
is, as it approached zero) the more symmetrical was the alpha
recorded from both hemispheres.   The higher the score, the more
asymmetrical was the alpha recorded from both hemispheres.

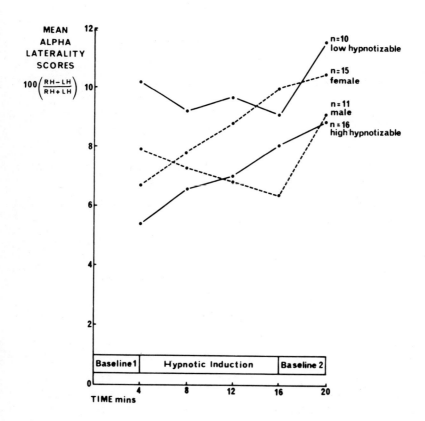

Fig. 5.   Mean integrated alpha laterality scores for the high and
low hypnotizable groups and for males and females

TABLE 5

INTEGRATED ALPHA LATERALITY SCORES FOR HIGH AND LOW HYPNOTIZABLE
GROUPS

Experimental Conditions	High Hypnotizable N=16 Mean	SD	Low Hypnotizable N=10 Mean	SD	Mean Difference	t
Baseline 1:						
Eyes-closed	5.39	8.47	10.22	11.55	-4.84	-1.22NS
Hypnosis 1	6.58	8.81	9.17	15.15	-2.60	-0.55NS
Hypnosis 2	7.01	12.54	9.67	12.19	-2.65	-0.53NS
Hypnosis 3	8.08	13.95	9.11	16.00	-1.03	-0.55NS
Baseline 2:						
Eyes-closed	8.85	11.79	11.56	9.91	-2.71	-0.60NS

NS=Not Significant
One integrated alpha score unit = 0.82 microvolts

b.Group differences. There were no significant differences
between the high hypnotizable and low hypnotizable groups in
laterality scores during the experimental conditions (Table 5).
The shapes of the graphs (figure 5) for the two groups were different and indicated different trends. The graph for the high
hypnotizable group showed a gradual increase in asymmetry of alpha
with more alpha generated from the right hemisphere as the experimental session continued. The graph for the low hypnotizable
group did not show the same gradual increase but fluctuated during
the experimental session. The low hypnotizable group showed a
trend for more asymmetrical alpha activity than did the high
hypnotizable group.

c.Sex differences. Figure 5 and Table 6 show the mean alpha lat-
arality score for males and females. There were no significant
differences between males and females in laterality scores during
the experimental conditions (Table 6). The shape of the graph for
the the females was similar to that of the high hypnotizable
group, and the graph for the males resembled that of the low
hypnotizable group. This suggested an interaction effect between

sex and laterality of alpha activity. This was not found. A two-way analysis of variance, laterality of alpha by sex, showed a non-significant interaction term (F=0.59, p>0.05). The reason for the similarity in the shapes of the graphs was because the high hypnotizable group was comprised mostly of females and the low hypnotizable group was comprised mostly of males.

TABLE 6

INTEGRATED ALPHA LATERALITY SCORES FOR MALES AND FEMALES

Experimental Conditions	Males N=11 Mean	SD	Females N=15 Mean	SD	Mean Difference	t
Baseline 1:						
Eyes-closed	7.93	10.26	6.74	9.85	1.19	-0.30NS
Hypnosis 1	7.30	13.61	7.80	10.05	-0.49	-0.10NS
Hypnosis 2	6.96	11.23	8.82	13.24	-1.86	-0.38NS
Hypnosis 3	6.37	13.92	10.02	15.13	-3.65	-0.63NS
Baseline 2:						
Eyes-closed	9.08	10.66	10.50	11.54	-1.41	-0.32NS

NS=Not Significant
One integrated alpha score unit = 0.82 microvolts

DISCUSSION

1.Alpha activity, hypnotizability, and the hypnotic state

The results indicated certain relationships of alpha activity with hypnotic susceptibility and the hypnotic state.

High hypnotizable subjects generated significantly higher alpha levels than the low hypnotizable subjects in both hemispheres during the experimental conditions. This supported the findings of recent studies[2].

The EEG alpha recordings significantly differentiated the hypnotic state from the awake eyes-closed resting baseline state. For the total group of subjects lower alpha levels were recorded from both hemispheres, during the hypnotic conditions than during the baseline conditions. This supported the work of other researchers[2].

It was contrary to the findings of other workers who found higher alpha levels during hypnosis than during the baseline peri- ods[2].

2. The hypnothesis of hemispheric specialization in hypnosis

The hypothesis that the right hemisphere was specialized for hypnosis was not supported. It has been argued that since there was generally more alpha activity recorded from the right hemisphere than from the left during states of lowered arousal, hypnosis must involve the right hemisphere more than the left[1]. The present study found that for the total group of subjects more alpha activity was recorded from the right hemisphere than from the left but this difference was not significant. There were also no significant differences in mean asymmetry of alpha scores between the high hypnotizable and low hypnotizable group.

The failure to support the above hypothesis requires some expla- nation. First, hypnosis may not be as completely lateralized as other functions, and both hemispheres may be equally involved during hypnosis. This may explain the findings in the present study that the high hypnotizable subjects showed more symmetrical alpha activity than the low hypnotizable group. Evidence for this concept of incomplete lateralization in the case of speech and visuo-spatial functions was provided by Bradshaw et al.[5] According to these researchers although these functions appeared to be processed mainly by the left and right hemisphere respectively "this specialization was not exclusive and a kind of continuum existed between left and right hemisphere". A similar continuum or gradient of specialization across the hemispheres may also exist for hypnosis.

Second, the method of bilateral EEG recordings used in this study, Lippold's method, may not have been sensitive enough to detect hemispheric differences. Despite the advantage of this technique over conventional electrode placements, it cannot be determined that the record from each side is the "true uncontam- inated" one without mapping the isopotential lines for each subject. Lippold's method ignored differences in head circumfer- ences and made an assumption that the alpha occipital generators were usually located 5 centimetres out from the inion, and that electrodes placed on an arc of radius 10 centimetres from these generator sites represented the isopotential contour originating from them.

It would have been more accurate in this study to have used the common average reference electrode placement system. This method has been shown to provide EEG records from each side of the head that were uninfluenced or "uncontaminated" by the other[2]. It follows the 10-20 System of the International Federation and provides a standardized electrode array which takes into account intersubject differences in head circumference.

Third, the choice of electrode sites may have been important in determining the extent of bilateral asymmetry. It has been shown that interhemispheric asymmetry of alpha activity depended significantly on the location of electrode placements[2]. Higher alpha abundance was found at left sides T3 and C3 and at right sides P4 and T6. Although asymmetry was found at the occipital positions, O1 and O2, there was no significant differences in the amount of alpha between these two positions. The present study's use of the O1-P3 and O2-P4 electrode sites may have accounted for the failure to find significant differences between the alpha activity recorded from the two sides of the head.

Fourth, the EEG alpha parameter used in this study, integrated amplitude, may have been a relatively insensitive measure in detecting significant differences between the two hemispheres. The frequency parameter of the EEG may be more likely to detect asymmetrical differences than amplitude. Amplitude reflects hemisphere "dominance" (a difference in "quantity" shown by asymmetrical amplitudes) whereas frequency reflects hemisphere "independence" (a difference in "quality" as shown by asymmetrical frequencies)[2].

3.SUMMARY AND CONCLUSIONS

The findings of the present study contribute to the increasing
evidence that the level of alpha activity appears to be related
to the degree of hypnotic susceptibility .
1.High hypnotizable subjects generated significantly high alpha
levels than the low hypnotizable subjects.
2.The EEG recordings significantly differentiated the hypnotic
state from the awake eyes-closed resting baseline conditions.
Lower alpha levels were recorded from both hemispheres during the
hypnotic conditions than during the baselines.
3.The hypothesis that the right hemisphere was specialized for
hypnosis was not supported. Although there were marked trends in
the direction expected. More alpha activity was recorded from the
right hemisphere than from the left. A number of suggestions
were offered for the failure to support this hypothesis: that
hypnosis may not be completely lateralised; the method of EEG
recording; sites of electrode placements and choice of EEG
parameter used were inadequate to detect asymmetrical differences.
Further research with the above methodological considerations in
mind need to be carried out to further explore the hypothesis of
hemisphere specialization.

REFERENCES

1.Foenander, G., Burrows, G.D., Debenham, P., and Hjorth, R.,
(1977) The Electroencephalogram, Alpha Activity and Hypnosis.
Aust. Jrnl. Clinical Hypnosis, 5, pp86-104.

2.Foenander, G., and Burrows, G.D. (1979) EEG Alpha Activity in
Hypnosis : A Review of the Literature. Aust. Jrnl. Clinical &
Experim. Hypnosis, 7, (In Press).

3.Morgan, A.H., MacDonald, H., and Hilgard, E.R. (1974) EEG Alpha:
Lateral Asymmetry Related to Task and Hypnotizability.
Psychophysiology, 11, pp 275-282.

4.Lippold, O. (1973) The Origin of The Alpha Rhythm. Churchill
Livingstone, London.

5.Bradshaw, J.L. (1972) Asymmetry and Delayed Auditory Feedback.
Jrnl. Experim. Psych. 94, pp 269-275.

Hypnosis 1979
G.D. Burrows, D.R. Collison and L. Dennerstein

BIOFEEDBACK AND HYPNOTIZABILITY

JEAN HOLROYD, KEITH NUECHTERLEIN, DAVID SHAPIRO, AND FREDERICK WARD
Department of Psychiatry and Biobehavioral Sciences, UCLA, 760 Westwood
Boulevard, Los Angeles, California 90024 (USA)

Both hypnosis and biofeedback are used to control a variety of physiological responses, including reduction of arousal or stress states. In clinical
applications, tension headache has been treated by hypnosis as well as by EMG
feedback from the frontalis muscle. Essential hypertension has been treated
by hypnosis and also by blood pressure biofeedback and EMG frontalis muscle
feedback. Both hypnosis and biofeedback may focus the subject's attention on
certain sensory information to change physiological responses usually not
thought to be under voluntary control. However, it is not clear that hypnosis
and biofeedback operate on the same principles. For example, individuals who
are good hypnotic subjects may not necessarily be good biofeedback subjects.
Roberts et al[1] found no relationship between hypnotizability and skin temperature control. Dumas[2] reported that high hypnotizable subjects did not learn
the EEG alpha increase/decrease operation which medium or low hypnotizable
subjects learned. In addition, biofeedback and hypnosis were found by
Engstrom[3] to be equally effective for altering the skin temperature of high
hypnotizables, but biofeedback was more useful for most low hypnotizables.

The aim of this study was to examine the relationship between hypnotizability and the ability to alter physiological functions by means of biofeedback and hypnosis techniques. This relationship has both theoretical and
clinical import.

In the present study, hypnotizability was related to competence in learning two kinds of physiological self-regulation: reducing frontalis muscle
activity (EMG) and lowering the blood pressure. Frontalis EMG reduction is
probably easier and under greater voluntary control than blood pressure reduction. Therefore the two tasks vary in susceptibility to voluntary control.

Eight highly hypnotizable and eight low hypnotizable subjects were selected from a pool of paid university volunteers who had been given an hour
of previous experience with hypnosis using a modification of the Harvard
Group Scale of Hypnotic Susceptibility.[4] "Highs" scored 10 or above on the
Stanford Hypnotic Susceptibility Scale, Form C,[5] whereas "Lows" scored 4 or
below.

Each subject spent one session attempting to reduce blood pressure and
another session on a separate day attempting to lower EMG. Within each
session the subjects used both hypnosis and biofeedback in counter-balanced
order. Thus we had a repeated-measures, within-Subjects design, as shown in
Figure 1. One "High" and one "Low" subject participated in each of the eight
separate orders of experimental conditions. The independent variables were
Group (High, Low), Treatment (Hypnosis, Biofeedback), Focus (EMG, blood
pressure), and Trials (5 during baseline, 25 during hypnosis or biofeedback).
The dependent variables were EMG, blood pressure, heart period (inversely related to pulse) and skin conductance.

Subjects	Day 1		Day 2	
High Low	EMG Focus		Blood Pressure Focus	
4 4	H FB	1, 2	H	FB
	FB H	3, 4	FB	H
	Blood Pressure Focus		EMG Focus	
4 4	H FB	5, 6	H	FB
	FB H	7, 8	FB	H

Fig. 1 Order of Biofeedback (FB) and Hypnosis (H) Conditions

We expected to find that subjects would be capable of greater control of
EMG than of blood pressure. We also hypothesized that "Highs" would do better
than "Lows" in the hypnosis condition, whether for lowering frontalis activity
or for reducing blood pressure. We never really reached consensus about hypotheses for the "Low" hypnotizables. Would they do better with biofeedback
because that requires directed motivation? "Lows" are thought to be more motivated and perform better on most experimental tasks.[3] On the other hand,
that very task motivation might interfere with achieving the passive mental
state seemingly required for successful biofeedback learning. Engstrom[3]
found that the "Lows" who were successful at biofeedback were also the ones
for whom alpha density increased during temperature biofeedback training.

There were two parts to each treatment session--a biofeedback period and a
hypnosis period. An attempt was made to make each treatment as similar as
possible to typical clinical conditions. Subjects were seated on a comfortable recliner in a dimly lit room. The hypnotist was present during hypnosis
treatment but left the room during biofeedback treatment after instructions
were given. During biofeedback the subjects tried to reduce the rate of

auditory clicks. The feedback was based on the amplitude of integrated EMG activity and, in the case of blood pressure, on the changing beat-to-beat estimate of systolic blood pressure.

The necessary instruments for measuring blood pressure, EMG, respiration, skin conductance, and heart rate were attached at the start of each session. There was a 5-minute baseline period before each 25-minute treatment condition, and also a 5-minute "break" with casual conversation immediately following the first treatment period. For the purposes of data analysis, we divided each treatment into 25 one-minute "trials." We used the tracking cuff method developed by Shapiro et al[6] to monitor continuous changes in blood pressure. The cuff was inflated for 45" of each one-minute trial and was deflated during the last 15" to permit blood to flow through the arm again. Physiological measures were taken continuously and averaged for every 5" during the 45 seconds of cuff inflation, yielding nine values per minute. Thus, the blood pressure cuff was inflated once a minute for 45 seconds whether the subject was focusing on reducing EMG or blood pressure and whether biofeedback or hypnosis was being administered.

Instructions for the biofeedback period included general and specific directions on how to relax: "In order to lower your forehead muscle tension you can think of relaxing your entire body, or you can simply think of relaxing your forehead muscles completely by letting all the little muscles relax and get soft and limp. Sometimes visualizing or imagining being in a relaxing situation helps. Do anything which you feel might help. The mild feeling of pressure in your arm and any sounds you may hear can be a part of your deeper and deeper relaxation."

During hypnosis the subject simply listened to the hypnotist read from a prepared script. An induction was read from the Stanford Clinical Hypnosis Scale[7] followed by suggestions similar to the instructions given for biofeedback, interspersed with several two-minute periods of silence. A subjective estimate of hypnotic depth[8] was requested after the induction and after 23 minutes of the 25-minute treatment period.

All personnel working with the subjects in the laboratory, including the experimenter who administered the biofeedback and the hypnosis treatments, were blind as to the hypnotizability level of the subjects.

RESULTS

For purposes of this presentation, analyses were made of changes in the four dependent variables (blood pressure, EMG, heart period, skin conductance) for each focus separately. Analysis of covariance was used to adjust for differences in baseline values. Results significant at the p <.05 level are reported.

More physiological changes suggesting general relaxation occurred when people were focusing on muscle activity than when they were focusing on blood pressure. There was a reduction in blood pressure, pulse rate, EMG, and skin conductance when trying to relax the forehead muscles. When subjects tried to lower their blood pressure, only the pulse and EMG indicated general relaxation. In fact, skin conductance actually increased in the biofeedback attempt to lower blood pressure.

When subjects were asked to focus on frontalis relaxation, differences between "High" and "Low" groups or between Biofeedback and Hypnosis treatments were not significant in terms of main effects. That is, High Hypnotizables did no better and no poorer than Low Hypnotizables, and hypnosis was no more nor less effective than biofeedback. However there were some interesting and heuristically meaningful interaction effects. "Highs" reduced frontalis tension more initially, but "Lows" caught up and surpassed them (Figure 2). This interaction seems to occur because of an initial paradoxical increase in EMG for "Lows" trying to use hypnosis to reduce frontalis activity (Figure 3). The same increase is seen for "Highs," but not to such a great degree. After 25 trials biofeedback and hypnosis seem equally effective for Low Hypnotizables. Somewhat surprisingly, a trend toward greater and faster frontalis relaxation through biofeedback is noted for High Hypnotizables (Figure 3). The paradoxical increase in EMG during early hypnosis trials can be seen more clearly when "Highs" and "Lows" are combined (Figure 4). I shall discuss that finding later, after presenting the remainder of the data. The greatest change in EMG seemed to occur during the first 15 minutes for hypnosis and during the first 10 minutes for biofeedback (Figure 4).

Blood pressure was only weakly responsive to attempts to lower it by blood pressure biofeedback and hypnosis. Consequently, the absence of significant differences between Highs and Lows or between Biofeedback and Hypnosis treatments was not surprising. There was a nonsignificant trend toward a treatment by group interaction in the opposite direction from that we expected: "Lows" tended to be more successful at lowering blood pressure with hypnosis than with biofeedback, whereas both methods of treatment were equally successful with "Highs" (Table 1). It is interesting that although blood pressure was not decreased significantly over experimental trials when subjects focused on its reduction, significant decreases did occur as an indirect effect when subjects tried to lower their frontalis muscle activity using either hypnosis or biofeedback.

TABLE 1

BLOOD PRESSURE CONTROL[a]

	Highs	Lows
Hypnosis	105[b]	106
Biofeedback	105	109

a   Treatment x Group Effect   p   .10

b   Values adjusted by analysis of covariance

Pulse rate, measured here inversely as heart period, appeared to be a sensitive response measure during both the blood pressure and the EMG tasks. Pulse rate decreased over trials whether subjects were trying to lower blood pressure or EMG, but especially when the focus was EMG - a significant focus x trials interaction (Figure 5). When the focus was blood pressure, hypnosis was significantly more effective for slowing pulse than biofeedback (hypnosis heart period = 957; biofeedback heart period = 939; p   .05).

In summary, High hypnotizable subjects performed no better than low hypnotizable subjects on any of the tasks under any treatment condition. In fact, with the possible exception of attempts to modify blood pressure, hypnotizability was not associated with differential overall effectiveness of hypnosis or biofeedback. Secondly, frontalis muscle activity is more easily reduced than blood pressure. Thirdly, reductions in the various physiological functions, including blood pressure, are more readily achieved when subjects are trying to reduce frontalis EMG than when they are trying to reduce blood pressure.

DISCUSSION

Our questions about what individual differences predict response to either hypnosis or biofeedback were not fully answered by this study. Now we seek to understand why high hypnotizable subjects did not do better than low

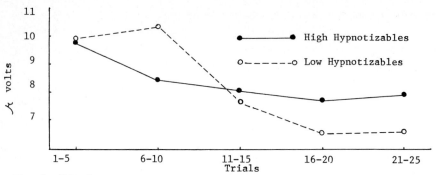

Fig. 2 EMG changes over grouped trials when focusing on muscle relaxation
(Values adjusted by analysis of covariance.)

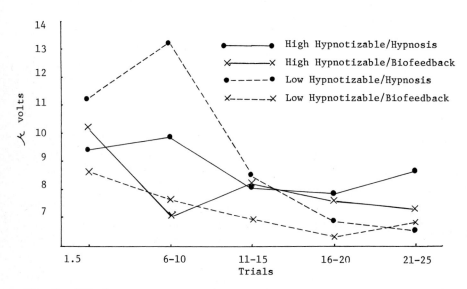

Fig. 3. EMG changes over grouped trials when focusing on muscle relaxation
(Values adjusted by analysis of covariance.)

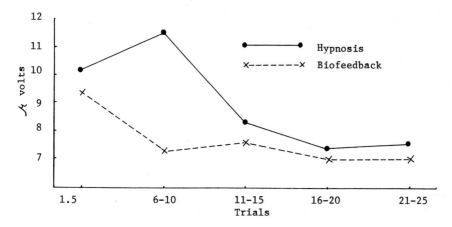

Fig. 4 EMG changes over grouped trials when focusing on muscle relaxation. (Values adjusted by analysis of covariance.)

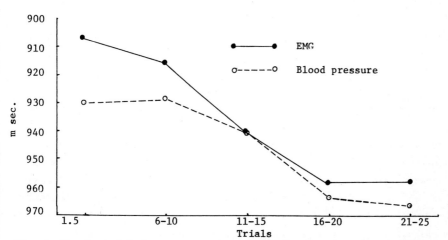

Fig. 5 Heart period changes over grouped trials when focusing on blood pressure or forehead muscle tension. (Values adjusted by analysis of covariance.)

hypnotizable subjects when employing hypnosis to change physiological responses. We have considered two possibilities:

(1) Blood pressure cuff inflation once each minute, to the point at
which systolic sound is not heard, is a significant pressure stimulus with
sudden onset. The impact of that repeated event may have interfered with
maintenance of sufficient hypnotic depth to permit the high hypnotizable
subjects to perform optimally in the hypnosis condition. This possibility
could be partially checked by examining self-report data on perceived hypnotic depth. A quick glance at the data--which will be analyzed in greater
detail later--suggests that high hypnotizable subjects were able to maintain
moderate trance depth (seven on a scale of zero to ten) despite that interference.

(2) Group differences under the hypnosis condition may have been diminished because the low hypnotizable subjects were more highly motivated to
perform the experimental tasks.[3] However, if that were the case the low
hypnotizable subjects probably should have performed better than the Highs
in the biofeedback condition. They did not.

Failure of the Lows to excel in the biofeedback task also constitutes lack
of support for Dumas'[2] hypothesis that Lows are superior at attending to
external stimuli such as the auditory feedback signal. Dumas had found that
Highs could not learn an alpha increase/decrease response with biofeedback
and suggested that Highs attend instead to internal, possible hallucinatory,
stimuli.

Originally we had planned to double the size of our sample if we noted
results that suggested group differences but were not statistically significant with this modest sample size. Since we selected subjects from the ex-
tremes of the hypnotizability dimension, we expected to find rather clear
differences if the results were to be clinically meaningful. The data we
obtained do not encourage us to increase sample size. Individual differences
in the ability to change physiological responses using hypnosis or biofeedback do not appear to be related to individual differences in hypnotizability.
Analysis of other data we have collected, such as responses to state and
trait anxiety questionnaires and debriefing interview data may shed further
light on our questions about individual differences in treatment response.

One of the general findings is clinically meaningful, however. When
subjects tried to lower forehead muscle activity whether by hypnosis or

biofeedback, many more generalized physiological changes occurred than when they were trying to lower blood pressure. This has direct implications for training a general relaxation response. If one is trying to induce general relaxation, one would probably do better to focus on muscular relaxation than on blood pressure reduction.

The paradoxical increase in EMG during trials 6-10 when subjects were attempting to relax their forehead muscles using hypnosis may be an artifact of the induction procedure. At about that point in the induction subjects were told, "You can change your position any time you wish. Just be sure you remain comfortable and relaxed." They were also asked to estimate their subjective depth, and would have been giving a verbal report at that time.

Finally, we have not yet completely analyzed the physiological response data and the previously mentioned questionnaire and interview data. A more complete report will be forthcoming.

1. Roberts, A. H., Schuler, J., Bacon, J., and Patterson, R. Individual differences and autonomic control of skin temperature. Journal of Abnormal Psychology, 1975, 84, 272-279.
2. Dumas, Roland A. Cognitive control in hypnosis and biofeedback. Unpublished manuscript, 1976.
3. Engstrom, R. Hypnotic susceptibility, EEG-Alpha, and self-regulation. In Schwartz, G. and Shapiro, D. (Eds.) Consciousness and Self-Regulation. N.Y.: Plenum Press, 1976.
4. Shor, R. E. and Orne, E. C. Harvard Group Scale of Hypnotic Susceptibility. Palo Alto: Consulting Psychologists Press, Inc., 1962.
5. Weitzenhoffer, A. M., and Hilgard, E. R. Stanford Hypnotic Susceptibility Scale, Form C. Palo Alto, CA: Consulting Psychologists Press, 1962.
6. Shapiro, D., Reeves, J. L., Greenstadt, L., Dolan, P., Cobb, L. F., and Lane, J. D. Blood pressure control using a beat-to-beat tracking cuff method: Preliminary observations. Psychophysiology, 1979, 16, 175-176 (Abstract).
7. Hilgard, E. R., and Hilgard, J. R. Hypnosis in the relief of pain. Los Altos, CA: Wm. Kaufmann, 1975.
8. Tart, C. Quick and convenient assessment of hypnotic depth: Self-report scales. The American Journal of Clinical Hypnosis, 1978-79, 21, 186-207.

© 1979 Elsevier/North-Holland Biomedical Press
Hypnosis 1979
G.D. Burrows, D.R. Collison and L. Dennerstein

RELAXATION AND BIOFEEDBACK: CLINICAL PROBLEMS IN RESEARCH WITH ESSENTIAL HYPER-
TENSIVE PATIENTS

MARISTELLA GOEBEL, Ph.D., GEOFFREY W. VIOL, M.D., GLORIA LORENZ, R.N., and TODD
S. ING, M.D.
Renal and Hypertension Section, Veterans Administration Edward Hines, Jr.,
Hospital, Hines, Illinois, U.S.A. 60141

INTRODUCTION

Research in biofeedback with essential hypertensives has been criticized in
recent reviews[1,2] for lack of experimental controls, inadequate baselines and
follow-up, few subjects, and use of normotensive subjects rather than patients.

In addition to research deficiencies, however, hypertension research has inherent clinical problems. Even with the most carefully controlled experimental
procedures, these clinical problems remain. The least we can do is recognize
them.

During our six-year research project in the behavioral management of hypertension we have become aware of at least five categories of clinical problems:
1) the sampling errors of sphygmomanometric measurements, 2) the errors involved
in slight variations of posture, 3) clinical problems during establishment of a
stable baseline, including noncompliance and a possible delayed response to medication reduction, 4) motivational contingencies in the research design itself,
and 5) excessive scientific rigidity on the part of the clinician-researcher.

CLINICAL PROBLEMS

1. The sampling errors of sphygmomanometric measurements

Figure 1 shows the true intra-arterial variation (30 mm Hg) of both systolic
and diastolic blood pressure for about 50 heartbeats, as described by Tursky[3]
for one patient. Readings that might result from two different cuff deflations
are shown in the diagonal lines superimposed upon the intra-arterial measures.
Any cuff deflation samples systolic blood pressure at one instant and diastolic
blood pressure at another instant. It is evident that any combination of readings could be derived, depending on time of initiation of inflation and rate of
deflation. The best one can do with an indirect cuff measure is to take many
readings and be aware of the range of readings of any patient under uniform
conditions--e.g., quiet sitting for five minutes. The need for an adequate

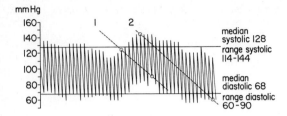

Fig. 1   Intra-arterial recording showing beat-to-beat variability of systolic and diastolic blood pressure, with two imaginary cuff deflations superimposed. (After Tursky[3].) Copyright c 1974 by Aldine Publishing Company. Reprinted, with permission, from CARDIOVASCULAR PSYCHOPHYSIOLOGY (New York: Aldine, Publishing Company.)

determination of blood pressure variability is one reason why the extended base-line is so important in clinical research with hypertensive patients.

2. The errors involved in slight variations of posture.

In planning our investigations we agreed that independent measures of blood pressure would be taken by the physician and by the psychologist, with the patient seated upright and his arm supported at heart level. We were surprised to discover that the physician's sphygmomanometric readings were about 10-20 mm higher than the psychologist's readings on the Arteriosonde machine[4,5]. The "physician effect" was ruled out in one series of comparisons by using simulta-neous but independent measures taken by two trained non-physicians. A study systematically ruling out human error, instrument error, conditioning to a par-ticular setting, and the "physician effect" produced the results in Table I.

These clearly implicate the conditions of seating--on an examining table, with back unsupported and feet dangling but with arm supported; and in an easy chair (upright position) with arm supported. When in another sub-study the physician and the psychologist took simultaneous but independent readings using a T-connector and a common cuff, they agreed very well under either condition of seating ($r = .98$, systolic; $r = .89$, diastolic). But the two conditions of seating were significantly different. Diastolic blood pressure was particular-affected by the two conditions of seating. It is evidently not sufficient to specify that "blood pressure was taken in the seated position, upright." The postural tensions of an unsupported back and dangling feet are probably respon-sible for the higher readings on the examining table.

TABLE I

EASY CHAIR VS. EXAMINING TABLE BLOOD PRESSURE READINGS, SEATED UPRIGHT

Means of 3 readings taken after 5 minutes of quiet sitting. N = 20.

Patient #	EASY CHAIR[a]		EXAMINING TABLE[a]	
	Baumanometer[b]	Arteriosonde[b]	Baumanometer[b]	Arteriosonde[b]
1	126/83	127/77	131/89	129/89
2	187/103	186/101	191/114	191/118
3	137/96	125/86	137/96	140/97
4	141/93	143/98	154/107	145/115
5	115/89	117/88	120/93	122/89
6	123/78	121/78	127/95	128/101
7	125/80	129/79	136/94	136/93
8	138/89	144/85	145/99	151/103
9	153/104	151/100	151/110	151/112
10	120/91	130/92	135/105	138/107
11	141/61	150/63	157/70	162/70
12	137/91	139/86	148/109	146/101
13	109/76	115/72	115/85	118/85
14	111/77	118/75	112/79	112/82
15	123/80	127/80	138/87	136/86
16	167/72	173/69	168/83	172/81
17	111/71	113/68	136/88	137/88
18	148/81	153/83	157/90	154/86
19	109/77	111/73	113/91	114/86
20	108/81	101/83	109/90	102/87
Means =	131.5/83.7	133.8/81.6	139.0/93.7	140.0/93.8

[a] $p < .001$ for all differences between chair and table.
[b] No significant difference between Baumanometer and Arteriosonde.

In one case (Patient #17) the differences were 24 mm Hg for systolic, 20 mm Hg for diastolic. Obviously, the welfare of individual patients could be at stake if medical decisions did not consider the conditions of "sitting upright." Also, we did not wish a patient's participation to be protracted much beyond the minimum 6 months of our study with his blood pressure in the upper borderline range. On the one hand, in order to provide sufficient maneuverability to lower blood pressure during the experimental stage of our study, and on the other hand to safeguard the patient's welfare, we decided to try to stabilize blood pressure in the *lower* part of the range 130-150/90-100 during baseline.

TABLE 2

PARTIAL RECORD OF PATIENT ILLUSTRATING NONCOMPLIANCE & SUBSEQUENT OVERMEDICATION

Medication and Remarks	Dates	Means
Pre-Study: Methyldopa 500 mg qid, Hydralazine 25 mg qid, Chlorthalidone 25 mg qid		
Changed to: Propranolol 80 mg bid, Hydralazine 50 mg bid, Hydrochlorothiazide 50 mg qam	Feb 25 '78	141/90
	.....	
	Apr 22 '78	115/82
	May 6 '78	149/93
	May 13 '78	123/77
	.....	
Dropped from study. Unstabilized.	June 3 '78	156/93
Asked to rejoin.	June 10 '78	118/73
Dropped from study. Unstabilized.	June 24 '78	168/104
	.....	
Third attempt in study; admitted noncompliance.	Oct 7 '78	97/67
Feeling tired.	Oct 11 '78	110/78
Medications reduced after 4 weeks stabilization:	Nov 4 '78	109/74
Propranolol 40 mg bid, Hydralazine 50 mg bid,	.....	
Hydrochlorothiazide 50 mg qam. Low pressures		
maintained. Ran out of medications.................Jan 27 '79		157/96
	.....	
Hydralazine ceased, with approval.	Feb 17 '79	116/79
	.....	
Suspected "self-regulation."	Mar 3 '79	142/90
Told he could have legitimate medication reduc-	Mar 10 '79	116/81
tion if he stayed low 2 weeks. Did so, boasting		
to other patients and feeling good.	Mar 17 '79	118/80
Lower readings due to compliance, not to experi-		
mental treatments. Baseline duration 57 weeks.		

3. Clinical problems during the baseline phase.

Noncompliance. Patients are known to be noncompliant in taking medications when they experience untoward effects. Table 2 shows the record of such a patient in our study. This problem is related to maintaining an accurate baseline for blood pressure on medications. Signs of this clinical problem are wide fluctuations between readings on different days during baseline measurements, together with complaints of unwanted effects. We have found that noncompliant patients are likely to be over-medicated; when they present with high readings they are likely to have their medications increased. When they finally do comply (after analyzing their low-high readings with the investigators during research), they may have a marked sustained drop in blood pressure. These patients can be helped to remain compliant by pointing out that if they keep their blood pressure low for two or three sessions they may have their medications legitimately decreased. It is evident that unless stabilization is achieved during baseline there will be a large error factor in any subsequent comparisons that are to be made with baseline readings. This error factor may be in favor of the learning procedures if the baseline sample includes many high readings, and against the learning procedures if the baseline sample includes many low readings. Adequate clinical counseling can reduce this error factor.

The patient in Table 2 was in an elastic baseline phase for 57 weeks, and his lower readings were probably due to his increased compliance. Using a baseline of uniform length may give the experimenter a false sense of scientific exactitude, but it may be misleading, both clinically and experimentally. We have specified stabilization for *at least six weeks following the last medication adjustment* in our study. Had we accepted the patient for the experimental phase in March or April, 1978, our experimental results for him would have been erroneous, and alterations unrelated to experimental treatments would have been observed.

Delayed response to medication adjustment in the baseline phase. It is not logically to be expected that relaxation and/or biofeedback would raise the blood pressure of patients who are stabilized on medications. Therefore when a rise is noted after seeming initial success in lowering blood pressure by one of the learning techniques, and when situational factors do not seem to be likely explanations, one must entertain at least the possibility that medication reduction in the baseline period has had a delayed effect. This is another reason for a long enough baseline to permit changes to become clear.

It may be noted that the delayed rise after medication reduction is also evident in some cases in our control group--a circumstance that supports the probability of delayed response to medication adjustment. If there is any sign of a rise in the sixth week after medication, it is advisable to wait until the blood pressure stabilizes for six weeks.

4. Motivational contingencies in the research design itself.

In addition to the usual need to motivate patients to apply experimental procedures at home and at work (which is met by using a variety of teaching devices), we found quite accidentally during two pilot studies that a small change in experimental design itself could greatly affect the motivational contingencies[6].

Table 3 shows the designs of Pilot Study 1 and Pilot Study 2. During Pilot 1 we had reduced medications during the experimental phase as soon as patients succeeded in lowering their blood pressure through relaxation and/or biofeedback. This process was repeated several times. The patients were highly motivated because of the prompt reward they received for blood pressure lowering. As a result the measure of success (medication reduction) was 57.5% in Pilot 1.

TABLE 3

DESIGNS OF TWO PILOT STUDIES ON RELAXATION AND BIOFEEDBACK WITH HYPERTENSIVES

Pilot 1 (N=15)	Pilot 2 (N=18 plus 4 controls)
8 weeks + (baseline), once/week, medication constant.	6 weeks + (baseline), once/week. Medication adjusted, BP borderline range for 6 weeks.
8 weeks (learning), twice/week, medication adjusted, home practice.	12 weeks (learning), 6 weeks twice/week, 6 weeks once/week (fading). Medication constant, home practice.
8 weeks (fading and follow-up), once/week, medication adjusted, home practice.	6 weeks (follow-up), once/week. Medication adjusted, home practice.

We made the "small" change in Pilot 2 of changing medication during the baseline phase and holding it constant during the experimental phase. Pilot 1, unfortunately, had confounded the effects of medication reduction and of learning, and hence no statistical analysis could be done on blood pressure changes. The change to the "cleaner" design of Pilot 2 did permit a clear analysis of blood pressure changes, as shown in Table 4.

It should be added that these were tonic (between-session) changes, rather than merely phasic (within-session) changes, and hence are not only statistically significant, but also clinically significant. But the changes in Pilot 2 eliminated a very powerful reinforcer, as shown by medication reduction of only 25.2% in Pilot 2.

Because of research demands, our main study is proceeding along Pilot 2 lines. But there is little doubt that the motivational contingencies inherent in the design of Pilot 1--with its immediate reinforcement for success being repeated as often as success occurred--were clinically superior to those inherent in the design of Pilot 2.

TABLE 4

PILOT STUDY 2: DECREASE IN BLOOD PRESSURE (BP), PHASE 1 TO PHASE 2

Pt.	BP End 1	BP End 2	Difference[a]
1	140/92	124/81	16/11
2	122/90	117/85	5/5
3	128/92	120/82	8/10
4	140/85	138/85	2/0
5	151/95	147/99	4/-4
6	141/90	139/88	2/2
7	141/88	129/81	11/7
8	148/97	136/92	12/5
9	135/89	127/86	8/3
10	130/91	127/84	3/7
11	136/92	120/87	16/5
12	134/88	129/94	5/-6
13	106/87	112/91	-6/-4
14	151/101	144/89	7/12
15	137/98	124/83	13/15
16	162/96	145/85	17/11
17	128/97	123/95	5/2
18	123/94	120/85	3/9

[a] $p < .0005/.005$, one-tailed t-tests.

5. Excessive scientific rigidity on the part of the researcher.

An important clinical consideration under the heading of motivation can be described as the inflexibility and rigidity of the researchers themselves, in the way they may apply an otherwise unexceptionable research design. Some investigators are aware when they fail in this regard and are their own harshest critics. Frankel and colleagues[7], for instance, used a variety of psychophysiological procedures during clinical research in blood pressure reduction with all subjects, teaching each technique briefly according to a fixed schedule (so that probably none was mastered), and they speculate that overconcern for scientific exactitude might have led to clinical inefficiency. They state that the need to combine clinical and research objectives is probably the most challenging problem in the area of behavioral therapies.

Surwit and colleagues[8] likewise state that a "rather limited amount of training and attention" may not have been adequate in their study, and that "an expectancy of success" might have been missing.

Chandra Patel, who is known for her clinical sensitivity to her patients, stresses the importance of the placebo effect provided by a confident clinician and has commented on the relationship between biofeedback clinician and patient as similar to the relationship between teacher and pupil[9,10]. This clinical attitude is one which all researchers, but particularly those involved in hypertension research (which is par excellence subject to non-specific, relational factors) might strive to emulate.

SUMMARY

Conflicting results in research on the use of relaxation and biofeedback with hypertensive patients may well be the result of failure to consider certain clinical problems inherent in such research. The researcher-clinician will be aware of motivational and other clinical problems that can affect an otherwise unexceptionable research design. Clinical problems identified in this paper include such vagaries of measurement as blood pressure changes from heart beat to heart beat and the effects of slight variation of sitting postures; the problems of compliance and medication adjustment, requiring flexibility in baselines in order to achieve stability; and the effects of the research design itself upon motivational and reinforcement contingencies. The objective of combining experimentally rigorous procedures with a clinically flexible approach is indeed the most challenging goal when the very object of the research is the clinical effectiveness of the procedures themselves.

REFERENCES

1. Blanchard, E.B. and Young, L.D.: Clinical applications of biofeedback training. Arch. Gen. Psy. 30:573, 1974.

2. Frumkin, K., Nathan, R., Prout, M., et al.: Nonpharmacologic control of essential hypertension in man: A critical review of the experimental literature. Psychosom. Med. 40:294, 1978.

3. Tursky, B.: Indirect recording of human blood pressure. In Obrist, P.A., Black, A.H. et al. (Eds.): Cardiovascular Psychophysiology. Chicago; Aldine Publishing Co., 1974, p. 97.

4. Viol, G.W., Goebel, M., Lorenz, G. and Ing, T.S.: Seating as a variable in clinical blood pressure measurement. Amer. Heart J., 1979 (In press).

5. Goebel, M.: "Blood pressure was taken in the seated position," or Another variable in the vagaries of blood pressure measurement. Am. J. Clin. Biofeedback 1:87, 1978.

6. Goebel, M.: Relaxation, biofeedback, and hypertension: Dialogue between researcher and clinician on implications of research design. Am. J. Clin. Biofeedback 1:36, 1978.

7. Frankel, B.L., Patel, D.J., Horwitz, D., et al.: Treatments of hypertension with biofeedback and relaxation techniques. Psychosom. Med. 40:276, 1978.

8. Surwit, R.S., Shapiro, D. and Good, M.I.: Comparison of cardiovascular biofeedback, neuromuscular biofeedback, and meditation in the borderline essential hypertensive. J. Consult. Clin. Psychol. 46:252, 1978.

9. Patel, C.: Biofeedback as treatment with particular emphasis on hypertension. Biofeedback Research Society Meeting Abstracts, Colorado, Springs, 1976.

10. Patel, C.: Biofeedback-aided relaxation and meditation in the management of hypertension. Biof. and Self-Regulation 2:1, 1977.

AUTHOR INDEX

J. Baillie   55
A. Barabasz   9
M.A. Basker   173
A.E. Bernstien   87
B.G. Braun   141
G.D. Burrows   33, 113, 319

P.S. Clarke   95
D.R. Collinson   79
H.B. Crasilneck   1

A.M. Damsbo   157

D. Elton   113
J.C. Erickson III   195
F.J. Evans   47
D.M. Ewin   269

E. Fiore   261
G. Foenander   33, 319

G.C. Gass   293
J. Gerschman   33
L. Girard-Robin   285
T.J. Glenn   201
H.K. Goba   71
M. Goebel   345
L. Goldstein   17
M. Gross   133

E. Hackett   165
J.C. Hancock   165
R. Hirvenoja   121
J. Holroyd   335
D.J. De L. Horne   55

O. Ihalainen   121
T.S. Ing   345
S. Inglis   127

J.A. Jackson   293
G.S. Jennings   139
J.A. Jensen   231
U.J. Jovanović   105

R. Kampman   121
R. Karlin   17

G. Lavoie   285
G. Lorenz   345

N. Malcolm   209
K.M. McConkey   311
C. MacL. Morgan   181
D. Morgan   17

K. Nuechterlein   335

G. Pettitt   63
N. Phillips   277
Z. Pleszewski   253

A. Rappaport   189
P. Reade   33
C.A.D. Ringrose   223

M. Senk   239
D. Shapiro   335
S. Sharma   149
P.W. Sheehan   25
J.F. Simonds   201

G.V. Stanley   113
H.E. Stanton   215

K. Thomas   97
K.F. Thompson   41

L.-E. Unestähl   301

G.W. Viol   345

F. Ward   335

M.D. Zannoni   247

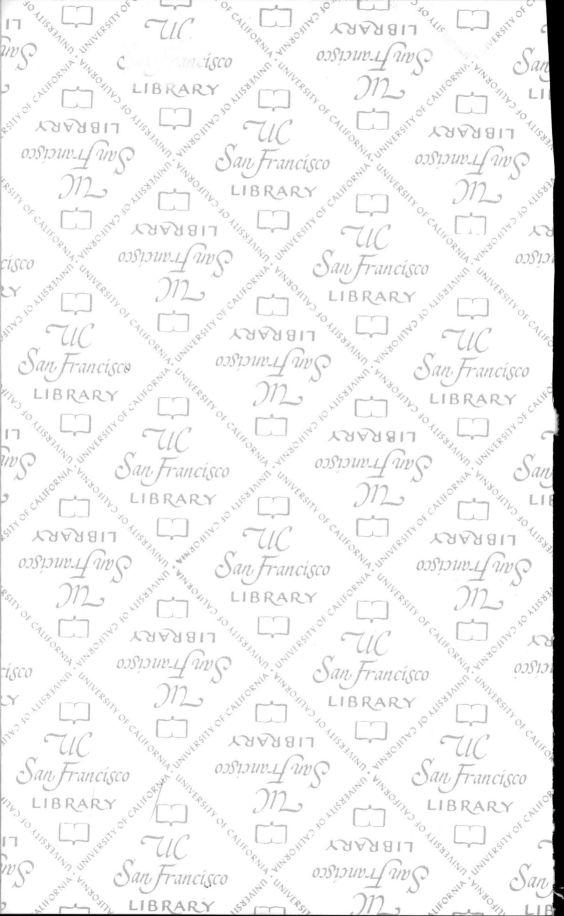